THE WORLD OF COMPUTERS

APPLICATIONS & PRINCIPLES

SECOND EDITION

THE WORLD OF COMPUTERS
APPLICATIONS & PRINCIPLES
SECOND EDITION

Rob Kelley, B.A., M.Ed.
Department Head
Westmount Secondary School
Hamilton, Ontario

Educational Advisors
Dennis Haynes
Anthony Viola, Jr.

John Wiley & Sons

Toronto   New York   Chichester   Brisbane   Singapore

Canadian Cataloguing in Publication Data
Kelley, Rob, 1947 -
The world of computers: applications and principles

2nd ed.
First ed. (1982) published under title: The world of computers and information processing.
ISBN 0-471-79527-5

1. Computers. 2. Electronic data processing. I. Title.

QA76.K45 1991   004   C90-094487-0

Editors: Marg Bukta
                    Sarah Kennedy

Cover Design: Landgraff Design
                    Associates Ltd.

Text Design: James Loates

Illustrator: James Loates *illustrating*

Contributing Illustrator:
                    Rob Kelley
                    (Dynamic Graphics, Inc.)
                    (Volk Clip Art, Inc.)

Production Co-ordinator:
                    Cheryl Teelucksingh

Typesetting: Jennifer Loates
                    Loates Desktop Publishing

Printer: John Deyell Company

Printed and bound in Canada
10   9   8   7   6   5   4   3   2

Computers are entering more and more areas of our lives. With each passing week, we read about a new computer breakthrough, a new computer use, or a new type of computer altogether. It seems that almost everything we work at, everything we do, and everything we use is now connected directly to computers. (Even this book was produced using desktop-publishing software.) Computers help astronauts to fly spaceships, doctors to operate more successfully, artists to be more creative, engineers to build better and safer airplanes... Computers run our television sets, our microwave ovens, our car engines... the list goes on and on. Computers are everywhere.

You will discover through this course that computers are tools. To be able to make them work for you to their fullest, you must understand how they work and how to apply them.

On the cover you can see two figures moving on a platform of computer circuitry. They are exploring the world of computers to discover the many different computer applications in the world of today and tomorrow. This is a new world for these two people but they know that their future careers, enjoyment, and security depends upon how well they learn to work with computers.

There is no doubt that your life in the twenty-first century is going to be computer based. How and where do you think computers will be part of your life?

List five things you use now that involve a computer somehow. Beside the item, tell how the computer is involved.

Now, write down ten ways in which you think you are going to be affected by computers in ten years' time; ten ways in which you think computers will change the way you live. It could be in the things you buy or the jobs you do. It could be in the way you talk to people or in how you go shopping.

At the end of the course, look at the list you have made. Make changes to it based on the knowledge you have gained. Keep the list. In ten years, look at it again to see how close you really were.

To those
who seek to
improve
what has
come before

TABLE OF CONTENTS

Chapter 9
Impact on Society

Chapter 10
Controversial Issues

Chapter 11
The Future

UNIT 4 Computer Programming

Chapter 12 Simple Sequential Structures

Chapter 13
Repetition Structures

Chapter 14
Selection Structures

Chapter 15   An Introduction
to Turbo Pascal

ACKNOWLEDGMENTS

The World of Computers, Second Edition is a comprehensive study of computers and their uses. To bring such a text to fruition required the cooperation of many teachers, educators, businesses, and government agencies. We thank them for their support and assistance.

Dennis Haynes, assistant head, Delta Secondary School, and Anthony Viola Jr., computer site administrator, Hill Park Secondary School, both in Hamilton, Ontario, acted as advisors, critics, and editors. Their input was invaluable. A sincere thank you to both of them for their patient, intelligent, and constant help.

In addition, students at Barton Secondary School field-tested the software applications. They completed the end-of-chapter material in word processing, spreadsheets, data base, and graphics. This included successfully completing the research projects with apparent enjoyment and with little difficulty.

Reviewers from across Canada provided ideas, direction, and suggestions. Their help was greatly appreciated. These reviewers included:
Charmaine Boyce and Friedl Ballaban, Westwood Secondary School, Mississauga, ON

Larry Noonan, L.J.N. Publishing, Inc.
Linda Engh, Springbank Community High School, Calgary, AB
Larry Colquhoun, Business Education Department Head, Dr. E. P. Scarlett Senior High School, Calgary, AB
Bette Grace, Technology Department Head, Ft. Langley Junior Secondary/Fine Arts School, Fort Langley, BC.

A special thank you to: Paul Swan, cartoonist, Dallas, Texas; Sandy Dean, cartoonist, Pensacola, Florida; Digital Equipment Corporation for their illustrative material; Sarah Kennedy, editor, John Wiley & Sons Canada Limited, who successfully managed the photo research for the text; and Marg Bukta, freelance editor, who went beyond the normal editorial functions by testing material and making excellent suggestions for improvements.

Special thanks as well to Joseph Gladstone, Acquisitions Editor for John Wiley & Sons Canada Limited, for his professional encouragement and support.

CREDITS

PREFACE

The World of Computers, Second Edition is an introductory computer textbook designed to provide a broad spectrum of information, concepts, and skills essential to the development of computer literacy and computer applications.

The chapters are written as independent modules and so it is not necessary to teach them sequentially. Teachers may design a program to meet the needs of the specific classes being taught. The author does recommend though that section one of the text be used first. This will ensure that all students begin with a similar understanding of what a computer is.

Almost a decade has passed since the first edition of *The World of Computers* was published. Much has changed in the world and the classroom in that time. Computer labs in schools, licensed software, and computer education in a variety of subject areas are now the norm.

It is because of the future needs of students, the current classroom requirements, and the new developments in curricula that this text concentrates on four major areas of study:

• Computer Hardware Systems
• Software Applications
• Computer Uses and Their Impact on Society
• Computer Programming

In addition, to increase student understanding and give the material greater depth, sections on computer history, careers using computer technology, and general problem-solving techniques are included.

The Second Edition provides many new innovative features:

1. **Key Concepts and Vocabulary:**
   a special list is presented at the end of each chapter that acts as a quick reminder of the content of the chapter or as a chapter review.

2. **Stress on Applications:**
   the Second Edition provides nine chapters specifically devoted to hands-on learning of a variety of essential generic software packages.

3. **Challenge Projects:**
   a wide range of projects are developed within each chapter to provide the students with the opportunity to use integrated software to combine graphics and text or to use a combination of computer software and mechanical layout techniques.

4. **Application Projects Included in the Main Body of the Text:**
   following each topic in the software applications chapters there are hands-on projects to give students immediate reinforcement.

5. **End of Chapter Projects:**
   at the end of every chapter there is a set of projects to provide students with practice using new material and processes. These projects vary in length and complexity and are presented in an order of increasing difficulty.

6. **Careers:**
   every chapter starts with a list of many of the jobs available in computer and computer-related industries.

7. **Clarity in Project Presentation:**
   each project is identified as to its major focus and purpose. Where helpful, references to the relevant text pages are provided.

8. **Variety of Projects:**
   there are four different types of projects:
   - short, text-imbedded, immediate follow-up projects
   - end-of-chapter skill specific projects
   - end-of-chapter skill blending projects
   - major projects involving several types of application combined.

9. **Chapter Summaries:**
   at the end of each chapter a quick summary is given for review and study purposes.

Our field tests have shown that the students find the projects to be varied, enjoyable, challenging, and useful. The projects are designed to expand the students' understanding and appreciation of the power of computers and the scope of applications available to them.

Our society is becoming more complex and technologically oriented. This makes it more important than ever that our students be computer literate. This textbook is designed as a resource and a guide to assist you in empowering your students with an ability to work comfortably and skillfully with what is, to some people, an intimidating technology.

In this age of information management, *The World of Computers, Second Edition* is an exciting journey for your students toward understanding the information machine and its applications.

UNIT 1

HARDWARE AND SOFTWARE: AN OVERVIEW

Chapter 1   AN INFORMATION PROCESSING MACHINE

*T*his one-chapter unit talks about the "nuts and bolts" that make up a computer. It clarifies the technical terminology, explores computer careers, and narrates a short history of the computer's evolution. For the newcomer to computers it provides the basic understanding needed for success with the later chapters.

Microcomputer systems have become progressively more complex since their debut in 1978. For the potential computer owner and user, an understanding of the inter-relationships between hardware and software is a necessity—even if only to avoid making a bad purchase. For the student, an understanding of the system will enhance the use of the machine and its software. It provides the students an opportunity to see both the computer's power and its limitations.

Chapter 1

AN INFORMATION PROCESSING MACHINE

66 This is a completely new type of societal technology quite unlike any of the past. Its substance is information, which is quite invisible. 99

Yoneyi Masuda
The Information Society

OBJECTIVES

By the end of this chapter, you will be able to:

1 Define the following computer terms: hardware, software, processor unit, peripherals, operating system, language processor, printout, main memory, auxiliary memory, processor unit, MPU, analog computer, hybrid computer system;

2 List the five essential functions of any computer system, and give examples of computer components that perform each of those functions;

3 Explain the purpose of an operating system and a computer language within a computer system;

4 Name and describe four categories of computers;

5 List several computer-related careers and their educational requirements;

6 Briefly explain the characteristics of each of the four generations of computers.

WORKING IN THE WORLD OF COMPUTERS

CAD Specialist
designs cars and bridges with a computer

Computer Consultant
advises people on what hardware and software to use

Computer Operator
responsible for operating large computer systems

Computer Technician
repairs computers

Data Entry Clerk
enters information into computer systems using pre-designed screen forms

Numerical Control Clerk
plans and enters blueprint information into a computer-controlled machine

Programmer
plans and writes computer programs

Spreadsheet Analyst
uses spreadsheet software to manipulate and analyze numerical data

Systems Analyst
studies ways in which computers can be used more effectively in an organization

Word Processing Operator
prepares memos, letters, and other documents for an organization

1.1 INTRODUCTION

*T*he computer is one of the most exciting technological achievements of the last 40 years. Just as mechanical machines help people to extend their physical power, computers are helping them to expand their thinking ability by providing high-speed processing of information. Computers are becoming an extension of the way humans analyze information and solve problems. The knowledge of how to use a computer to manipulate information, and the expertise to program it, have become highly desirable skills, both in the workplace and the home.

This chapter provides an overview of the various system components related to computers: the hardware, the software, and the users. It examines the relationship between the machinery that makes up a computer system and the instructions that "bring it to life".

Studying the interrelationships of these elements will help you to develop a greater understanding of how computers operate. Also, a general knowledge of computer hardware, software, careers, and recent history will broaden your overall understanding of computer systems.

Specific chapter topics include the hardware components that perform the five functions of a computer system, the roles that manufacturers' software play within computers, some common categories of application software, several computer-related careers, and a look at the historical evolution of computers.

1.2 A COMPUTER SYSTEM

*W*hat makes up a computer? Well, computers actually consist of several devices linked together to form an operational unit. For this reason, it is more accurate to refer to a complete computer as a **computer system**. All the electrical, mechanical, and magnetic parts that make up a computer system are called **hardware**. These hardware devices might include a monitor, keyboard, disk drive, printer, and the processor unit. The main part of the computer, the processor unit, contains the circuit boards, which are capable of storing and processing information. This device controls the flow of information that travels throughout the computer system. All the other devices attached to the processor unit, such as a printer or a monitor, are referred to as **peripherals**.

Another necessary but invisible element that forms part of all computer systems is the set of programs that, with the help of the processor unit, operates the computer. A **program** consists of a series of instructions designed to guide the computer step by step through some process. On a broader scale, all the instructions that combine to make a computer operate in some required manner, including system instructions provided by the computer manufacturer, are referred to as **software**.

*A*ll computer systems have five essential features — input, output, storage, processing, and control. Each of these features represents a specific task or function that the computer can perform. This section describes the various alternative hardware components that can be used to perform each of these functions. Although some may differ from the hardware you are currently using, an awareness of substitute devices will strengthen both your general understanding of computers and your ability to adapt to new computer environments when necessary.

Input

*E*ach computer has one or more devices that allow instructions to be fed into the system, the most common being a keyboard much like the ones found on typewriters. The user keys in the instructions to obtain whatever action or information is required from the computer. The traditional QWERTY keyboard, named after the six top left alphabet keys, is usually surrounded by many special function keys that pertain directly to the operation of the computer.

Along with the keyboard, an assortment of special pointing devices, such as a mouse, trackball, light pen, graphics tablet, and joystick, have become increasingly popular tools for communicating with a computer. Each of these devices provides speed and directional control over the placement of the cursor (the blinking underscore or square on the screen), which indicates where the computer's attention is currently focused within a certain program.

Some microcomputers, such as the Commodore Amiga and the Apple Macintosh, are dependent on a mouse for selecting options from the on-screen menus. The mouse and trackball devices are also often part of educational, networked computer systems, such as the Commodore, ICON, IBM, and Tandy networks, which cable several workstations together to share software stored on a common large-capacity disk drive.

The mouse is a hand-size input device that moves over the surface of a desk top to control the cursor's movement on the screen. A "mechanical mouse" contains a small roller ball underneath the unit that allows it

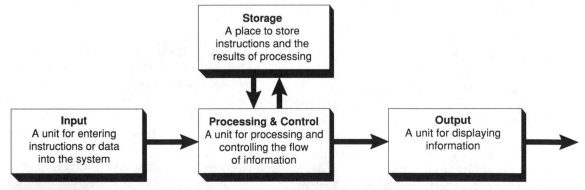

Figure 1.1 This diagram illustrates the five functions of any computer system. Separate devices are generally used for input and output, while the storage, processing, and control functions are represented by circuit boards and chips inside the computer.

to roll smoothly along the surface. An "optical mouse" contains a tiny light and light-capture hole underneath the unit, and is restricted in movement to the limits of a special reflective surface called a "mouse pad". In addition to these variations, mice operate with or without a "mouse tail" — a cord connecting the mouse to the computer.

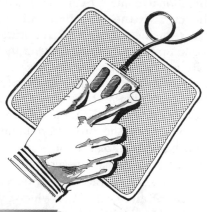

Figure 1.2 The mouse controls the directional movement of the cursor on the screen and is currently the most popular pointing device.

The trackball is also a hand-held input device. It sits flat on the desktop or is permanently embedded in the microcomputer's keyboard surface. The smooth roller ball, which faces upward, turns in whatever direction the user's fingers move it, causing the cursor to move in the same direction across the screen.

Many designers and engineers prefer to use a stylus, light pen, or mouse together with a flat drawing surface called a "graphics tablet" because of the increased cursor control these devices offer. This combination of input devices permits them to draw elaborate computerized images working on a desktop, as they would with a pen and paper. The images created by the pointing devices are immediately transferred to the screen through a connecting cable. Upon request, the computer can store the entire graphic design for later recall.

If textual information is already typed, a different kind of input device, called a page scanner, can be used. This time-saving device digitizes text and graphics into signals that the computer can understand. Once it is digitized, an entire page of data can be transferred directly into the computer's memory, which is useful for people who create newspapers and flyers because it enables them to input text or images without having to retype or redraw them. Material is fed into the scanner as easily as it would be into a photocopier.

Within the decade, manufacturers will combine artificial intelligence with voice input to give computers the ability to hear and understand entire phrases spoken aloud by the user. Voice-activated microcomputers will provide the first generation of truly user-friendly machines. They will lead to a whole range of consumer-oriented products that respond to voice input, such as household and office appliances that turn on or off by voice command. A voice-activated word-processing system that types as you speak is an example of this kind of innovation. These microcomputers will first combine, and then eventually replace, keyboard input with voice input for most future data entry.

Output *T*he next of the five computer functions can also be performed by several hardware devices. The output from a computer—statistics, textual information, sound, or graphics —can be displayed in a variety of ways, a common method being to display it on a visual screen or monitor. The output, which appears on the screen, can be cleared, coloured, or modified to suit the user's needs. There are different types of visual screens. A common model is a large, bulky monitor called a "cathode ray tube" (CRT), which closely resembles a home television set. Another type is a lighter, flat monitor called a "liquid crystal display" (LCD) screen, used with portable laptop and pocket computers.

The clarity and amount of detail that a monitor can project is referred to as its "resolution". Low- to medium-resolution images can be achieved with a regular, composite video screen. The finer detail required by such items as schematic or architectural drawings can only be achieved with higher-resolution monitors.

In addition, the resolution of any style of monitor can be greatly enhanced with a computer engineering technique called "bit mapping". This technique uses extra memory to address each pixel (picture element on the screen) separately, which results in tremendous control over the design and colour combination of computer graphics.

Monitor resolution often presents a problem for programs that include graphics. Usually, graphics designed for high-resolution screens will not run on lower-resolution screens.

If a copy of the display is required, a printer can be used. When the information appears on a piece of paper, it is called a **printout** or hard copy. Inexpensive printers generally are dot matrix printers, which form the print characters with a mosaic of tiny dots. More expensive models might include a daisy wheel printer, which provides "letter-quality" output for business letters and formal reports.

The most expensive type of desktop printer, capable of reproducing fine quality graphics, scanned photographs, and textual material, is the laser printer. It works with a

Bar Graphs

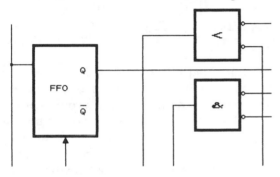

Circuit Diagrams

Arabic Characters

UPC Bar Codes

Chinese Characters

Figure 1.3 Today's printers are capable of producing various types of characters, fonts, and symbols—even dot matrix printers. Often it's the software that determines the quality of output, rather than the printer.

combination of laser light and a photocopying process, and is well suited for printing professional-looking flyers, newsletters, newspapers, and magazines.

Sound, music, and voice output can also be generated from a computer system. Various tonal qualities can be reproduced with a sound generator. More elaborate musical output can be generated by miniaturized music synthesizer chips that often contain multiple channels for imitating several musical instruments at the same time. Voice output requires a voice synthesizer chip and a stored library of sound-wave patterns, so that the output imitates human speech. All forms of sound output require a small speaker inside the computer.

"What's taking the new man so long? I just sent him for some extra RAMS."

Storage

The third function of any computer system is its "storage" capability. Most microcomputer systems have two storage areas—internal and external. The first area is found inside the processor unit and is referred to as **main memory** or internal memory. It usually appears in the form of integrated cir-cuits called "Random Access Memory" chips, or RAM. These integrated circuits continue to store programs as long as the electrical current remains on. When the power is shut off, however, all information contained in RAM vanishes like the digits on a pocket calculator.

A second memory chip, called "Read Only Memory", or ROM, is used for the permanent storage of system software provided by the manufacturer. This memory cannot be modified or erased by the user. It remains intact even when the power is shut off.

The amount of main memory a computer has is usually measured in groups of 1000 bytes. A "byte" is the amount of space it takes to store one number or one letter of the alphabet in code. The Greek letter "K", meaning 1000, is often used in abbreviations, as in "64 K of main memory", which is translated to mean "64 000 bytes of main memory". One screenful of information requires 4 K of storage, so a computer with 64 K bytes of main memory could hold approximately 16 screenfuls of information.

The other type of storage area found in computer systems is called **auxiliary memory** or external memory. It can be provided by connecting extra devices to the computer. These devices can store information on reusable, long-lasting media such as cassette tapes, floppy disks, high-speed hard disks, or optical videodisks.

Diskettes, hard disks, and optical disks are random- or direct-storage media. When a program is requested from these media, the storage unit first consults its index, then moves directly to the program's location. The program can be loaded into main memory within a few seconds, with the speed of transfer being dependent on the size of the program and type of storage medium being used.

Floppy disks are inexpensive, low-volume storage media for microcomputers. They have become steadily smaller since they were introduced in the 1970s; they are currently available in four diameters (still referred to in non-metric measurements of 8", 5.25", 3.5", and 2"). Unlike the first two floppy disks, which have a flexible covering, the 3.5" size, sometimes called a "minidisk", is housed in a rigid plastic cover to protect the data during handling.

Figure 1.4 — **Computer disks are available in four sizes. A 2" disk, not shown here, has recently been created that can hold one million bytes, but it is currently not widely used.**

Courtesy of JVC Magnetics Corporation

To obtain greater storage capacity, users can purchase a different type of device called a "hard-disk drive". This high-speed, magnetic unit contains one or more smooth aluminum platters coated with metal oxide (similar to the coating on floppy disks and magnetic tape). These rigid platters spin at speeds of up to 150 km/h, providing very fast response to hovering read/write magnetic heads. The storage capacity of such media ranges from 20 to 600 megabytes. A megabyte refers to one million bytes of character storage, which is equivalent to storing 125 one-page business letters.

Optical laser disk players can read information from metal circular platters, called videodisks, with the help of laser light. Videodisks can store "still" photographs or motion pictures and two separate sound tracks, in addition to normal computer output. The unit can randomly locate any frame in five seconds or less. Pictures can be superimposed on a computer monitor, while the processor is displaying output from a computer program. Videodisks are capable of holding a gigabyte (one billion bytes) of character storage.

Videodisks used for the permanent storage of computer material appear under several names, such as optical disk and CD-ROM, which stands for "Compact Disk-Read Only Memory". Earlier versions of optical disks could not be erased or added to. However, several manufacturers are developing optical disks that can be both read from and written to by computer systems to give them the same storage flexibility as floppy and hard disks.

Processing and Control

*T*he last two functions of a computer system are combined as the "processing and control" functions. All the calculations, logic decisions, and comparisons and handling of information are done in one area, called the **processor unit**. Here, the miniature electronic memory and logic circuits operate the entire computer. The most important chip in the processor unit is called the *microprocessor unit (MPU)*. This is the actual computer reduced to a wafer of miniaturized circuits; it provides the machine with its processing capability.

Name	Description	Capacity
Floppy Disk	Removable, flexible, inexpensive, magnetic storage medium composed of mylar plastic	Measured in thousands of bytes
Hard Disk	Fixed, rigid, expensive, high-speed, magnetic storage medium composed of a metal platter coated with mylar plastic	Measured in megabytes (millions of bytes)
Optical Disk	Removable, rigid, low-cost, optical storage medium composed of highly reflective metal read by laser light	Measured in gigabytes (billions of bytes)

The microprocessor contains an arithmetic and logic unit, a control section, and sometimes a small memory buffer. The arithmetic and logic unit (or ALU) contains the electronic logic circuits that are designed to perform such functions as addition, subtraction, multiplication, and division. It also contains the circuitry designed to perform such logical operations as comparing one number to another and indicating the results. This comparison feature gives the computer its decision-making capability and allows alternative pathways to be taken throughout a program (a process known as branching).

The control section refers to circuitry that controls the sequence of operations in a program. It contains several special memory locations called "registers". The control register accepts one instruction at a time, analyzes it, and performs the action with the help of the arithmetic and logic unit.

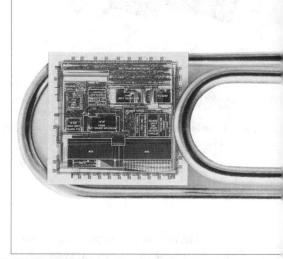

Figure 1.5

This wafer-thin circuit sitting on a paperclip is a miniature microprocessor unit.

Courtesy of Bell Labs

1.4 SYSTEM SOFTWARE

*T*he computer manufacturer must include a program with the machine (stored on a floppy disk or internal memory) to make the computer function. This program, called an **operating system**, must be present before any other software can be run.

The operating system handles routine functions, such as detecting which keys have been struck on the keyboard, displaying information on the screen, and handling information as it travels to and from peripherals like the disk drive or the printer. It also controls the operation of the computer system by providing the "intelligence" that allows the microprocessor to act as the "traffic director" for the flow of information throughout the computer.

Computer Languages

*A*nother type of manufacturer's software is a program classified as a language processor or, more commonly, a **computer language**. Its purpose is to translate instructions the programmer provides into electrical impulses that the computer can understand. A computer language acts like an "English teacher" by filtering and accepting only the correct syntax (grammar, punctuation, and construction) and the correct spelling of commands. Some examples of computer languages are BASIC, C, COBOL, FORTRAN, and Pascal.

Figure 1.6

Many versions of computer languages are marketed to software developers. This one is designed by one of the originators of the BASIC language, John Kemeny.

Courtesy of True BASIC, Inc.

1.5 APPLICATION SOFTWARE

*I*t is helpful for computer users and programmers to be able to distinguish between different general classifications of application software. The term "application software" refers to programs, other than "system software", that are written to assist people in handling certain tasks such as performing specific calculations, writing letters, or retrieving information. Software that specifically makes the manual tasks of writing, filing, drawing, and computation easier and quicker is commonly called "productivity software" and includes word processors, spreadsheets, and data bases. There are many categories of application software. The following chart highlights some of the more common classifications.

Broad Classifications of Application Software

Classification	What It Does
Word Processing	Assists user in creating, editing, printing, and filing documents
Spreadsheet	Helps user manipulate numerical data in a row-and-column format
File Manager	Stores and retrieves records for preview or to form reports. Groups of data are recorded in a routine format and stored in separate files
Data Base	Allows the integration of materials from several files to form reports; a multiple-file manager
Computer-assisted Instruction	Helps students learn facts or develop skills through a series of lessons, simulations, and tests; "teaching" software
Desktop Publishing	Allows the user to combine graphics, words, and photographs into a newsletter, newspaper, or magazine format; a sophisticated word-processing application
Accounting	Includes modules for payroll, inventory control, accounts receivable ledger, accounts payable ledger, general ledger, and sales ordering
Graphics Design	Allows the user to create illustrations, artwork, pictures, animation, and business graphs
Entertainment	Provides simulation, logic, and arcade-style distractions for fun

*D*igital computers are capable of following step-by-step instructions, performing calculations, making logical decisions, and storing and retrieving large amounts of data.

There are four categories of digital computer. The smallest type, called a **pocket computer**, is a portable, hand-held model. A keypad allows letters, numbers, and special commands to be entered. A tiny screen displays the output. Many pocket computers are designed so they can be connected to other devices, such as another computer or a printer. Business briefcases are available that snugly hold the pocket computer, auxiliary storage, and a modem to communicate data over the telephone line, if necessary. Salespeople, engineers, scientists, and managers enjoy the compactness of this model.

The next type is a portable **laptop computer**, so called because it can sit comforta-

bly on your lap while you use it. A full-size keyboard is the input device, and a thin, full-size display screen the output device. The whole unit folds up into the shape of a small, lightweight briefcase when not in use. Business people like this model when they are away from the office or for recording minutes at meetings. University students may use them for taking notes while listening to lectures.

The third and most popular category is the **microcomputer**. It is a large, desktop model commonly used in schools, business offices, and at home. It contains a full-size keyboard, a large cathode ray tube screen, internal or external disk drives, and a desk-model printer. Sometimes referred to as a "personal computer", it can only be used by one person at a time. The processor unit comes in both horizontal and vertical "tower-style" versions.

In an office setting, when many computers are used all day, the fastest microcomputer is sometimes employed as a "file-server" for a group of less powerful workstations that are connected in a network to the fileserver with coaxial cable. The fileserver distributes application software to the workstations, "routes" output to a shared printer, and may also store information generated by each workstation.

Mainframe computers are the largest of these four types. Most of the basic computer functions are housed in separate, but interconnected, floor-model machines that operate at very high speeds. Sometimes these devices are so numerous that they occupy a small room. The term mainframe refers to the oversized processor unit. Large corporations, various levels of government, and the military prefer the speed and volume of information that a mainframe computer is capable of handling. A mainframe can also communicate with hundreds of users almost simultaneously. The largest and fastest mainframes are called "super-computers".

Figure 1.7 A hand-held, programmable pocket computer with a one-line display screen and complete alphanumeric keypad.

Courtesy of Tandy Corporation

Figure
1.8

The semicircular design of the processor unit is a unique characteristic of the Cray super-computer. High-end models can process one billion instructions per second.

1.7 HYBRID COMPUTER SYSTEMS

*I*n addition to the popular digital computer, there are two other types of computer system that are more specialized and limited in function—the analog and hybrid computers.

An **analog computer** is a device that measures a physical quantity, such as air pressure, temperature, or velocity, and compares it to a preset level. For example, when a cruise-control device in a car is turned on, it locks the engine into a certain speed. If the car travels up or down a hill, the cruise control compensates for the change in speed by increasing or decreasing the flow of air and gas to the carburetor. In this way, the engine's performance is adjusted to maintain a constant speed. Other examples of analog devices include furnace thermostats, air conditioner thermostats, heat-sensing fire alarms, and automatic pilots in aircraft.

A **hybrid computer system** is a combination of the analog and the digital computer. Usually, analog computers act as input or output peripherals, while the digital computer provides the processing and instructions for the system.

An example of a hybrid computer is the system used to monitor the status of a space shuttle and its rocket launcher, both on the launch pad and in flight. Analog sensors located at critical points within the aircraft measure real physical quantities, such as heat, air pressure, fuel levels, motion relative to the horizon, and acceleration. These sensors produce continuous signals that vary with changing conditions. The analog gauges and gyros (multi-directional sensors) are connected to "analog-to-digital" circuitry that converts the measurements to digital signals. These converted signals can then be displayed in the cockpit for the astronauts to see and relayed to the control centre for a team of engineering specialists to monitor on their individual computer screens.

Figure 1.9

Engineers in a NASA control room monitor the orbital flight of a space shuttle.

Courtesy of NASA
Lyndon B. Johnson Space Center

Another application of a hybrid computer system is a computerized manufacturing assembly line. Here, several analog devices measure and check product specifications, while the digital computer uses this information to decide what manufacturing processes the product should go through next.

1.8 OPEN AND CLOSED ARCHITECTURE

*T*he type of microcomputer a person chooses often limits what can be done with the system. The type of housing and general design considerations given to a computer can be grouped into two broad categories—open and closed architecture.

In smaller, less expensive microcomputer systems, the operating system, and sometimes the language processor, are permanently stored inside the computer. ROM chips store these software packages, which immediately become active when the computer is turned on. These microcomputers, such as the Commodore C-64 and early Atari machines, represent a style of design referred to as **closed architecture**. This means that neither the computer's circuitry nor the manufacturer's software can be altered internally to improve the system's performance or to adapt it to some new use.

Other computers require the user to insert a DOS (Disk Operating System) disk into the disk drive before turning on the machine. The diskette contains the computer's operating system (and sometimes a computer language), which the machine needs in order to function. Having the manufacturer's software stored externally on disk allows companies to make software improvements without altering the equipment. Also, third-party vendors may design and sell add-on circuit boards to enhance the system's performance and capability. Microcomputers with this type of design, such as the Apple IIe, Compaq, Dell, and IBM PC, are referred to as having an **open architecture.**

The type of system preferred will depend on the use to which it is put. The more expensive and more flexible open architecture system may not be necessary for simple computer applications.

1.9 INSIDE THE PROCESSOR UNIT

*T*he main printed circuit board that channels the flow of information and distributes electrical power to the system is called the **motherboard**. Vertical "daughterboards" that operate peripherals or provide separate functions are attached to it.

The most significant chip in a computer, usually found on the motherboard, is the microprocessor. The power of the computer is often described in terms of the speed with which the microprocessor processes information. Much like the different sizes and powers available in automobile engines, computers also come in different engine sizes: 8-bit, 16-bit, and 32-bit microprocessors.

The size of the microprocessor usually determines three things—the speed of operation, the amount of main memory that the computer can directly control, and the special abilities of the system.

The first limitation refers to the maximum number of operations that the chip can process per microsecond. This is described as its megahertz rating, similar in concept to a car engine's horsepower rating. The larger the processor, the more millions of operations will be processed per microsecond. For example, the 8-bit processor contained in a C-64 or Apple IIe microcomputer operates in the range of 0.5 to 2.0 megahertz, while some of the current microcomputers with a 32-bit chip can operate at speeds of 33 megahertz, or 16 times as fast as the top 8-bit processor.

The size of the microprocessor also determines how much main memory can be directly addressed, or controlled. Eight-bit processors can address a maximum of 64 000 bytes of memory. Sixteen-bit processors can address ten times as much. Thirty-two-bit processors can address 256 times as much as the smallest processor can.

The last limit created by the size of the microprocessor relates to special features that require a high speed to operate. For example, performing true three-dimensional animation is only possible when the processor reaches the 32-bit size. Other special features that require tremendous speed include voice recognition and multitasking. The latter refers to the ability of a computer to run several tasks simultaneously.

1.10 PEOPLE WHO WORK WITH COMPUTERS

*U*sing computers to process information has caused many changes in the traditional business office and simultaneously created new jobs. **Word processing operators** key in, print, and electronically file business letters, memos, and minutes of meetings.

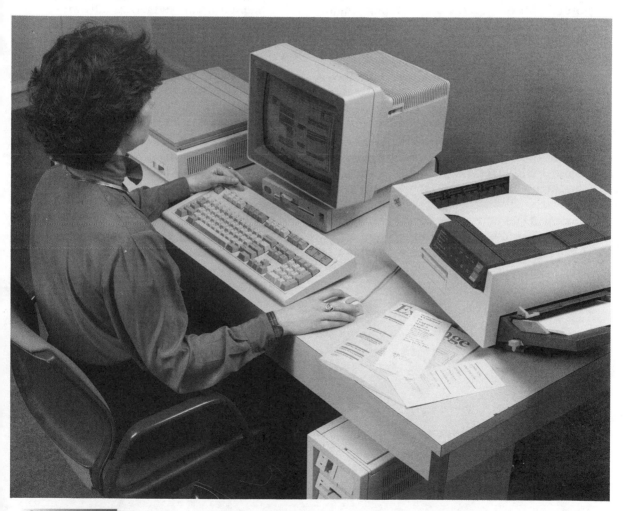

Figure 1.10

A word processing operator keys in a business letter from a hand-written draft.

Courtesy of Mohawk Data Sciences Ltd.

The job requires a good working knowledge of English or French (or both), keyboarding skills, and an ability to create, print, proofread, and edit professional-looking documents. Educational requirements include a high school or college diploma, with an emphasis on office administration.

Jobs involving the collection and manipulation of statistics need employees trained as **spreadsheet analysts**. Insurance companies, accounting and budget departments, research facilities, and government taxation offices, all of which concentrate on financial and numerical data, may employ several people who are adept in the use of spreadsheet software. This software is capable of performing calculations on the data, as well as generating printed reports. Educational requirements include a business degree from a college or university, in addition to spreadsheet expertise.

Many large corporations and government buildings have their own computer departments with powerful mainframe computer systems run by specially trained people. **Data entry clerks** prepare information in a suitable form for the computer to read. They key in data at workstations, proofread and edit it for correctness, and store the information on hard disks for later transmission to the mainframe computer. Information to be entered might concern company payroll, inventory updates, sales orders sent in from various locations across the country, and banking transactions. Educational requirements are usually a high school or college diploma in office administration and keyboarding skills.

Departments with their own mainframe computers may also have people who write or modify specialized application software. A **computer application programmer**, for example, plans and writes software for specific uses. A senior programmer assigned to a project might spend several months planning, writing, and correcting the steps involved in a program. Junior programmers, usually with less than five years' experience, work on existing programs under the supervision of a senior programmer.

Writing computer programs is a job that requires problem-solving skills, patience, determination, and attention to small details. Programmers usually have a college degree in data processing or a university degree in computer science. Typically, they are skilled in at least two of the major programming languages (BASIC, COBOL, PL1, Pascal, and C) and have an in-depth knowledge of the manufacturer's software.

1.11 OTHER COMPUTER-RELATED JOBS

Computer-related jobs are not restricted to traditional office areas. Businesses that design and manufacture specialized products for factories often have employees who work as **numerical control operators**. When a new product or part is ordered, this person translates the details of a blueprint into computer commands and stores them on magnetic disk or magnetic tape. When completed, the information is fed into a computer-controlled machine that follows the instructions to cut, shape, and grind the raw materials into a finished product. A numerical control operator needs a strong technical and math background, with an emphasis on mechanical drafting, algebra, geometry, calculus, and computers.

Computer-Aided Design (CAD) specialists may be mechanical engineers or blueprint specialists who are also trained in the use of "computer-aided design" workstations and in drafting and engineering concepts. These people design automobiles, bridges, and manufacturing parts right on the computer screen and then print detailed blueprints of the design. This work requires a college degree in manufacturing and design, or a university degree in mechanical engineering.

Figure 1.11

Computer industrial systems are programmed by numerical control operators, who combine an understanding of factory systems with programming knowledge.

Courtesy of Cincinnati Milacron

One of the highly paid, non-traditional programming roles is that of a **systems software programmer**. These specialists develop operating systems and computer languages for computer manufacturers. Major manufacturers such as IBM, Apple, Commodore, and Unisys have their own staff of systems software developers who make their latest models of computer operate. IBM's mainframe software development facility for the North American market is located in Toronto. A supercomputer company located in Edmonton also has its own staff.

There are also several independent companies such as Quantum Software (located in Ottawa), Phoenix Corporation, and Microsoft Corporation that concentrate on the development of operating systems as their product, which they sell commercially. Other companies that concentrate their software development on computer languages include Waterloo Systems (a Canadian company), True BASIC, Digital Research Corporation, PC-Brand, MPB Software, Systems Technology Incorporated, and Borland International.

Systems Software programmers must have a university degree in computer science and often a post-graduate degree in some specialized area of software development but don't necessarily need to have many years experience in the industry. The members of the system-development team for the Apple Macintosh microcomputer, all in their early twenties, were chosen for both their creative thinking and their computer skills. Bill Gates, the president of Microsoft, a multi-billion dollar software corporation, was in his twenties when he invented the Disk Operating System (IBM DOS) for the IBM PC microcomputer.

Many universities and corporations have people developing specialized software that "thinks" for itself and often speaks human languages. During the 1990s, research into this type of software, referred to as "artificial" or "machine" intelligence software, will produce the next major revolution in computers—the "Fifth Generation". **Artificial intelligence programmers** experiment with symbolic computer languages, game-playing strategies, robotics, and speech synthesis. Post-graduate degrees in computer science (M.A. or Ph.D.) are usually required for this work.

1.12 COMPUTER EVOLUTION

*T*he historical development of computers is fascinating. Computers have only been mass-produced commercially for about three decades, and yet each decade has brought enormous improvements in their design and capabilities.

In order to assist with the 1890 census, Herman Hollerith, a statistician with the U.S. government census bureau, designed a way to store information using punched holes on cardboard cards. He invented the Hollerith Code: the combination of holes needed to represent any letter, number, or symbol on the cards. In 1924, his ideas were purchased by the International Business Machines Corporation, today more commonly known as IBM.

Another innovator, James Powers, invented similar equipment to handle cardboard cards, using a different code with rounded punched holes. Eventually the company he founded became part of UNIVAC, a forerunner to the Unisys Corporation. Together, IBM and UNIVAC dominated the card-handling equipment market for several decades.

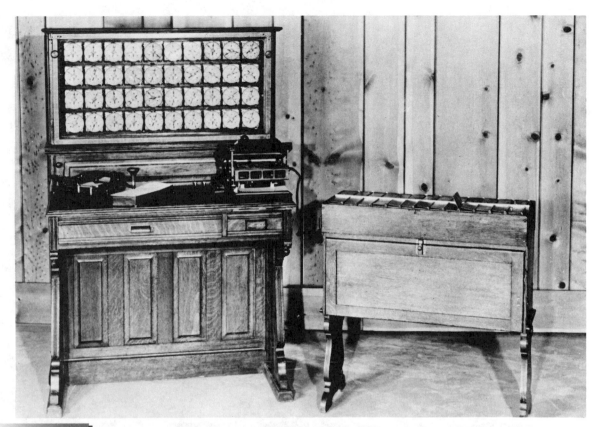

The Herman Hollerith Tabulating Machine was the forerunner to early computer systems. It punched coded information onto cardboard cards to facilitate machine handling.

Courtesy of IBM Canada Ltd.

The First Experimental Computers

During the Second World War (1939-1945), the U.S. military began secret development of its first computer. Howard Aiken, together with IBM, built a computer composed of both electrical and moving mechanical parts that operated on a system of electrical relays, switches, and gears. Instructions were punched onto rolls of paper tape, and once the machine started on the first instruction no further assistance was required.

A short time later, America's first completely electrical computer was designed by an engineer named John Mauchly, along with a graduate student named J. Presper Eckert. The computer, called **ENIAC** (Electrical Numerical Integrator and Calculator), had no moving parts. Electrical impulses, instead of gears, were used for counting. The machine weighed 30 tonnes and contained 18 000 gas-filled glass vacuum tubes and several kilometres of electrical wire. The computer required so much power to operate (130 000 watts) that it is claimed that all the lights in West Philadelphia used to dim when it was turned on.

Figure 1.13
ENIAC was the first completely electrical computer in North America. It generated a great deal of heat and was in frequent need of repair.

Courtesy of Unisys Corporation

The ENIAC operated on the decimal system (0, 1, 2, 3, 4, 5, 6, 7, 8, 9), similar to the way humans performed ordinary arithmetic. It was originally designed as a specialized military computer. One of its early test runs contained equations for the infamous "Manhattan Project", which created the two atomic bombs dropped on Japan, forcing that country's surrender during World War II.

After the ENIAC, many research laboratories, most of them associated with universities in Britain and the United States, began to construct their own experimental models of electrical computers. Between 1946 and 1954, three important ideas were put forth that are part of the design of modern computers.

The first innovation, the "stored program concept", was documented by the brilliant mathematician John von Neumann. This feature permitted a computer program to be held inside the computer, while the processor unit worked on it without further human intervention. Prior to this discovery, instructions had to be fed into the computer on paper tape, or by rearranging hundreds of removable plug wires into a special pattern on a panel. Because the program was stored electrically inside the computer, the person using it could alter the instructions whenever necessary, even when the machine was operating.

Another idea von Neumann recommended, which eventually increased computer speeds, was to replace the ten decimal numbers used for counting with "binary numbers". Since electrical switches can be either on or off, the binary system, which only has two numbers (0 and 1), seemed a

Figure 1.14 A photo of John von Neumann taken around 1954.

logical way to store information electrically in coded form.

The third development, made by Grace Hopper, a captain in the U.S. Naval Reserve, was the creation of a "compiler program" called COBOL to translate human instructions into binary so that a computer could follow them. The compiler also gave error messages to the programmer when any instructions were incorrect.

1.13 DEVELOPMENT OF A COMPUTER INDUSTRY

*T*he electronic computer industry, as we know it today, began with the creation of the **UNIVAC 1**. Its prototype (original experimental model) received tremendous publicity by correctly predicting the victory of Dwight D. Eisenhower in the U.S. presidential election before all votes were counted. In 1954, Sperry Rand mass-produced 48 identical models of the UNIVAC 1. It was the first "general-purpose computer", designed to help with a variety of applications in business, scientific fields, and the military. At the time, marketing people estimated that the total world need for these computers might reach as high as 200 units! Sperry Rand also introduced magnetic tape machines as a method of transferring stored data quickly.

Sperry Rand's early lead in the computer industry proved to be short lived: IBM also began producing a "general-purpose computer". Superior marketing techniques and computer designs soon gave IBM the largest share of mainframe computer sales in North America, and it is still the market leader today.

The first successfully mass-produced desktop microcomputers were built in 1978 by Apple Computer Inc., with a modular component model simply called "Apple", a forerunner to the Apple IIe. Competitors soon followed their lead. Commodore Business Machines brought out a computer

Figure 1.15 The Univac 1 was the first mass-produced mainframe computer system. It used magnetic tape drives as auxiliary storage devices.

Courtesy of Unisys Corporation

called the "PET", which had a green mono-chrome screen and a cassette deck built into a single sealed unit. Both microcomputers proved popular in schools, although not in the business world. Finally, in 1981, IBM marketed its first IBM PC (Personal Computer), supplying convincing proof that microcomputers could be used effectively in business and government offices. Today, after several "generations" of machines, IBM only holds 20 percent of the micro-computer market. Smaller, innovative companies such as Apple, Compaq, Dell, Digital Equipment, and Hewlett-Packard have provided faster and less expensive versions that are favoured by customers.

1.14 COMPUTER GENERATIONS

*V*arious improvements in electronics and software have increased the speed and reliability of computers. Each improvement created a new computer generation, or series.

Computers built during the period of the UNIVAC 1 (1954-1958) are referred to as the *first generation of computers*. Their circuits were made up of gas-filled glass vacuum tubes and kilometres of electrical wires. Sheets of magnetic rings called "cores" served as internal storage, while magnetic tape units could be added to provide external storage. Programs were awkward to write because the computer only accepted instructions in binary code—that is, patterns using the numbers 0 and 1.

In the *second generation of computers* (1959-1964), solid transistors replaced the hot, unreliable, glass vacuum tubes. These floor-model computers were smaller, faster, cooler, and less likely to break down. Three different types of storage devices could now be attached to the computer. In addition to the magnetic tape, a cylindrical magnetic

Figure
1.16
The first three generations of computer circuitry are shown in this photograph. The largest item is a circuit panel containing eight gas-filled vacuum tubes. Second-generation circuitry, shown at the left, is represented by a plastic circuit board containing several transistors. The modules in the foreground are examples of third-generation transistor chips.

Courtesy of IBM Canada Ltd.

drum device or a circular magnetic disk unit were also available. Committees of programmers designed standardized computer languages called FORTRAN and COBOL. For the first time, people could communicate with computers using English commands or phrases instead of just numbers.

The *third generation of computers* (1965-1969) was characterized by tiny transistor chips called "integrated circuits". These integrated circuits reduced and combined the wiring and transistors of earlier computers into miniature circuit patterns occupying only five square millimetres.

One notable feature of this generation was "interactive processing". For the first time users were allowed to communicate directly with the processor unit, asking questions and getting responses almost immediately. Another feature called "teleprocessing" allowed users at computer terminals to have information processed by a computer several kilometres away. People no longer had to be in the same building, or even in the same city, as the computer they were using.

The *fourth generation of computers* (1970-199?) contains microprocessors that are a complete processing unit on a chip. The miniaturization of the processing unit has encouraged the development of modern-day desktop microcomputers, laptop computers, and pocket computers, as well as calculators, digital toys, and appliances. Magnetic disks have become the favoured method for storing data.

The *fifth generation of computers* promises to be capable of artificial intelligence, and to be able to both speak and understand spoken languages. This may give rise to computers and appliances that talk and think for themselves. Can you imagine having your household fridge tell you to "Remember your diet!" as you open the door to look for a late-night snack, or ordering "Robby", your personal domestic robot, to fetch you a coke while you watch your favourite television show?

Figure
1.17

Fourth-generation circuitry introduced a complete computer on a single chip. The computer chip, shown here on a penny, contains the logic, control, and memory registers necessary to operate an entire microcomputer system. It is also referred to as a microprocessor unit.

Courtesy of Rockwell International

*M*ost computers consist of several devices linked together to form an operational unit. For this reason, it is more accurate to refer to a computer as a computer system. The main part of the computer is the processor unit; any devices attached to the processor unit are referred to as peripherals.

Hardware includes the electrical, mechanical, and magnetic parts of a computer system. Programs, or software, are the instructions that make a computer operate. All computer systems perform five functions—input, output, storage, processing, and control. Each of these functions is usually carried out by an individual device in a computer system.

Computer manufacturers sell two major software components as part of a computer system. The first, an operating system, must be present before any other programs can be run. It provides the intelligence that allows the microprocessor to act as "traffic director" for the flow of information throughout the computer.

The second software component, a computer language, translates the instructions a programmer provides into electrical impulses that the computer can understand and perform. The computer language acts as an "English teacher" by filtering and accepting only statements that contain the correct syntax and spelling.

Programs developed for home or office use are referred to as application software. There are several types of application software, such as word processors, spreadsheets, file managers, data-base managers, and accounting packages.

Competition among computer hardware and software manufacturers ensures graduates of a constant supply of computer-related jobs, including those of word processing operators, spreadsheet analysts, programmers, numerical control operators, CAD specialists, system software developers, and artificial intelligence programmers.

The evolution of computers began with cardboard cards and encoding systems developed by Herman Hollerith and James Powers, whose ideas were purchased by two of the major computer manufacturers today—IBM and Unisys.

analog computer	data entry clerk	microcomputer	processor unit
artificial intelligence programmer	ENIAC	motherboard	program
	five functions	numerical control operator	software
auxiliary memory	hardware		spreadsheet analyst
CAD specialist	hybrid computer system	open architecture	systems software programmer
closed architecture		operating system	
computer application programmer	laptop computer	peripherals	UNIVAC
computer language	mainframe computer	pocket computer	word processing operator
computer system	main memory	printout	

CHECKING YOUR READING

*T*hese are general questions that may require factual recall, reading comprehension, and some application of the knowledge gained from this chapter.

A Computer System

1. Explain the concept of "hardware" and give two examples.

2. What is computer "software"? Give an alternate name for software.

Five Functions of Any Digital Computer System

3. Name the five basic functions of any digital computer system.

4. Name five different types of input device used to enter information into a computer system.

5. What is a computer printout?

6. Why is information stored in main memory RAM vulnerable?

7. Why is the "microprocessor" the most important computer chip in the processor unit?

System Software

8. Describe the role of a computer's "operating system".

9. (a) What is an alternate name for a "language processor"?
   (b) What purpose does it serve?

Application Software

10. Name and describe the uses of each of the following software applications.
    (a) word processor
    (b) spreadsheet
    (c) file manager

Types of Digital Computers

11. Name the four categories of digital computers.

12. Who would use a pocket computer?

Hybrid Computer Systems

13. (a) Define analog computer.
    (b) Describe how a thermostat analog device can control room temperature.

14. (a) What is a hybrid computer system?
    (b) Briefly describe an example of a hybrid computer system.

Open and Closed Architecture

15. Explain what is meant by "closed architecture".

16. What two features of an "open architecture" microcomputer make it different from the other style?

Inside the Processor Unit

17. What two functions are provided by a "motherboard"?

18. What three things does the size of a microprocessor determine in a computer?

People Who Work with Computers

19. Name five businesses that might need an employee trained as a spreadsheet analyst.

20. What does a data entry clerk do?

21. Describe one other computer-related career that may not be located in a traditional office.

Computer Evolution

22. (a) Name the first mass-produced computer.
    (b) How did it receive a lot of publicity?

23. To what does the phrase "computer generation" refer?

APPLYING YOUR KNOWLEDGE

*T*hese questions assume an understanding of the material presented in the chapter, and provide new situations that may require evaluation, analysis, or the application of your newly acquired knowledge.

1. A pocket calculator has several features that are similar to those on a computer. List each of these items, then, beside each one, state which function (input, output, storage, processing, or control) the item represents. Items: display screen, keypad, memory button, logic circuits, clear button.

2. When a consumer product is labeled "digital" it often means that the product contains a computer chip (example: digital pocket calculator). Name three additional products with that label, and explain what the computer circuitry is used for in each case.

3. Mainframe computers are the largest of the four types of digital computer. List the following users of this size of digital computer: (1) government, (2) large corporations, and (3) the military. Beside each organization, give at least two uses it has for the computer. Make all of the items different.

4. Suppose that you are in charge of finding staff for a new computer company. What type of computer expert would you advertise for in the newspaper to get each of these following tasks done?

   (a) design new computer models interactively on the screen;

   (b) write, edit, and print letters to customers;

   (c) keep track of monthly revenue and expenses;

   (d) write updated versions of company operating system;

(e) write programs that make the computer think for itself.

5. Computers come in all sizes and levels of complexity. Suggest which of the four categories of digital computer is most appropriate in each of these situations, and then explain why.

(a) field engineer working on the construction of a bridge;

(b) head office of a national bank;

(c) university student attending lectures;

(d) high school student who has to prepare a printed report for history.

6. Suppose your parents gave you sufficient funds to purchase a computer for use at home, provided that you used it to do school work rather than play games.

(a) List five separate hardware items you would need in order to have a complete modular computer system.

(b) What manufacturer's software would you also need?

7. Large commercial airliners have an automatic pilot mechanism that can be used to control the plane while the pilot relaxes. The automatic pilot control is actually a combination of analog and digital computers. Name three pieces of data that the device needs as input to keep the plane on course for you while you have a coffee.

8. Imagine that you are travelling alone in a space shuttle 30 km above the earth. Radio communications are not working, and you have only a computer to keep you informed of what is happening with the shuttle. Name five things essential to survival you would like the computer to keep track of for you.

INDIVIDUAL PROJECTS

*T*hese are research projects that may require materials from outside the classroom.

1. Want Ads

Using both local and national newspapers as resource material, find want ads for ten different computer jobs. Fasten each clipping neatly to a separate page. Underneath each clipping, prepare a brief description of the job (50-word minimum). The description should be researched from your textbook and library resources, and include job description, educational requirements, and approximate annual salary. Cover the ten pages with an attractive title page.

2. Ads for Computer Hardware

Using newspapers and computer magazines as resources, find ten different advertisements for computer systems and computer hardware (peripherals, circuit boards). Fasten each clipping neatly to a separate blank page. Underneath each clipping, prepare a brief description of the product, including the product name, manufacturer, uses for the product, and its price. Cover the ten pages with an attractive title page.

UNIT 2   SOFTWARE APPLICATIONS

*T*his six-chapter unit explores the most popular software applications in the work place: word-processing, spreadsheet, data-base, computer-graphics, desktop-publishing, and integrated software. The chapters provide both a conceptual understanding and a hands-on, working knowledge of each of these types of software.

The chapters are not written for any specific computer system, and thus allow the use of any available program, on any microcomputer used in the schools.The topics are independent of each other, and thus can be taught in any sequence. Any section can become the main focus of the course.

Chapter

2

WORD PROCESSING

66 Word processing probably accounts for over half of all the computer use in North America, and is usually one of the first programs an adult purchases for his or her computer. 99

OBJECTIVES

By the end of this chapter, you will be able to:

1 Define the following computer terms: word processing, document, window, status line, cursor, scrolling, printout (or hard copy), proofreading, copyediting, screen editing, word wrap, WYSIWYG;

2 Use a six-step word-processing cycle to key in, edit, save, and print a one- or two-page document;

3 Use special print features such as boldface, italics, underlining, and different font sizes or styles in a document when something needs to be emphasized;

4 Differentiate between a file name and a document title;

5 Type multi-paragraph documents with proper spacing, and sub-headings where required;

6 Create professional-looking memos and business letters;

7 Recognize and use proofreaders' marks while editing.

WORKING IN THE WORLD OF COMPUTERS

Computer Consultant
prepares a printed report for a client

Department Manager
organizes proposals and reports for senior managers to consider

Fiction Writer
writes fiction novels to sell to a publisher

Newspaper Columnist
creates a daily or weekly column for a newspaper

Radio Announcer
prepares printed copy to read while "on the air"

Speech Writer
creates imaginative speeches for politicians

Teacher
uses a word processor to create lessons and assignments for students

Television Newscaster
writes and revises printed copy to read on the news broadcast

Word Processing Operator
prepares memos, letters, and other documents

2.1 INTRODUCTION

*H*ave you ever noticed that teachers tend to award higher marks to typed reports and assignments than to hand-written ones? That is probably because typed assignments are more attractive to look at and easier to read. This preference for typed material is also found among managers in almost all business and government offices across Canada.

The typewriter was the first portable device to provide quality typed output, and reigned unrivaled as an office machine from 1873 to 1980. The first mass-produced Remington typewriters could only print capital letters, much like early computer printers. During the 1970s however, a desk-size computer, referred to as a dedicated word processor, was developed by such companies as AES Ltd. and Wang Ltd. to specialize in screen editing of typed documents. Their cost (approximately $20 000) and their large size (like a piece of office furniture) prevented wide-spread adoption. However, during the 1980s smaller, less expensive, desktop microcomputer systems including a keyboard, a visual display screen, and a printer became popular replacements for office typewriters.

Word processing refers to the use of a computer for keying in, editing, saving, and printing documents. **Documents** include memos, letters, reports, assignments, essays, or anything else you might want in print. Word processing probably accounts for over half of all the computer use in North America, and usually is one of the first types of program an adult purchases for his or her computer at home or at work. Anyone who has touch-typing skills, in addition to computer skills, will be more efficient at producing documents. Some of the more popular commercial word-processing soft-

ware for microcomputers includes *Ami*, *Microsoft Works*, *Microsoft Word*, *WordPerfect*, and *WordStar*. Less sophisticated but easier to use software for school computer labs includes *Appleworks*, *First Choice*, and *PC-Write*.

2.2 VIEWING A DOCUMENT ON THE SCREEN

*U*nless you have a very short memo, most computer screens will not show the entire document that you are working on. The screen is similar to a **window** that allows you to view only part of the document, in the same way that a real window lets you see only part of the scene outside of a building. However, by using the appropriate keys on the keyboard, such as the directional cursor keys, or the PgUp and PgDn keys, or a pointing device, such as a trackball or hand-held mouse, the document you are working on can be **scrolled** (moved vertically or horizontally) across the screen to bring into view that part of the document that you want to work on.

The Status Line

*M*ost word-processing software divides the screen into the "window", or working area, and the **status line**. The latter appears either at the very top or at the very bottom of the screen. It contains useful reminders for the person at the keyboard. Although the order of the information varies from program to program, at least three things are usually displayed.

The first is the document's file name. A **file name** is a short word, or hyphenated phrase, used as a label for disk storage and retrieval. All documents must be given a unique file name for the computer to be able to tell them apart. Sometimes the file name is preceded by a disk-drive reference

Typical Word-Processing Screen

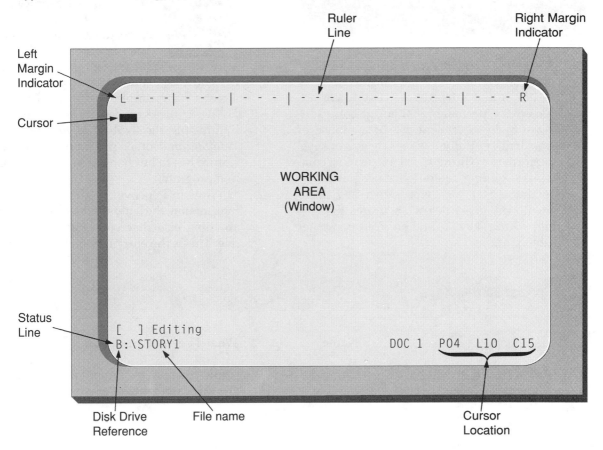

like "A:" or "2:". This tells the computer which disk drive (or other storage device) to use when more than one is available.

A file name is not the same as a document title. A file name is a label for filing purposes. A **document title**, on the other hand, is the title that you place at the beginning of your document to assist the reader.

The second item displayed in the status line is the page number of the document you are working on. An indication such as "P04" would mean that you are currently working on page four of the document.

The third item displayed in the status line would be the current location of the cursor on the screen. The display "L10 C15" would mean that your cursor is sitting on

line ten in column fifteen. The **cursor** is the blinking underscore or lighted square that tells you where the computer's attention is currently focused on the screen.

Most word-processing programs have a feature called **word wrap**. This feature allows the program to take your cursor to the beginning of the next line automatically when a preset margin is reached. It will also bring with the cursor any word from the end of the previous line which was too long to fit within the margin requirements.

The advantage of word wrap is that you do not have to worry about pressing the "Return" or "Enter" key at the end of each line. This feature will increase your keyboarding speed tremendously.

*O*ne of the advantages of using word-processing software over the traditional typewriter is that mistakes are easy to correct. No error is permanent. Although some software makes excellent use of a mouse or trackball, typically five keys (or sets of keys) perform the editing functions on most computers. *Editing* refers to locating and correcting errors in a word-processed document. The chart below illustrates the special editing keys found on most computer keyboards.

Typeover Mode or Pushright Mode

*N*ot all word-processing software begins with the same default positions for data entry. Fortunately, most software permits the user to change the way in which the letters are entered on the screen. For example, in *WordPerfect* and *PC-Write*, these modes are easily invoked by pressing the INSERT key on or off. In *WordStar* and other programs, the default feature has to be changed in the configuration program.

While in Typeover Mode, as you key in information, the letters and words type over anything else that you may have on the line. This is the entry mode we will use.

Special Editing Keys

Keys	Name	What They Are Used For
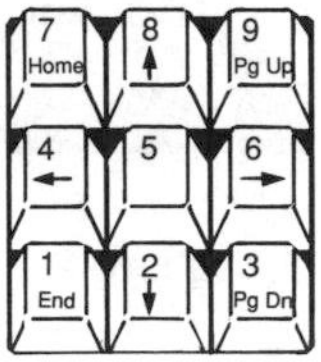	Cursor keys	Allow you to move around on the screen in any direction without erasing anything
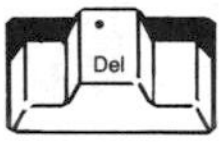	Delete Key	Deletes the character ahead of the cursor. A forwards eraser
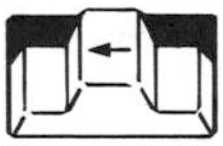	Backspace Key	Moves the cursor backwards, erasing as it goes. In some software, this key may move backward without erasing
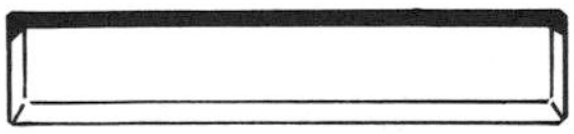	Space Bar	Moves the cursor forward, either inserting spaces or erasing as it goes. A forward eraser in "typeover mode"
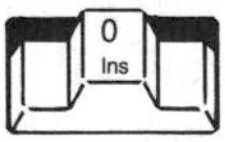	Insert Key	Permits missing letters or words to be "inserted"

While in Pushright Mode, as you key in information, any previous words on the screen are pushed ahead of the letters being entered. This is equivalent to continuously having the INSERT feature turned on. If your program automatically begins in this mode, turn off the INSERT mode as soon as you begin.

Practice Assignment   **(20 mins.)**

Screen Editing

The following statements have errors in them. First, key in the statements exactly as they appear. Then, using only the editing keys specified, make the corrections. (Note: students using Ámi or Microsoft Works software, or an ICON or Macintosh microcomputer, may handle the editing differently by highlighting sections of the text, and selecting "pictured" options. Those students should refer to their teacher for further instructions.)

Phrase to Type In	Suggested Editing Keys to Use for Corrections
1. Word procesing is eazy.	Use the BACKSPACE key to erase backwards. Re-enter the words.
2. Judy Judy Smith is the singer.	Use the cursor key to move to the second "Judy" in from the margin. Place the cursor on "J" and press the DELETE key five times.
3. This process of finding and correcting errrors on the screen is callled editing.	Move to words with extra letters using the cursor keys. Use the DELETE key to remove unwanted letters.
4. Microcompters are multi-purpose.	With the cursor key, move to the "t" in the first word. Press the INSERT key. Type in the missing letter. Turn off INSERT by pressing the key again.
5. Key in your first and last name leaving letters out of each word.	Move to missing letter position with the cursor key. Press INSERT. Key in the missing letter. Turn off INSERT by pressing that key before moving again.

Microcomputer workstations that share a hard drive and printer may never use a personal diskette to store documents. However, if your workstation permits the use of a floppy disk, you will need to format the disk before saving anything on it. *Formatting* is a process that prepares a new disk to match the computer with which it is to be used. During the process, the computer organizes the blank disk with circular tracks, pie-shaped sectors, and an index to store file names. Formatting tends to be "machine-specific", which means that a diskette formatted for an

Apple IIe will not work in an IBM PC. Old disks can be formatted as well, but the process will erase everything currently stored on the disk. If you use a floppy disk for storage, make sure that it is formatted before attempting the next practice assignment.

The command to format a floppy diskette varies with the machine that you are using. Consult the manual or your teacher for specific information. If you are using an IBM PC, for example, the formatting command might appear as follows:

FORMAT A:/S/V

The letter "A" is the disk drive location. The "S" is an option that places a system file on the disk to give it some "intelligence", and the "V" is an option to permit the user to place a volume label (directory label) on the disk, such as "PETE'S DISK" or "PETE FRANKIN", for identification.

Practice Assignment   (15 mins.)

Creating a Document

For this practice assignment, you will need a formatted diskette in the disk drive on which to save your work (if a floppy disk drive is available). Using the word-processing software, key in the following paragraph, with single spacing between each line. When you have completed the data entry, proofread your work and correct any errors. Save the corrected document on your disk using the file name "Story1", then print a hard copy on the printer.

Why Word-Processing Software?

Word-processing software permits the user to key in, edit, save, and print documents using a microcomputer. This is handy because students can use such software to prepare school assignments that have a "polished" appearance. Often, typed assignments receive higher marks than hand-written ones. This is probably because printed assignments are more attractive to look at and easier to read. Students who know how to manipulate a word processor have an "edge" over those who do not.

2.5 SPECIAL PRINT FEATURES

*I*n word processing, there are usually several ways to emphasize important concepts on paper. The word or phrase can be **underlined**, or printed in **boldfaced** characters (made darker by double-striking the characters), or the font size can be changed, as can the font style.

Only some programs permit a change in font size. **Font size** means that the physical size of the letter is changed, or scaled to larger or smaller versions of itself. When available, larger font sizes can be used for preparing cover pages for assignments and making document titles stand out.

Variations in font style are also only available on some software. **Font style** refers to a change in the actual style of the lettering. Examples might include condensed letters, or those with a shadow effect. One font style that is standard in most word-processing programs is *italic*, which is useful for emphasizing names of books and foreign or unusual words.

The latest innovation in word processing is software that lets you see on the screen exactly what will appear on your printout. This means that differences in font sizes, styles, and formatting, such as boldface and underlining, will appear exactly as designed on the screen. This final view can be seen through a "print preview" option on newer versions of software such as *WordPerfect* and *WordStar*. In other software, such as Ámi Professional and Macintosh programs, this finished view appears all through the text as you enter material. Programs that have this continuous finished view are often referred to as **WYSIWYG** (What You See Is What You Get) software.

Common Highlighting Features

Highlighting Feature	How It Appears
Underlining	<u>microcomputer</u>
Boldfacing	**microcomputer**
Font Size	microcomputer
Font Style	*microcomputer*

Practice Assignment

(20 mins.)

Highlighting in Documents

Key in this assignment as shown. Include in your printout the underlining, boldfacing, or printing in italics. Centre your title. Save your completed document on disk with the file name "Uncle Harry" and make a printout.

<u>Uncle Harry</u>

Uncle Harry was a strange fellow. During the winter he always wore a crumbled trench coat, brown leather shoes, badly in need of repair, and an old grey hat with the brim turned upwards. He liked to quote from a book called *Poems For Weary Travellers* and tell stories of his adventures as a youngster in a small eastern township. His light blue eyes seemed to sparkle, and his beer belly would jiggle when he laughed. I miss his laugh most of all.

2.6 WORD-PROCESSING CYCLE

*T*he use of word-processing software for writing essays, reports, or research papers, where the original material must be created by you, involves a series of six steps. Each of these steps has certain skills attached to it that are easy to master.

**Step 1
Researching
& Composing
the Report**

*M*ost assignments that you are given in school involve looking up information, or certain facts, which you then organize into a coherent paper or report. This is called the research stage. It is here that you use the school library, class materials, personal interviews, or resources from outside the school to gather the information you require. First you outline the details in point form under various headings, then you rearrange the wording and order of the ideas so that the entire report will communicate a clear message to the reader. This stage is called "composition". Time spent in researching and composing will lead to a well-organized and thoughtful report later on.

**Step 2
Keying in
the Report**

*U*sing the microcomputer and word-processing software, you key in your report, composing correct sentences and adding phrases and ideas that will attract the interest of your reader. You have to also consider the format of the document so that it will be visually pleasing. For example, the main title should be centred at the top of the page, whereas subtitles are placed at the left-hand margin. Usually two lines are left blank after any title, before the paragraphs begin. Setting the left- and right-hand margins at ten character spaces or one

inch each will ensure an attractive white border on either side of the document. The resulting line length is referred to as a 65-stroke line. The margin settings can be altered for different types of output. Remember to save your completed document on disk with a unique file name.

**Step 3
Print a
Draft
Document**

*T*he first printed copy of your document is called a *draft document* because changes will probably have to be made. This first printout is also referred to as "version one". (When changes are made and another printout is obtained, it is called "version two", and so on.) Most printers have a "draft mode" that makes a very quick printout of your document by producing lighter characters than are needed for the final copy. This is sufficient for the early stages, and saves time and costly printer ribbons.

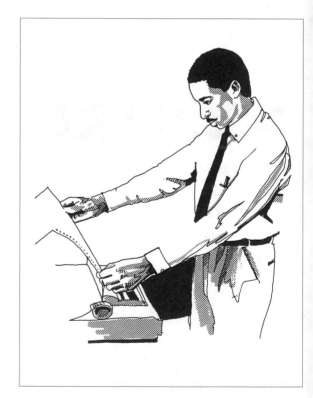

At this stage you **copyedit** your material using your draft copy printout. Identify any errors in spelling, grammar, or punctuation, and write the corrections on the printout. Programs that check spelling and grammar would help to locate errors. It would be wise, however, not to rely on them entirely because of their inability to identify all the possible mistakes a document may contain.

You may also wish to consult with the original question sheet, or your teacher, to make sure the format of the document (the spacing and general layout) is as requested.

Bring the copyedited version of the draft printout to your computer workstation, and key in the corrections to the original document on the screen. The task of correcting the errors identified in the copyedited version by making changes on the screen is called *screen editing*.

When the changes have been entered into the original document on the screen, another draft is printed. The first and second printouts are then compared to make sure that all the changes have been made. Comparing and checking printouts is called **proofreading**.

Steps three, four, and five may have to be done several times, producing several different versions of the same document, until all the errors are corrected. Some software requires that each new draft of the document be saved with a new file name, such as Harry1, Harry2, etc.

This is the version that you plan to hand in to your teacher for marking, or to your boss in the workplace. All previous versions were just printed for editing purposes. The quality of print of the final version should be dark and clear, all the errors should have been removed, and all special print features should be included. Remember to remove the edges of the computer paper containing the tractor-feed holes, if any, and separate the printout into individual sheets if there is more than one page. Prepare a cover page or title page and staple it and the report together before handing them in. Keep in mind that, as a student, or as an employee, you will be judged by the quality and appearance of the work that you submit, not just the quantity.

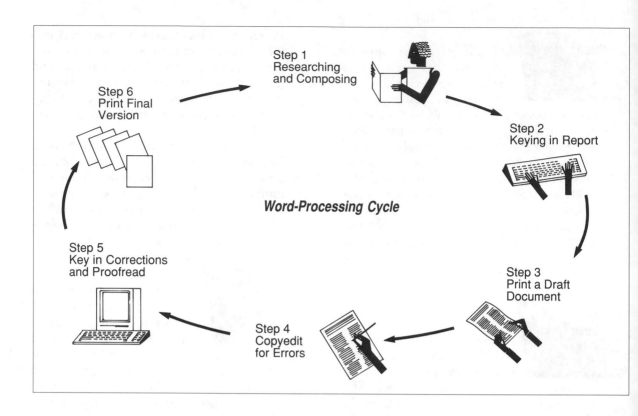

Word-Processing Cycle

Step 1
Researching
and Composing

Step 2
Keying in Report

Step 3
Print a Draft
Document

Step 4
Copyedit
for Errors

Step 5
Key in Corrections
and Proofread

Step 6
Print Final
Version

The Biography

This assignment is similar to the type given to newspaper reporters. It contains all six steps of the word-processing cycle including the first step—researching your topic.

Your task is to interview a classmate and collect information about that person on a sheet of paper. Cover about 12 points that will make an interesting write-up. Then, using the computer, compose a one-paragraph biography for that student similar to the sample provided. Save the file using the file name "Biograph", then print a draft document. Let the person you interviewed read it for factual accuracy. You should then copyedit it for wording, spelling, grammar, and punctuation. Using your pen or pencil, make the corrections right on the printout. Next, use the computer to key in the changes on the screen, then resave it, and print a second draft to compare with the first, making sure the changes are correct. This is called proofreading. When you are satisfied with its appearance, use a double-strike or near-letter-quality option to get a darker print and print the final document.

SUSAN WALKER

Susan is 16 years old and lives within five blocks of the school. She works part-time at McDonald's three nights a week, usually on weekends. At school she plays in the school band, which practises at lunch time, and she is one of the eight members of the cheerlead-ing team. She enjoys swimming, dancing, reading romance novels, and watching come-dies on television. Her favourite recording artists are The Bangles and The Rolling Stones.

2.7 DOCUMENT PROTECTION

*B*ecause data is in electronic form within the computer's main memory, it tends to be vulnerable to erasure. In a computer lab there are many accidental threats to docu-ment destruction. For example, the power may fail because someone kicked a power cord with their feet, or because a mainte-nance person flicked a switch while check-ing electrical circuits. Thunderstorms can also cause a power outage throughout the school. Removal of power for whatever reason will automatically erase anything stored in temporary main memory, includ-ing your document and the word-process-ing software.

Your floppy disk is also vulnerable to data destruction. Any document that you store on the disk is held there with only a weak field of magnetism (similar to the static on a comb when your hair is dry). Getting your disk dirty or smudging the read/write surface with your fingerprints could easily make the disk unreadable.

Here are some suggestions that you should follow to protect your documents and all the effort that went into their crea-tion.

Suggestions for Protecting Your Document

(1) Save your document on disk as often as possible while working, to avoid having to re-key an entire document after an electrical accident.

(2) Print the latest version of each docu-ment as a backup in case the disk be-comes corrupted (which means it is no longer usable).

(3) Keep floppy disks in their protective envelope when they are not being used inside the disk drive. This protects them from dust, grime, and static electricity.

(4) If possible, make a backup copy of your disk and all its files at the end of each workday.

2.8 SOFTWARE TOOLS TO ENHANCE WORD PROCESSING

*T*here are five additional software programs that you can use to enhance word processing. Some expensive software may already have some of these features built in. Because of their extra memory requirements, usually only computers with a hard disk drive and a very large memory can use them adequately.

"What do you mean... File unavailable? You just stored it!"

Spelling Checker

A **spelling checker** can search through your document at a very fast pace, checking the spelling of each word against a data dictionary of 50 000-200 000 words that it has stored on the hard disk. When it finds a word that is not in its data dictionary, it displays some possible correct spellings from which the user can choose the most appropriate word. Some spelling checkers have a feature that lets you add words of your own to a "personal dictionary". This is useful if you are working with specialized vocabularies for such

topics as computers, psychology, law, or medicine. You can also get the program to check the spelling of just one specific word, rather than scan the entire document.

Although they are probably the most helpful of the word-processing tools in the group, most spelling checkers have three limitations. The first is the tendency to use American spelling references, rather than Canadian. The second is their inability to deal with people's names or place names. When the spelling checker scans a line and encounters words such as "Fred Jenkins" or "Toronto" it stops scanning and asks you what you want done with them, as if they were spelling mistakes. The third weakness is an inability to recognize words that are spelled correctly but are grammatically wrong, such as "He went too the store four a loaf of bred." The words "too", "four", and "bred" are grammatically incorrect but are spelled correctly, so the spelling checker would not spot them.

The spelling checker will replace any word that you specify and automatically readjust the line length to accommodate any difference in the number of characters.

Thesaurus

A second add-on tool for people who use word processors is a **thesaurus**, which is similar to *Roget's Thesaurus*, a book used by writers. With a few keystrokes, this program will display alternative words with a similar meaning for the word that you would like to change in your document. Suppose you have used the word "large" in your document, and you want a similar but more appropriate word. The program will look up its index and return with a list, such as "big, great, huge, colossal, enormous, immense". You can then select one of those alternatives and the computer will replace the original word with the new word and readjust the line length to compensate for any difference in the number of characters.

Grammar Checker

*T*his software program scans through any document you have created and checks for sentence length, incorrect punctuation, incorrect use of grammar, and some other points, and suggests what should replace each highlighted section of text. It tends to work best with technical report writing and worst with fiction writing because its rules of "thinking" do not allow for some kinds of statements. Suppose that in a mystery short story you wrote the following:

> Crash! Sam jumped at the sudden interruption to his thoughts about the murder victim.

Some grammar checkers would give this response:

> "*** Crash! Incomplete sentence. Lacks subject and predicate."

This type of analysis would discourage even the most enthusiastic of mystery writers. It prevents what literary critics call "artistic licence"—deviations from grammatic form or rule that help to enhance the meaning or keep the reader's interest.

Document Outliner

*T*he fourth major word-processing add-on tool is called a **document outliner**. It is used to plan the sequence and details of a report or story in point form before composing the real thing. It uses headings and "bullets" to list the details of each section. It will not make your story more accurate or imaginative, but can help to make it better organized so that the reader can follow it more easily. It is an alternative to using a pen and paper to organize the details on a topic before beginning the first draft.

Idea Generator

*T*he last of the five major word-processing add-on tools is the **idea generator**, a program that helps people to be more creative. It contains several subprograms that provide creative problem-solving strategies to make your brainstorming sessions more productive. For example, it may suggest that you focus solely on the people to be included in an essay, or solely on the goals involved in the proposed document. It may give you a list of selected words or phrases, and then ask you to describe how they would fit into your sentences (development of metaphors), and so on. Your answers can then be organized and printed as a report. This tool can be used for document processing, or as a general problem-solving tool when analyzing tough or vague problems that require innovative thinking. City planners, politicians, business leaders, environmentalists, futurists, and many others could all benefit from this type of strategic-thinking software.

DOONESBURY   **by Garry Trudeau**

A Newspaper Column

Your task is to set your screen for a narrow, single-column article, similar to those in magazines or newspapers. Set the column to be a 25-stroke line, or 2.5 inches. Make up a three-paragraph short story about a local teenager who sees a house on fire and rushes in to save a two-year-old baby and the baby's mother. They are lying unconscious on the floor of the house. When the story is completed, check your document for spelling and grammatical errors. Save your file using the file name "News", then make a printout of your news column.

2.9 WRITING MEMOS

*T*he ability to write professional-looking memos is often the key to drawing immediate attention to your ideas or requests. Word processing is an easy way to create and print memos that will impress both your colleagues and top management.

Corporate memos usually appear in a standard format. Without some standardization, memos would become too varied and difficult to read. Consider the following example of a well-designed corporate memo. It contains two sections—the heading and the body.

Memo Heading

*A*s you can see in the example opposite, the title "MEMO" appears at the top. The date and the names of the recipient and the sender appear underneath, against the left-hand margin. No addresses are given because memos are a company's internal form of communication. However, it is proper to give the name and title (or department) of both the sender and receiver.

The Body of the Memo

*T*he content of the communication is contained in what is referred to as the "body" of the memo. It begins with a title in capital letters that is preceded by the word "SUBJECT" or the letters "RE:" which is the abbreviation for "REGARDING". The title should always indicate what the memo is about and be different from other memo titles you have used recently, because people often refer back to memos by their title as well as their date.

If you are on familiar terms with the receiver, you can begin with the person's first name. Otherwise, use a formal style, such as Mr., Mrs., Miss, or Ms., or leave out the name entirely. The remainder of the memo contains the content of the message. You may sign your first name, just include your initials, or have nothing at all at the bottom. If someone else types the memo, their initials would appear last.

Strategies for Writing Effective Memos

(1) Personalize the memo, if possible, by beginning with the person's first name in the body section.

(2) Use positive-sounding words and phrases that will make the reader glad to be reading your memo. These would include phrases such as "I appreciate...", "your work is excellent", and "you'll like this idea".

(3) Keep the memo short and to the point. The idea is to bring the reader's attention to something that you believe is important, not to tell him or her a long story.

Example of a Memo

MEMO

1992/03/21

TO: Wally M. LeRoy
              Director of Marketing

FROM: Marie Fawcette
              Product Manager

SUBJECT: MEETING TO DISCUSS NEW PRODUCT

Wally, our team has just come up with an exciting product idea for a new video game cartridge based on the Star Wars theme.

Could we arrange a meeting for Friday at ten o'clock so our team can present the idea to your marketing group? We're aiming the cartridge at the 12- to 15-year-olds and are looking at a possible June 30 deadline for product announcement. One possible distribution method for sales is through department stores and specialty computer stores.

Your work on the last project was excellent, and we're looking forward to working with you again.

Budget Request Memo

Using the corporate memo style discussed in this chapter, ask the company president for a $240 000 increase in your advertising budget. The money will be used to promote three new models of electric guitar that the company has developed since the original budget was set. You are the Vice-President of Advertising, and the memo is to be sent to Earl Lewis, President. The business is called Harmony Guitar Corporation. Include two logical reasons for the proposed budget increase. Before you begin you should review the example of the memo and the *Strategies for Writing Effective Memos* mentioned on page 46. Save your file using the file name "Memo". Make a printout.

2.10 BUSINESS LETTERS

*F*ormal **business letters**, as well as memos, tend to have a standard format to their layout. This section will illustrate a particular business letter style called *full block style*, which is commonly used in most companies today. In this style of business letter there are no indentations. All lines, even those that start new paragraphs, begin at the left-hand margin. This style also follows a special form called "open punctuation", which omits commas and periods at the ends of the lines containing the date and address, unless they end with an abbreviation. This style makes typing much easier and faster because there is no centring or tabbing and less punctuation.

Like the memo, the full-block-style business letter contains a top section and a body. The top section contains the date, the recipient's name, title, corporate name, and address, and the salutation. The *salutation*, meaning the conventional opening used in a letter, can begin in several ways, such as "Dear Sir/Madam", "Dear Sir", or "Dear Mrs. Peachtree".

The body section contains your message with each different idea outlined in a new paragraph. The *closing* is used to signal to your reader that your letter is finished. It is the phrase just above your signature, and can appear in several forms including "Sincerely", "Yours truly", or "Sincerely yours". Your full name and title or department is typed below your hand-written signature (just in case no one can read your signature). Consider the following example of a "full-block-style" letter.

Example of a Full-block-style Letter

**INDEPENDENT
GAS RETAILERS**
1923 James Street
Toronto, Ontario
M6B 1L2

1992/11/30

Mrs. Mariam Ali
Supervisor of Marketing & Distribution
Webco Petroleum Company Limited
225 Main Street W.
Calgary, Alberta

Dear Mrs. Ali

Thank you for the excellent service over the years. Deliveries to our independent
gasoline outlets have, for the most part, been on time and as requested.

We have encountered a small problem that I thought should be brought to your
attention. During the past two months, some service stations in the Kitchener-
Waterloo area of Ontario have not been receiving their orders for high octane on
time. The dealers have forwarded their complaints to me at head office. I know
that you have an excellent reputation for filling orders, and would not wish to see
it tarnished by this incident. When you have a chance, would you please look into
this for me?

Sincerely

R. L. Bateman

Rick L. Bateman, President
Independent Gas Retailers Association

2.11 TIPS FOR EFFECTIVE LETTER WRITING

*I*t is important to remember that even when you are angry the person receiving the letter will respond much better, and be more likely to do as you ask, if you treat them nicely. If you have something negative to express, begin with a compliment so that the criticism to follow will not seem so harsh. Never order someone else to take action—persuade them instead. Many of the same strategies that apply to memos also apply to letter writing. To the right are some to remember.

Letter-Writing Strategies

(1) Personalize the salutation if you know the recipient by using their first name; otherwise, use the formal style.

(2) Use positive-sounding words and phrases.

(3) Be brief and to the point (1-2 pages maximum).

(4) If you have to communicate something negative, mention something positive or complimentary first, and then explain the situation without expressing anger.

2.12 PROFESSIONAL PROOFREADING SYMBOLS

*M*anagers, manuscript editors, secretaries, and students can all benefit from a collection of standard proofreading symbols. These are standard paper-editing notations used when proofreading draft documents.

A knowledge of some of the more frequently used symbols will assist you in making corrections. It will also help you to tell someone else what changes are to be made, when the proofreading and data-entry functions are being performed by different people. The following table lists several symbols used in the proofreading stage to edit documents.

Proofreaders' Symbols

Instruction	Symbol	Example	Corrected Version
Insert comma	⋏	large heavy item	large, heavy item
Insert period	⊙	This is it	This is it.
Insert space	#	hardcopy	hard copy
Close up space	⌒	print out	printout
New paragraph	¶	¶ The second item	The second item

Instruction	Symbol	Example	Corrected Version
Delete	ℓ	the ~~the~~ computer	the computer
Make upper case	≡	<u>ibm</u> computer	IBM computer
Make lower case	/	the /Computer	the computer
Spell out	(Sp)	(Sp)/10 printouts	ten printouts
Align	‖	the system if available	the system if available
Transpose	⁓	the machine new,	the new machine
Run in	⟶	It's time.⟩ ⟨Let's go.	It's time. Let's go.

Interpreting Proofreading Symbols

This assignment can be done both orally, as a discussion on recognition and interpretation of the proofreading symbols, and at the keyboard to practise editing skills.

(a) First, see if you can explain the meaning of the various corrections to the class.

(b) Then, using your computer, key in the corrected version of the document. Save it with the file name "Symbols" and make a printout.

The Proofreader's Dilemma

Alice and her partner Jodie were working on a Library research paper together for their computer course They have selected the topic — "Computers In Banking" and spent 2 days looking up information and making making rough notes. Yesterday, they spent an hour in the lab composing and printing a draft version of their report. Today jodie was on a field trip and alice working alone, was having great difficulty interpreting her partner's penciled corrections. "If only we had learned proofreaders' symbols," Alice said to herself a with sigh.

Word processing refers to the use of a computer to type, edit, save, and print documents, such as memos, letters, essays, reports, and assignments. Except for those with a vertical-style monitor, most computer systems will not let you see a complete page all at once. The user can usually view only part of a document through a "window", similar to the way a person can only see part of the scenery outside a building when looking through a window.

The word-processing cycle is a series of six steps that people perform when they are creating a document "from scratch". The six steps are: Researching and Composing the Report, Keying in the Report, Print a Draft Document, Copyedit for Errors, Key in the Corrections and Proofread, and Print the Final Version.

There are five major programs that may be part of the user's word-processing software library. A spelling checker is a fast scanning program that points out possible spelling errors; a grammar checker operates in a similar fashion, but scans for grammatical mistakes; a thesaurus provides alternative words with a similar meaning to the one that you have highlighted; a document outliner helps writers plan and organize the content of their document; an idea generator provides a number of strategies to make brainstorming sessions more productive.

Two forms of standard written communication in the business world are the corporate memo and the business letter. Although there are several variations in style, only the most popular format for each is provided in this chapter.

Proofreaders' symbols are standard, paper-editing notations used when proofreading draft documents. A knowledge of some common symbols will assist you in making corrections. It will also help in communicating the corrections to someone else when the proofreading and data entry functions are performed by different people.

boldface	font size	spelling checker
business letter	font style	status line
copyediting	grammar checker	thesaurus
cursor	idea generator	underlining
document	italic	window
document title	memo	word processing
document outliner	proofreading	word wrap
file name	scrolling	WYSIWYG

CHECKING YOUR READING

*T*hese are general questions that may require factual recall, reading comprehension, or some application of the knowledge gained from this chapter.

Introduction

1. Define "word processing".

2. Suggest three tasks relating to your courses in school that might be done more effectively with word processing.

3. List four commercial word-processing programs that people can purchase for office or home use.

Viewing a Document on the Screen

4. Why do some people refer to the display screen as a "window"?

5. Translate the letters of the acronym WYSIWYG and explain its meaning.

6. What three things do most word-processing programs display in the status line?

7. How does a file name differ from a document title?

8. Explain what the following information, contained in this status line, means.
   A:STORYONE   P10   L5   C15

Simple Screen Editing

9. Which keys on the keyboard permit the following actions?

   (a) Move around on the screen without erasing anything;

   (b) Erase as the cursor moves backwards;

   (c) Erase as the cursor moves forward;

   (d) Place a missing letter into a word.

Formatting a Diskette

10. What does the process of "formatting" do to a blank diskette?

11. Explain what is meant by the phrase "formatting tends to be machine-specific".

Special Print Features

12. List four different ways to emphasize something important in a document.

13. Give an example of what is meant by each of the following: (a) font size; (b) font style.

The Word-Processing Cycle

14. What resources can students refer to when researching a topic for a school project?

15. To what does "version one of a draft document" refer?

16. What three tasks are performed when someone "copyedits" a document?

17. Define "screen editing".

18. What is meant by "proofreading"?

19. Before handing in a final version of a document for marking, what three things should you remember to do?

20. List the six steps in the word-processing cycle.

Document Protection

21. Suggest two different problems that people may have with computer data, and also suggest a solution for each one.

Additional Software Tools

22. What three weaknesses do many spelling-checker programs have?

23. If you were using a thesaurus program, what would you expect it to do?

24. Why do most fiction writers avoid grammar-checker programs?

25. What function does a document outliner perform?

Writing Memos and Letters

26. Why is it important to write a professional-looking memo, rather than a casual-style one, within a corporation?

27. (a) What does the abbreviation "RE:" mean?
    (b) What alternative word can be used instead?

28. (a) What is a "salutation" in a letter?
    (b) Give one example.

29. (a) Why is a closing used in letters?
    (b) Give an example of a typical closing.

30. Interpret the meaning of the proofreading symbols in the following examples.
    (a) pocket, laptop, microcomputer, and mainframe
    (b) the mpu operates at 20 megahertz
    (c) the the best desktop microcomputer
    (d) vertical-style monitor
    (e) theprintout

*T*hese are more practice assignments that require the use of word-processing software. They will help you develop keyboarding, editing, and proofreading skills before you begin assignments to be marked.

1. One Story—Two Versions

Complete the missing blanks in the story by inserting an appropriate word as you type. Save the document using the file name Version1 and make a printout. Key in the story a second time, using different descriptive words. Save the second story as Version2, and make a second printout.

MR. TWILLIGER
Version One

Mr. Twilliger was a strange _____. His _____ hair and slightly graying _____ gave him a wild appearance as he slowly walked along the _____ carrying an old_____. His baggy _____ flapped in the wind. "I wonder if my _____ will remember me after all these years?" he thought as he approached the familiar _____.

2. Lab Time Request

Key in the following memo completing the missing parts as you go along. Save the document with the file name "Memo" and make a printout.

MEMO

Today's Date

TO: (enter your teacher's name)
           Computer Studies Teacher

FROM: (enter your name)
           (enter course code)

SUBJECT: AMOUNT OF COMPUTER TIME

Mr./Ms. _____, I appreciate the time and effort that you take with us in class to help us understand the computer software. Your dedication to the subject and willingness to help students individually with their problems is commendable.

Would it be possible to arrange for our class to get more lab time on the computers during the week? This change would prove to be very helpful in the completion of our assignments for you.

3. Creative Fiction

Using your imagination, create a one-page short story that begins with the phrase "Once upon a time ...". Some theme suggestions for your story include sports, adventure, science fiction, romance, western, or some experience from real life "spiced up" a bit.

Save your story on your disk with the file name "TallTale". Then print a hard copy, copyedit the printout, and key in the changes. Continue the process until you are happy with your final version.

*E*ach of these assignments requires the use of a word processor. Your teacher will provide a list of printer options that will indicate how to get the printer to perform functions such as underlining, boldfacing, italics, and enlarged lettering. Type and attach a title page to each assignment before handing it in for marking.

SECTION 1 NON-RESEARCH PROJECTS

These projects emphasize various types of document creation and editing skills. They do not require any research.

1. Thinking Computers

Using your word processor, key in, edit, save, and print the following document. Print the title in boldface or enlarged letters. When typing with single spacing, leave two blank lines after the title and between each paragraph.

ARTIFICIAL INTELLIGENCE

Artificial intelligence is a relatively new field. It refers to software design that will allow computers to think and make decisions on their own. The research topics include robotics, gaming theory, (such as chess and checkers), giving computers the ability to see and recognize objects, and giving them the ability to understand and speak the English language.

Although this field is very exciting to researchers, not all people are equally as enthusiastic. Some scientists fear that the long-run outcome of this type of study may be the loss of an enormous number of both "white-collar and blue-collar" jobs, the development of more sophisticated warfare applications, and major decisions that affect humans being made by machines. Movies such as *War Games*, *The Terminator*, and *Robo Cop* indicate the extreme negative views some fiction writers have of artificial intelligence in the future.

Whatever the outcome, these types of machine may soon appear. It is predicted that a prototype computer, to rival humans in almost all thinking processes, will be developed within our lifetime. The computers that you are now working on will seem like tinker toys by comparison.

2. Pete's Restaurant

Set up this menu for Pete's Restaurant using similar column layouts and titles to those shown below. Use boldfacing or enlarged letters for the main title. Use "Menu" for a file name, and request a printout.

PETE'S RESTAURANT MENU

A la Carte

French Fries	$1.00
Onion Rings	$1.25
Small Tossed Salad	$1.75
Soup of the Day	$1.50

Main Dishes

Fish & Chips	$3.50
Hamburger & Fries	$3.99
Liver & Onions	$4.89
Chili Dog	$2.00

Beverages

Coffee	$ .75
Milk (large)	$ .75
Milk Shake	$1.50
Pop	$ .75

Desserts

Sundaes	$3.50
Pies	$1.75
Jello & Whipped Cream	$1.25
Rice Pudding	$1.25

3. A Fun Kinda' Guy

Key in, save, and print the following sample of a criminal record file. Special emphasis will be needed—the title in boldface or large letters, underlining, and italics wherever indicated.

CRIMINAL RECORD FILE   # 51690

CRIMINAL: (you make up a name)
            Alias—Biff Griffen

AGE: 28

ADDRESS: (you make up the address)

HISTORY: Auto Theft   1981 08 14
            Breaking & Entering 1985 09 05
            Weapons Possession 1988 12 24
            (add another entry here)

COMMENTS:

Escaped custody before trial—(enter a date) Warrant pending for arrest. Armed and dangerous.

---

4. The Troublesome Tour

Your boss at the City Travel Agency, where you work as a travel agent, is angry that the Hamilton Hilton Hotel did not have enough room for your clients during a pre-arranged package tour to Hamilton. The hotel manager, Jim Henderson, had over-booked the rooms on account of a convention. As a result, 40 clients on the tour had to find rooms at other hotels for the night and were, not surprisingly, upset. Your boss has asked you to write to the manager expressing your concern. Since this is the first mishap, you still want to use the hotel as a stopping point on future tours.

Using the full-block style for the business letter and the four writing strategies suggested in the chapter as a guide, create a suitable letter to send to Mr. Henderson. Use today's date and the address listed below. You are the signer.

> Hamilton Hilton Hotel
> 150 King Street West
> Hamilton, ON
> L8E 2G7

SECTION 2 RESEARCH PROJECTS

5. Technical Report on New Product

Prepare a full one-page technical report on a new computer hardware or software product. Use the advertisements found in computer magazines or newspapers provided by your teacher or librarian. The report is to appear in the following format.

```
*********************************
   TECHNICAL REPORT ON
      NEW PRODUCT
   BY (insert your name here)
*********************************
```

NAME OF THE ITEM:

MANUFACTURER:

COST:

DESCRIPTION OF WHAT IT DOES:

TYPICAL USERS:

ADVANTAGES OVER COMPETITORS:

6. The Glossary

This is a two-page assignment that requires researching the definitions of ten computer terms (five definitions per page, evenly spaced). Each term must be boldfaced and underlined with the definition part in regular type. The beginning title must be in boldface or large type. All terms must be organized in alphabetical order.

Definitions:

Computer Applications
Supercomputer
Videodisk
Word Processing
Industrial Robot
Spreadsheet
Computer Ombudsman
Teller Terminal
Number Cruncher
Computer Graphics

Sample Layout:

GLOSSARY OF COMPUTER TERMS

(a) **COMPUTER APPLICATIONS:**
This refers to the uses that ...

(b) **COMPUTER GRAPHICS:** etc.

7. Computer Applications Report

This is a full one-page report with sub-headings on one specific computer application taken from the chapter called *Computer Applications*. First read a section that looks interesting, make some personal notes, then type up the report as shown below. Sample topics include: Office Administration, Computers in Factories, Computers Help Researchers, Helping to Serve Customers, Computers that Teach, and Keeping Track of Moving Vehicles. The title is to be in boldface or enlarged letters. The sub-headings are to be boldfaced and underlined.

Sample Layout:

```
*****************************
COMPUTER APPLICATIONS
REPORT ON (insert title here)
BY (your name)
*****************************


DEFINITION OF APPLICATION:




WHAT PEOPLE DO WITH THIS
APPLICATION:




DETAILED DESCRIPTION:
```

8. Controversial Issues Report

This is a full one-page report on some specific "Controversial Issue" taken from the chapter with the same title. Examples of topics include: Can Computers Think?; Computer Theft; Robots; Computers and the Courtroom; Enhanced Human Intelligence; The Controlled Society; and Invasion of Privacy.

Your task is to read the article and make some personal notes. Next, type the report in your own words using the format shown below. The title is to be in boldface or enlarged letters, and the sub-headings are to be in boldface and underlined.

Sample Layout:

```
************************************
        CONTROVERSIAL ISSUE
    REPORT ON (insert title here)
     BY (insert your name here)
************************************
```

WHAT THE CONTROVERSY IS ABOUT:

POSITIVE ASPECTS OF THE ISSUE:

NEGATIVE ASPECTS OF THE ISSUE:

Chapter 3

ELECTRONIC SPREADSHEETS

ELECTRONIC SPREADSHEETS

ELECTRONIC SPREADSHEETS

66 Productivity tools are abundant. People trained to use them are not. 99

OBJECTIVES

By the end of this chapter, you will be able to:

1 Define the following terms: spreadsheet, label, value, formula, function, template;

2 Write spreadsheet formulas to manipulate numerical data;

3 Design templates to suit particular spreadsheet applications;

4 Save, load, print, and manipulate templates as files;

5 Use the graphics option on some spreadsheets, and convert spreadsheet data into an appropriate line, bar, or circle graph;

6 Solve challenging problems using the six steps of the "spreadsheet cycle".

WORKING IN THE WORLD OF COMPUTERS

Accounting Clerk
keeps a running total of various costs and expenses related to a business

Budget Manager
compares the actual year-to-date financial figures with projected ones so that the organization does not go over budget

City Planner
estimates costs of city improvement plans before bringing them before council for discussion

Economist
uses a spreadsheet to estimate various economic trend indicators, such as the Gross Domestic Product and the Inflation Rate

Entrepreneur
uses a spreadsheet to keep track of the costs and expenses of starting up a new business

Insurance Agent
estimates premium costs to customers based on insurance claims

Political Analyst
uses a spreadsheet to count incoming votes from across the city to predict election results

Sales Manager
keeps track of sales by territory, by salesperson, and by customer, to obtain an overall picture of how well products are selling

Sport Statistician
uses a computer and a spreadsheet to analyze statistics of various sports

Spreadsheet Analyst
uses spreadsheet software for numerical analysis of data

3.1 INTRODUCTION

*J*ust as people turn to word-processing software to organize words into documents, they can also turn to spreadsheet software to calculate and organize numbers into reports. The term "spreadsheet" is not new. It was originally used to describe large, wide sheets of columnar paper. The computer software of the same name is simply an electronic version of that large sheet of paper. Specifically, an **electronic spreadsheet** is a computer program that provides a multi-columned workspace in which users can process and analyze large quantities of numerical data very quickly. It is a very popular program in finance departments, where it is used for a type of financial analysis that predicts future trends in expenses and revenues, and also in research departments to organize and process statistical data almost instantly. In seconds spreadsheets can perform calculations that would often take minutes or even hours to do by pen and paper, or with a calculator.

Other tasks spreadsheets have been applied to include home budgeting, bank account tracking, investment analysis, market research data, analyzing medical or scientific data, manipulating geography field data, and forecasting population or voting trends. Forecasting is making guesses about the future, a popular feature with many spreadsheet users. Generally, spreadsheets can be used for virtually any task that requires the manipulation of monetary figures or numerical data.

There are many sophisticated commercial spreadsheet programs available to users including *Framework, Lotus 1-2-3, Lucid 3-D, Microsoft Excel,* and *PlanPerfect.* Simpler and less expensive versions used in schools include *Appleworks, Microsoft Works, PC-Calc, VP-Planner, VisiCalc,* and *Words and Figures.*

The first spreadsheet software, called *VisiCalc,* came on the market in 1978 with versions for the Apple computer, and later the IBM PC. *VisiCalc,* more than any other program, is credited with popularizing desktop microcomputers for home and office use. It made the tedious work of multiple numerical calculations easy. Office workers loved it!

Spreadsheets are particularly useful for asking "what- if" questions. These questions help predict what effect a present change in figures will have on the future. For example, suppose a student is considering placing her summer earnings of $3500 into a daily interest savings account. She asks herself "What if I invested the money in a term account, or what if I purchased a Canada Savings Bond instead?" She can use a spreadsheet to calculate and display the earned interest and future balance for each type of investment by simply entering different interest rate formulas. This allows her to compare the results and select the best option. The spreadsheet could then be saved on disk and updated with current interest rates whenever additional money becomes available for investment.

BRITAIN [POUND]	.5275	.6547
CANADA [DOLLAR]	7218	1.3858
FRANCE [FRANC]	1423	7.0250
JAPAN [YEN]	.00604	165.45
SINGAPORE [DOLLAR]	.4505	2.2200
SOUTH AFRICA [RAND]	.3650	2.7397
SPAIN [PESETA]	0709	141.79
SWEDEN [KRONA]	402	7.1350
SWITZERLAND [FRAN	486	1.8825
W. GERMANY [MARK]	537	2.2040

*T*he spreadsheet can be both longer and wider than your viewing area. Your screen acts as a **window**, allowing you to view only a certain section of the sheet at any one time. You can move or "scroll" the window viewing area in all four directions using the directional cursor keys, the PgUp and PgDn keys, or pointing devices such as a hand-held mouse or a trackball, depending on your type of hardware and the software you are using.

The spreadsheet is organized as a grid of horizontal and vertical lines forming rows and columns. In some software the grid lines are visible, while other programs leave them out. The rows are numbered down the left side of the grid. The columns are labelled horizontally along the top with letters of the alphabet. Where the rows and columns intersect, a space or **cell** is formed. The address of each cell, also called its "location" or its "coordinates", is defined by the intersection of rows and columns. For example, the very first cell in the top left corner of the grid is location A1 (column A, row 1).

You can think of the spreadsheet as a blank checkerboard pattern that you can hop around on using the cursor. To place something on any one of the checkerboard spaces, you first move the cursor to that location. Next, you key in the data. It will not appear at the location of the cursor, but instead will appear on the **status line**, usually found at the top or bottom of the screen. The status line displays both the coordinates and the contents of the cell where the cursor is currently located. Only when you press the "Return" or "Enter" key does the data get stored in that location. This permits corrections or changes to be made before the data is stored.

*T*he cells in a spreadsheet can accept three types of data—labels, values, and formulas. A **label**, also referred to as text, is an entry that cannot be manipulated mathematically. Labels include titles at the top of the spreadsheet and headings on the rows and columns that clearly indicate the purpose and content of the spreadsheet.

A **value** is a number that can be manipulated mathematically. It can be a whole number, a decimal number, a dollar figure, or a percentage. Values are always entered as "raw data"; that is, there are no other symbols, such as commas, dollar signs, percentage signs, or spaces, attached to them. These symbols are added later when you **format** particular cells to include such features. Formatting defines the form a cell or group of cells will take. For example, you can designate cells to contain only integers (whole numbers) or to contain only dollar figures, and so on.

In the following "Dance Ticket Sales" example, the word "revenue" represents a label, the number 70.00 represents a value, and all the values in column "C" have been formatted after they have been entered to convert them to dollar figures with two decimal places.

Spreadsheets, which are basically powerful calculating tools, require formulas to make them work. A **formula** is a mathematical expression made up of cell locations and math operators such as addition, subtraction, multiplication, and division (+, -, *, /). In some spreadsheets the "@" symbol is required in front of all formulas; in others, it is only required in front of a formula that contains a "function". A **function** is a pre-defined command, such as SUM, AVERAGE, MINIMUM, MAXIMUM, or COUNT, that the software will perform on

Sample Spreadsheet

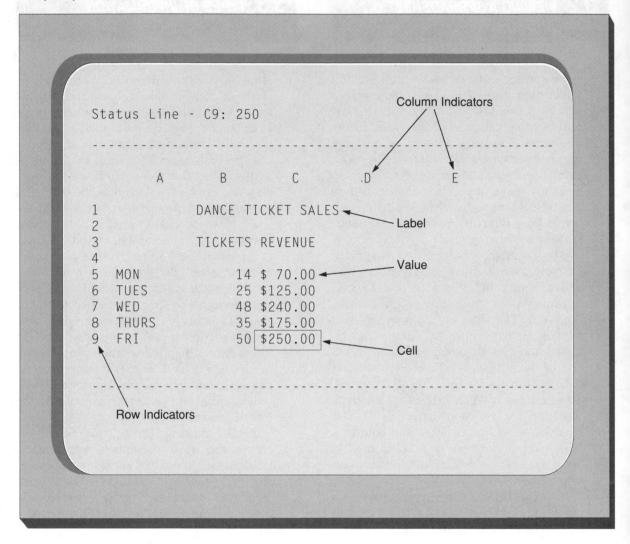

Status Line - C9: 250

Column Indicators

         A   B   C   .D   E

1   DANCE TICKET SALES   Label

2

3   TICKETS REVENUE

4   Value

5 MON   14 $ 70.00

6 TUES   25 $125.00

7 WED   48 $240.00

8 THURS   35 $175.00

9 FRI   50 $250.00   Cell

Row Indicators

a value or given range of values. Also, some spreadsheets may require a set of dots rather than the colon when indicating a series of cells. For example, SUM(A1:A20) may be entered as SUM(A1...A20). Each spreadsheet program tends to have its own style for writing formulas. Refer to your software manual, or class notes, for additional instructions.

Unlike values and labels, formulas remain hidden from view in the spreadsheet,

and appear only in the status line. Any time values or formulas in the spreadsheet are altered, any data affected by the change is immediately recalculated and displayed on the screen. You can view any formula by moving the cursor to the cell where it is located. The expression will then be displayed in the status line. Opposite is a chart of some sample formulas and functions typically used in a spreadsheet.

Sample Spreadsheet Formulas

PROCESS REQUIRED	SAMPLE EXPRESSION
Adding Two Numbers	(A1+A2)
Subtracting Two Numbers	(A1-A2)
Multiplying Two Numbers	(A1*A2)
Dividing Two Numbers	(A1/A2)
Series of Calculations	(A1+A2+A3)*(B2/B4)
Adding An Entire Row or Column	@SUM(A1:A20)
Average An Entire Row or Column	*@AVG(A1:A20)
Smallest Number in Row or Column	@MIN(A1:A20)
Largest Number in Row or Column	@MAX(A1:A20)
Number of Items in Row or Column	@COUNT(A1:A20)

* Spelling variations include AVE, AVER, AVERAGE.

3.4 REUSABLE TEMPLATES

*O*ne useful feature of spreadsheets is that the designer can "build" a reusable template. A **template** is a pre-designed shell or mask on the screen with none of the actual data inserted. It provides an organized format for information to be entered into or retrieved from a computer system. A spreadsheet template would include titles, row and column headings, formatting, and the insertion of formulas wherever needed.

There are many applications that benefit from a reusable template; for example, customer invoices or itemized sales slips, weekly or monthly budgets, company payrolls, income statements for businesses, teacher's mark records, or any projects in marketing, politics, science, or medicine that require a repeated format, but use different data.

To create a reusable template, design your shell with all the necessary components except the data. Then, save the shell as an empty "master template". Make a copy of the template and give it a different file name, so that two copies of the same file exist on your disk. One of these files is your "master template", the other is a "working copy". To distinguish them on your disk directory, you may wish to use file names that reflect their contents. For example, files recording student marks might be stored on disk with the following names.

MARKS   Working copy of spreadsheet with data

MRKS_TEM   Master template without any data

One exception to building templates without data occurs with the use of the AVERAGE function. When data to perform this function is missing, you get a "division-by-zero" error. To remove the error message during the template design stage, insert the value "1" in the appropriate data column so that the formula can be calculated.

"I don't know what you guys see in these computers..."

3.5 BUILDING A SPREADSHEET

*E*ach problem to be solved on a spreadsheet has its own requirements, such as the number of rows and columns to be used, the types of formulas, and so on, but the pattern for setting them up is similar. Consider the following situation in which a school store, operated by members of the senior marketing class, is keeping track of sales by category.

**Step 1
Put in the
Labels**
*T*he first step is to give your spreadsheet a title. Usually the first row of the spreadsheet can be used for that purpose. Next, label the rows and columns. The second row of the spreadsheet is left blank to separate the title from the rest

of the data. The third row can be used for the horizontal column labels, and the fifth row in column "A" can be used to begin the vertical row labels. To improve readability, designers usually leave a blank row to separate column or row labels from the figures to be entered under them later.

In some spreadsheet programs, a cell may only allow a limited number of characters to be entered, so you must keep your labels short (other than the title), or be prepared to use two cells for each label, which will produce a column two cells wide. For example, if the label "Thursday" is too long for one cell, you can use its abbreviation (Thurs.). The WIDTH command (if available) can solve this problem by allowing you to expand the width of a column of cells and thus key in the entire word.

Spreadsheet with Labels Keyed In

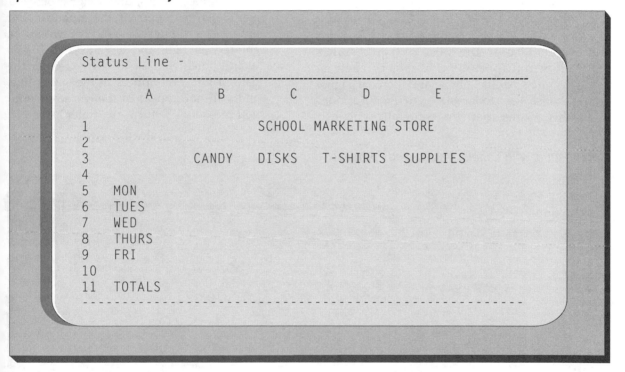

```
 Status Line -
 -------------------------------------------------------------------
          A         B         C         D         E
 1                      SCHOOL  MARKETING  STORE
 2
 3                 CANDY    DISKS    T-SHIRTS   SUPPLIES
 4
 5     MON
 6     TUES
 7     WED
 8     THURS
 9     FRI
 10
 11    TOTALS
 - - - - - - - - - - - - - - - - - - - - - - - - - - - - - - - - - - -
```

**Step 2
Enter the
Formulas**

*I*n this school store example, the bottom of each product column requires a total. To enter the formula for each column, move your cursor to the B11 location in the totals line, and press the "@" key to begin the formula. (Microsoft Works requires that an = sign precede all formulas instead of the @ sign.) The formula for cell B11 is @SUM(B5:B9), which will add all the entries from cells B5, B6, B7, B8, and B9. Press the enter key to store the formula there. The answer to the formula will automatically appear at location B11 in the totals column once the data is entered. Move the cursor across row ten and continue to enter summing formulas for the "C", "D", and "E" columns.

*I*n the example of the School Marketing Store, the data entries are money figures, which should be represented with a dollar sign and two decimal places. This can be done with the formatting feature. In most spreadsheets, special commands can be called up, or invoked, with the slash key (/). For example, if you press the slash key and enter the letter "F" for Format, a sub-menu of options will appear in the status line, or in an alternate line called a command line. You will usually be asked if you are formatting a label or a value. Choose the value option. Another submenu appears with choices such as decimals, dollar signs, and percent signs. Choose the dollar sign (currency) option. This means that you want all figures to

appear with a dollar sign and two decimal places. The program will also ask you which cells in the spreadsheet are to be formatted in this way. This is sometimes called the "range" to be formatted.

*E*nter the numbers in the appropriate cells. This is done by moving the cursor to the cell and keying in the figure. Remember to enter raw data without commas, spaces, dollar signs, percentage signs, or letters of the alphabet. For example, a value such as $12.50 would be entered as 12.5, and a value like $18.00 would be entered as 18. As you enter the data, it will first appear in the status line, and will not appear in the cell itself until you press the "Return" or "Enter" key.

Spreadsheet with Labels, Values, and Formulas

```
Status Line - B11: @SUM(B5:B9)
-----------------------------------------------------
            A         B         C         D         E

1                    SCHOOL MARKETING STORE
2
3                  CANDY     DISKS   T-SHIRTS   SUPPLIES
4
5    MON          $12.50    $18.00    $ 4.00    $ 2.30
6    TUES         $14.25    $ 2.00    $ 0.00    $ 1.15
7    WED          $17.50    $ 4.00    $ 8.00    $ 3.25
8    THURS        $12.75    $ 4.00    $ 0.00    $ 5.00
9    FRI          $10.25    $ 6.00    $12.00    $ 2.30
10                ------    ------    ------    ------
11   TOTALS   *   $67.25    $34.00    $24.00    $14.00
12                ======    ======    ======    ======
-----------------------------------------------------
```

* Hidden formula in cell B11 is shown on status line

In the example of the School Marketing Store, the spreadsheet complete with labels, data, formulas, and formatting appears at the bottom of the previous page. The final totals have been calculated by the computer using the formulas hidden in those particular cells (B11, C11, D11, and E11).

Dance Ticket Sales

The student council has asked you to keep track of both the total number of tickets sold and the total revenue received from the dance ticket sales. Set up a spreadsheet with a title, labels, and spacing similar to the example shown below, then enter the data and the formulas in columns "B" and "C" so that the totals will be calculated. Format the ticket column to accept only integers, and the revenue column to accept only dollar figures with two decimal places. Insert single lines for addition and double lines to indicate completion of the columns. This can be done if you first enter a space with the space bar before keying in the single or double line. (Normally the symbol "—" means subtract, and the symbol "=" means equal. Inserting a space before them indicates a label rather than an operation.) Save the spreadsheet with the file name "Dance" and make a printout.

DANCE TICKET SALES

	TICKETS	REVENUE
MON	14	$ 70.00
TUES	25	$125.00
WED	48	$240.00
THURS	52	$260.00
FRI	75	$375.00
	------	-------------
TOTALS		$
	====	========

3.6 SPREADSHEET COMMANDS

*M*ost spreadsheets contain a number of special commands to help the user either design the template or manipulate the data in some way. These commands are normally hidden from view and can only be called into action with a special keystroke. Some examples include pressing the slash key, the ALT key, or the ESC (escape) key, or using a mouse or trackball to point to a special area, usually the left-hand corner of the screen. A series of optional commands, referred to as a *command menu*, appears. Not all spreadsheets use the same command names, or have the same number of options from which to choose . Generally, however, about ten special commands are provided. The following chart lists some of the more popular commands, their abbreviations, and a description of their functions.

Spreadsheet Commands

Command	Abbreviation	Description of Use
Copy	C	Copies the contents (data or formula) of one cell to another
Delete	D	Erases an entire row or column
Format	F	Alters the way numbers or labels appear. Formats can include $ signs, % signs, number of decimal places, and placement of a label
Graph	G	Creates business-style line, bar, and circle graphs from raw data in the spreadsheet
Go to	Goto (or >)	Moves you immediately to any cell that you specify
Insert	I	Inserts an entire blank row or column within an existing spreadsheet
Load	L	Retrieves a previously designed spreadsheet from disk storage. May also be called FILE command
Print	P	Prints a hard copy of the entire spreadsheet (even the part not shown on the screen). Usually permits the addition of a title, or the printing of just part of the data
Replicate	R	Copies large sections of a spreadsheet from one area to another, including formulas, which the software rewrites to fit the new location. May be part of the COPY command
Save	S	Stores a spreadsheet (data and/or template) on disk. Alternatively called FILE which contains load, save, and delete options
Width	W	Adjusts the width of columns

*O*ne of the most powerful and time-saving commands listed in the chart is called replicate. *Replication*, or copying, refers to the duplication of data or formulas in different parts of a spreadsheet without the need to retype them. It is often desirable to repeat certain formulas for several different rows or columns within a spreadsheet.

Suppose, for example, a teacher has 25 students in a class, and wants to design a template to record their marks from various assignments and tests during the term. The calculations for totalling one student's mark are the same for every other student.

Once the formulas are entered for the first student, the "replicate" command can be used to repeat the same formulas for all the other students. The spreadsheet software automatically figures out what new cell locations are required for the formula in each new row or column. This process is referred to as a "relative cell reference", which means that the formula should change to reflect its new location in the spreadsheet. You can also request "absolute cell reference", which means that the formula should not change to reflect its new location. You can use the latter if you wish to repeat the same answer in another location, rather than a different answer.

Spreadsheet Formulas Designed with Replicate Command

```
Status Line - E3: @SUM(B3:D3)
-------------------------------------------------------------------
          A          B          C          D          E

1    STUDENT     ASSIGN1    ASSIGN2     TEST 1     TOTAL
2
3    Aikin, J        10          8         88     * 106
4    Brixo, L         8          7         71
5    Dean, D          6          7         68
6    Eckert, M        9         10         95
7
8
9
-------------------------------------------------------------------
```

* Formula for cell E3: @SUM(B3:D3) is replicated for cells E4, E5, E6, and so on

3.7 BUSINESS GRAPHICS

*O*ne of the useful features found in many spreadsheets is the capability of producing simple or elaborate business graphics. **Business graphics**, sometimes called "value graphics", refers to the creation of specific types of graphs based on the statistical data provided by spreadsheets. This visual display of data may appear in the form of a line graph, bar graph, or circle graph. Variations, such as a stacked bar graph or exploded circle graph, can also be made. This feature is valuable because people tend to interpret data more quickly and easily if it is presented as a picture rather than as a table of data, which is what spreadsheet printouts tend to resemble. The row and column headings from the spreadsheet can be used as labels on the graphs, and the raw data can be represented in the form of a line, a vertical bar, or a section of a circle.

Line Graph

A line graph gets its name from the line that joins several plotted points on the graph. The computer first plots the points on the horizontal and vertical axes using values found in the spreadsheet. Then the dots are connected by a trend line. Using the past trend as a guide, the future direction of the line (unchanging, increasing, decreasing) can be forecast. This graphing technique is useful for making predictions about future statistical trends based on the behaviour of past trends.

The line graph, like all well-designed graphs, should contain a main title and appropriate labels for both the x-axis and the y-axis. These additions help the reader understand what the graph represents. Consider the spreadsheet data for "Monthly Computer Sales" on the next page, and the line graph created from it.

Figure 3.1

The graphic detail on most modern microcomputers is enhanced by their high-resolution monitors.

Courtesy of IBM Canada Ltd.

Sample Spreadsheet and Line Graph

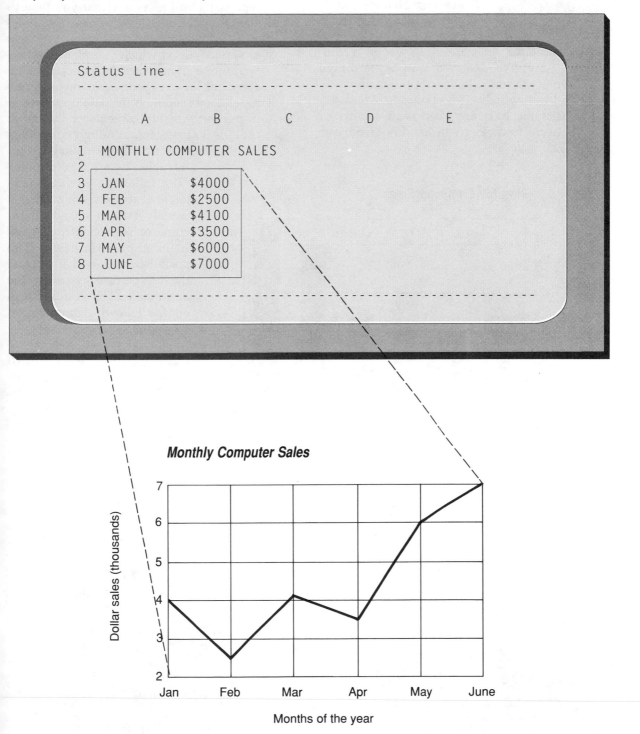

Status Line -

	A	B	C	D	E
1	MONTHLY COMPUTER SALES				
2					
3	JAN	$4000			
4	FEB	$2500			
5	MAR	$4100			
6	APR	$3500			
7	MAY	$6000			
8	JUNE	$7000			

Monthly Computer Sales

Dollar sales (thousands)

Jan Feb Mar Apr May June

Months of the year

Bar Graph

*T*he bar graph is easy to interpret. Each bar is a different length, so changes in values are easily seen by a comparison of the bars. Bar graphs are drawn two ways: vertically (bars pointing upward), and horizontally (bars pointing sideways). Often the bars are filled with colours or patterns to make them stand out from one

a whole. For instance, if the complete circle represents all the money that you plan to spend this month, then the pie-shaped sections could represent the various products or services upon which you plan to spend your money. The larger the monetary value of a category of expenditure, the bigger its pie-shaped section. If the data is expressed in percentages, the contents of the entire circle is 100 percent, although computers may round up, making the total higher than 100 percent.

The following example of a circle graph gives a student's weekly budget based on income of 30 dollars per week from a part-time job. The spreadsheet uses that total as the 100 percent figure for the entire circle. The student budgets the following amounts on these categories.

LUNCH	$ 7.50
FUN	$10.00
SCHOOL	$ 2.00
CANDY	$ 5.00
INVEST	$ 0.50
CLOTHES	$ 5.00

Monthly Computer Sales

Dollar sales (thousands)

7
6
5
4
3
2
1
0

Jan Feb Mar Apr May June

Months of the year

another on the screen. Additional graph options may include a three-dimensional view or "stacked bars" in which different data values are placed one on top of the other and distinguished with different colours or patterns. Bar graphs are excellent for comparing data from month to month but less good for showing trends.

The Circle Graph

*T*he circle graph, also called a pie chart, is in the shape of a circle and is divided like a pie into several sections. Usually, each section represents a percentage of

Weekly Budget

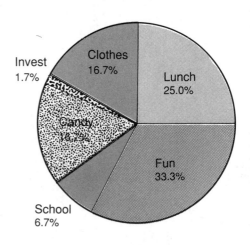

Premier Electronics Ltd.

Charles Wickham, the owner of Premier Electronics Ltd., a business that imports and distributes audio and video equipment, needs some assistance in tracking the company's monthly sales. He asks you to design and print three things: (1) a spreadsheet with the company name, data, formulas, and labels. It should also contain the total sales figure for the six-month period; (2) a line graph that illustrates the dollar sales by month; (3) a bar graph that illustrates the dollar sales by month. Both graphs should have the title "Monthly Sales Figures" and the axis labels "Months" and "Dollar Sales".

Sales Data: (in millions of dollars)

Jan.	$3 250	April	$5 800
Feb.	$5 500	May	$4 000
Mar.	$6 750	June	$7 000

3.8 SPREADSHEETS AS PROBLEM-SOLVING TOOLS

Most of the spreadsheet problems presented in this chapter are clearly defined. You know how the output is to appear because an example of its layout, including titles, labels, and sample data, is supplied and the list of data to be used is given. In "real life" situations this information is not usually provided. You may even find it faster and easier to use pen and paper and maybe a calculator, instead of a spreadsheet, to solve a problem. The decision on when to use a spreadsheet depends on the three criteria shown below. ("Number crunching" means that many calculations are involved.)

Three Criteria for Selecting a Spreadsheet

(a) The task is a large number-crunching one.

(b) The task will be repeated in the future.

(c) The task will justify the time spent constructing and testing a spreadsheet.

Suppose that it is nine o'clock on Friday morning and you are sitting at your desk in an office-supply wholesale company. Your manager comes to you and asks for a list of the week's orders showing details of products purchased by the firm's 25 retail customers. He wants the list by noon so that he can begin the employee work schedules for next week.

This problem has all the criteria that make it suitable for a spreadsheet. It is a fairly large task involving "number crunching"; it is a task that will be repeated weekly; and there is sufficient time to construct and test the spreadsheet (three hours). In this example, no data is given; you will have to collect the sales orders from elsewhere in the company and key in the appropriate information.

3.9 THE SPREADSHEET CYCLE

Problem solving with a spreadsheet can be expressed as a series of six steps.

(1) Determine What Is Required

Determine what output is expected, how it is to appear (as a chart, or graph, or both), and where the necessary data can be found. Apply the "three criteria for selecting a spreadsheet" to decide whether the task should be done mentally, with pen and paper, with a calculator, or by computer. If you fulfill all three criteria, then use a spreadsheet program to complete the task.

(2) Research Your Data

In business, the task given to you often involves the collection and organization of data into a readable report for management. Usually the data is scattered among other reports or among several printed resources, or is stored in other people's memories. Regardless, your job is to research the data—to find out where the data is located and retrieve it for use in your report. Your research may involve phoning or interviewing people, looking up documents, writing letters or memos (if you have time), or going to the library.

(3) Design the Template

The third stage, designing the template to be used in the application, is the part you are probably most familiar with so far. It involves selecting a title, row and column labels, and formulas to process the data. Spacing is important in a spreadsheet to ensure that other people can read it without your assistance. Usually, designers leave one blank row after the title and another after the column headings. A line is inserted in the row above a column total to indicate that addition or subtraction has occurred. A double line under a figure indicates that it is final.

Enter some "test data" to see if your formulas are correct. Use simple numbers that you can estimate in your head and check the answer generated by the formula. Do any of the columns or rows need special symbols, such as dollar signs, commas, percent signs, etc? If so, use the FORMAT command to assign the appropriate symbols. When you are satisfied that the template design is correct, erase the sample data with a CLEAR or NEW command.

It is important to save your template without any data in it. This master template can be used again and again, as long as the original is kept blank.

(4)   Enter the Data

At this stage, you turn to the data gathered from your research. Retrieve a copy of the spreadsheet template stored on disk and enter the data into the appropriate cells. If you must store the completed spreadsheet, choose a different file name so that it is stored separately from the original master template.

(5)   Report Generation

You have a choice of printing the information as a table or in one of the three main types of business graphs. Managers usually want to see both formats. Most spreadsheet software will let you create some form of graph by highlighting the relevant columns or rows of data.

If a spreadsheet is too wide for your printer, some programs offer the option of printing it sideways.

(6)   Verify Your Report

It is easy to print good-looking spreadsheets and graphs that are worthless because they are based on incorrect information. Check your work before handing it in. Compare the notes from your research with the data in the table and make sure you did not make any mistakes. Calculate one of the totals in your head or on paper to verify its accuracy. Use a set of "test data" for which you have already worked out the answers in the template and compare the program's results to your own. Are they the same? If not, maybe a formula needs repair.

Finally, is the output what your teacher (or employer) asked for? If not, your design may have to change. It is not uncommon for users to print several "draft versions" of a spreadsheet before they are satisfied with the result.

*J*ust as people use word-processing software to organize words, they use spreadsheet software to calculate and organize numbers. An electronic spreadsheet is a computer program that provides a checkerboard-like workspace made up of cells that are organized into rows and columns. It is basically a calculating tool for any task that requires the manipulation of numbers. Spreadsheets are particularly useful for making "what-if" calculations that permit comparisons between alternative situations or allow guesses to be made about the future based on past trends.

Applications include home and office budgeting, bank account tracking, investment analysis, market research analysis, data analysis, and trend forecasting.

The cells in a spreadsheet can accept three types of data: "labels", which are words used to make titles and headings, "values", which are numbers, and "formulas", which are mathematical expressions that the software can process. The combination of these three types of information allows a user to create templates to process numbers from virtually any source. Since all data must be entered "raw", those cells which require symbols such as a comma, dollar sign, percentage sign, or space must be formatted to include these features.

Typical output from a spreadsheet is a table of data arranged in rows and columns. However, some spreadsheets also permit the conversion of this data into a graph. Commonly used spreadsheet graphics include line graphs, horizontal and vertical bar graphs, and circle graphs (also called pie charts).

Unlike textbook problems, most real-life problems are poorly defined and come without test data. Use the series of six steps presented in this chapter to systematically solve these problems.

Shoe

CHECKING YOUR READING

*T*hese are general questions that may require factual recall, reading comprehension, and some application of the knowledge gained from this chapter.

Introduction

1. What is a spreadsheet?

2. List five tasks to which spreadsheets can be applied.

3. (a) What use are "what-if" questions?
   (b) Give an example.

Viewing a Spreadsheet on the Screen

4. In what way does your computer screen act as a "window" when you are working with a spreadsheet?

5. What is a "cell"?

6. Why is a spreadsheet similar to a blank "checkerboard"?

7. How do you get information to stay in a cell once you have typed it?

Types of Information

8. What three types of information can a spreadsheet accept?

9. Explain what these two types of data refer to.
   (a) label
   (b) value

10. (a) How is a dollar sign or percentage sign added to raw data in a spreadsheet?
    (b) What happens when you enter raw data into a spreadsheet with dollar or percentage signs attached?

11. (a) What is a "formula"?
    (b) Give the formula for adding two numbers located in cells C5 and C6.
    (c) Give the formula for adding a column of numbers located in cells C5, C6, C7, C8, and C9.

Reusable Templates

12. (a) Define "spreadsheet template".
    (b) What is the purpose of a template?

13. How do you create a "reusable template"?

Building a Spreadsheet

14. List the four steps required to build a spreadsheet.

Spreadsheet Commands

15. What spreadsheet commands can be used to perform the following functions? (Answers will vary with program being used.)
(a) Place a dollar sign and two decimal places on each value in a specific column.
(b) Store your spreadsheet for later use.
(c) Get rid of an unnecessary row.
(d) Place a blank column between two existing columns.
(e) Make a printout of your spreadsheet.
(f) Copy the same formula into four different cells.

Business Graphics

16. Define "business graphics".

17. List three types of business graphics commonly used with spreadsheets.

18. Suggest the most appropriate type of graph to accomplish the following:
(a) Illustrate how different items represent percentages of a total figure.
(b) Compare data.
(c) Show trends in values.

Spreadsheets as Problem-solving Tools

19. What are the three rules for deciding whether or not to use a spreadsheet?

20. What is meant by the term "report generation"?

21. Suggest two ways to verify your report.

APPLYING YOUR KNOWLEDGE

*T*hese questions assume an understanding of the material presented in the chapter, and provide new situations that may require evaluation, analysis, or the application of your newly acquired knowledge.

1. The Three Rules

(Orally)

For each of these examples, suggest which of the following solution options would be most appropriate—mentally, pen and paper, calculator, or a spreadsheet.

(a) You must figure out your term average accurate to one decimal place.

(b) Your manager asks you to calculate the office budget balance every Friday.

(c) Your parents ask you to calculate the amount of sales tax they will have to pay when they purchase a new stereo set for the house.

(d) As student council treasurer, you are responsible for keeping track of the revenue earned and expenses incurred for each of the school's eight different committees.

2. Spreadsheet Formulas

(Orally)

Suggest the appropriate formula for each of the following:

(a) Add a series of numbers located in cells A1 to A20.

(b) Divide the answer located in cell A21 by a number stored in cell A30.

(c) Indicate the number of actual entries in a column which includes cells B3 to B20.

(d) Find the largest number in a series of numbers stored in cells A10 to Z10.

3. Forecasting Sales

(includes a line graph)

Sal Mineo, the owner of a large music store, has asked you to prepare a spreadsheet and a line graph. The spreadsheet is to list the sales in dollars and the average annual sales figure for a period of six years. The line graph is to show the sales trend and the forecast, using the average sales figure, for the next year. Include appropriate labels for the spreadsheet and the graph. Give each the title "Mineo's Music Store Sales".

Sales Data:

1989	$18 000
1990	$25 000
1991	$22 000
1992	$21 000
1993	$26 000
1994	$25 000
1995	(projected figure obtained through formula calculation)

4. Stoney Creek's Annual Budget

(includes circle graph)

The mayor of the town of Stoney Creek has requested a spreadsheet and a circle graph that will show how the town's annual budget is spent on various projects. The spreadsheet will contain a total figure for expenditures and include figures expressed as both dollar amounts and as percentages. The circle graph, however, will display only the percentage figures. Give both the graph and the spreadsheet the title "Stoney Creek's Annual Budget", in addition to specific labels for each expenditure. You may have to reduce the length of the labels.

City Expenditures:

Street Repairs	$120 000
Parks Maintenance	$ 85 000
Garbage Collection	$290 000
Office Salaries	$455 000
Buses	$333 000
Police Protection	$250 000
Fire Protection	$200 000

SPREADSHEET PROJECTS

Students should understand all the concepts presented in this chapter before attempting these comprehensive projects.

1. Marks Register

Miss Faraway, the geography teacher, has asked you, as the class computer expert, to set up a spreadsheet. It should allow her to record marks for 12 students in one of her senior classes. The spreadsheet should contain the elements shown below. Also, set up formulas that will calculate the total and average for each test, to appear at the bottom of each column of test marks. Leave a blank row after the headings and another before the column totals and average marks.

Sample Layout:

Grade 12 Marks Register			
STUDENT	TEST 1	TEST 2	TEST 3
Avery	66	69	72
Bauer	82	79	81
Denniger	67	61	55

Data:

Student Name	Test 1	Test 2	Test 3
Avery	66	69	72
Bauer	82	79	81
Denniger	67	61	55
Huszti	52	64	56
Monroe	90	91	93
Nissan	67	67	66
Penchant	48	51	54
Rapallo	75	70	71
Smythe	67	66	59
Thompson	45	53	60
Wilson	77	71	80
Wong	88	83	78

2. Walter's Carpet Cleaning

Walter Fisken, a university student, runs his own carpet-cleaning service every summer to raise money for school. He's not sure exactly how much money he makes per month because he is too busy to do the bookkeeping. He has asked you to help him develop a spreadsheet template that compares revenue, expenses, and net profit (revenue minus expenses) for the three summer months. Create a spreadsheet, similar to the sample layout shown below, with single lines where addition or subtraction are necessary, and double lines to indicate final figures.

Sample Layout:

WALTER'S CARPET CLEANING			
ITEM	JUNE	JULY	AUG
Cleaning Revenue	$720	$800	$825
Cleaning Supplies	$ 80		
Helper's Wages	$200		
Telephone	$ 40		
Truck Expense	$ 50		
Total Expenses	$	$	$
Net Profit	$	$	$

Data:

Revenue	720	800	825
Cleaning Supplies	80	90	110
Helper's Wages	200	225	225
Telephone	40	45	41
Truck Expense	50	75	70

3. Basketball Stats

Jim Cunningham, the senior basketball coach, needs someone to design a special spreadsheet to monitor the progress of his 12-member team. He has a battery-operated laptop computer with spreadsheet software, but lacks the knowledge to design an appropriate template. The team is scheduled to play a four-game regular season. The coach wants statistics on "Total Points/Season"

for each player, and the "Highest" and "Lowest Points Per Game". Design a spreadsheet template, similar to the layout below, and enter the test data to prove that it works.

Sample Layout:

BASKETBALL STATISTICS					
Player	Game 1	Game 2	Game 3	Game 4	T. Pts.
1st.	45	12			57
2nd.	2	6			8
3rd.	10	8			18
High Score	45	12			
Low Score	2	6			

Data:

	Game 1	Game 2	Game 3	Game 4
Miles Hei	45	12	8	24
Fred Hook	2	6	4	3
Pete Moss	10	8	0	14
Wayne Kafta	0	12	8	10
Larry Quinn	15	6	20	18
Sonny Side	12	26	14	12
Bo Tye	4	8	12	8
Gerry Bean	3	0	0	0
Izzy Able	12	22	35	28
Mack Roni	2	8	10	4
Dan Druff	4	10	10	10
Ben Dover	22	30	16	18

4. Sales Staff Payroll

The sales division of a television manufacturing company has an incentive policy that rewards their salespeople with a 1/4 % (.0025) commission based on their monthly sales (in addition to their regular $400 monthly salary). The manager has asked you to prepare a spreadsheet that will display the employee number, name, sales, monthly salary, commission earned, and total pay for each of the salespeople. All money figures are to be expressed with dollar signs. In addition, the commission earned and total pay figures are to be accurate to two decimals places.

Sample Layout and Data:

```
SALES DIVISION PAYROLL    OCTOBER 19 —

NO.  NAME       SALES       REG. COMM. TOT.
                            SAL.        SAL.
100  F. Wilson  $ 85 000    $400
112  R. Asken   $ 72 000    $400
130  D. Trump   $110 000    $400
145  H. Marcos  $ 60 000    $400
103  C. Kent    $ 25 000    $400
                ------------ ------ --------- -------
TOTALS          $           $    $         $
                ======      ====  =====   ====
```

5. City Elections

(includes circle graph)

The city election centre is in charge of recording vote tallies from the six district voting polls across the city. The three candidates running for the office of mayor are V. Agro, P. Radski and F. McMann.

Design a voting record template, similar to the example shown below. It should accept totals for each candidate by district, calculate each candidate's total, and give the percentage that each candidate's total represents of all ballots cast. Create a pie chart with appropriate labels and a title to illustrate the percentage votes per candidate.

Sample Layout:

```
ELECTIONS FOR THE OFFICE OF MAYOR

CENTRES    AGRO  RADSKI  McMANN
North
South
East
West
Central
Mountain
           ----------  --------------  ----------
Totals

Percent       %          %          %
           ======     ======     ======
```

Data:

	Agro	Radski	McMann
North	1450	1320	2298
South	231	55	1200
East	1110	2317	3102
West	578	791	343
Central	1490	1589	1860
Mountain	910	880	1200

6. Investment Analysis

(includes bar graph)

Marilyn Reise, a grade ten high school student, works part time as a sales clerk in a department store. So far she has managed to save a total of $2500, which she keeps in a daily interest savings account. After studying investments in one of her courses, Marilyn has decided to compare the outcome of four ways of investing her money over a two-year period. Create a spreadsheet template as shown in the example that follows. Format the interest and balance columns to make them display the figures with dollar signs and two decimal places. Also, using the balance figures from the second year, create a bar graph to compare the outcome of each of the four types of investment.

Sample Layout:

```
INVESTMENT COMPARISON CHART

TYPE         FIRST YEAR   SECOND YEAR
             INT.   BAL.  INT.   BAL.
             ($)
Savings
Bank Term
Trust Co.
Mutual Fd.
Original Principal = $2500
```

Data:

Daily Interest Savings Account = 6.0 % annually or 0.00016 % daily interest
Bank Term Deposit = 9.5 % paid annually
Trust Company Term Deposit = 10.5 % paid annually
Equity Mutual Fund = 12.0 % paid annually

*T*hese are advanced-level problems. It is recommended that students read and comprehend the section "Spreadsheets as Problem-solving Tools" before attempting these problems.

1. Wilson's Music Centre

(multiple uses of one template)

Denver Wilson operates a music shop in one of the local shopping malls. He needs a computerized "sales slip generator" that will allow his sales clerks to enter data on the keyboard, and calculate and print the customer's sales slip. Design a template that will outline the headings contained in a typical retail sales slip. Include the formulas to calculate the cost for each item purchased, the subtotal, the provincial sales tax, and the final total. All money entries are to be formatted as dollar figures. Your task is to print separate sales slips for three customers using the identical spreadsheet template for each one.

Suggested Operating Procedure:

(a) Save the completed template without any data on your disk. Clear the screen.
(b) Reload the template. Enter the data for the first customer. Print the spreadsheet.
(c) Do *not* save the spreadsheet. Clear the screen. Reload the original blank template before beginning entries on the next customer.

Customer Data:

George Harrison
19— 10 10
6 Guitar Strings @ $2.00 each
2 Guitar Magazines @3.50 each

Sally Armstrong
19— 10 11
1 Yamaha Electronic Keyboard $ 1 625.00
1 Beginner's Keyboard Book $ 8.50

Mickey Fox
19— 10 12
1 Fender Telecaster Guitar $ 950.00
4 Flat Guitar Picks @ $ 0.25 each

Sample Layout:

WILSON'S MUSIC CENTRE
200 MAIN STREET
TORONTO, ONTARIO
M3J 1K7

CUSTOMER:
ADDRESS :
DATE :

QTY.	DESCRIPTION	UNIT PRICE	COST

SUBTOTAL $
PROVINCIAL SALES TAX $ ____
TOTAL $ ____

2. Chequing Account Dilemma

Mr. Kim Woo, the manager of a small variety store, is unhappy with the monthly reporting system that the bank uses to inform him of the balance in his chequing account. Two things make him unhappy. The first is that mailing the bank statement is too slow: he never knows what his current bank balance is from day to day. Writing cheques that "bounce" becomes more likely. The second is that the "Particulars" column in the bank statement does not give enough background information about each transaction; for instance, to what company was a cheque sent, or from where did revenue come? Mr. Woo needs a record of what the transactions were for.

He has turned to you for assistance. His last bank statement appears below. Some of the statement abbreviations are: D D - Direct Deposit, ATM - Automatic Terminal Machine, S C - Service Charge.

Sample Bank Statement:

BANK OF BRITISH COLUMBIA
1020 Burnard Street
Vancouver, BC
V6G 154

Acct. #
1090-591

Mr. K. R. Woo
Eastside Variety
56 Riverside Drive
Vancouver, BC
V6F 1T3

November 30, 19—

DATE	PARTICULARS	DEPOSIT	WITHDRAWAL	BALANCE
Nov. 1	Previous Balance			$ 110.00
1	D.D.	$ 500.00		$ 610.00
2	Cheque 105		$ 55.80	$ 554.20
5	ATM		$ 50.00	$ 504.20
4	Cheque 106		$ 28.50	$ 475.70
8	D.D.	$ 550.00		$1025.70
15	ATM		$ 50.00	$ 975.70
21	Cheque 112		$ 25.00	$ 950.70
28	S.C.		$ 4.00	$ 946.70

Chapter 4

DATA-BASE SOFTWARE

DATA-BASE SOFTWARE

66 Within the next five years, expert systems—artificial intelligence—will be in the personal computer marketplace. Programs will soon be available to serve as your librarian, tax attorney, or personal physician. **99**

Ira Goldstein *"The OMNI Book of High Tech Society 2000"*

OBJECTIVES

By the end of this chapter, you will be able to:

1 Define the following terms: file manager, data-base manager, file, record, field, template, searching, sorting, key to the search, key to the sort, report generation, test runs, and data structures;

2 Distinguish between a horizontal-format and a vertical-format file manager;

3 Manipulate a file by searching, sorting, and performing calculations prior to displaying the report;

4 Use a six-step strategy for solving problems with a file manager;

5 Describe three types of data structures used in data-base managers.

WORKING IN THE WORLD OF COMPUTERS

Airline Reservation Clerk
enters flight requests into flight files

Customer Order Clerk
enters phone orders into customer order files

Hospital Nurse
keys in and retrieves information about patients

Hotel Clerk
enters hotel reservations into a data base

Librarian
uses both CD-ROMs and data bases in searches for library users

Personnel Manager
tracks records of employees with a data file management system

Police Officer
keys in licence plate numbers for ownership verification

Political Historian
does searches of files for information on famous politicians

Shipping Desk Supervisor
checks computer files for contents, receiver, and completion of shipments

Travel Agent
enters details of vacationer's trip into a file

*A*pproximately 50 000 new publications (books, journals, and magazines) are printed worldwide each year. They include topics on the entire set of human knowledge. It has been estimated that the amount of information in the world doubles every 15 years. The amount of scientific knowledge available when you retire will be almost 100 times what it was when you were born. This presents professional people, such as lawyers, doctors, engineers, computer consultants, and business managers, with a problem: information overload. With all the various sources of information, and with new ideas and inventions being created each year, how can an individual or an organization keep up to date, or even find the facts needed to do an effective job?

One of the solutions is to store the facts in a computer system and retrieve the information in a way that is useful to the task at hand. Several publishing companies now issue CD-ROM disks with entire sets of books on them. For example, you can purchase a reference disk called *Microsoft Bookshelf* that contains the *Houghton Mifflin Spelling Verifier and Corrector*, *Roget's II: Electronic Thesaurus*, *Bartlett's Familiar Quotations*, *The Chicago Manual of Style*, and several other items. The new 21-volume *Oxford English Dictionary*, produced every five years in England, can be purchased as a CD-ROM disk. *The New Grolier Electronic Encyclopedia* (21 printed volumes) takes up less than 30 percent of a CD-ROM disk, but lacks photos and illustrations, and the *McGraw-Hill Encyclopedia of Science and Technology* now appears on disk as well as in printed book format. Several magazines can be purchased on a floppy disk instead of in print.

In addition to having one's own personal volumes of information, people can search through computerized materials stored in distant locations. Students at York University, for example, can access the library catalogue using a computer and modem. The system tells the browser the title and author of books, and whether or not a particular book is currently available. You can also do topic searches by title, subject, or key word and receive a condensed summary of the work.

Lawyers can use a telephone connection, a modem, and a desk-top microcomputer to access a centralized library of court-case decisions when they are researching material for a client. Business managers can access data on their own business, such as weekly sales, inventory updates, and income and expense summaries. Anyone who needs to research a topic, and owns a computer with the right software, can simply "let their fingers do the walking".

A knowledge of how to create and use data files or data bases is useful for people in the workplace, at school, and in the home. This chapter introduces the components of these information-management software packages.

"Gee! My first computer date! I wonder what he'll be like?"

4.2 ORGANIZATION OF DATA FILES

*A*n organized collection of similar information is referred to as a **data file** if it is stored together as a single file under one file name in the computer, or as a **data base** if it is stored as several different but related files. People now commonly refer to both single and multiple files as a data base. This incorrect designation only creates a problem when selecting software. A **data-file manager**, for example, can only deal with information from one file at a time, whereas a **data-base manager** can select and organize information from several files at the same time. The latter is both more powerful and more difficult to learn.

To better understand the "invisible components" of electronic files, it may be helpful to some readers to imagine a data file as an office folder stored in a filing cabinet. The file folder can be retrieved, opened, processed, closed, and placed back into the filing cabinet when it is no longer needed. The documents within the file folder are the records. The documents in an individual file would hold similar information organized in a uniform way, and would be related to each other by the headings used to describe the information. Electronic filing systems use similar terminology and processes to the manual method described above.

Generally speaking, the terms "files", "records", and "fields" are part of any file-management vocabulary. Any organized collection of similar data can be referred to as a "data file". Each data file can be subdivided into a number of units called **records**, which are organized in an identical pattern and contain similar types of information. Each record can be further subdivided into smaller sections called **fields**, which contain specific information by heading, such as "name" or "address".

4.3 HORIZONTAL-FORMAT FILE MANAGERS

*S*oftware companies tend to design their data-entry and output screens in either a horizontal or a vertical format. In horizontal-format file managers, such as *Appleworks* and *WATFILE*, each record is entered and displayed as a single horizontal line. (Some programs allow alternate styles.)

For example, suppose your local police station has a computerized "Criminal Record Data File" in which they store records of those individuals who are convicted of indictable offences. The information for each criminal is entered as a single line, sectioned into several fields. A sample criminal file might appear as shown on the following page.

The whole group of items is the criminal file. The last entry, "Mandel, Joseph", is an example of a single record within the file. It provides information on only one criminal. The vertical highlighted section including assault, arson, theft, and murder is a single field found in all the records. In this case, the field contains the criminal offence. Each record in this file contains three separate fields—name, offence, and conviction date. The number of fields and their maximum widths varies with the software package. Records are usually larger than the screen, and can be seen by scrolling with the cursor keys.

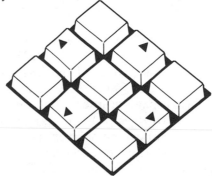

Example of a Criminal File (Horizontal Format)

	NAME	*Field* OFFENCE	CONVICTION DATE
	Grimely, Biff	Assault	1991 09 06
	LaFlame, Hilda	Arson	1985 01 10
	Lightfinger, Laurie	Theft	1988 07 21
Record	Mandel, Joseph	Murder	1992 08 30

4.4 VERTICAL-FORMAT FILE MANAGERS

*T*he majority of file management programs tend to be in a vertical format. In this type of program, after the initial title screen a menu of options usually appears that allows you to perform several different tasks, such as creating, deleting, searching, sorting, and printing files. The data-entry and display screens, sometimes referred to as "templates", are arranged so that only one record appears on the screen at a time, and each field of information in the record usually has a separate line to itself. This format is much easier to read and interpret than the horizontal format because it resembles a normal page of information and the entire record usually fits on the screen. Examples of the more popular vertical-format file managers include *Filing Assistant, Microsoft Works, PFS File*, and *Q & A*.

To illustrate the vertical format, we will refer to how a data-file manager might be used in educational institutions. By law, schools must keep records of all their students, past and present. To accomplish this, each school must establish a "Student Records Data File" to assist staff in recording and storing information.

A single student record would contain similar information about all students, such as name, address, phone number, date of birth, and grades received. A typical template might appear as shown on the right.

In the sample student record, there are six different fields of information listed vertically, each with its own field name. Field names are sometimes referred to as "prompts" because they tell the person entering the data what is expected on each line. An individual record within a file is retrieved in much the same way a cook flips through a series of recipe cards looking for a particular dish.

Example of a Student Record (Vertical Format)

```
              WESTDALE SECONDARY SCHOOL


   STUDENT NUMBER:          109 462 39

   STUDENT NAME:            Phillips Jodie

   DATE OF BIRTH:           1979 07 15

   MAILING ADDRESS:         100 Main Street
                            Kingston, ON
                            K7K 6N2

   HOME PHONE NUMBER:       536-7079

   COURSES TAKEN:           English      81
                            French       65
                            Business     75
                            History      63
```

4.5 CREATING A DATA FILE

A data file is easy to create, but first you must design a screen template that will accept the data. A **template** is the shell or mask superimposed on the screen so that information is entered in an organized, identical pattern. It contains the headings or field names that prompt you on what type of information is expected.

Suppose you wish to create a "birthday data file" that keeps track of the birth dates of all your close friends and relatives. This information can be used as a reminder to send them a card or buy them a present. Useful information for such a file might include Name, Birthdate, and Favourite Presents.

In a horizontal-style data manager, the field names appear in a straight line across the screen. The data is entered in rows underneath them. Each field in the data file is defined by you to be a specific length. Always pick the length of your longest entry so that both short and long items can be entered. In this case, the "Favourite Presents" field is the longest and is set at a width of 30 characters. Spaces for names are typically 20 characters long.

Example of a Horizontal-Format Template

```
NAME                BIRTHDATE    FAVOURITE PRESENTS
- - - - - - - - - - - - - - - - - - - - - - - - - - - - - - - - - - - - - - - - - -

Trimble, Peter      05  19       Model building, chocolates

Mavis, Aunt         09  04       Sewing wool, porcelain art

Ralph, Uncle        07  10       Carpenter tools, funny cards


3 out of 3 records
- - - - - - - - - - - - - - - - - - - - - - - - - - - - - - - - - - - - - - - - - -
```

A template with similar content can be designed for a vertical-format data file. In this situation, the field names appear down the left-hand side of the screen rather than across the top. Usually a colon is required to mark the end of the field name.

Example of a Vertical-Format Template

```
                    BIRTHDAY DATA FILE        Record #1


NAME:                          Trimble, Peter

BIRTHDATE:                     05 19

FAVOURITE PRESENTS:            Model building, chocolates
```

4.6 SCREEN-DESIGN CONSIDERATIONS

Did you notice that in both formats the field name is in capital letters and the data within the field is in upper- and lower-case lettering? This is a simple way to make the distinction between the field name and the data when reading the entries.

In both examples, you have to make decisions at the start about the order in which the data is to be entered, and how much space to leave in each field. Should the birth-date come first or second? How many characters will the longest name have? Should the last name come first, such as "Trimble, Peter" or should it be written "Peter Trimble"? This latter question is important if you are planning to have the program arrange the list alphabetically later on. Altogether, there are five decisions that are required at the design stage. These include number of fields, name of fields, order of placement, size (length), and type of data (integers, decimal numbers, alphabetic, mixed, dollar figures).

More screen layout decisions are required by the vertical format than the horizontal format. The vertical format should have a title at the top indicating the type of data being shown. In this case, the title is "Birth-day Data File". Also, to assist readability, the answers to the prompts should line up one underneath the other regardless of where the colon ends. This creates an even left-hand margin to the data as well as a separate, even left-hand margin for the field names. As is the case with a textbook or a newspaper, any information provided with a straight left margin is much more readable than that with a ragged left-hand margin. Some programs, such as *Filing Assistant*, actually use the colon as an indicator of where the answer is to be placed. In that situation, line up all the colons to create your even left-hand margin for the data.

Evenly Aligned Data

```
NAME:        Williams, Fred

ADDRESS:     126 Main Street
             Toronto, ON
             M6B 1L2

AGE:         15
```

Unaligned Data

```
NAME: Williams, Fred

ADDRESS: 126 Main Street
         Toronto, ON
         M6B 1L2

AGE: 15
```

Stolen Cars

Design a template for a "Stolen Car Data File" that the local police can use to look up the licence plate numbers of vehicles they suspect to be stolen. The file should contain licence plate numbers, the make of car, the owner's name, and the status (stolen, or ok). After the template is completed, enter the data listed below. To test your file, call up any car by the licence plate number and determine who owns it and if the car has been reported stolen or not.

Data:

LICENCE	MAKE OF CAR	OWNER	STATUS
KIP 560	Dodge	Jenkins, Fred	ok
HOT 888	Pontiac Firebird	Golly, Lyle	stolen
GYF 123	Toyota Celica	Fisher, Alice	ok
WOW 876	Corvette	Wolenski, John	stolen
REV 101	Oldsmobile Cutlass	Grenier, Wendy	ok
DIDI 10	Honda Civic	Gandi, Pooja	ok

Figure 4.1   Ottawa police have computer terminals installed in their cars through which they can have radio access to the Department of Motor Vehicles' computer (Toronto) for ownership information, and also to their local computers for any outstanding warrants.

Courtesy of Digital Equipment Corporation

4.7 MANIPULATING A DATA FILE

*O*nce an information data file or data base has been created, there are three ways it can be processed. The information can be searched, sorted, or mathematically manipulated. When **searching** a data file, the program is looking for a specific item that you have requested, using some criterion, such as a person's last name. The criterion that you provide for the program is called the **key to the search**. Most data managers will permit any of the field names to be used in the "key". Consider the following example based on the practice assignment above. The "key to the search" is a specific car licence number which can be owned by only one person.

Search for a Specific Record

```
FIELD TO BE SEARCHED?    Licence
ITEM?                    WOW 876

WOW 876  Corvette
Wolenski, John      stolen
```

You can also request the software to seek and display all the items that meet some specification. Using the same data file, notice how the software retrieves several records to meet the single criterion. The "key to the search", in this case, is the word "stolen" found in the Status field.

Search for a Group of Records

```
FIELD TO BE SEARCHED?    Status
ITEM?                    stolen

HOT 888 Pontiac Firebird
Golly, Lyle              stolen

WOW 876 Corvette
Wolenski, John           stolen
```

Most file managers have a set of symbols (<, >, =, *) that permit more detailed searches, such as asking the program to display all records that contain a specific range of values. Imagine that the contents of a furniture and appliance warehouse are being monitored by an "Inventory Data File". It can be used to find out how many items are in stock at any point in time.

INVENTORY DATA FILE

PRODUCT #	DESCRIPTION	QTY.	SELLING PRICE
2010	Colour TV Sony 21"	125	$ 895.00
2020	Colour TV Console	400	$ 995.00
2030	VCR Stereo 4 heads	205	$ 499.00
2040	VCR HiFi 2 heads	113	$ 399.00
3010	Lazi-Boy Recliner	200	$1 200.00
3020	Korna 4-seat sofa	118	$ 749.00

Since some fields have numbers in them, you can ask the software to search for a particular numerical range. Suppose a department store manager wants to clear out all inventory products with quantities of 200 or over by putting on a sale. You can request a search for all products with a quantity greater than or equal to 200, to see what is available.

Search for a Particular Range

```
FIELD TO BE SEARCHED?   Qty.
ITEM?                   >= 200

2020 Colour TV Console
400                  $  995.00
2030 VCR Stereo 4 heads
205                  $  499.00
3010 Lazi-Boy Recliner
200                  $1 200.00
```

Sorting a Data File

A second function that can be performed on a data file is called sorting. **Sorting** refers to the re-arrangement of records within a file into some particular order, such as alphabetically (A-Z or Z-A), or numerically (low to high or high to low).

This feature is helpful when you wish to visually scan the contents of a file on the screen or on a printout. It is much easier to find a particular name or value in a list when the items are organized sequentially. Suppose, for example, that the user of the "Inventory Data File" wanted the products listed alphabetically instead of by product number.

The field that is the one to be sorted is referred to as the **key to the sort**. In the case below, the key to the sort was the "Description" field. Other sorting possibilities would have been to rearrange the Inventory Data File from highest to lowest quantities, or from highest to lowest selling prices.

Mathematical Calculations

A third function that most file managers can perform is simple mathematical calculations on specific fields within the data file. Calculations are performed using four math operators (+, -, *, /) and the locations of the fields. For example, if you wished to multiply the contents of the third and fourth fields, you would enter the following formula into field five, where you want the answer to appear.

F3 * F4

File Sorted Alphabetically

INVENTORY DATA FILE

PRODUCT #	DESCRIPTION	QTY.	SELLING PRICE
2020	Colour TV Console	400	$ 995.00
2010	Colour TV Sony 21"	125	$ 895.00
3020	Korna 4-seat sofa	118	$ 749.00
3010	Lazi-Boy Recliner	200	$1 200.00
2040	VCR HiFi 2 heads	113	$ 399.00
2030	VCR Stereo 4 heads	205	$ 499.00

If that calculation were performed on the Inventory Data File, the contents of the "Quantity" field and the "Selling Price" field would be multiplied together to give a total retail value of each product. Most systems require that you ask for the calculations with an equation, using the field names rather than their positions, as in this example. Notice that TTL is used for the TOTAL, since some programs have a specific math command called TOTAL or SUM.

CALCULATE TTL = PRICE * QTY

Some file managers also permit the use of certain functions such as COUNT, AVERAGE, MAX, MIN, and TOTAL on data files to provide further information about the file.

NUMBER OF RECORDS = 6
TOTAL TTL = $985 639
AVERAGE QTY. = 193.5

```
INVENTORY DATA FILE

PRODUCT #     DESCRIPTION          QTY.      SELLING PR.        TTL

2020          Colour TV Console    400     $   995.00      $398 000.00

2010          Colour TV Sony 21"   125     $   895.00      $111 875.00

3020          Korna 4-seat sofa    118     $   749.00      $ 88 382.00

3010          Lazi-Boy Recliner    200     $1 200.00       $240 000.00

2040          VCR HiFi 2 heads     113     $   399.00      $ 45 087.00

2030          VCR Stereo 4 heads   205     $   499.00      $102 295.00
```

Practice Assignment

(25 mins.)

Football Eligibility

Jack Hawkins, the football coach at a local high school, wants to use a data-file manager to screen his football "tryouts" for eligibility. In addition to having a certain weight (greater than 76.5 kg), each player must also have passed all courses in the last semester. Design a template that will accept the data provided below. Arrange the players' names alphabetically, and then get the computer to print a list of only those tryouts who meet both the weight and credit criteria.

Data:

Name	Weight	Courses Failed
Lauzo, Ralph	69.5	0
Rizzo, Joe	81.0	0
Neumann, Fred	69.5	1
Knuckle, Bob	90.0	0
Keminski, James	69.5	0
Jenkins, Wally	72.0	1
Hammer, George	76.5	2
Tidy, Tom	78.5	0
Wilson, Albert	81.0	0
Ulik, Yeman	78.5	1

Report generation refers to the organization of information selected from one or more files into a formal document.The report can be displayed on the screen, or presented as hard-copy output. Usually the report contains data selected from several or all records contained in a file, and acts as a summary of the file's contents. Most data-file managers permit the fields to be reorganized into any order or left out of the report, if they are not needed by the reader.

For example, a police station may have access to a large criminal record file listing all the people convicted of indictable offences in the city for the last 20 years. However, the detective doing the search may be interested in only those criminals found guilty of pickpocketing within the last five years. The data-file manager would search through the entire file, and select only those records that meet the two criteria (pickpockets, last five years). The report could be displayed with any title that you wish, and with the fields of information arranged to suit the user.

Most file managers require that the user answer a series of questions about the format (setup) of the report before printing. This gives the user the opportunity to make any changes in the style and content.

The following set of questions is typical of most report generators.

Questions from the Computer   **Answers from the User**

```
1.  TITLE OF THE REPORT?              Pickpockets

2.  NUMBER OF FIELDS TO BE PRINTED?   5

3.  SPECIFIC FIELDS TO                1, 4, 5, 3, 2
    BE PRINTED?                       (or listed by file name)

4.  PRINT FIELD NAMES?                Yes

5.  NUMBER OF COPIES?                 1
```

Hospital Duty Roster

The administrators of the Henderson Mercy Hospital have asked you to assist them in the design and testing of a duty roster. The file is to be used by the head nurse to create a daily list of people on duty, and should contain the information shown below. To test your file, generate a "Hospital Duty Roster for Monday", and a separate one for Tuesday. Both lists are to be sorted alphabetically by last name. Neither of your reports should contain the names of people who are on their day off on the day of the report.

Data:

PERSON'S NAME	DAY OFF	SPECIALTY	YEARS EXPERIENCE
Fleming, Wanda	Monday	Pediatrics	5.0
Latham, Glenna	Wednesday	Obstetrics	3.5
Peachtree, Lyle	Friday	Emergency	3.5
Jenkins, Kim	Thursday	Surgical	0.5
Po, Won	Sunday	Radiologist	10.0
DiPoso, Toni	Saturday	Lab Technician	8.0
Manly, Steve	Wednesday	Emergency	12.0
Rickers, Cathy	Tuesday	Pediatrics	1.0
LaFleur, Rose	Friday	Geriatrics	2.5
Clare, Mary	Thursday	Surgical	4.6

4.9 PROBLEM SOLVING WITH A FILE MANAGER

Working with data-file managers and data-base managers is probably most challenging when you are required to solve a problem from scratch. This means that you must look up the information to enter into the file, as well as design an appropriate screen template to accept the data. Generally, problem solving with a file manager can be expressed as a series of six steps.

(1) **Determine What is Required**

Determine what is expected by the target user as output (on the screen or printer) from the data file you establish. Ask questions such as: "What types of report are required?" "What type of information will be in the reports?" The answers to these questions will help you decide what to store in your data file.

(2) **Research Your Data**

Most commercial file managers are empty. They have no data stored in them. It is up to the user to collect the information on whatever topic the file is to contain. The information may come from your home, community, school resources, or even personal experiences.

(3) **Design the Template**

The next step is to design the template or mask that overlays the screen and helps the user to enter data. Five decisions are required in the template design: (a) number of fields required; (b) field names; (c) order of placement; (d) length of fields (number of characters); (e) type of data within each field. Remember that more screen-design considerations are required for a vertical-format than a horizontal-format file manager.

(4) **Enter the Data**

Using the template as a guide, enter each record into the file and save the file when the entries are completed. Make sure that your entries are accurate: a data file is only useful if the data is accurate, factual, and complete.

(5) **Report Generation**

The information in the file can be processed by searching for specific data, sorting data into a particular order, or performing mathematical calculations on numeric data. The processed information can then be displayed on the screen, or printed on paper as a finished report. The action of creating reports with their own titles and layout is called "report generation".

(6) **Verify Your System**

One way to check the accuracy and usefulness of your newly designed data file is to perform several "test runs". A **test run** is a procedure used to discover any present or potential failure of the system's components that would stop it from achieving its intended purpose.

For example, you might perform some test runs on the file by asking for specific items or sorting data to see if the content and the field names are sufficient to produce the types of report that you expected in step number one. If the test runs indicate a weakness, edit the template to add/delete/modify the required sections. Continue this process of making test runs and modifications until the file design and content match your needs.

4.10 MORE POWERFUL DATA-BASE MANAGERS

When the particular job you are working on requires interaction between two or more files to produce the necessary reports, a more sophisticated and expensive data-base manager is required. Commercial packages of this nature include *Clipper, dBASE, Foxbase, FoxPro, Oracle, Paradox, RBase*, and *Smart Software. WATFILE Plus* also has multiple file-handling capabilities, but is described more generically as an information management system, rather than a data base.

Typical users of data bases include large corporations or government agencies that have access to centralized files. Departments may need information from several files to produce their reports. The payroll department might want information about the sales staff from the "Personnel File", such as Social Insurance Number, Rate of Pay, and Employee Number, and also information from the "Product Sales File" such as Amount Sold by Sales Staff. Neither file alone could provide all of the required data. But parts of each file can be assembled and processed to produce the required output—employee paycheques.

Not all data-base managers operate in the same way. The files in a data base are organized according to some predefined model, called the data structure. A **data structure** specifies relationships between multiple files in a data base. This is important to know because it restricts how your files can be organized, yet still be able to relate to each other.

There are three types of data structures currently used in data-base managers. The first is called a "hierarchical" (or tree) structure. Its name comes from its top-down, tree-like structure in which there is a "parent-daughter" file relationship. The top file (the parent) is related to its two children (two daughters) who are, in turn, related to their two children (two more daughters). To get to information stored in the third file down, you have to search through the mother, her daughter, and her granddaughter.

A second type of data structure is called a "network structure". The relationship between the files is very specific, although it varies between different data bases. To search for an item, you have to follow a very specific path through the files until the data is reached.

The third type of data structure is called a "relational structure". This is what the letter "R" in front of the software called *RBase* stands for. In a relational data base, there are no pre-existing paths to worry about. The data is listed in tables, and users can browse through the files and arrange all or parts of the data to suit the task. Relational data-base managers tend to be ideal for developing applications on decision making, or where free-style thinking is necessary to search for relationships among different files. Typical users might include newspaper research departments, secret intelligence agencies, medical research facilities, and large corporations controlling multiple subsidiaries. Generally speaking, data-base management systems are for the "power users"; that is, those people who have a strong understanding of how the files are constructed and related to each other, as well as a professional need to manipulate large quantities of complex data.

*A*n organized collection of data is referred to as a data file if it is stored together under one file name, or as a data base if it is stored as several different but related files. A data-file manager can only process one file at a time, whereas a data-base manager can manipulate several files simultaneously.

The terms "files", "records", and "fields" are part of any file-management vocabulary. A file is the organized collection of data that can be subdivided into units called records. All records within a file are organized in a similar pattern, and contain similar information. Each record can be further subdivided into smaller sections called fields, which contain specific information such as name or address.

Information-management software can be currently grouped into two broad classes. A horizontal-format file manager organizes information in straight lines across the screen. One line represents one record. Vertical-format file managers, on the other hand, organize information vertically like a page of information. One screen full of data represents a single record. Vertical-format file managers generally require more screen-design considerations than the horizontal style, but the extra effort pays off in clarity and readability.

Information stored in a file can be sorted alphabetically or numerically, searched for particular items, and manipulated mathematically if numeric data is available. This processing often takes place just prior to report generation—when reports are organized and printed.

A Data Base Problem-Solving Cycle can be expressed as a series of six steps: (1) determine what is required; (2) research your data; (3) design the template; (4) enter the data; (5) manipulate and display the data; (6) verify your system.

More complex tasks may require information from more than one file. To manipulate multiple files, a more powerful, expensive, and complex program called a data-base manager is required.

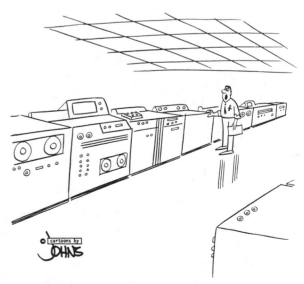

"I still say this is a clothes dryer!"

data base

data-base manager

data file

data-file manager

data structure

field

horizontal-format file manager

key to the search

key to the sort

record

report generation

searching

sorting

template

test run

vertical-format file manager

CHECKING YOUR READING

*T*hese are general questions that may require factual recall, reading comprehension, and some application of the knowledge gained from this chapter.

Organization of Data Files

1. What is a "data file"?

2. How does a data-base manager differ from a data-file manager?

3. Write the following data into your notebook. Using circles and arrows, indicate which part of the illustration would represent (a) a data file; (b) a single record; (c) a field.

SUPERHEROES

Superman	Clark Kent	Flies
Batman	Bruce Wayne	Batmobile
Cyborg	Steve Austin	Bionic Legs

4. When using a horizontal-format file manager, how can you see additional fields that are out of view on the screen?

5. Why is a vertical-format display easier to read?

6. What is a "screen template"?

Screen-Design Considerations

7. List the five decisions required at the design stage of any data file.

8. List two screen layout decisions that are specific to vertical file managers.

Manipulating a Data File

9. (a) To what does the term "searching" refer?
   (b) Explain the phrase "key to the search".
   (c) If a police officer is searching for only criminals convicted of theft, what would you suggest as the "key to the search"?

10. To what does "sorting" refer?

11. List four ways of sorting fields.

12. Explain the phrase "key to the sort".

13. Give an example of how mathematical calculations within a data file could be helpful.

14. List five commands that can be used to perform certain mathematical operations in some data-file managers.

15. Define "report generation".

16. Explain how fields in a record can be manipulated to change the content of a final report.

Problem Solving with a File Manager

17. List the six steps to problem solving with a file manager.

18. (a) What purpose do "test runs" on a newly designed data file serve?
(b) When does the procedure of conducting test runs stop?

More Powerful Data-Base Managers

19. (a) When is a data-base manager required?
(b) Give three examples of names of commercial data bases.

20. (a) What is a "data-file structure"?
(b) Why is it important to know about the way in which data is organized within a data base?

21. List the three different types of data structures used in data-base managers.

22. Suggest two general types of application to which relational data-base managers are ideally suited.

*T*hese questions assume an understanding of the material in the chapter, and provide new situations that may require evaluation, analysis, or the application of your newly acquired knowledge.

1. File Maintenance Problem—The Class List

Usually, files are not static. Records are added, modified, or deleted during the process of using them. These tasks are referred to as "file maintenance". This practice question involves creation, data entry, and maintenance of the records in a file.

(a) Create a template for the following records, then enter the data.

Data:

STUDENT NAME	YEAR	NO. OF CREDITS
Kim Jung	12	24
Wayne Toolie	11	14
Georgette Summers	10	8
Hank Belick	12	23
Wanda Demeric	10	9
Louis Thomas	10	7
Kelly Rimmer	11	16
Valerie Emard	12	24

(b) During the summer three students took summer school courses to improve their standing. Make the following changes. Display the modified file on the screen when completed.

Wanda Demeric	one additional credit
Wayne Toolie	two additional credits
Louis Thomas	one additional credit

(c) Three new students have been added to the class list and one student has been deleted. Modify the file to accommodate these changes.

New Student - Harold Damion 12   23
New Student - Wong Ho   11   16
New Student - Anthony Perche 11   17
Delete - Georgette Summers   10   8

(d) Make a printout titled "UPDATED CLASS LIST" with today's date on it and include all the changes mentioned above.

2. File Maintenance Problem—Grocery Store Price List

(a) Create a template to hold the following records, then enter the data.

Data:

PRODUCT NAME	SUPPLIER	UNIT PRICE
Noxema Shaving Cream	Harvey's Wholesale	$1.29
Glad Garbage Bags	Kitchen Products Ltd.	$6.99
Primo Spaghetti	Primo Products	$2.15
Primo Sauce	Primo Products	$1.75
Scott Paper Towels	Kitchen Products Ltd.	$0.55
Scott Family Napkins	Kitchen Products Ltd.	$1.19
Alymer Green Beans	Premier Distributors	$0.95
Alymer Asparagus	Premier Distributors	$1.15

(b) Four companies have sent price changes. Modify the records to reflect the new prices.

	NEW PRICE
Glad Garbage Bags	$7.05
Primo Spaghetti	$2.18
Primo Sauce	$1.75
Noxema Shaving Cream	$1.25

(c) The grocery store decided to add three new product lines to their displays. Add the following records:

Jergens Hand Lotion	Harvey's Wholesale	$3.50
Beautiful Hair Shampoo	Walter's Distributors	$1.13
Alymer Corn Nibs	Premier Distributors	$1.10

(d) Two companies no longer distribute the following products. Delete them from the list.

Scott Family Napkins

Alymer Asparagus

(e) Make a printout titled "UPDATED PRODUCT LIST" with today's date on it, and include all the changes mentioned above.

*S*tudents should have read and understood the concepts in this chapter before attempting these comprehensive problems.

1. The Medical File

Doctor Wainwright, a medical practitioner, has just purchased a microcomputer system. He wants to construct a computerized medical reference file that any member of his nursing staff can turn to for assistance in their diagnosis of symptoms. The file is to contain the Name of the Disease, Symptoms, and Recommended Cure. Your task is to design a template for the screen that will accept the data to be entered by the nursing staff. Next, type in the data for the medical file. Your printout, called MEDICAL DATA FILE, will list the diseases alphabetically along with the symptoms and the cure.

Data:

Common Cold	Sneezing, Runny Nose Bed Rest, Analgesic
Broken Limbs	Cannot Move Arm or Leg Rigid Cast, Analgesic
Bronchitis	Lung Congestion Sore Throat Expectorant, Analgesic
Sprained Ligament	Movable, Pain Analgesic
Pneumonia	Lung Inflammation Fever Antibiotics Hospital
Severed Spinal Cord	Paralysis Surgery Keep Immobile
Abrasions	Broken Skin, Bleeding Antiseptic, Bandage
Pinched Spinal Cord	Extreme Pain to Limbs Surgery, Keep Immobile
Head Concussion	Headaches, Dizziness Hospital
Heart Attack	Pain in Arm or Chest Hospital

2. Sports Cars

One of the major automobile manufacturers is concerned about losing its share of the North American sports car market. The general manager has asked you to set up a data file that will provide up-to-date information on both imports and domestic models. Your task is to design a template that will accept the data that the manager needs. The data includes the Name of the Sports Car, Country of Origin, Units Sold in Canada, and Price. The printout, called SPORTS CAR DATA FILE, will list the cars alphabetically. (If you know of recent price increases in the cars or model changes, please update the information when entering the data.)

Sample Screen Field Names:

SPORTS CAR
COUNTRY
UNITS SOLD
PRICE

Data:

Porsche Carrera 54 Germany 2500 $100 000	Corvette ZR-1 U.S.A. 10 000 $65 000
Toyota Supra Japan 5000 $45 000	Mazda RX7 Turbo Japan 5000 $35 000

Ferrari 328 GTSi	Lamborghini
Italy	Italy
2000	1800
$110 000	$225 000
Firebird Trans Am GTA	BMW 725 CSI
U.S.A.	Germany
8000	400
$30 000	$90 000

3. Library Reference

Mr. Morgan, a librarian, is interested in a sample data file that would illustrate its usefulness as a book-searcher system for students who come to the library. He has given you 16 books and the information about each one. Your task is to set up a template to accept the data, then enter the facts he has provided. Mr. Morgan wants three different lists when you are finished:

(1) All books sorted alphabetically by title

(2) All books sorted alphabetically by author

(3) Only books in the science fiction category

Data:

The Tommyknockers
by Stephen King
(Gothic Horror)

Octagon
by Fred Saberhagen
(Science Fiction)

Deep Lie
by Stuart Woods
(Spy Thriller)

Outbreak
by Robin Cook
(Medical Thriller)

The Right Man
by Sandra Field
(Romance)

Odyssey Three: 2061
by Arthur Clarke
(Science Fiction)

A Touch of Class
by Rita Rainville
(Romance)

Sphere
by Michael Crichton
(Science Fiction)

Black Alert
by Alan White
(Action Thriller)

Foundation
by Isaac Asimov
(Science Fiction)

Trump
by Jerome Tuccille
(Biography)

Firefox Down
by Craig Thomas
(Spy Thriller)

Alien Nation
by Alan Dean Foster
(Science Fiction)

The Zurich Axioms
by Max Gunther
(Investment Advice)

World of One
by Charles
  Templeton
(Contemporary
Fiction)

The Alley Cat
by Yves Beauchemin
(Contemporary
Fiction)

4. The Racing Track

Faraway Raceways is a race track where the best race horses from all across the country compete for prizes. The owner, Zucho Mondale, has requested a data-file retrieval system which would help stable owners with their decisions for purchasing new horses. The data file is to contain the following information: Name of the Racing Horse, Number of Wins, Number of Races Entered, and Prize Money Earned. To help you, Mr. Mondale has provided the data shown on the following page. You are to prepare two separate printouts.

(a) "Top Runners" is to contain all the information on only those horses that have ten or more wins.

(b) "Top Earners" is to list the information on the horses arranged from highest to lowest earnings. Leave out the data on number of races entered.

Data:

Race Horse	Wins	Races Entered	Money Earned
Fast Francis	12	15	$50 000
Winning Edge	3	8	$ 3 000
Slow Poke	0	10	$ 250
Sassy Sally	4	5	$ 1 200
Charley's Pride	9	12	$ 4 000
Fancy Pants	13	14	$55 000
Foxy Lady	10	15	$27 000
Charming Gent	6	10	$ 5 500
In The Money	4	8	$ 3 500
Sweet Heart	11	13	$17 000
Dad's Game	3	6	$ 1 500
Fred's Frolic	11	16	$29 000

5. Career Search

The school guidance department has asked you to assist them with the establishment of a data file on various careers about which students have requested information. The career data is organized into three fields: Occupation, Education Required, and Salary after five years on the job. (If you are aware of any salary increases, please update.) When you have completed the data entries, indicate the file's usefulness by generating these two different reports.

(a) "Interesting Careers" lists all the careers in the data file sorted alphabetically by occupation.

(b) "High-Income Careers" lists only those careers in the data file that have an income of $30 000 or more, sorted from highest to lowest.

Data:

Registered Nurse	Waitress
4 years university	Grade 12
$38 000	$18 000
Truck Driver	Construction Worker
Grade 10	Grade 10
$22 000	$23 000
Store Manager	Criminal Lawyer
3 years college	8 years university
$30 000	$100 000
Bank Clerk	Veterinarian
Grade 12	8 years university
$18 000	$75 000
Chartered Accountant	Doctor (generalist)
7 years university	8 years university
$80 000	$120 000
Psychiatrist	Doctor (specialist)
12 years university	10 years university
$110 000	$150 000
Newspaper Reporter	Teacher
4 years university	5 years university
$35 000	$40 000
Data Processing Mgr	Real Estate Sales Person
3 years college	6 months college
$38 000	$30 000

6. Best Stocks

Investment Counsellors Ltd. is a business that provides investment advice to clients for a fee. The counsellors need to provide clients with three different types of report when they are discussing investment strategies. Data on the company includes name, number of shares sold last week, value of any dividends (profits) issued, and the price being asked for one share on the stock market. The manager wants these three reports:

(a) "Listing of All Companies" shows all the stocks listed alphabetically by company name.

(b) "Top Dividend Companies" shows only those companies with dividends greater than $1.50, sorted from highest to lowest.

(c) "Companies By Price" prints only those companies that have more than 50 000 shares sold, with the price per share sorted from highest to lowest.

Data:

Company Name	Shares Sold	Dividends	Price/ Share
Edmonton Oil	65 000	$1.25	$15.00
Sears Ltd.	100 000	$0.75	$23.50
Canada Cement	75 000	$1.50	$32.00
Royal Bank	15 000	$2.19	$45.00
B.C. Lumber Ltd.	80 000	$2.00	$25.00
Sask. Potash Ltd.	32 000	$0.75	$ 5.50
IBM Canada Ltd.	125 000	$1.75	$99.00
Scotia Bank	45 000	$0.56	$15.25
Compaq Computers	56 000	$1.15	$31.60
Kimberly Clark	34 000	$1.00	$56.90
Howard Johnsons	12 000	$0.15	$18.00
Noranda Mines	2 000	$1.10	$ 6.50
Epson Printers	76 000	$2.80	$20.50
Levis Co. Ltd.	20 000	$0.50	$19.00
Stelco Ltd.	300 000	$1.75	$28.00
Ford Canada	175 000	$2.00	$15.00
Cape Breton Coal	15 000	$0.90	$15.00
General Electric	80 000	$1.00	$26.00
Nfld. Fisheries	8 000	$0.85	$ 9.50
Petro-Canada	16 000	$1.40	$ 7.25

PROBLEMS THAT REQUIRE DATA RESEARCH

These problems require some research to gather the data prior to establishing the data file. These are general-level questions.

7. The Music Collection

Most students have a personal library of music tapes, CD-ROMS, or albums that they like to listen to. Your task is to design a data file composed of your top 15 favourite selections using information from your personal music collection or from current albums on the market. The template for the screen will contain four fields—Title, Recording Artist, Music Category, and For-mat. Some suggested music categories include Country Music, Show Themes, Punk Rock, Soft Rock, Hard Rock, and Instrumental. Format means either tape, disk, or album. There will be two printouts of your data base.

(a) "Recording Artists" lists all the albums sorted alphabetically by artist.

(b) "Music Collection" lists all the albums sorted alphabetically by title.

8. Compatibility Search

This assignment simulates a dating service and is based on certain criteria. To obtain the data, conduct actual interviews with students in the school, starting with people in your classroom. Ask them their name, age, height, favourite type of movie, and main hobby. Movie categories might include comedy, western, action, romance, thriller, science fiction, and mystery. If you are overly shy, you may wish to create fictitious data. You need 15 entries. Three printouts are required.

(a) "Complete List" contains the entire file sorted alphabetically by last name.

(b) "Compatible By Age/Height" contains only those entries that are a suitable age and height, and sorted alphabetically by last name.

(c) "Compatible By Hobby" contains only those entries that have a particular hobby.

Sample Layout and Data:

NAME	AGE	HT.	MOVIES	HOBBY
Kovac, Kim	15	165	Comedy	Walking
Simpson, Jim	16	173	Action	Baseball

9. Adventure Holiday

A specialized travel agency provides challenging "adventure tours" around the globe for tourists who want a little risk in their lives. The manager has asked you to assist them with their data file, which will be used by the travel agents. In addition to the five tours shown opposite, add ten others. Each entry should indicate the country, city, cost, and risk factor rated out of ten. More ideas for the data may be obtained from travel agency brochures or the weekend travel section of your newspaper.

Sample Inquiry:

A customer wishes to know about all the tours costing $1200 or less, and with a risk factor of five or greater.

A Sample Response to Inquiry:

COUNTRY	CITY	COST	RISK
Ireland	Belfast	$ 1 000	6
Libya	Tripoli	$ 1 100	8

Incomplete Data:

COUNTRY	CITY	COST	RISK
China	Beijing	$ 779	4
Ireland	Belfast	$ 1 000	6
Libya	Tripoli	$ 1 100	8
Kenya	Nairobi	$ 1 325	3
Colombia	Bogota	$ 1 580	9

(Add ten additional records to complete the file.)

*T*he following problems involve data creation, sorting, and searching.

1. Airport Luggage

Vancouver International Airport requires an information system that will provide information on luggage ownership, weight of contents, flight number, destination, and surcharges, if any. You are required to create ten additional passenger records to bring the file up to a total of 20 records. Four separate reports are required.

(a) A printout sorted by passenger name of any of these three flights—959 (London), 928 (Osaka), or 924 (Paris)

(b) Three separate lists of all passengers owing money for having luggage in excess of 20 kg., sorted by weight and name for all three flights—959, 928, and 924

Incomplete Data:

Passenger	Luggage Weight	Flight No.	Destination
Smees, J.	20	959	London, England
Michalsky, W.	22	959	London, England
Ormerod, P.	18	959	London, England
Hoffman, J.	23	959	London, England
Krar, G.	25	959	London, England
Holinaty, S.	15	928	Osaka, Japan
Perrault, D.	25	928	Osaka, Japan
Chu, L.	29	928	Osaka, Japan

Passenger	Luggage Weight	Flight No.	Destination
Lew, D.	19	928	Osaka, Japan
LaForme, B.	28	928	Osaka, Japan
Macdonald, M.	23	924	Paris, France
Solino, F.	21	924	Paris, France
Lareau, G.	27	924	Paris, France

(Add seven more records using just those three flight destinations to complete the data file.)

2. Junior Hockey

A new rule has been implemented in a local hockey team to control unsportsmanlike players. Any player who accumulates five or more demerits during a five-game season will receive a First-Level Suspension, which involves an automatic two-game suspension and a $1000 fine. An accumulation of ten points in a season will result in a Second-Level Suspension, which involves a season suspension and a $5000 fine. The incomplete data on the team's players requires ten more entries for a total of 20 records. The following two reports are required:

(a) "Players with First-Level Suspension", which is to include the player's name, team name, total demerits, and the two minor punishments.

(b) "Players with Second-Level Suspension", which is to include the player's name, team name, total demerits, and the two harsher punishments.

Incomplete Data:

PLAYER	TEAM	G1	G2	G3	G4	G5
Zablocki, T.	Black Hawks	1	2	0	0	2
Swan, R.	Maple Leafs	3	0	0	1	0
Archer, L.	Black Hawks	1	0	0	1	3
Berendt, K.	Canucks	1	3	0	0	1
Buchan, F.	Flames	0	0	0	0	0
Cihocki, S.	Canadians	1	0	2	2	0
Gajic, S.	Oilers	1	1	1	1	3
Panker, T.	Oilers	3	3	1	2	2
Hannibal, E.	Canucks	5	1	2	0	3
Prong, I.	Canadians	0	2	3	1	0

(Add ten more entries to complete the data file.)

3. Top Canadian Corporations

A publisher of a major business journal has requested an information system containing data on the top 20 money-making corporations in Canada. The file must contain information on the Company Name, Product or Service Provided, Chief Executive Officer (CEO), and his/her Salary. The incomplete data file requires a total of 20 records. Once your file is created, print three different reports with appropriate titles that would be of interest to the readers of the business journal.

Incomplete Data:

Company Name	Product/ Service	CEO	Salary
Olympia & York	Real Estate	Reichmann Bros	$1 200 000
K.C. Irving	Timber	Irving Bros	$1 000 000
Petro-Can.	Petroleum	Wayne Henley	$ 125 000

(Add sufficient records to create a 20-record file.)

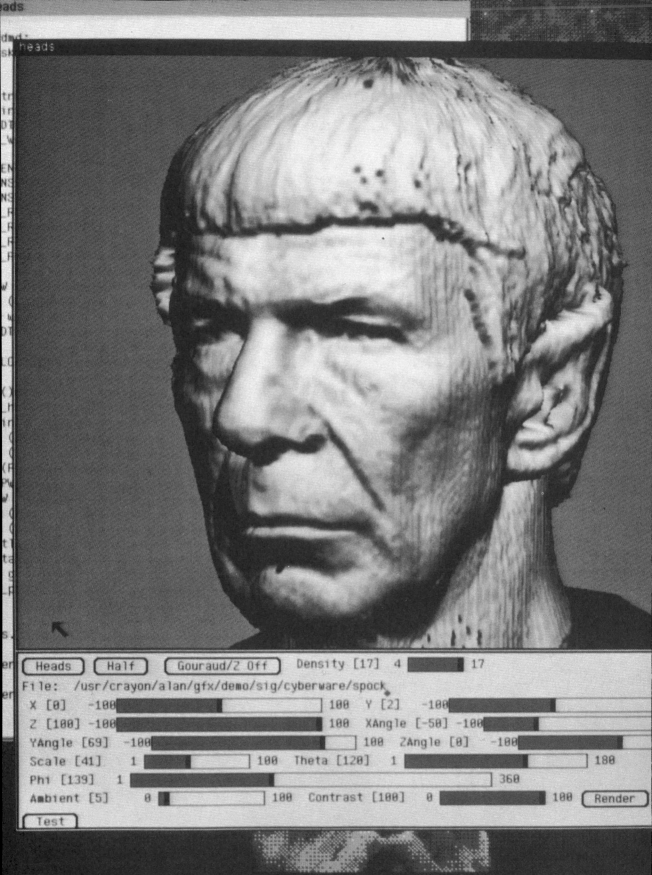

Chapter 5

GRAPHICS-DESIGN SOFTWARE

66 A computer's versatility is limited only by the user's imagination. 99

OBJECTIVES

By the end of this chapter, you will be able to:

1 Define the following terms: computer graphics, line drawings, shadow effect, clip art, graphic layout, text, fonts, page scanners, hand scanners;

2 Identify six different categories of graphics-design software, and describe an example of output from each one;

3 Create simple two- and three-dimensional images using a free-style drawing program;

4 Create a poster or flyer using a graphics assembly program, such as *PrintMaster* or *Print Shop*;

5 Create a fill-in-the-blank business form using forms-design software;

6 Create a simple, computerized slide show presentation using desktop presentation software.

WORKING IN THE WORLD OF COMPUTERS

Architect
uses CAD software to design blueprints of structures such as buildings or bridges

Graphic Illustrator
uses free-style design software to create images for magazines or books

Hair Style Consultant
shows clients how different hair styles, superimposed on their digitized facial image, alter their appearance

Interior Decorator
uses specialized room layout software to illustrate room changes for clients

Landscape Consultant
draws pictures of the way the land around a building can be made more attractive

Mechanical Engineer
uses computer-aided design software to plan production details of mechanical parts

Office Secretary
uses form-design software to create specialized forms for office use

Plastic Surgeon
shows prospective patients how their face will appear after surgery by altering the client's video image

Sales Order Clerk
enters sales orders into a pre-designed template on the screen

Video Graphics Designer
creates short computer graphics sequences and videotapes them for use in commercials

5.1 INTRODUCTION

*O*ne of the more creative and exciting applications of microcomputers is their use as a drawing tool to create computer graphics. **Computer graphics** refers to any image created on the screen or printer and generated by a computer, including simple line drawings, creative artwork, diagrams, maps, elaborate illustrations, cartoons, scanned images, engineering diagrams, and business charts. Programs that can create these images are referred to as graphics-design software. Features such as text insertion, titling, labelling, colouring, and page-layout capabilities, are also often included as part of the program.

Many careers require computer graphics skills. An illustrator who draws artwork for a magazine or newspaper must be familiar with graphics software. Engineers who design rockets, buildings, bridges, engines, or automobiles create and manipulate three-dimensional scaled images of the object on the computer. Landscape consultants and interior decorators use land-topography diagrams or room-layout diagrams to show their prospective clients how changes will look.

Plastic surgeons using a camcorder attached to a computer can capture the image of a person's face. Then, using an assortment of different noses, chins, ears, and eyebrows, the surgeons can alter the original image by superimposing the changes and printing out a suitable new face for the potential client to consider prior to surgery.

New ways for computers and graphics to interact are being developed every year, as with the transfer of subjects from camera to monitor, called **video digitizing**. This chapter provides a brief overview of the various categories of graphics software, and presents opportunities to understand and practise some of the easier modes of interaction.

5.2 CATEGORIES OF GRAPHICS SOFTWARE

*G*raphics-design software can be quite specialized in what it allows the user to do. Usually each program concentrates on a specific type of graphics design, rather than attempting to meet all the user's needs. Graphics software can be divided into eight broad categories: (1) free-style drawing, (2) graphics-assembly, (3) forms-design, (4) computer-aided design (CAD), (5) desktop presentations, (6) animation, (7) business graphics, and (8) desktop publishing. Since "business graphics" is covered in the chapter on spreadsheets, and "desktop publishing" is the topic of the next chapter, only the first six categories will be described in this chapter.

5.3 FREE-STYLE DRAWING

*T*he first category, which includes **free-style drawing software**, also referred to as "paint programs", and the more advanced "graphics illustrators", allows the user to create images from "scratch". The images can be drawn as simple line diagrams, and altered pixel by pixel, for shading or colouring. A number of commercial drawing programs can perform this task, including *Colour Draw, CORELDRAW, Deluxe Paint, Dr. Halo, GEM Draw, Macdraw, Pixel Paint, PC Paint*, and *PC Paintbrush*. Typically the screen consists of a drawing area, and a "tool box" of options along the left- or right-hand side (called side bars) from which to choose drawing features. Tools may include specific shapes, such as a circle, square, or rectangle, or symbolic drawing tools, such as a pencil for drawing, an eraser for rubbing out errors, a spray can for blending colours or shading, a fill command, and an array of colours and patterns with which to fill in the picture.

Generally, free-style drawing programs are aimed at people who have some artistic ability. The drawing area is blank, and, although symbolic drawing tools are provided, the talent must be supplied by the user. An example of a simple two-dimensional **line drawing** is shown below left. It gets that name because the image is simply lines with some shading added. Since it appears to have only length and width, but no depth, it is described as being two-dimensional.

Creating a Three-Dimensional Perspective

*T*he ability to create three-dimensional perspectives helps make images look real. Making an image appear to have three sides (length, width, and depth) instead of just two is simple. First, create a two-dimensional line drawing; then add extra lines to give the illusion of an extra dimension. For example, suppose that we begin with the drawing of a square on the screen. The three-dimensional representation of a square is a cube. By extending three corners behind the image, an illusion of depth is created, as illustrated in the two diagrams below.

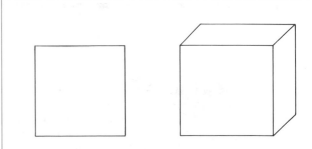

Another technique used to provide the illusion of depth is to add a **shadow effect** to the drawing. This makes the viewer think that the object on the screen is casting a shadow because of an off-screen light source. If we were to add the shadow technique to the cube already drawn, the image might look more realistic. A circle can be turned into a ball with the shadow effect on the object as well as behind it. The "spray can", which provides a fine black-coloured spray, can be used to create the shadow effect.

Simple Line Drawing

Using a free-style drawing program (paint program), draw a reasonable copy of one of the images shown at right. Then, using the graphics tools provided in the program, improve the image by adding things or modifying existing lines to give it a three-dimensional appearance. Add a title to the drawing, put your name in the upper right-hand corner, and get the computer to save and print your graphic design. You may go through several drafts of the drawing before you are satisfied with the final printed version. Make sure successive editing stages are saved before you leave your work-station.

Tracing an Outline

One way to develop professional-looking images, without drawing them from scratch, is to use a photocopier to make transparencies from the originals. You can then temporarily tape the transparency to the screen and, using a mouse or trackball to direct the cursor, trace the outline of the image. This works for cartoons, diagrams, maps, or virtually anything that has clearly defined shapes and lines. The image can then be altered using the software graphics tools to produce shading, patterns, colours, and labels.

Another method of getting professional-looking images is to use special input devices called **page scanners** or **hand scanners**, which use laser light to scan the origi-

nal image from a book, magazine, or newspaper and transfer it to the screen. These devices tend to be expensive and have limited clarity (maximum 400 dots per 2.5 square centimetres versus 2500 dots per 2.5 square centimetres for many originals). Another limitation of image scanners is that some accompanying programs do not allow you to manipulate the image once it is transferred to the screen. You must save the image on disk and then load it into a separate free-style drawing program to be able to alter it. Even then, some images cannot be altered because of incompatibility between files. However, if you can alter and print them, scanning is a fast way of getting sophisticated-looking graphics.

Tracing an Image

Tape to your computer screen a transparency of an image you have brought in, or an image provided by the teacher. Using your computer's mouse, trace the outline of the image. Remove the transparency when the tracing is done. Then continue to alter and modify the image to improve its appearance. When completed, add a title at the top and type your name in the upper right-hand corner. Save your work on disk, then print the graphic.

Figure 5.1 A graphics illustrator traces an image of a futuristic jet fighter using a special Hewlett-Packard digitizing board. The image was stored in the computer and was later rotated and animated for a cockpit sequence in a Star Wars movie.

Courtesy of Computing Canada

Not all graphics-design programs require a lot of artistic talent. A **graphics-assembly program** has pre-drawn images, borders, and specialized lettering that can be "assembled" or arranged into whatever design the user needs. Usually, the software has one or more types of format in which assembly is permitted, including posters, long banners, greeting cards, personalized stationery, calendars, certificates, and cartoons. Examples of this type of software include *PrintMaster, Print Shop, Principal's Assistant, Certificate Maker, Print Magic,* and *Garfield Deluxe*.

Pre-drawn images stored on disk as individual picture files are referred to as **clip art**. There are several vendors that sell programs called *clip art libraries,* which contain 50-100 picture files to be used with specific programs. Specialized, scalable (its size can be adjusted) lettering is also used in this type of program. The style of letter, such as Times Roman, Western, and Balloon, is called the typeface. The size or treatment of the letter is called the **font**.

The nice feature about graphics-assembly programs is that they are highly **user friendly**. You can usually learn how to operate the software without ever looking in the manual, and still get sophisticated-looking, helpful documents. This accounts for the software's broad appeal to all age levels.

Effective Graphic Designs

The one skill required of the user is **graphic layout** — the positioning of the various elements (fonts, clip art, and borders) within a specific format. While graphics-assembly software will print virtually anything, the results may be ineffective at communicating a message, or simply be unattractive. Here are some suggestions for producing effective graphic designs.

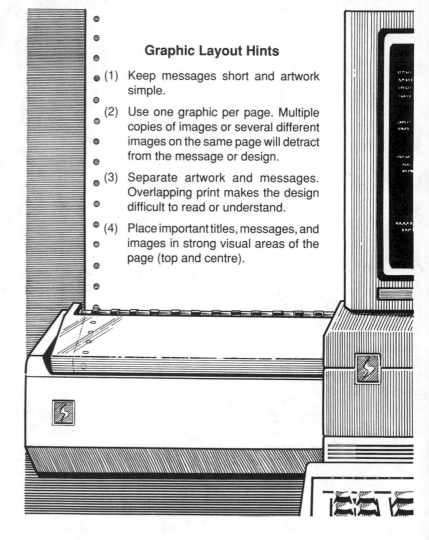

Graphic Layout Hints

(1) Keep messages short and artwork simple.

(2) Use one graphic per page. Multiple copies of images or several different images on the same page will detract from the message or design.

(3) Separate artwork and messages. Overlapping print makes the design difficult to read or understand.

(4) Place important titles, messages, and images in strong visual areas of the page (top and centre).

Copying a Poster Design

Using a graphics-assembly program such as *Printmaster Plus*, or *Print Shop*, design and print a vertical poster similar in content, spacing, size of type, and layout to the one shown to the right. (The clip art and font can vary if your program does not provide the particular ones used here.)

GOLF LESSONS

KING'S FOREST GOLF CLUB

WEDNESDAY EVENINGS
6:30 — 7:30

5.5 FORMS-DESIGN SOFTWARE

Several **forms-design software** packages are designed to produce ruled forms for businesses, schools, and offices. The forms might include a sales invoice, a checklist, an inventory list, an application form, or nearly any type of fill-in-the-blank-style form that you imagine. The programs usually present you with a blank working area and a sidebar menu of options for constructing the business form. Options might include vertical lines, horizontal lines, square corners, t-intersections, two or three sizes of font for titles and prompts, and various patterns for decoration.

Examples of forms-design software include *FormTools, FormFiller, FormWorx, Per-FORM*, and *Xerox Formbase*. Most of these programs also contain a data-file manager component, which permits the user to design a form on the screen and then use that form as a screen template to enter data into a special data file. For example, a clerk who takes orders over the phone might fill in the template on the screen while simultaneously talking to a customer. The computer prints the customer's order, which is sent to the warehouse so workers can find, box, and ship the required products.

Forms-design programs are mostly used to design and print one master copy of a form, which is then photocopied for office use.

Designing a Sales Order Form

Using a forms-design program, design and print a sales order form for Premier Wholesalers Limited, 100 Main Street West, Victoria, BC. The heading should contain the customer's name and address, the date, and the sales order number (upper right-hand corner). The sub-headings should include Quantity, Description, Unit Price, and Extension. The company sells televisions, stereo sets, and VCRs to retail stores, which usually buy 10-50 sets at a time.

SALES ORDER # _____

PREMIER WHOLESALERS LTD.
100 MAIN STREET WEST
VICTORIA, BRITISH COLUMBIA

DATE _____ 19 ___

CUSTOMER: _____

ADDRESS : _____
_____
_____

QUANTITY	DESCRIPTION	UNIT PRICE	EXTENSION

5.6 DESKTOP PRESENTATIONS

*O*ne of the newer types of graphics software, **desktop presentations**, lets the user create something that resembles a slide show on the computer. This is useful for business people who put on demonstrations at conventions and trade shows. Also lecturers and presenters can have a series of computer images projected onto an overhead screen, or shown on a large monitor, instead of using a traditional overhead projector.

Typically, desktop presentation software is capable of producing text, word charts, free-style graphics, borders, clip art, flashing screens, an assortment of colours, fades, dissolves, overlapping images, limited animation, and sometimes even sound. If a music synthesizer circuit board is inserted inside your computer, you can create sound at the keyboard, save it on disk, and orchestrate it with the series of images in the presentation. Hardware sometimes permits the music to be played through a public address system for an impressive "full-bodied" sound.

Examples of commercial presentation software include *PC Emcee, PC Paint, PC Screen Presenter, Show Partner FX, Slide Shop, Storyboard Plus,* and *VCN Concorde.*

Students taking courses in marketing or entrepreneurship can use the presentation software to design a 30- or 60-second commercial on a product or service. History students can use it to make a presentation on "Famous Canadians". Geography students can teach other students a particular topic, such as "Cloud Formations", complete with diagrams, titles, labels, explanations, and the sound of thunder in the background.

Each "slide" or "frame" is designed individually using specialized editors provided with the program. These frames are saved on disk, and numbered for future reference. Then you tell the computer in what order you wish the images to appear on the screen (example: 1, 4, 2, 5, 3), how many seconds each frame should stay on the screen, and how you wish each frame to disappear (slow dissolve, side wipe, slide top down, or overlaid by next picture). This information is saved as an executable file (referred to as a **script editor**) with an appropriate file name. Any time these executable files are loaded and run, the computer will automatically follow the instructions you have provided. The audience will then see and hear a computerized slide show presentation.

Practice Assignment (5 h)

Desktop Presentation

In teams of two or three students, plan a series of five frames to advertise the sale of your school yearbook. It costs $18.00, has a durable hard cover, and includes several colour pages. The messages that appear on the screen should include the yearbook name, its cost, and special features such as autograph pages, candid shots, personal write-ups on graduating students, and group photos of all school teams. Enhance the presentation with different size fonts, varying colours, artwork, and special effects.

5.7 COMPUTER-AIDED DESIGN

No other graphics package can do the fine, intricate, scalable line drawings that a **computer-aided design (CAD)** software package is capable of doing. With the help of specialized wide-body printers called "plotters" you can print detailed blueprints of engines, cars, or boats, or architectural drawings of houses, apartment buildings, office towers, or complete layouts of newly designed computer chips, or topographical maps of land contours.

Mechanical and electrical engineers,

Figure 5.2 This student is looking at graphs produced by a table-top drum plotter. Notice the four different pens poised above the roll of printer paper. They can plot graphs in four different colours.

Courtesy of California Computer Products

architects, blueprint draftsmen, and car-tographers (map-makers) all use this type of graphics software. Often special input tools, such as flat-surface graphics tablets with hand-held pointing devices, are used to create the lines. Examples of commercial CAD or CADD (computer-aided design and drafting) software include *Autosketch*, *De-signCAD 3-D*, *Drafix CAD Ultra*, *East CAD*, *Generic CADD*, and *Mathcad*.

5.8 ANIMATION SOFTWARE

The last of the six categories of graphics software described in this chapter is **ani-mation software**. These programs create moving graphic images, such as a man walking, or a bird flying, by treating the image as a single unit that can be made to assume several different positions. The user types direction and image changes into an executable file, and the computer generates the action automatically. Some animation packages have their own set of commands, similar to programming commands, to in-dicate movements, colours, dissolves, and wipes. Commercial animation packages include *Grasp* and *Show Partner FX*. Some desktop presentation software also includes limited animation capabilities.

Animation software is not as easy to use as it sounds. Often it requires the memori-zation of a set of commands, some artistic talent, and a flair for making attractive, simple stories. People who use this type of graphics software include graphics consul-tants (for television), video-advertising de-signers, and business people (for enhanc-ing desktop presentations).

Animation Project

In teams of two or three students, use animation or desktop presentation software to create an animated sequence of some object, such as a ball, truck, bird, or symbol.

The resulting program should contain at least five different "poses" of the object, although there is no limit to the number of frames allowed in the sequence. If possible, include a suitable title in the presentation.

A computer graphic is any image generated by a computer and presented on the screen or printer. Images include simple line drawings, creative artwork, diagrams, maps, elaborate illustrations, cartoons, scanned images, engineering diagrams, and business charts. Most graphics-design software also includes features such as text insertion, colour, and page layout capabilities.

Graphics software can be divided into eight broad categories: free-style drawing, graphics assembly, forms design, computer-aided design (CAD), desktop presentations, animation, business graphics, and desktop publishing.

Free-style drawing programs, or "paint programs", and the more advanced "graphics illustrators" allow the user to create images from scratch. Typically, the screen consists of a drawing area and a sidebar of drawing tools from which to choose.

Graphics-assembly programs come with pre-drawn clip art, a variety of fonts, and the ability to position these elements anywhere within the particular format being designed.

Forms-design software produces ruled, fill-in-the-blank forms for businesses, schools, and offices. Typically, a master copy of the form is produced with the software, and then additional copies are made by photocopying. Some forms-design programs also include a data-file manager. This permits the user to create a fill-in-the-blank screen template and enter data directly into a data file for storage and reference.

Desktop presentation software is ideal for business people who put on demonstrations at conventions and trade shows. The software can also be used for lectures, instead of transparencies and an overhead projector.

Computer-aided design (CAD) software produces fine, intricate, scalable line drawings, which are usually ouptut on a specialized wide-body printer called a "plotter".

Animation software includes specialized packages for preparing moving figures. Typically, such software requires the user to learn a set of commands, as well as requiring skills in artistic drawing and in planning storyboards: the latter are skills similar to those used by movie makers.

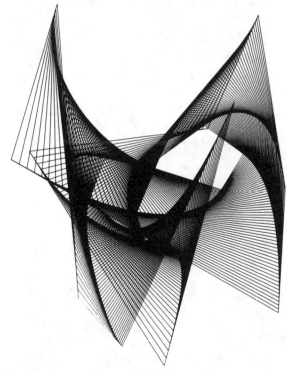

animation software

clip art

computer-aided design (CAD)

computer graphics

desktop presentations

fonts

forms-design software

free-style drawing software

graphics-assembly programs

graphic layout

hand scanners

line drawings

page scanners

script editor

shadow effect

user friendly

video digitizing

CHECKING YOUR READING

These are general questions that may require factual recall, reading comprehension, and some application of the knowledge gained from this chapter.

Introduction

1. What is a "computer graphic"?

2. Give five examples of computer-generated graphics.

3. List four careers that would require a working knowledge of graphics-design software, and give an example of how it might be used in each career.

Categories of Graphics Software

4. Why are there so many different types of graphics-design program?

5. List eight categories of graphics-design software.

Free-style Drawing

6. What other names are applied to the category called "free-style drawing"?

7. At whom is free-style graphics software aimed commercially?

8. What is a two-dimensional line drawing?

9. Suggest two ways of making a simple line drawing look more realistic.

10. Suggest two methods of getting an image from a magazine into a computer.

11. What is the disadvantage of scanners?

Graphics-Assembly Software

12. What is a graphics-assembly program?

13. Name two graphics-assembly programs people can purchase.

14. Why are graphics-assembly programs easy to use?

15. One skill required of a user of graphics-assembly software is "graphics layout". Explain to what that process refers.

16. Suggest what is wrong with these poster designs:

    (a) Jennifer made a marketing poster with the same image in 15 different spots.

    (b) The title on the dance poster read "Hallowe'en Dance this Friday Night at Nine O'Clock - Costumes Required", all in the same large block letters.

    (c) Fred's student council campaign poster had the words "Vote for Fred" overlaying an image.

    (d) Susan's "Bake Sale" flyer had the title at the bottom of the flyer underneath some artwork and other details.

Forms-Design Software

17. Give three examples of forms an office worker might create with a forms-design program.

18. How can a forms-design program be used with a data-file manager?

Desktop Presentations

19. Who uses "desktop presentation software"?

20. How can music be added to this type of program?

Computer-Aided Design

21. For what type of artwork is "computer-aided design" made?

22. Suggest four people who would use CAD software in their work.

Animation Software

23. Why is some animation software not easy to use?

24. List four different jobs that require animation software.

*T*hese questions assume an understanding of the material presented in the chapter, and provide new situations that may require evaluation, analysis, or the application of your newly acquired knowledge.

1. Simple Line Diagrams

Using free-hand drawing software, draw one of these suggested images: pine tree, snowman, sports car, rabbit, scissors and paper, or television set. Add extra features such as shading or shadowing to enhance the image. Title, save, and print the finished drawing.

2. Three-dimensional Images

Using free-hand drawing software, draw a two-dimensional image of the front of a house, barn, or toy block. Then, using line extensions and the shadow effect, create a three-dimensional image. Title, save, and print your creation.

3. Illusion of Distance

Repetitive images that get smaller toward the centre of the screen tend to create the illusion of distance. Draw a picket fence, with flowers and grass growing around it, that gets smaller as it extends from the left-hand side of your screen (largest part of your fence) to the middle of your screen (smallest part of your fence).

4. Map Tracing

Bring in a map that shows streets and major buildings of the countryside, town, or city where you live. Make a transparency of the section of the map where your home is located. Using the pointing device attached to your computer, trace the main streets and buildings that will provide directions to your house. Remove the transparency from the screen. Enhance the map with a drawing of your house and directional arrows indicating the best route, and type your name and address in one corner of the map. Save your work on disk and make a printout.

5. Cartoon or Superhero Tracing

Bring in a fairly large cartoon character, or superhero image, and make a transparency of the picture. Using your computer's pointing device, trace the outline of the image. Enhance the image in some way by adding more detail. Title, save, and print your graphic.

6. Graphics-Assembly Advertising Poster

The Grad Committee at your school has asked you to create an advertising poster, similar to the one shown below, for their bake sale. The students bake the items themselves with the help of their parents and use the proceeds to raise funds for the graduation dance. Cookies, tarts, brownies, pies, and muffins will be on sale.

BAKE SALE

Cookies, brownies, tarts, pies, and muffins

MONDAY AT NOON. CAFETERIA

*S*tudents should have read, understood, and practised the easier problems from this chapter before attempting these comprehensive problems in graphics design. Problems will require the selection of the most appropriate software for the task.

1. Advertising Posters for Student Council

The Student Council needs to advertise two events and they have come to you, as a computer expert, to create two posters for them. The first is for a School Dance in the cafeteria on Wednesday May 31 at 8:30 p.m. The cost is $5.00 per person, and it is the last school dance of the year. The council wants the words "School Dance" to be printed in the largest font on the poster. The second poster is to remind students to "Vote" for their favourite candidate in the upcoming student council elections. The voting will take place in home rooms on Friday June 2.

2. One-bedroom Apartment Design

A local Institute of Advertising and Design has offered a $5000 scholarship to any interested students who submit their own version of a graphic layout of a one-bedroom apartment. The apartment is to have a kitchen with refrigerator, stove, microwave, cupboards, and sink; a three-piece bathroom; a large living room with at least two windows looking out over a balcony, and a door to the balcony; and a large bedroom with a window and walk-in closet. The people marking the design are looking for an "open concept" with plenty of room for moving around and with fixtures arranged in convenient, easy-to-reach places. Extra features that obviously should be available, but are not mentioned here, will be considered positively as well. The space for the design must be a rectangle, with the length of the entire apartment being exactly twice the width. Each completed room is to be labelled for identification, and a main title is to appear at the top.

Sample Apartment Design

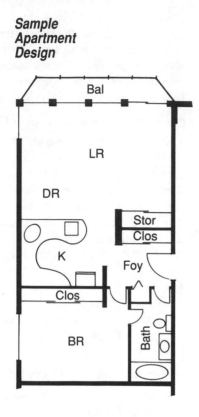

3. Credit Application Form

The manager of a large department store called "Greenways Department Store" has asked you to create an application form for customers who want to apply for credit cards. The form is to be used to "screen" the applicant for past credit history, current ability to pay debts, and current financial position. You may wish to study similar forms to see how they are laid out. Both the company name and the words "Credit Application Form" are to be printed in large, bold, block letters at the top of the sheet. Each entry section is to be "boxed", and the entire form is to be enclosed with a rectangular border.

4. New Sports Car Design

An automobile manufacturer is running a contest for the best new sports car design. The first prize is their top-of-the-line $80 000 sports car. Your graphic design is to be filled in as a completed picture, and should include a side-view of the car with body panels, windows, tires, door handles, etc. The judges are looking for an image of a fast and powerful machine with low wind resistance. Also, they expect you to give your creation a unique name.

5. A Scenic View

One of the projects for a senior art class is to draw an outdoor scene showing trees and a brook meandering off into the distance. The best design is to be used on the cover of a brochure that invites people to view school art exhibits next month during open house. You may wish to include people, (such as a boy or girl fishing or relaxing under a tree), or animals (a deer or raccoon taking a drink) in the scene. The final design should provide a three-dimensional perspective with shadow effects that gives the viewer the illusion of depth as the brook heads off into the distance.

6. New Stamp Design

Canada Post is looking for new stamp designs for next year's issues of first-class stamps. Your design is to be the size of a page; it will be photo-reduced and engraved on the actual printing plates by the corporation's design shop. Sample images may include sports, a Canadian bird or animal, a black outline of a city skyline, a train engine, or any other image agreed to by your teacher. If the image is to be in colour, and you do not have access to a colour printer, you may wish to have it marked on the screen rather than printed. Include the word "Canada" and the price of the stamp in the design.

7. Teaching Unit

Design a minimum five-screen teaching unit on computers for someone who has never taken a computer course before. The topic must be something included in this course; you must provide information that helps the viewer learn the basic elements of that topic. The screens are to be manually flipped by the user, rather than automatically timed. They should show variety in layout, colour, word charts, and graphic images. Some possible teaching units might include: components of a computer system, categories of graphics software, general software classifications, computer careers, or any other topic agreed to by your teacher.

8. Animated Travel Sequence

The owner of a local travel agency called "Marlin's Travel" has asked you to design a 30- or 60-second travel theme with some animation included. The owners plan to place a large monitor and computer in their store window to attract the attention of passing customers. The sequence should include the name of the travel agency in the first or last frame, and images such as ships, planes, a small island with a palm tree and setting sun, or people playing tennis or swimming. Animation should be part of the display, but does not need to be used in every frame. Any worded sections should be in large letters with very short messages to hold the audience's attention. Musical accompaniment can also be added if that feature is available in your software.

Chapter 6

DESKTOP PUBLISHING

DESKTOP PUBLISHING

DESKTOP PUBLISHING

"" Home publishing has become a new cottage industry. With a microcomputer and a colour laser printer, even small interest groups can publish their own polished-looking newsletter, newspaper, or magazine. **""**

OBJECTIVES

By the end of this chapter, you will be able to:

1 Define the following terms: desktop publishing, laser printer, scanner, template (page layout), nameplate, headline, text, clip art, typeface, font;

2 Design and print a one-page, two-column newsletter;

3 Recognize and use good design features when creating documents.

WORKING IN THE WORLD OF COMPUTERS

Advertising Designer
designs and prints advertisements and flyers for clients

Conference Organizer
creates and prints brochures for participants at conferences

Consultant
organizes attractive reports for clients

Investment Counsellor
prints monthly investment newsletters for clients

Lecturer
uses software to create professional-looking handouts for the audience

Magazine Publisher
creates page layouts with scanned photos, illustrations, and articles

Parts Distributor
prints illustrated catalogues of parts from which companies can order

Public Relations Officer
creates and prints pamphlets to present a positive image to the public

School Principal
creates and distributes periodic newsletters to parents about special school events

Software Distributor
publishes an illustrated catalogue and price list for customers

6.1 INTRODUCTION

*T*he heavy, metal typesetting machines and messy black-ink printing machines currently found in printing shops are gradually being replaced by high-quality laser printers and high-speed desktop microcomputers. The once separate functions of reporting, editing, typesetting, and printing can now be performed by one individual working with a computer system.

The use of a computer system to design and print professional-looking documents, using a combination of text and graphics, is referred to as **desktop publishing**. Documents produced on this type of system include newsletters, newspapers, magazines, brochures, manuals, catalogues, and books. Some Canadian magazines, product catalogues, and training manuals are produced entirely on these newer systems by a small staff of one to four people.

Desktop publishing requires the use of special software that permits the integration of scanned images, columns of text, and various sizes and types of lettering. Examples of desktop-publishing software include *Gem Desktop Publisher; Express Publisher; NewsMaster; Newsroom; PFS: First Publisher; Professional Page; Publish It; Ready, Set, Go;* and the most expensive, difficult to learn, and sophisticated entries—*Ventura* and *Pagemaker*. To produce even simple one-page documents using any of this software will require four to five hours of work when the user is first learning. Once the techniques are mastered, however, the same document can be created in 15-20 minutes.

The best screen-design feature to have in a program is referred to as **WYSIWYG** (pronounced "wizzywig"), meaning What You See Is What You Get. This allows the user to see on the screen exactly how the page will appear when printed, including pictures and enlarged titles. Some less sophisticated programs do this as a "Page Preview" function. However, good software lets you design interactively on the screen while in WYSIWYG mode. Examples of easy-to-use, interactive, WYSIWYG-mode programs include *GEM Desktop Publisher*, *NewsMaster*, and *Express Publisher*.

6.2 SPECIALIZED HARDWARE

*P*rofessional publishers usually require four expensive hardware components to produce quality documents that will look attractive to customers. The complex processing of lengthy documents that combine text with pictures requires a computer with a high-speed microprocessor chip, and a minimum of one or two megabytes (million bytes) of main memory. The large amount of memory is needed to hold the desktop-publishing program, along with a working space to assemble the document being created. Slower computers may take as long as five to ten minutes just to assemble and print one page. At that rate, a 100-page document would take over 16 hours to produce.

The second hardware component required for desktop publishing is a high-resolution monitor with either an EGA (enhanced graphics adapter) or VGA (video graphics array) circuit board to control it. The high-resolution monitors are necessary to allow the designer to see the fine details of an assembled page on the screen.

Vertical monitors, screens that are taller than they are wide, are favourites among publishers because one entire page can fit on the screen. Extra-wide monitors are also useful for previewing two facing pages on the screen at the same time to make sure the layouts blend together in an attractive manner.

The third hardware component is a specialized printer called a **laser printer**. Laser printers are quiet, non-impact printing devices that use a method similar to the one used by a photocopier to produce very high-quality output, typically 300 dpi (dots per square inch), at the rate of four to ten pages per minute. Some less expensive, 24-pin dot-matrix printers are also capable of producing that quality of output, but not at that speed. Colour laser printers can produce documents in four or more colours.

This is a useful feature for designing attractive reports, brochures, and magazines.

It is not only printers that are responsible for creating high-quality images. Software such as *Express Publisher* and *The New Print Shop* use special printing instructions called "printer drivers" to produce high-quality images and text even on the least expensive category of printer — the 9-pin dot matrix.

The last hardware component used by publishers is a **flat-bed scanner**, sometimes referred to as a "digitizer". This device will transfer any photo or graphic image placed on its surface into the computer. It digitizes the images bit by bit, and reassembles them inside the computer's main memory. This digitized graphic can then be saved on disk as a file, and used inside a newsletter or catalogue that will be developed later on.

Scanners require special software to help the computer translate the image. Usually scanning-device manufacturers provide different programs for text and graphics. This means that words and pictures must be scanned and entered into the computer as separate files. Xerox corporation has software that can recognize up to 150 different type styles, and can also translate handwriting. This text-scanning feature can save people a lot of time by not requiring them to key in information that is already printed in some other document.

A less expensive alternative to the flat-bed scanner is a portable version called a **hand-held scanner**. It fits easily into the palm of your hand, and is capable of scanning and digitizing a ten-centimetre wide picture at one time. This limits its usefulness to small images and short paragraphs, each of which must be saved as a separate file.

6.3 PRE-DESIGNED TEMPLATES

A desktop publishing **template**, or **page layout**, is an outline created for the entry of text and graphics. Its boxed-in areas are usually shown as dotted lines, and do not appear when the page is printed. The template acts as a guideline on the screen, so you can see where the main title ends and the body of the newsletter, with its separate columns and artwork, begins. It can be saved as a shell and used over and over again for similar tasks.

Most people who use desktop-publishing software on a regular basis favour templates because they help to create a uniform

Page Layout

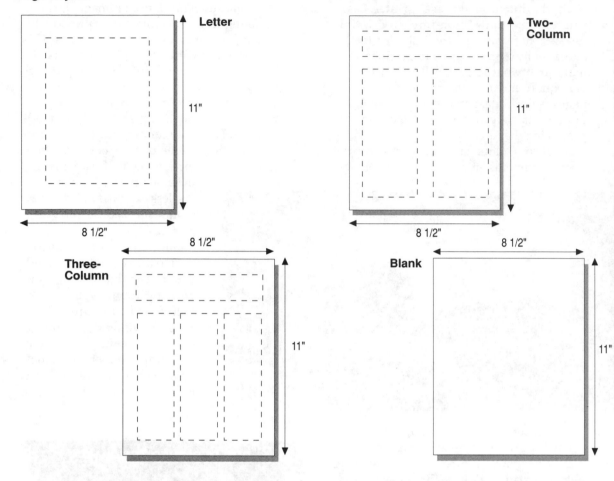

appearance from one issue or document to the next. Templates also save development time on future issues by allowing the user to save the original layout on disk. A template for an entire page can be seen if you choose the "Page Layout" option in most programs.

A standard template for a newsletter might contain a horizontal, boxed section across the top for the name, two equal- sized, vertical columns for the articles, and a boxed section somewhere on the page in which to place a scanned picture or artwork. This is referred to as "two-column format". Other formats may include blank, letter, and three-column.

6.4 COMPONENTS OF A NEWSLETTER

A simple way to begin desktop publishing is to try a one-page newsletter. This form of communication is frequently used in industry and government as an information bulletin to instruct clients on new products or to inform employees about company policies. Schools also use this format to keep parents up to date about school events. Newsletters are similar to one- or two-page newspapers with a specific theme or focus. They contain four main elements—a nameplate, headlines, text, and graphics.

The **nameplate** is the horizontal area across the top of a page in which the title appears. Text typed in this area goes all the way across the page without regard to the column separators on the page below. The two- or three-word title entered in the nameplate will be identical on each issue of the newsletter, providing "product recognition". Unlike other titles, nameplates often make use of stylish fonts and unusual layouts. To be called a nameplate, this section should include some additional information, such as the publication date, volume or issue number, price, and logo or picture. When this top area does not include any additional information, it is simply called a "banner" or "letterhead". Bars or ruler lines the width of the page are put below most nameplates to delineate the title from the rest of the newsletter.

A nameplate on a school newsletter might be called the "Westdale Reporter" or "High Ridge News". Industrial or government newsletters might be titled "Electronic Products Update", or "Department Policy Sheet". Once established, the type and size of lettering in the nameplate stays the same to ensure easy recognition by readers.

A **headline** is the title of an article contained within a document. Headlines are usually restricted to one or more columns to match the width of the article they are describing. The one exception is a "banner headline", which stretches across the entire page and is used when very important news is being announced, such as "World War Three Begins", or "Liberals Sweep Into Power". Headlines use the same typeface throughout the newsletter. Though their size may vary, they should be smaller than the nameplate, and should be kept to a maximum of three to six words.

It is important that the headline reflect the content of the article that it is describing. Journalists are known for their use of creative headlines, which may contain alliteration, such as "Barton Bears Bash Blues" (referring to an article on football), or a play on words, such as "Hang Gliding Hits New Highs", or a metaphor, such as "War On Poverty", to capture the reader's attention.

The written portion, or **text**, usually takes up 70% of the page and fills most of the body of the newsletter. Each article begins with a headline in large type to indicate the topic. Sometimes it contains smaller subtitles (one column wide) throughout to indicate shifts in focus or to break up long sections of text, making them easier to read.

The
WESTDALE REPORTER

Issue Number One

Designing a Nameplate

Using desktop-publishing software and a two-column template form, create a nameplate for a newsletter entitled SCHOOL NEWS. Additional information should include the publication date and issue number in smaller letters. Save the design with the file name SCHOOL and make a printout.

6.5 COMPUTER GRAPHICS

The last main element of a newsletter is graphics. **Computer graphics** include scanned photographs or images, cartoons, line drawings, business graphs, and clip art. These images are added to the newsletter to enhance the appearance of the document, support the substance of the article, or break the monotony of the columns of text for the reader.

Many software companies sell graphic **clip-art libraries**, which are collections of pre-drawn pictures and images that can be used with your desktop-publishing program. These images are stored on disk and can be retrieved for use in any document. Clip art is saved on disk in several different formats, however, which makes some libraries incompatible with some software. Make sure that you purchase clip-art packages that will work with your particular program.

To bring clip art into your document, it is necessary to select the particular title (file name) each image is stored under and load it into the computer's main memory through the desktop-publishing program. The image may float temporarily on your screen to allow you to position it wherever

Sample Clip-Art Library

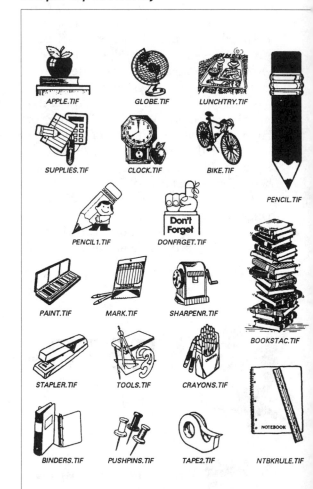

you wish. You must then "stamp" or "fix" the image to a particular spot before the computer can enter text around it.

Most programs also have a "clip-art editor", which is similar to a "paint program". Before you "fix" the image to a particular spot, this editor can be used to enhance or alter the image. It may also allow you to **rotate** the image, **crop** it (cut off unimportant parts), and **size** it (enlarge or shrink it, also referred to as scaling).

Reasons for Using Clip Art

*C*lip art can be used to support the article being written, or simply as a decoration. Supporting the content of the article makes more sense to the reader because the image matches the topic being discussed. When used as a decoration, the image may have no relevance to the topic, and may possibly confuse the reader. Whenever possible, choose clip art that will match your topic.

Nameplate ———

Logo ———

Headline ———

Clip art ———

Text ———

Highland News
Issue One

HIGHLANDERS IN FIRST PLACE

In an exciting semi-final game at Ivor Winn Stadium last night, the Highlander Seniors beat the Barton Bears 14-1. George Fisher and Tony Fioso made the two touchdowns in the second half of the match.

Quarterback Gomer Pyles completed 14 out of 15 passes for a season total of 145. The "sweep" and "rollout" patterns that proved so successful throughout the season, also proved to be the Bears' downfall.

Honourable mention goes to defensive captain Dan Crusher for breaking the school record for the most tackles in any one game. Dan repeatedly smashed through the Bears' linemen for a total of 18 tackles. The new record ensures his name in the school's Sports Hall of Fame.

UPCOMING EVENTS

Spirit Week   October 15-19

Monday -- Outdoor Barbecue

Hot dogs and hamburgers will be served on the back lawn by staff members. The $2.00 lunch also includes a pop and dessert.

Tuesday -- Air Band

Ten different acts will be presenting their versions of famous rock stars live on stage. Loads of fun.

Wednesday -- Milk Chug-A-Lug

The student council is hosting a milk Chug-A-Lug contest in the gymnasium during the lunch hour. Prizes for the winners.

Thursday -- Football Finals

Highlanders Seniors play the Eastdale Bulldogs for the city championship. GAC/BAC committees will be selling pop and popcorn at the game.

Friday -- Victory Dance

Dance to celebrate Highlander's victory. Admission $4.00 per person. Doors open at 8:30 p.m.

Figure 6.2

This document, created with *NewsMaster II* software, contains all the elements of a newsletter—nameplate, logo, headlines, text, and graphics.

Two-Column Newsletter with Clip Art

Using desktop-publishing software, retrieve the file called SCHOOL, which contains the nameplate that you designed in the previous practice assignment. The articles for this newsletter are to be created by you (as the reporter) and may cover topics such as sports, special events, upcoming dances, tips for studying for exams, or interesting classroom projects from a particular course. Do not include gossip or negative feelings. As a reporter, your duty is to present the facts in a neutral, unbiased, and positive manner. Include at least one clip-art image to support your article.

6.6 TYPEFACES AND FONTS

Desktop-publishing software lets you select from several different typefaces and sizes of lettering, referred to as **fonts**, to assemble your document. A typeface is the particular design of a set of characters and symbols. Typical names of typefaces include Times Roman, Helvetica, Cooper Black, and many others. Because names can be copyrighted, each company has their own set of names for their particular typefaces, even though the styles might be identical to those used by other software companies. Each of those typefaces forms the basis for a "font family" that includes special variations on the characters, such as boldface, italic, and shadow.

Helvetica Thin	Helvetica Condensed Italic	**Helvetica Black Condensed**
Helvetica Thin Italic	Helvetica Extended	**Helvetica Black Condensed Italic**
Helvetica Light	**Helvetica Bold**	**Helvetica Black Extended**
Helvetica Light Italic	**Helvetica Bold Italic**	**Helvetica Compressed**
Helvetica Light Condensed	Helvetica Bold Condensed	**Helvetica Extra Compressed**
Helvetica Light Condensed Italic	**Helvetica Bold Condensed Italic**	**Helvetica Ultra Compressed**
Helvetica Light Extended	**Helvetica Bold Extended**	Helvetica Bold Outline
Helvetica	**Helvetica Heavy**	Helvetica Rounded Bold
Helvetica Italic	**Helvetica Heavy Italic**	**Helvetica Rounded Bold Italic**
Helvetica Condensed	**Helvetica Black**	Helvetica Rounded Bold Outline

Figure 6.3 This is the Helvetica family of fonts, with 30 special "attributes" or variations applied to the same typeface. Only top-of-the-line desktop-publishing programs would provide access to an entire family of fonts.

Users can select from a range of sizes of fonts. While the names given to fonts vary from one software package to the next, there is a standard way to refer to font height: by points. A one-inch character is 72 points high, a half-inch character is 36 points high, a quarter-inch character is 18 points high, and so on. Another way to look at it is that "Roman 24" is exactly twice as high as "Roman 12". The larger the number, the larger the point size and the height. The collection of characters for each of these different fonts is saved on disk and often requires a great deal of storage space.

Some programs, such as *Express Publisher*, or *Pagemaker*, let you enlarge or shrink the size of the lettering at random using a process called scaling, rather than requiring you to save the different font sizes as specific files. Both methods produce fonts of different sizes which can be printed with a dot matrix printer.

A word of caution for selecting type styles—use only one or two different typefaces per document. Text is easiest to read when it is all of the same font type and font size. The more variations in font and typeface a document contains, the more difficult it becomes for the reader to interpret. Textbooks, for example, tend to use one font for 98 percent of the printing. Headlines and captions for pictures or illustrations are usually in another font to distinguish them from the body of the text.

*B*ecause in the English language we read documents from left to right and top to bottom, certain areas on the page have stronger visual impact on the reader than others. The horizontal strip across the top, for instance, is a high-impact area. This is why almost all newsletters, newspapers, and magazines place their nameplate there. The centre section is also strong. The weakest area is the lower left-hand corner. It tends to be overlooked most often, which is why warning labels, such as those found on cigarette packages, are located in this spot. The labels meet the requirement of being on the front of the package, but are located in an area that has a weak visual impact.

Differences in visual impact are actually a cultural phenomenon. Documents in Chinese and Japanese characters, for example, are written and read in vertical columns from right to left and top to bottom. Nameplates on newsletters for those markets should be the first vertical column on the right for highest impact.

Consider the following diagram that illustrates the locations of high-, medium-, and low-impact areas on a page. Headlines and pictures should always be located in a high or medium area for maximum visual impact on the reader.

Roman 10 -Point

Roman 15-Point

Roman 20-Point

Roman 25-Point

Roman 30-Point

Roman 35-Point

Roman 40-Point

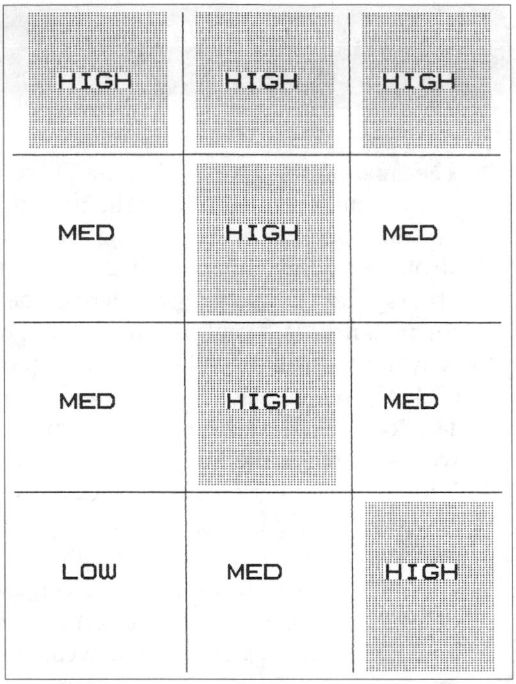

HIGH	HIGH	HIGH
MED	HIGH	MED
MED	HIGH	MED
LOW	MED	HIGH

Figure 6.4 When designing the layout for a page, consider using the areas of highest visual impact for the placement of the nameplate, headlines, and pictures.

6.8 DOCUMENTS WITH MANY COLUMNS

*H*ave you ever noticed the format of everyday sources of information such as magazines or newspapers? Typically, magazines use a three-column format, and wide-body newspapers use a six-column format. The more columns available to the page designer, the greater the variations in page layout that can be achieved.

As in newsletters, the nameplate in newspapers occupies the entire top row on the first page. Below it, pictures and headlines break the monotony by having different column widths. Headlines are extended to cover the exact number of columns the article they accompany occupies. Similarly, a picture or chart will stay within the number of columns the related article takes up on the page.

Automatic Wrap-to-Fit *M*ultiple columns also provide interesting possibilities for wrapping text around the shape of a picture in a magazine article. Some software permits the text to outline the contour (shape) of a picture while still staying in the same column. Text may wrap around both sides, one side only, or, if the picture has even margins, appear only above or below it. "Automatic wrap-to-fit" tends to be used primarily in magazines and newsletters. Newspapers prefer to use square and rectangular boxed images and pictures in their layouts.

The secret to making interesting but professional-looking documents is to vary the wrap-to-fit feature and the title- and image-placement techniques on each page, so that the reader does not find the pattern monotonous. In addition, use a minimal number of typefaces and fonts to ensure easy readability.

Summary of Good Design Suggestions

1. Choose clip art that will match your topic.

2. Place titles and images in high-impact areas whenever possible.

3. Use only one or two typefaces and fonts per document.

4. Limit the width of headlines and pictures to the number of columns the related article takes up.

5. Use a wrap-to-fit option to contour words around images for added interest.

PRACTICE MAKES PERFECT

Desktop publishing involves the use of text, graphic clip art, and titles. Learning to manipulate this type of software can be quite time-consuming. Perseverance, practice, and reading the manual are the best methods of mastering complex software. Ironically, less expensive software often presents the most roadblocks in layout and design, even for simple tasks. Expect to spend several hours just learning to design a nameplate when beginning.

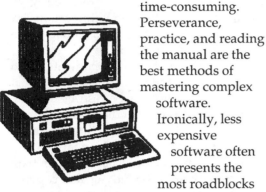

Figure 6.5

Most desktop-publishing software requires that you enter the text first. Next, a clip-art image is superimposed onto the text. Finally, a "wrap-to-fit" command arranges the text around the contours of the image automatically.

6.9 DEVELOPING THE PROFESSIONAL LOOK

*O*ne way to develop a professional appearance for your document is to study samples of magazines, newspapers, or brochures that you find attractive. Each document category has its own distinctive page-layout format. Each business has its own particular style for using titles, text, graphics, and columns. By copying a particular style, you can create a document that looks similar to the professional ones you admire.

Practice Assignment

(90 mins.)

Copying a Magazine Format and Style

Bring one of your favourite magazines into class. Select a particular page that appears attractive to you. Set up a template identical to the layout on the page. Create a one-page document as close to the original as possible using similar fonts, nameplate, and text. If a scanner is available, insert the exact picture into your document. If a scanner is not available, select a suitable image from your software's clip-art library to accompany the article. Save your document with the file name "MAGCOPY". Print your document. Hand in both the original page (or a photocopy of it) and your printed version. Staple an appropriate title page to your assignment before handing it in.

Desktop publishing refers to the use of a computer system to design and print professional-looking documents that contain a combination of text and graphics. Documents include newsletters, newspapers, magazines, brochures, manuals, catalogues, and books. Specialized software and hardware are required to produce complex documents.

Like word-processing software, desktop-publishing software usually comes with pre-designed templates that can be used to create documents with specific formats. The templates appear on the screen as dotted lines, but do not appear when the page is printed.

A one-page newsletter contains four main elements—a nameplate (the horizontal area across the top where the title is inserted), headlines (the titles of particular articles), text (the content of the articles), and computer graphics (images or pictures inserted to accompany an article). To assist designers, clip-art libraries can be purchased to add to your program's collection of insertable pictures.

Desktop-publishing software gives you control over the typefaces and fonts used in the document. Font sizes may be adjusted using a "point-system" or scaled interactively in a WYSIWYG (What You See Is What You Get) mode.

The effective placement of pictures and headlines requires a knowledge of the high and low visual-impact areas on a page. Adjusting the dimensions of a picture is referred to as "sizing" it, and cutting off unimportant sections of a picture for greater impact is referred to as "cropping" it.

Multi-column format documents, such as newspapers and magazines, require that pictures and headlines be restricted to the number of columns that the article takes up on the page. If an article is three columns wide, for example, the title and any accompanying picture should be no wider than those three columns. Studying and copying attractive page layouts used in your favourite magazine can assist you in producing professional-looking documents.

8/12

© 1987 Universal Press Syndicate

"Pizza's here."

clip-art libraries	flat-bed scanner	nameplate	text
computer graphic	fonts	rotate	typeface
crop	hand-held scanner	size	visual impact chart
desktop publishing	headline	template (page layout)	WYSIWYG
family of fonts	laser printer		

CHECKING YOUR READING

*T*hese are general questions that may require factual recall, comprehension, or some application of the knowledge gained from this chapter.

Introduction

1. Explain the term "desktop publishing".

2. List five different types of document that can be produced with desktop-publishing software.

3. (a) Translate the acronym WYSIWYG. (b) Why is this a good feature to have in desktop-publishing software?

Specialized Hardware

4. Name four expensive hardware components required to produce professional-quality documents, and explain why each one is needed.

Pre-designed Templates

5. (a) What is a "template"?

(b) Describe two advantages of using templates.

6. Describe the layout of a standard template for a two-column format newsletter.

Components of a Newsletter

7. Name the four elements of a newsletter.

8. In order for a banner or letterhead to be called a "nameplate" what information, in addition to the title, should it contain?

9. What is a "headline"?

Computer Graphics

10. (a) What is a computer graphic? (b) List six different examples of computer graphics.

11. What are "clip-art libraries"?

12. When a clip-art image is loaded into a desktop-publishing document, why does it tend to float temporarily on the page?

13. To what do these actions refer? (a) crop an image; (b) size an image; (c) rotate an image.

14. Explain the best way to use clip art in a document.

Typefaces and Fonts

15. Define the terms "typeface" and "font".

16. Why is it wise not to use more than two typefaces in a document?

High-Impact Areas

17. If you were preparing a newsletter for a Chinese or Japanese community, where would you place the nameplate on the page? Why?

18. According to the chart on high-impact areas, where would be the best place on a page for the following items? (a) nameplate; (b) one important photograph; (c) an unimportant item, such as a UPC code (patch of stripes for pricing and inventory information).

Documents with Many Columns

19. How many columns do these publications usually have? (a) newspapers; (b) magazines.

20. How many columns wide should titles or pictures be in relation to the width of the articles they accompany?

21. To what function does the phrase "automatic wrap-to-fit" refer?

APPLYING YOUR KNOWLEDGE

These are additional questions that will require some application of the knowledge from this chapter, and provide some practise on specific components of a newsletter.

1. Practising Banner Designs

Most newsletters and newspapers have a standard banner across the top of the front page that helps to identify the particular publication. For each of the following, design an appropriate banner along with a graphic logo, if the software permits.

(a) "The Forester". This publication is aimed at employees who work in provincial parks.

(b) "The Medical Journal". This one is read by doctors and medical specialists.

(c) "Mohawk Racetrack". This is a publication read by race-horse enthusiasts.

2. Comparing Two- and Three-Column Formats

Select a short article from a magazine. Using the content from the article, create a two-column format flyer, save it, and print it. Then, using the same content from the magazine, but a three-column format, create a second flyer, save it, and print it. Include one graphic, and a banner called "The Right Stuff". Compare both versions, and decide which look is better suited for the material.

Students should have read, understood, and practised the concepts in this chapter before attempting these comprehensive questions.

1. The Product Catalogue

Superior Sporting Goods Ltd., a wholesale company that sells all types of sports equipment to schools, professional teams, and retail stores, has hired you as the computer expert to design a product catalogue for their business. The manager wants pictures, product descriptions, and wholesale prices for each item. Include an attractive cover page for the catalogue, a total of 20 different products, and a final page with the mailing address - Superior Sporting Goods Ltd., 447 Portage Avenue, Winnipeg, Manitoba, R3C 3B6.

2. The Training Manual

Microcomputers Unlimited, a service company that provides computer software training to corporations for a fee, has asked you to design a five-page training manual, including an attractive cover page, for business people who take their courses. The manual, complete with pictures and illustrations, is to be used to guide a beginner through a particular process step by step. Your main topic is "How to Format a Diskette" and should include Formatting Procedures, a labelled picture of Parts of a Diskette, Cautions in Disk Handling, and Accessing Your Disk Directory.

3. Company Newsletter

Ted Ringer, the manager of Beaver Foods Ltd., has asked you to publish a three-page newsletter for the company's 800 plant and office employees. You are to make up an attractive nameplate and logo for the front page. He suggested a two-column format with pictures and headlines covering three different sections—The Company Bowling League (The Eager Beavers), Company Policy News, and Special Announcements for birthdays, weddings, awards, etc. The style is to be chatty, positive, and informal so employees will enjoy reading it. You are also the reporter who must seek the news for the paper. Be creative in your articles.

4. The Dating Service Brochure

One of the money-raising projects the student council has decided upon is a dating service. Interested students submit a short write-up on their interests in music, sports, movies, hobbies, and favourite characteristics in people. This write-up, along with some representative image, such as a record, people dancing, or a sports figure, will be printed in a brochure. Interview ten people in the class (both guys and girls) about each of the items mentioned above. Then prepare a brochure, complete with title page, called "The Dating Service" that lists the names and interests of each of the ten people. Make the write-ups positive-sounding, interesting, and flattering.

Chapter 7

CHALLENGE PROJECTS FOR INTEGRATED SOFTWARE
INTEGRATED SOFTWARE
INTEGRATED SOFTWARE

66 Integrated software combines the utility of several productivity programs into one powerful system. 99

OBJECTIVES

By the end of this chapter, you will be able to:

1 Define integrated software, clipboard, importing, exporting, electronic page layout, mechanical page layout;

2 Use up to five different computer programs, or one integrated software package, to complete one project;

3 Transfer images and text between different software packages to create professional-looking output;

4 Work cooperatively in teams of two or three students to complete a project.

WORKING IN THE WORLD OF COMPUTERS

Advertising Specialist
uses integrated software to blend diagrams, graphs, and charts into ads

Department Manager
prepares written reports with charts and diagrams for senior management

Economist
incorporates statistical charts into articles to illustrate economic trends

Financial Newsletter Writer
includes charts and graphs in newsletters to clients

Journalist
writes articles that may include charts and diagrams

Political Aide
creates parliamentary updates with charts and graphs to send to voting constituents

Publisher
uses artwork, diagrams, charts, and graphs to illustrate and supplement text in magazines and books

Statistical Researcher
prepares reports and graphs based on numerical data to verify some topic

University Professor
writes books and articles that include charts and diagrams about topics in his or her speciality

*M*any software packages on the market today are separate, individual programs that do not necessarily communicate well with other software packages. For example, the clip-art library from one graphic program, such as *Print Shop*, may not work with a program developed by another company, such as *Printmaster*. Articles created on one word-processing program may not work with a desktop-publishing program you wish to use to print sophisticated-looking output. This can be very frustrating for computer users who wish to combine output from various programs.

However, some software packages, referred to as **integrated software**, contain a collection of programs with a common menu that permits the passing and merging of text, graphs, and clip art. An integrated software package may contain a word processor, a spreadsheet, a data base, some graphic capability, and a communications program that permits you to use a modem.

Apple Macintosh and NeXT microcomputers provide easy systems with which to use integrated software because of their unique operating systems and screen interfaces. There are also DOS software packages that provide similar transfer capabilities, such as *Ability Plus, GEM Desktop, Enable, Framework, Microsoft Works, PFS: First Choice*, and *Smart Software System*.

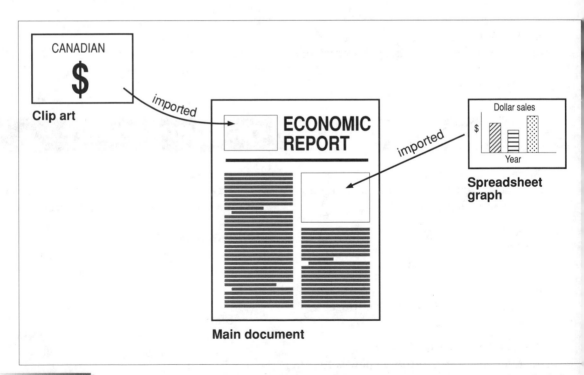

Main document

Figure 7.1 When integrated software is used, the main document usually contains the word-processed text. Illustrative material generated elsewhere, such as clip art, spreadsheet tables, or graphs, is imported to become part of the main document.

*T*he key feature of true **integrated software** is its ability to transfer the contents of one file into another, and position the new content anywhere the user requires it within a particular document. This is usually done with the help of a clipboard. A **clipboard** is a temporary file used to hold items in transfer between different programs.

Suppose you used a word-processing program to create a report on student enrollment by grade level, and saved it as a particular file. Then, you switched to a spreadsheet program, and created a bar graph with the actual data. The graph would be saved in its own file. Since these two files would be separate, they would have to be merged together into one single file. The actual merging procedure varies with different software packages.

Normally, graphs and clip art are merged into a larger, main document containing the word-processed text, rather than the other way around. The integrated software package then allows the user to move the graph into a certain spot within the document before "fixing" it to that spot. If the graph is too big, it can be scaled down to a smaller image. The text can then be wrapped to fit around the graph, and the merged text and graph can be printed as a single document. This process of arranging the text and graphics together with the help of the computer is called **electronic page layout**.

If you create a chart or graphic with one program and transfer it elsewhere, that transfer is referred to as **exporting**. If you transfer an image that was created elsewhere into a document, that process is called **importing**.

7.2 HIGH-END WORD-PROCESSING SOFTWARE

*U*sers may wish to substitute "high-end" word-processing software, such as *WordPerfect* (version 5.0 or greater) for integrated software packages. These more expensive professional-level programs may contain several fixed size typefaces, scalable typefaces, a graphics editor, a clip-art library, and importing and exporting capabilities. The purchase of add-on programs including other clip-art libraries, other typefaces, and spreadsheet programs can raise the price of these programs to, or even beyond, the price of integrated software packages without matching the entire range of capabilities.

The output from "high-end" word-processing software is very impressive when laser printed and reasonably impressive when produced on a dot-matrix printer. The quality of the output on dot-matrix printers depends on how well the program's "printer drivers" work.

Example of Word-Processing Add-On Programs

Title	What It Provides	Price	Publisher
WordPerfect	Word-processing program with various scalable typefaces, graphic editor, clip-art	$499.00	WordPerfect Corporation
PlanPerfect	Spreadsheet with line, bar, and circle graphs	$250.00	WordPerfect Corporation
DataPerfect	Data-file manager	$375.00	WordPerfect Corporation

Title	What It Provides	Price	Publisher
Glyphics Font Manager	A font selection system with six extra typeface libraries	$98.00 plus $125.00 for each library	Swifte International Ltd.
Clip Art	Clip art picture files (180) to use in WordPerfect	$6.00	The Software Labs
Total Cost for System		**$1 978.00**	

7.3 MECHANICAL PAGE LAYOUT

Not all schools will have access to integrated software packages or "high-end" word-processing programs. Fortunately, those packages are not necessary as long as you have the individual programs required to perform the separate tasks. You can print the items separately, cut and trim the items, assemble them on the page, tape or glue them, and then photocopy the assembled documents. This process of printing, cutting, assembling, and pasting, called **mechanical page layout**, is what many professional designers do to get their elaborate combinations of graphics and type on the same page. Instead of photocopying the results, they photograph the pages and then have them professionally printed (usually in colour).

In the classroom, for example, you may wish to create a logo or trademark with special drawing software, print it, cut it out, and tape it to the top of a word-processed document. A good photocopier can then blend the text and letterhead together.

Basic tools used in mechanical page layout include a pair of scissors (or lettraset knife), paper glue or scotch tape, a ruler for drawing lines and measuring distances, a thin, black, felt-tipped pen for drawing, graph paper to use as a layout guide underneath your sheets, and some correction fluid to use as a cover-up.

Five individual programs that would satisfy the requirements of the projects in this chapter include a word-processing program, a spreadsheet program with graphics capabilities, a data-file manager, a graphics-assembly program (*Print Master Plus* or *The New Print Shop*) and an animation or desktop presentation program. Other optional programs, such as free-style drawing, forms-design, and desktop-publishing, would also be helpful.

*T*his chapter presents four different team projects. They may require printed output from up to five different software packages, and will require team planning, group cooperation, and some leadership coordination. In each case, you take the role of a particular company which has been given several document-creation tasks to complete. In none of the cases are you told what software to use; that is up to your team to figure out. All of the programs, however, have been previously described in this textbook, and you can refer to those descriptions for clarification.

THE HOLIDAY PACKAGE

Project 1

*R*obert L. Kendall owns an advertising agency in Toronto, Ontario, that handles clients who want specific advertising campaigns created for their product or service. Kendall's latest client, Jenkins Travel Agency, has requested a month-long advertising campaign for a Florida Holiday Package offering vacationers a week for two people in Orlando Florida, with accommodation, car rental, and flight for a total of $565.00. The location is close to various tourist attractions including Disney World, Sea World, and a Space Technology Museum.

Mr. Jenkins has asked for an attractive one-page flyer with graphics to hand out to customers, a smaller advertisement (10 cm x 12 cm) with less text to insert in the newspaper, and a catchy slogan for the campaign. You will also need to design a trademark logo for Kendall Advertising Limited which will appear as part of a letterhead on all their correspondence, along with their company name.

Addresses

Addresses required by this project include the following:

Jenkins Travel Agency
167 King Street
Toronto, ON
M9V 1L1

Kendall Advertising Limited
Unit 1490
2060 Front Street West
Toronto, ON
M7R 2B2

The Toronto Daily News
18091 Lakeshore Drive
Toronto, ON
M8S 2Z3

Project Correspondence

The correspondence for this project includes the following three items on special letterhead stationery for Kendall Advertising Limited.

(1) A business letter dated January 5, 199-, formally accepting the job offer, outlining the three items to be created, and including the cost of the service—$8000. It is signed by the agency's president, Robert L. Kendall.

(2) A business letter from Kendall Advertising Limited to the Advertising Department of

The Toronto Daily News requesting that an advertisement be placed in the Travel Section of the newspaper, beginning March 1, 199-, and running for four weeks. The price agreed upon by telephone is $495. The letter is dated January 10, 199-, and is signed by the president of Kendall.

(3) A Sales Invoice made out to Jenkins Travel Agency from Kendall Advertising Limited itemizing the tasks to be performed, and requesting payment of $8000 for services rendered. The invoice is dated January 23, 199-.

Summary of What to Hand In

(1) Three items of correspondence

(2) One-page advertisement flyer

(3) Smaller-sized, newspaper advertisement

(4) Logo and trademark for Kendall Advertising Limited to be used on all their correspondence

(5) Slogan for advertising campaign

(6) Computer-generated cover page for entire project

B.C. LUMBER CO.

Project 2

A large corporation in British Columbia called B.C. Lumber Company harvests several types of trees, including redwoods and jack pine, for processing into finished lumber or pulp wood for the newspaper industry. They have three logging camps and two processing plants scattered across the province. Their head office is in Vancouver.

The board of directors has requested a formal report from the research department (which your team represents) on profits over the last ten years, and statistics on logging-camp production. The president, Mr. H.

Avery, wants business graphics (bar, line, and circle graphs) along with the actual data to show to the board of directors. Mrs. Frauley, the Supervisor of the Research Department, has agreed to supply the information. All correspondence must include the corporate logo of B.C. Lumber Co. (designed by your team).

Addresses

B.C. Lumber Co.
1300 Robson Street
Vancouver, BC
V8L 1Y3

Mourihata Newspapers Inc.
2250 Sinto Street
Tokyo, Japan

Project Correspondence

All correspondence for this project will be on special letterhead paper which includes the corporate logo and company name for B.C. Lumber Co.

(1) Corporate memo from Mr. H. Avery to Mrs. Frauley dated July 16, 199-, requesting that

the information listed above be ready within one week.

(2) Corporate memo from Mrs. Frauley to Mr. Avery, dated July 24, 199-, stating that the data and graphics are ready. She also mentions that she hopes the data is as requested, and she is available to assist with the presentation to the Board of Directors.

(3) Business letter dated July 30, 199-, to Mr. Hito Mourihata, President & Chief Executive Officer of Mourihata Newspapers, Inc. The letter is an apology for the delay in getting pulp wood to their pulp and paper factory in Tokyo. The request for 12 000 metres of pulp wood for this year was not met due to declining wooded areas from which to draw. Estimated total available for delivery for this year 11 500 metres. (Make the letter sound apologetic and optimistic at the same time to hold that valued customer's continued good will.)

Research Data for Project

The data available to the research department is as follows. (You may update the data with additional figures of your own creation, if you wish to have more current data.)

Annual Profits

1983	$1.5 billion
1984	$2.9 billion
1985	$3.1 billion
1986	$3.5 billion
1987	$3.1 billion
1988	$3.0 billion
1989	$2.7 billion
1990	$2.6 billion
1991	$2.5 billion
1992	$2.4 billion

Lumber Data From Logging Camps

Camp One—Redwoods Logged
(in thousands of metres)

1988	12.56
1989	8.25
1990	8.50
1991	7.00
1992	6.50

Camp Two—Jack Pine Logged
(in thousands of metres)

1988	4.50
1989	4.75
1990	5.00
1991	5.10
1992	5.50

Camp Three—Mixed Timber Logged
(in thousands of metres)

1988	5.75
1989	5.90
1990	6.00
1991	5.75
1992	6.00

Summary of What to Hand In

1. Two corporate memos with B.C. Lumber Co.'s name and logo at the top

2. One formal business letter with the company's name, address, and logo in the letterhead

3. Four business graphs with titles and labels as part of a written report from your research department. The report describes profit and logging camp data for the company.

4. Four tables of spreadsheet statistics with appropriate titles, headers, and totals as an appendix to the report

5. A computer-generated cover page for the entire project

Project *3*

*F*erguson Latham is the chairperson of a fishing cooperative that operates out of St. John's, Newfoundland. Thirty-five trawlers owned by individual families provide the fish. The catch, composed mostly of cod, flounder, and sole, is brought in to the fish-packing plant in St. John's harbour, where the produce is processed and packaged for shipment to distant markets in Ontario, and along the New England coast in the United States. Many shipments are flown directly to famous fish restaurants, although the bulk of the catch is sold in frozen packages to national grocery store chains under the brand name "Atlantic Fisheries".

Lately, sales have been declining, and Mr. Latham has hired Feldman Advertising Consultants to analyze the situation and produce a suitable advertising campaign to increase the company's market share. Josh Feldman, President of the agency, has accepted the offer. He has promised to provide a printed report including graphic analysis and explanations of the current markets, to create a new brand name for their products, with a logo, and to come up with an advertising slogan. The campaign will also include a one-page advertisement to promote Atlantic Fisheries' new image.

Addresses

Feldman Advertising Consultants
156 Whalers Wharf, Unit B
St. John's, NF
A4C 1G8

Atlantic Fisheries Co-op Ltd.
1622 Front Street
St. John's Harbour, NF
A4C 1B8

Project Correspondence

(1) A business letter to Mr. Ferguson Latham, Chairperson of Atlantic Fisheries, from Feldman Advertising Consultants formally accepting the job offer, outlining the five items to be created, and including the cost of the service—$6580. A down payment of $1000 is required before the firm begins. The letter is dated February 12, 199-, and is signed by the president of Feldman Advertising Consultants.

(2) A sales invoice to Atlantic Fisheries Co-op from Feldman Advertising Consultants outlining the tasks performed and requesting payment of $5580, the balance of the fee for services rendered. The invoice is dated May 25, 199-.

Data for Project

Annual Sales by Fish

Cod	$450 000
Flounder	$110 000
Sole	$ 75 000
Other	$ 5 000

Annual Sales by Customer

Ontario Groceries	$360 000
Boston Restaurants	$ 45 000
New York Restaurants	$205 000
Cat Food Company	$ 15 000
Fertilizer Company	$ 15 000

Summary of What to Hand In

(1) Two items of correspondence (letter-head optional)

(2) A printed report for Atlantic Fisheries including a recommended brand name, logo, and slogan for the business along with three recommendations for changes. The report is to include two business graphs with labels and data illustrating current sales by fish and by customer.

(3) Two spreadsheet tables of statistics with grand total figures, titles, and headers. One is to show the percentage of total sales generated by each category. This is to be added to the report as an appendix.

(4) A one-page advertisement for promotion

(5) A computer-generated cover page for the entire project

THE WINTER CARNIVAL

Project
4

*T*he mayor of Jasper, Alberta, has hired your team to develop a promotional campaign for their annual winter carnival. Mayor Wayne Nester has sent your company (make up a name) a letter requesting a five-frame, computer-animated sequence, a flyer to advertise the carnival, a smaller format (10 cm X 12 cm) newspaper advertisement to place in national newspapers, and a suitable slogan and trademark logo for the event.

The winter carnival is to be held from December 20 to January 10 and offers downhill skiing, tobogganing, snow-shoeing, a Christmas Party, and a New Year's Eve Dance, and features the crowning of a Snow Queen. Out-of-towners can send for a brochure. The mayor hopes to attract families seeking a Christmas vacation, newlyweds, and tourists.

Addresses

West Edmonton Mall
17700 87 Avenue
Edmonton, AB
T5T 4V4

Jasper Winter Carnival
Jasper City Hall
Post Office Box 87
Jasper, AB
T5D 4V3

Your Team's Address
(make up your own)

Project Correspondence

All correspondence must include a letter-head with your company's name and logo at the top of the page.

(1) A business letter to Mr. Fisken, Sales Manager of The West Edmonton Mall, from your company, requesting permission and cost figures to set up a booth in the mall that would run the five-frame animated se-

quence advertising the winter carnival, and provide flyers and information to interested customers. The booth would stay active during mall hours from December 1 to December 22. The letter is dated September 15, 199-, and is signed by your company's president.

(2) A business letter to the mayor of Jasper from your company accepting the job of creating the promotional campaign for the Jasper Winter Carnival. It states the four items required by the city council, and agrees to the fee of $5000. It is signed by your company's president, and dated September 16, 199-.

Summary of What to Hand In

(1) Two letters of correspondence with company name and logo in the letterhead

(2) A full-page flyer to advertise the Winter Carnival

(3) A small format newspaper advertisement asking people to write for a brochure

(4) A five-frame animated sequence in colour to advertise the Winter Carnival

(5) A slogan and trademark logo included in both the newspaper advertisement and the animated sequence

(6) A computer-generated cover page for the entire project

*I*ntegrated software is a collection of programs with a common menu that permits the passing and merging of text, business graphs, and clip art. Such a package often contains a word processor, a spreadsheet, a data base, some graphic capability, and a communications program that allows the use of a modem.

The key feature of a true integrated software package is its ability to transfer the contents of one file into another, and position the new contents anywhere the user requires them within a particular document. Usually the main document contains the word-processing text. Illustrative material, generated elsewhere, is imported to become part of the main document. A temporary file called a clipboard acts as a holding file for items in transition. If you transfer a graphic created elsewhere into a document the process is called importing. If you transfer an item from the program you are using into another program the process is called exporting.

Because of cost, or software availability, users may wish to substitute a "high-end" word-processing package for the integrated package. These expensive word processors often contain features such as a graphics editor, a number of different fixed size typefaces, scalable typefaces, and a clip-art library. In addition, compatible programs, such as a data-file manager and a spreadsheet, can be purchased to generate complementary files that can be imported into the main document. The process of arranging the text and graphics together with the help of computer software is called electronic page layout.

An alternate method of preparing complex layouts is to use individual programs to create and print the separate parts of the document. Each of these items can then be cut and trimmed from its printed page, assembled on the main document, taped or glued in place, and photocopied. This process of putting a design together by hand is referred to as mechanical page layout.

"...And when I hit 'Gently Down the Stream,' you come in with 'Row, Row, Row your Boat.'"

clipboard

exporting

integrated software

electronic page layout

importing

mechanical page layout

CHECKING YOUR READING

*T*hese are general questions that may require factual recall, comprehension, or some application of the knowledge gained from this chapter.

Introduction

1. What problem might users encounter when attempting to combine output from various programs?

2. Define "integrated software".

3. Integrated software packages sometimes use a clipboard. Explain to what that refers.

4. (a) If an integrated software package is not available, what software might be substituted?
   (b) What limitations does the substituted software have?

5. Explain the difference between electronic page layout and mechanical page layout.

6. List four steps that are required in mechanical page layout to create a complex page of graphics and text.

7. List seven different tools that are needed to produce layouts done mechanically instead of electronically.

UNIT 3

USES AND SOCIETAL IMPACT OF COMPUTERS

*T*his four-chapter unit invites the students to broaden their vision of the computer as an element of change in society through readings, research, and discussion.

The section begins with a study of the variety of uses people have found for this technology beyond the class-room. Then it investigates the problems and controversies surrounding certain applications in society. Finally, the unit explores the direction this technology is taking and where it may be leading us, with particular emphasis on the Canadian setting.

Chapter 8

COMPUTER APPLICATIONS

COMPUTER APPLICATIONS

66 Computers are causing a change in society equivalent to the Industrial Revolution. Just as engines extend our physical powers, computers are extending both our mental and physical capabilities. 99

OBJECTIVES

By the end of this chapter, you will be able to:

1 Define the following computer terms: electronic mail, cybernated factories, process control, computer model, point-of-sale terminal, teller terminal, automated teller terminal, computer-assisted instruction, universal product code, strip coding, bulletin board, and dedicated processor;

2 Name four different types of office report and give an example of each type;

3 Explain how large factories and processing plants can operate without the need for human intervention;

4 Describe how researchers and engineers use computer models;

5 Describe how computer terminals help to serve customers in grocery stores and banks;

6 Describe how computer systems can help with traffic control in airports, train yards, and city streets;

7 List several consumer products that contain a dedicated processor.

WORKING IN THE WORLD OF COMPUTERS

Air Traffic Controller
uses computer-enhanced radar screens to identify airplanes

Automobile Manufacturer
employs programmable robots and assembly lines to manufacture vehicles

Bank Teller
keys information about customer accounts into a computerized banking system

Checkout Clerk
moves the UPC patch on grocery products across the scanning window embedded in the checkout counter

Journalist
requires a background knowledge in computer applications to write about them using a computer and a word-processing program

Office Worker
sends inter-office memos through the electronic mail system

Rail Yard Foreman
reads printouts of rail car manifest and destinations

Teacher
introduces students to the three roles computers can play: as teacher, as student, and as a tool

8.1 INTRODUCTION

*A*lthough computers have been available for over 40 years, until fairly recently, organizations that needed to use computers were forced to purchase or rent expensive and complex mainframe computer systems. As a result, the early applications of computers were restricted to research laboratories, government and business data-processing centres, and the military. The users of the systems tended to be engineers, business administrators, and computer specialists, all with college or university degrees.

With the arrival of the first mass-produced microcomputers in 1978, however, a personal computer revolution began. An older mechanical and manual office environment was beginning to be replaced with an electronic one. Typewriters, printing calculators, manual accounting systems, and tally sheets were phased out and replaced with microcomputers with interactive software. Computer use was no longer limited to university graduates; young children began to operate microcomputers with equal skill. Homes, schools, and offices all have found uses for this high-speed, information-processing machine.

The uses that people find for computers in society are referred to as **computer applications**. The applications may range from a factory assembly line completely run by computers to children's robotic toys responding to remote control signals. This chapter describes seven categories of the more common computer applications.

8.2 OFFICE ADMINISTRATION

*B*usiness offices have found computers to be invaluable for processing the "mountains" of paperwork needed to keep a typical business operating. Corporations and government agencies often have a separate data-processing department, supported by a mainframe computer system, to process such items as the company payroll, invoices to customers, cheques to suppliers, warehouse inventory, and production scheduling.

Types of Reports

*T*here are four categories of report generally produced by computers: scheduled listings, exception reports, predictive reports, and demand reports.

The term **scheduled listing** refers to a printout containing the complete contents of a particular file that is printed on a regular basis, such as once a week or once a month. Although it can be useful in certain circumstances, such a report, when overused, can create enormous amounts of irrelevant data. In a school, for example, an alphabetical list of the name of every student enrolled in a particular class is a scheduled listing. Other examples include term marks for all students, report cards, an itemized warehouse inventory, a telephone directory, and a voters list for an entire city.

An **exception report**, on the other hand, prints only the "exceptions to the rule", or items that require immediate attention. A lengthy, scheduled listing for school attendance, for example, could be reduced to one page by printing only the names of those students who were absent. Other examples include a list of honours students in a school, a printout of only those automobile drivers who have lost points this year for traffic violations, and a list of Canadian rock stars who have sold over a million records. This more efficient style of reporting is sometimes referred to as "management by exception".

Predictive reports are generated by using mathematical equations to forecast trends, and to assist planners in making decisions about the future. A printout that forecasts a company's sales trends to the year 1998 is an example of a predictive report. Weather reports, economic forecasts about the Canadian economy, and estimates of the amount of oxygen left inside a returning space shuttle are all predictive. These reports are usually displayed in the form of a graph or a table of statistics, or expressed in terms of probability of occurrence, such as a meteorologist saying "There will be a 10% chance of rain tomorrow."

Demand reports are created by selecting information from one or more files and arranging the information into a particular order requested by the user before displaying it on the screen. Of the four types of reports, a demand report gives the user the greatest control over the content and arrangement of the display. Often, demand reports concentrate on one item or one individual at a time.

Suppose, for example, a typical school data base contained several files such as student enrollment, days absent, total credits, guidance reports, and term average. The school principal could enter a request for any combination of such data, as in the example of a demand report at the top of the next column.

In that example, the computer would find information on Tom from several files, using the student number as a search reference. Since any combination of information can be retrieved upon demand to form the report, it is called a demand report.

Example of a Demand Report

```
STUDENT NAME:        WILSON, TOM
STUDENT NUMBER:      345527
NUMBER OF CREDITS:   24
DAYS ABSENT:         3
NUMBER OF LATES:     1
CURRENT SUBJECTS:    MATH
                     ENGLISH
                     ACCOUNTING
                     CHEMISTRY
```

Types of Reports

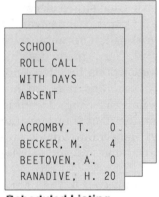

```
SCHOOL
ROLL CALL
WITH DAYS
ABSENT

ACROMBY, T.    0
BECKER, M.     4
BEETOVEN, A.   0
RANADIVE, H.  20
```
Scheduled Listing

```
ABSENTEES

BECKER, M.     4
McCURDY, E.   20
TINGLEY, T.    1
ZENNON, S.     3
```
Exception Report

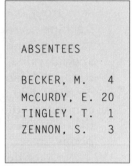

Predictive Report

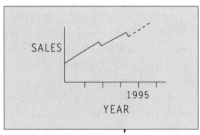

```
EMPLOYEE: MANDIK, V.

* SALES-TO-DATE: $14 350
* RANKING: 10th
* YEARS WITH CO.: 5
```
Demand Report

*O*ther computer applications in business and government offices include word processing and electronic mail. People who work with word-processing software use microcomputers to key in, edit, save, and print memos and letters. The keyboard, screen, and printer are gradually replacing the office typewriter, while the magnetic disk storage units are supplementing the multiple-drawer filing cabinets.

A system called **electronic mail** allows people to immediately transfer information such as memos and letters by computer. Messages are recorded and stored electronically, rather than on paper, so they can be sent from one workstation to another in fractions of a second. This is made possible by connecting workstations together with special cable. Workstations that are not connected can use an encoding/decoding device called a modem that translates the computer's digital signals into analog signals suitable for transmission along telephone lines.

Another device connected to the phone lines, called a **fax machine**, is used to transmit copies of documents from one building to another, even over great distances, such as between cities or countries. (Fax is an abbreviation for facsimile, which means exact reproduction.) This unit electronically copies the original piece of paper, line by line, and sends the coded information along the telephone lines to a similar device at the receiving end of the transmission. The document is then reassembled and printed as a photocopy of the original. Both computer modems and fax machines reduce the need for traditional mail service.

Electronic mail, however, has not solved the problem of delivering bulky parcels to various office locations. Some innovative corporations use "mailmobiles"—robotic, personal-delivery, mail-service vehicles that follow a hidden strip under the carpet, and stop at pre-destined points along the route to permit office workers to load and unload parcels and letters.

Figure
8.1 The "mailmobile" provides an alternative to electronic mail delivery in office complexes. Whenever it meets people in the hallway, its sensors stop its motor to allow them to pass.

Courtesy of Bell and Howell

8.3 COMPUTERS IN FACTORIES

*P*roduction plants have adopted computers to varying degrees. Many Canadian factories use machinery such as lathes, drills, and pattern cutters that operate automatically once the operator has programmed them. These machines tend to increase productivity but they require highly skilled technicians to program and operate them.

Some plants, including car factories in Windsor, Oakville, Cambridge, and Oshawa, as well as a parts plant in Toronto and a steel plant in Nanticoke, are **cybernated**. This means that computers control

Figure
8.2

Sparks fly as the assembly-line robots apply nearly 3000 welds to the metal frames of each car. The programmable, robotic arms are able to perform many assembly-line jobs such as welding, spray painting, and lifting.

Courtesy of Chrysler Corporation

and operate automated machinery along assembly lines to produce finished products. Robotic devices with interchangeable, multiple-purpose arms and reprogrammable memories can perform a given task repeatedly without complaint; they make "ideal" employees. Cybernation, however, has become a highly controversial issue because of its negative effect on the number of available manual-labour jobs.

The examples mentioned above represent varying degrees of a computer application called **process control**, which refers to the ability of a computer to operate machinery external to the computer system itself. In addition to manufacturing products, process control can also be used to monitor and control chemical plants, cold-rolling steel plants, power-generating stations, blast furnaces, and sewage treatment plants.

8.4 COMPUTERS HELP RESEARCHERS

*C*omputers are also excellent research tools. Advances in such fields as medicine, chemistry, engineering, aeronautics, economics, meteorology, and astronomy have been increasingly dependent on complex calculations that computers can provide. Researchers can test a theory by creating a computer model. A **computer model**, also referred to as a computer simulation, is a series of mathematical equations that represent variables in a real-life situation. By changing some of the variables in the model, researchers can observe what effect changes would have on the actual case being studied.

Suppose some mechanical engineers

have just completed the preliminary design for an expansion bridge that should allow vehicles to cross a particular waterway. How can they be sure that the bridge will not collapse once it has been built? The engineers have two choices. They can build the actual bridge and wait to see what happens. (This experimental method, of course, is extremely risky.) Or they can design a mathematical representation of the bridge (a computer model) and test it using a computer.

The computer model will include all the things that will put a heavy load or stress on the bridge such as cars, trucks, asphalt, concrete, cables, wind, temperature, and even a big snowfall. Once the model is completed, the engineers can experiment with different values (for instance, number of cars or weight of snowfall) until they arrive at the best combination of materials and design features to support the estimated maximum weight of the bridge.

Computer models, however, are only as accurate as the information used to design them. One engineer who designed a Canadian university library used a computer model to calculate the building's total mass. He needed this figure because the ground on which the building was to be erected could only hold a certain mass before compressing and sinking. Six months after the building's completion, it started to tilt and sink. The engineer was astonished! What had gone wrong? He checked the computer figures for several days before he discovered the answer: he had forgotten to include the mass of the two million books purchased for the library shelves. The computer had given the right answer for the information it had been fed, but, unfortunately, the engineer's information was incomplete.

Often, special peripherals are used to make computer modeling easier. A graphics designer, for example, may draw a picture directly onto a computer screen or a graphics tablet using a light pen. A special software program then automatically translates the lines and curves into mathematical equations. This allows the user to concentrate on the design features of the drawing, rather than on the complex mathematical formulas that the computer uses to represent them.

Training Simulators

*H*ybrid computer systems, which are a mixture of analog devices and a digital computer, also make excellent simulations for testing or training people to do certain jobs. Astronauts and airline pilots, for example, can be trained in on-the-ground **flight simulators**. These systems are realistic copies of space shuttles or airplanes that contain operational dials and switches, and can simulate the physical

Figure 8.3

This flight simulator is used to train airline pilots. Pneumatic pistons cause the simulator to move up or down or side to side in response to the pilot's flying skills.

Courtesy of C.A.E. Electronics Ltd.

Figure
8.4
An airport ground display with a mounted, mobile camera relays pictures to the flight simulator to provide the visual illusion of flying.

Courtesy of C.A.E. Electronics Ltd.

movements of flight and visual scenery that would be seen by the pilots through the cockpit window.

The computer attached to this device can be programmed to imitate actual flight conditions. Even such perilous occurrences as sudden storms, strong air currents, and engine failure can be simulated. With this device, training expenses are greatly reduced, and pilot reliability is increased.

Additional applications for computer simulations include weather predictions, marketing sales estimates, production forecasting for business, war games for the military, and various types of medical and scientific research. Computer modelling possibly represents the best example of a computer's capacity to extend human ability to analyze hypothetical situations and predict results.

8.5 HELPING TO SERVE CUSTOMERS

*H*ave you noticed the electronic cash registers most large stores are now using? These devices have become popular because they also act as a computer terminal. As a sale is recorded on the keyboard, the information can immediately be transferred to a computer for processing. Total sales, sales by department, and merchandise inventory can be determined from the recorded information.

Most terminals also allow a clerk to enter a credit card number to determine whether or not the card has been stolen, or if the customer's credit limit has been reached. Since this device is placed where the actual sale occurs, computer manufacturers call it a **point-of-sale terminal**.

Grocery Stores

*G*rocery stores combine a flat optical scanning window embedded in the checkout counter with the cash register terminal that can translate the UPC **(Universal Product Code)** stripes found on most grocery products. This scanning device (along with a hidden computer system) provides customers with immediate verification of each purchase by displaying the product name and price on a display screen which is set at the customer's eye level. (Some systems are designed to "say" the name and price out loud using a voice response unit.) The product information is simultaneously sent to the mainframe computer (usually kept in the store's accounting office), where each purchased item is subtracted from that product's inventory total.

The following morning, the computer that links all these cash registers can be requested to print a list of all items that need to be reordered.

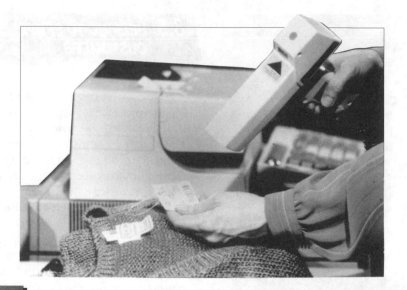

Figure
8.5

A laser scanner reads the Universal Product Code on the packages and sends the information to a computer system. The computer looks up the name and price of the article to send back to the point-of-sale terminal, and adjusts the inventory totals and sales figures.

Courtesy of IBM Canada Ltd.

Electronic Banking

*M*ost branches of financial institutions such as banks, credit unions, and trust companies use **teller terminals** to process banking transactions. These specialized computer terminals are directly linked to distant mainframe computer systems located in the company's head office.

Suppose a customer wishes to withdraw $100.00 from her savings account. The teller first checks to see if there is a sufficient balance in the customer's account to cover the withdrawal by keying in the customer's account number on the terminal keyboard. The computer uses the account number to locate the customer's balance on magnetic disk; then it displays the amount on a computer monitor for the teller.

By looking at the balance, the teller can decide whether or not to enter the latest transaction. If the transaction is entered, the computer automatically changes the customer's balance on the magnetic disk and updates the customer's passbook, when it is inserted into a printer.

Customers can also use an **automated teller terminal** located outside the bank to process banking transactions. Once the account holder inserts an identification card into a slot, and enters an identification number (password) with a keypad, the terminal will respond to requests to deposit, withdraw, or transfer money.

If a withdrawal is made, the machine slides the specific sum of money out of a second slot and provides the customer with a printed receipt of the transaction for future reference.

Automated teller terminals are often given "pet" names such as "The Green Machine" or "Johnny Cash" to encourage public acceptance. Systems are also named

tems to keep track of incoming and outgoing flights, as well as to reserve seats for passengers on various interconnecting flights. Some shopping malls and airports now have automated flight reservation machines for credit-card customers to book flights without any human assistance.

8.6 COMPUTERS THAT TEACH

*A*t all levels of education, there has been a dramatic increase in the use of microcomputers as learning aids. According to author Robert Taylor, educational applications generally fall into three categories. He suggested that computers can play the role of a "teacher", a "student", or a "tool" in the classroom.

The Computer as Teacher

*A*s a teacher, the computer presents facts and information on the screen, tests your understanding of the information, and offers remedial help if you get a low score on the tests. Software designed in this way is referred to as **computer-assisted instruction** or **CAI**.

Medical, engineering, and business administration students use computer simulations to increase their knowledge. Interns and nurses practise making diagnoses while studying a simulated human body and vital signs. Marketing and entrepreneurship students can make decisions about how to run a company with simulation programs such as "The Peanut Butter Company" or "Entrepreneurship" and can immediately see the effects of their decisions on the company's overall profit.

One popular testing technique is to employ multiple choice questions, which students can respond to at the keyboard. Lessons and tests can be displayed in any spo-

Figure 8.6

A printer updates a customer's passbook. Records of customer accounts are stored in the bank's head office several miles from the bank.

Courtesy of the Royal Bank of Canada

after their electronic network affiliation, such as "Cirrus", "Interact", "Plus System", and "Circuit"; they permit users to gain access to their bank accounts from any institutional outlet that bears that name anywhere in North America.

Other Point-of-Sale Users

*S*ervice businesses, such as banks, airlines, freight companies, hotels, and travel agencies, also use point-of-sale terminals to handle business transactions. Airlines, for example, use computer sys-

ken language, and for any grade level. CAI programs also allow students to work at their own speed, and at their own level of ability. Videodisk machines can be attached to the computer systems to allow sophisticated movies, sound, and actual photographs to enhance the lesson.

Computers as Learners *T*he second educational role the computer takes is that of "learner", in which the user teaches the machine how to perform some task using a computer language such as BASIC, Pascal, or PROLOGUE. In this mode, the student must learn to communicate with the computer using its limited vocabulary, and plan a logical series of steps that it can carry out on its screen, printer, or sound system peripherals. This type of interaction is referred to as **programming**.

The Computer as a Tool *T*he last category of educational computer interaction occurs when you use the machine as a "tool" to perform some particular task. Using word-processing software to create and print a report is one example; using a spreadsheet to compare and analyze statistical data is another. A data-file manager, a graphics program, and a music generator program are also "tools".

A computer literate student would be one who experienced all three learning environments during his or her education.

8.7 KEEPING TRACK OF MOVING VEHICLES

*T*raffic congestion in city streets, in crowded rail yards, and in the air over metropolitan airports is a frustrating problem for traffic controllers. Fortunately, computer systems have been designed to monitor the movement of vehicles and reduce traffic congestion.

Toronto, for example, has several kilometres of traffic lights under computer control. Optical scanners, mounted on poles, can detect the presence of cars at a stop light, or monitor the flow of traffic on a section of roadway. The computer can be instructed to give a certain route priority during rush hours. All the lights along this route will be green for a driver who is travelling within the legal speed limit.

Railway Traffic Control *R*ailway cars can also be monitored with optical scanners placed along the railway tracks. Each piece of rolling stock contains a pattern of coloured stripes, referred to as **strip coding**. This coding contains information as to the type of car (tanker, boxcar, or flatcar) and its serial number. The optical scanners can detect the code even if the train is moving at speeds up to 100 km/h. The information from the code is relayed to the computer system at the rail yard traffic-control centre. The serial number is then used to get more information about the car—owner, manifest, and destination—by searching the appropriate data file on disk. The information can be displayed on a lighted traffic board, on a display screen, or in the form of a printout.

Using these techniques, a computer system monitoring large rail yards, like those in Winnipeg, Toronto, and Montreal, can ensure that boxcars containing perishable products or other merchandise will be correctly routed and will arrive at their destination on time.

Air Traffic Control

Air traffic controllers rely heavily on computerized radar systems to prevent air disasters. It is common for several airplanes to be "stacked up" in the air, flying in levels several hundred metres apart, waiting for permission to land at some busy city airport. A computer system takes impulses from a radar scanner, which picks up a signal generated by most large airplanes from a device called a transponder, and superimposes an identification code on it. This identification code, for example, AC 209 (Air Canada, Flight 209), then follows the dot representing the airplane across the traffic controller's viewing screen. The system helps the controller to identify airplanes and communicate instructions to the pilots.

Figure 8.7

The optical scanner mounted on the pole is reading the coloured stripes on the railway rolling stock. This coded information is relayed to the rail yard's computer centre.

Courtesy of Canadian National Railway

Figure
8.8
The air traffic controller watches the symbolic representations of airplanes moving around on the computer-enhanced radar monitor.

Courtesy of Transport Canada

Without the "number-crunching" ability of large mainframe computer systems, traffic congestion would almost make modern-day travel an impossibility in large urban centres.

8.8 CONSUMER PRODUCTS

*E*lectronic appliance and toy manufacturers have found many uses for the integrated circuits produced by the computer industry. Computer chips are found in pocket calculators, digital watches, digital clocks, cassette decks, children's toys, electronic games, and programmable appliances such as microwave ovens, video cassette recorder/players, and home electrical, temperature, and security systems.

When a computer chip is limited to one specific purpose, as in the operation of the items mentioned above, it is referred to as a **dedicated processor**. This means that the set of instructions for operating the toy or appliance cannot be altered.

Many toy and electronic game manufacturers include voice and sound generators with their product. One popular learning aid called "Speak and Spell" responds to the user not only by displaying the words, but "speaking" them as well in a mechanically toned voice: "C-A-T ... Cat".

Computers can also be used to monitor and manipulate other appliances or devices with the help of home environment control programs. These programs allow the computer to centralize heating and cooling systems, fire and theft alarms, and lighting. Some creative people even use the computer to open and close curtains or vacuum rugs by remote control.

Figure
8.9
This popular learning aid provides both visual and auditory confirmation of a correctly spelled word. The device contains a keyboard, visual display screen, and voice response unit.

Courtesy of Texas Instruments Inc.

*I*nformation service companies, such as *InfoGlobe* (operated by The Globe and Mail in Toronto), are offering access to distant data bases in return for a per-minute fee. With a computer modem and a telephone line as the communication link, a microcomputer can be used to dial, make the line connection, and search for information stored in the service company's files. These systems permit people to watch the stock market figures, do library catalogue research, order tickets for airline flights or concerts, or view local real estate deals. Eventually, the service may be expanded to include major government services: education, medical consulting, legal advice, and electronic voting on political issues.

**Bulletin
Boards**

*O*ne variation in electronic information services is called a bulletin board. This service links many computer users to each other by permitting them to leave personal messages on "bulletin boards" that all members have access to. The messages, which are actually small computer files on a centralized hard disk, are then read by other members who respond to them with messages of their own. If the originators of questions leave their phone numbers, the person responding can send the answer directly to their computer system. Bulletin-board users must have a modem and access to a telephone line to link them together.

Commercial bulletin boards, such as *CompuServe*, which boasts 500 000 members, charge user's a fee to access their system. In addition, users may have to pay long-distance telephone charges depending upon the distance from which they call. Local bulletin boards operated by computer clubs or computer classes in different

schools, on the other hand, can access each other's files without paying any charges as long as they have the correct telecommunications software. Programs that perform the task of accessing bulletin boards or information service companies are usually provided on disk when you purchase a new modem.

**Homes
with Built-in
Computer
Systems**

*S*ome suburban model homes in Winnipeg were constructed with built-in computer systems. These computers can centrally control the environment, place automatic police and fire calls with the push of a button, and store messages for family members. Imagine a viewing screen in the kitchen that displays this kind of message:

"Susan ... Bob called. He got the concert tickets. Love Mom."

*C*omputer applications are the various uses that people find for computers. The two earliest uses for computers, dating back to the 1950s, were in business administration and research. There are four categories of report generally produced by computers for office use: scheduled listings, exception reports, predictive reports, and demand reports.

Computer modelling, which refers to a series of mathematical equations representing variables in a real-life situation, is the basis of most research. Such models are used in engineering, economics, and various fields of scientific study.

More recent computer applications include cybernated factories, retail point-of-sale terminals, computer-assisted instruction, monitoring of transport vehicles, and personal computing.

Cybernated factories use programmable robots along assembly lines to produce finished products. Probably the most controversial application of computers, this process reduces the need for the largest segment of factory employment: manual labourers.

Stores, banks, hotels, and travel agencies use the time-sharing capability of computer systems to help serve customers. Typically, the clerk interacts with a computer terminal that is connected to a mainframe computer located in some other location.

The development of table-top microcomputers has promoted the widespread adoption of computers as teaching aids. Schools use computers in three different ways: as a teacher, as a learner, and as a tool.

Traffic congestion in crowded urban centres can be reduced through the monitoring and control of vehicle movement. Automobiles, railway rolling stock, and airplanes can be digitally represented inside a computer system. This information can then be used to direct the flow of traffic.

Dedicated processors, computer chips with a fixed set of instructions, are used in many consumer toys and appliances. This represents an application of computer integrated circuitry, rather than an entire computer system, to the improvement of consumer products.

"Why are you still here? According to my computer, you should have been cured days ago!"

automated teller terminal

bulletin board

computer applications

computer-assisted instruction (CAI)

computer model

cybernated

dedicated processor

demand report

electronic mail

exception report

fax machine

flight simulator

information service companies

point-of-sale terminal

predictive report

process control

programming

scheduled listing

strip coding

teller terminal

Universal Product Code

CHECKING YOUR READING

*T*hese are general questions that may require factual recall, reading comprehension, or some application of the knowledge gained from this chapter.

Types of Reports

1. Not all computer-generated office reports are efficient. Describe both a scheduled listing and an exception report. Then explain why one type is more efficient than the other.

2. List two examples of a predictive report.

3. How is a demand report created? Give an example of a demand report.

Other Office Applications

4. What does a "fax machine" do?

Computers in Factories

5. Describe a cybernated factory. Why is this a controversial computer application?

6. Automated machines and cybernated factories are both examples of "process control". Describe the process and give some additional examples.

Computers Help Researchers

7. What is a "computer model"? Why are computer models popular among all types of researchers?

8. What is a "flight simulator"? How does it assist airline companies?

Helping to Serve Customers

9. What advantage does a "point-of-sale terminal" have over a cash register?

10. Some grocery stores have a specialized input device built into the checkout counter. Explain its function.

11. How does a bank teller know if he or she should process a withdrawal slip for $500.00 from a customer?

12. Some people do their banking after the bank is closed. How do they do that?

Computers that Teach

13. Give examples of how a computer can be used in education in each of these three roles:
    (a) computer as teacher
    (b) computer as learner
    (c) computer as tool

14. Translate the letters C.A.I. To what function of computer software does that label refer?

Keeping Track of Moving Vehicles

15. Why is it possible for a driver to travel across the city within the legal speed limit and always encounter green traffic lights?

16. Describe how railway rolling stock can be monitored even when the trains are moving.

17. How are computers used to assist air traffic controllers?

Consumer Products

18. What is a "dedicated processor"? What uses have manufacturers found for it?

19. What tasks can a home environment control program perform?

20. List five information services to which computer owners have access.

21. What two devices must a computer owner have to be able to use information service companies?

22. Explain what a bulletin board service does.

APPLYING YOUR KNOWLEDGE

*T*hese questions assume an understanding of the material presented in this chapter, and provide new situations that may require evaluation, analysis, or the application of your newly acquired knowledge.

(1) A sales manager in a large manufacturing company receives a 14-page printout each Monday morning from the data-processing department. The printout lists each salesperson, their weekly sales, and their year-to-date sales.

   It takes the sales manager an hour to review the list and decide what instructions to give the sales staff. With the goal of reducing the manager's paperwork, what would be a better method of reporting the data? Give reasons for your answer.

(2) Explain why a computer system capable of creating demand reports will take more time and expertise to set up than any other reporting technique.

(3) Several automobile manufacturers around the world have cybernated their factories.

   (a) Explain some advantages that this gives the company owners.

   (b) What type of employee is replaced by the programmable robots?

   (c) Suggest two jobs that a cybernated factory would create.

(4) Suppose a pharmaceutical company is inventing various types of chemical compounds in an attempt to develop a cure for a certain disease. How could the company ensure effective research without actually performing all the chemical combinations?

(5) How does a clerk in a retail store use a point-of-sale terminal to check if a customer's credit card is stolen or at its limit?

(6) Most grocery store items contain a Universal Product Code patch somewhere on the label or packaging.

(a) How does a laser scanner interpret the code?

(b) What information do you think the printed manufacturer's code contains?

(7) Many financial institutions have automated teller terminals on the outside wall of the building. What features prevent a thief from taking money out of your account?

(8) Suggest how computer-assisted instruction could be used to teach people how to type.

(9) Suppose that east-west traffic across the city is given priority during the evening rush hour. How would a computerized traffic system recognize if cars were stopped at north-south traffic lights, be able to assist them, and still keep the heavy east-west traffic flowing smoothly?

(10) Railway rolling stock has coloured "strip coding" on it which can be read by an optical scanner.

(a) What information do you think the permanent stripes contain?

(b) What can the centralized computer do with that information?

(11) Why is a computer chip in a digital watch referred to as a "dedicated processor"?

(12) Suppose that your family subscribed to a computerized information service. To what types of legal information would you be interested in getting access? Explain your answer.

*T*hese projects will require research, and are best worked on with a partner.

1. Bulletin Board Display

(2 weeks)

Plan and prepare a bulletin board display on computer applications that will illustrate either (a) a certain use of computers, or (b) a variety of computer applications. Give the display an appropriate title printed in large computer-generated letters. The final product will be judged for neatness, organization, picture variety, creativity, and effort.

2. Slide Presentation

(2 weeks)

Using a 35 mm camera and colour slide film, obtain at least 15 clear pictures of computer applications from your town or city. Arrange the slides into a pleasing theme, then show them to the class in the form of a slide-talk presentation. You are in charge of arranging for the loan of a camera and a slide projector. The final product will be judged for variety, clarity, effort, and your understanding of the content of the slides.

3. Using Bulletin-Board Software

(1 week)

This project can only be accomplished if one of the school's computers has a modem and access to a telephone connection. Your task is to contact a computer bulletin board and obtain printed answers to these five questions from another user on the bulletin board. Print your answers out in the same order as the questions below. When they are completed, prepare and attach a computer-generated title page.

(a) Name and location of user;

(b) Type of computer equipment the other person is using;

(c) Three positive uses the other person has discovered for bulletin boards;

(d) Two negative features about using bulletin boards;

(e) Description of one factual piece of information the other user has discovered while using a bulletin board.

1. Research Paper

(3 weeks)

Prepare a word-processed research paper on a specific computer application that you have researched in the library, in class, or at home. The information must come from at least three different sources, which must be listed at the back of the research paper in a bibliography. Whenever an idea other than your own is used in the body of the paper, a note of its source is required. The numbered notes may appear at the bottom of the page as footnotes or may be collected together as end notes on a "Notes" page placed before the bibliography.

Some suggested resources include books, computer magazines, news magazines, newspapers, encyclopedias, television documentaries, and personal interviews. Your final copy is to be double-spaced, with a 3 cm white border all around (60-stroke line). Cover your paper with a title page.

List of Topics

(a) Computerized Banking
(b) Industrial Robots
(c) Space Exploration and the Computer
(d) Computers and Law Enforcement
(e) History of Computer Uses Since 1945
(f) Computers and National Defence
(g) Computers in Transportation
(h) Computers in Hospitals
(i) Biography of John Watson—IBM
(j) Coming—A Cashless Society?
(k) Computer Viruses
(l) Computers in Retail Stores
(m) Electronic Funds Transfer Systems and Banking
(n) Electronic Theft
(o) Any other computer topic with the permission of your teacher

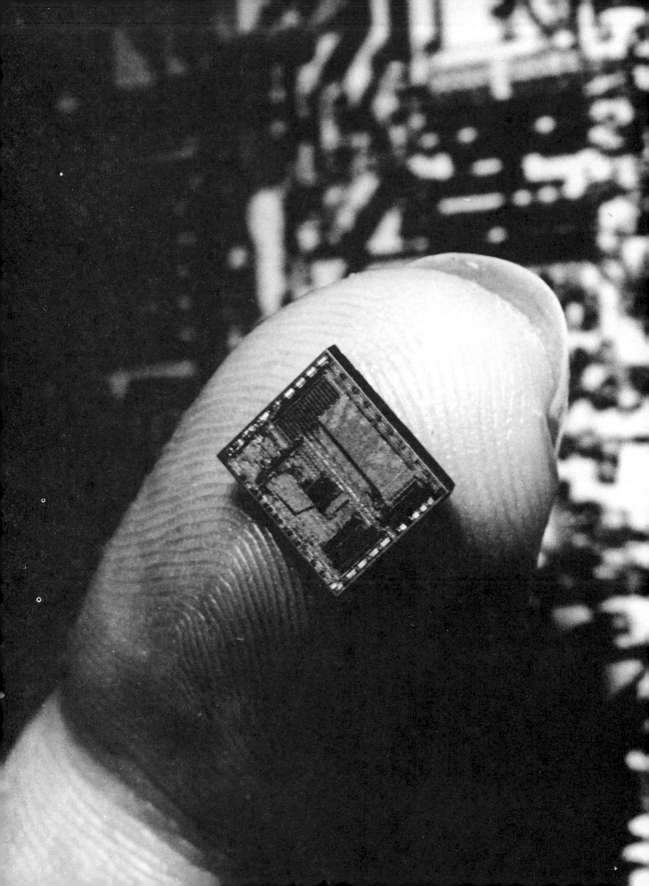

Chapter

9

IMPACT OF COMPUTERS ON SOCIETY

ON SOCIETY
ON SOCIETY

66 When one considers that an entire computer can be held on the tip of a finger, and its programming endlessly modified to serve any task, the impact of such a technology is awesome. 99

OBJECTIVES

By the end of this chapter, you will be able to:

1 Describe the positive impact of computers on productivity, intellectual achievements, and increased leisure time;

2 Describe some of the negative impact of computers on shifts in employment patterns, invasion of privacy, and the frustration of dealing with computer-oriented systems;

3 Define the term "electronic funds transfer system", and explain the possible trend towards a cashless society;

4 Explain that the impact of the microchip is not neutral, nor will it necessarily be applied to socially beneficial purposes.

WORKING IN THE WORLD OF COMPUTERS

Airline Owner
invests in automated flight-reservation terminals for shopping malls

Assembly-Line Worker
checks the quality of work produced by robotic devices

Bank Manager
needs a knowledge of computer banking systems in addition to accounting and finance

Biochemist
uses a computer to simulate molecular changes in experiments with genetic material

Car Manufacturer
utilizes stationary robotic arms along assembly lines to manufacture automobiles

Credit Card Manager
establishes a centralized data bank accessible to stores throughout the world by satellite transmission

Lawyer
accesses archive computer records of precedent cases to help clients

Politician
enacts legislation to protect citizens from electronic invasion of privacy

Robotics Technician
needs a knowledge of how to repair robots

Robot Engineer
designs and builds industrial, office, and domestic robots

World of Computers 181

9.1° INTRODUCTION

*C*omputers have a powerful effect on the way people live in our society. Unlike other fixed-purpose inventions such as the automobile, electric light, or television, computer-chip technology can be endlessly modified through its programming. It can guide spacecraft, teach, make medical diagnoses, search criminal files, draw three-dimensional pictures, talk, generate music, and even operate complete factories without assistance. There is almost nothing to which the miniaturized, programmable computer chip cannot be applied. That is what distinguishes it from other technologies of the past—its adaptability to almost any task.

Consider the impact of the automobile. It has contributed to the development of highways, suburbs, drive-ins, fast-food chains, traffic lights, petroleum refining, tires, and batteries, as well as the assembly line method of manufacturing, air pollution, traffic congestion, and jobs for one-sixth of the North American population.

Computer technology is having that kind of impact. It is affecting how we learn, the types of jobs available, our work habits, our leisure time, our job productivity, our rights to privacy, and the method by which we handle money; it is also causing shifts in employment patterns, and increasing our capacity to process ever more complex problems.

It is not enough to study the applications to which computers are suited. Any complex technology, if it becomes popular, can cause dramatic changes in society. We need to know the "why" as well as the "how" to survive in the "Age of Information". Things will not stay as you know them today. The super-intelligent, fifth-generation computers and talking robots of the next decade will alter almost everyone's lifestyle in some way, regardless of income level, role, status, age, or gender.

As individuals, most of us will not be able to alter the impact of such technology on our lives. However, an understanding of its effects may help us to accept and cope with the changes. This chapter will help you to explore some of the positive and negative societal influences of this ever-changing microtechnology.

9.2 INCREASED PRODUCTIVITY

*O*ne of the benefits of having a computer system is that it allows people to accomplish more tasks with greater speed and accuracy. More jobs being done within a given period can be described as an increase in productivity. Some computer specialists refer to this as "increased throughput".

Office secretaries, clerks, and managers, for example, can key in, edit, and electronically file a greater number of letters with fewer errors with a word-processing station than they could with an ordinary typewriter and manual filing system. Teller terminals allow financial institutions to handle an increase in the number and accuracy of banking transactions. Airline reservation clerks and travel agents, with their immediate access to flight times and passenger statistics, can complete a transaction in a fraction of the time that it used to take without the aid of a computer system.

9.3 EXPANDED INTELLECTUAL ACHIEVEMENTS

*J*ust as engines have increased what humans can achieve physically, computers have expanded what humans can achieve intellectually. Motors and engines provide us with the capability to fly, outrun any animal, travel enormous distances in a few hours, and lift loads a thousand times our human strength. Similarly, computers provide us with the means to process very complicated equations, predict future trends, draw three-dimensional rotating diagrams, and simulate situations that only our imagination can conceive.

Computers have provided scientific, medical, and technical researchers with improved methods of experimenting and proving assumptions. New discoveries and advances in space exploration, biochemistry, communications, weather forecasting, warfare, transportation, and engineering are increasingly dependent on the processing power of the computer.

Even advances in computer technology design are being made with the help of a computer. Some companies have programmed computers to design and test new computer chips that operate faster and more accurately than the chips doing the designing and testing. This self-improvement feature has caused much debate among scientists. What if computers are taught to think for themselves, and are then programmed to make themselves more efficient than their original models? This may lead to a world in which machines contain more "intelligence" than the people who designed them.

Norbert Wiener, who coined the word cybernetics, predicts that as machines learn (as they do in some university chess programs), they will develop unforeseen strategies at rates that baffle their programmers, and will go beyond the limitations of their human designers. In the future, a systems analyst may teach a computer to learn by itself. Within a few computer generations, that machine may develop a thinking ability many times that of the systems analyst and may, in effect, become the teacher. Mankind, at that point, may be taught by machines to view the world in new ways.

Science fiction writers often use the fear of such computers as the basis of their plots. In a story by Fredric Brown written about 30 years ago, a supercomputer was asked, "Is there a God?" After making sure that its power supply was no longer under human control, it replied, "There is now!"

*A*ll new technologies cause **job obsolescence**, either by reducing the number of people required or changing the skills required to perform certain tasks. When cars became popular in the early part of this century, blacksmiths, horse ranchers, saddle manufacturers, hay growers, and cobblestone street cleaners all lost their jobs. Their services were no longer needed.

A similar situation is occurring with the increased application of computer systems in today's society. Manual factory workers and office managers and staff who work at routine jobs are being displaced. The increased productivity of individual workers

using computers often means that fewer staff are required to perform the same quantity of work. Fewer employees means lower costs and higher profits for the organization. Reductions in staff also mean that fewer supervisory personnel are needed. All levels of work become affected. Ironically, the middle managers who recommend increased deployment of computers may also become redundant as a result of the process.

People who work as typists, filing clerks, mail clerks, office managers, shop foremen,

machine operators, typesetters, and assembly-line workers can all become unemployed as a result of increased use of computer technology. Their jobs can, in many cases, be done more quickly and at a lower cost with a computer. Automated machines in manufacturing and processing plants can work tirelessly without the need for coffee breaks, sleep, salaries, or vacations.

Imagine the job displacement when electronic mail and electronic newspapers become popular. Skills currently performed by thousands of workers will become obsolete. The new electronic systems eliminate the middlemen in the process of passing information from the sender to the receiver. Postal clerks, mail delivery personnel, courier service employees, typesetters, printing machine operators, photodevelopers, and many other traditional roles will be greatly reduced in number and may in time disappear altogether. Consider the chart to the right, which outlines several shifts in the job market caused by increased computer use.

In this chart, the left-hand column indicates the types of job that are in decline, and the right-hand column indicates the types of job that are increasing. Notice that in several examples, it is machines (shown in brackets) rather than people that are increasingly being used to perform the tasks.

Identifying Patterns of Change in the Job Market

*T*here are four observable patterns of change in the job market that can be deduced from the chart on page 185.

(1) Shift towards High-Technology Jobs

Almost all shifts are from relatively low-technology to high-technology jobs that may require more education or training and a different set of technical skills.

(2) Manual Labour Jobs Disappearing

There are large blocks of people, assembly-line workers for example, for

Shifts in the Job Market Caused by Increased Computer Use

JOBS IN DECLINE	JOBS INCREASING
Manual assembly-line jobs	(robots)
Machine repair	Robotics technicians
Machinists	Numerical control operators
Office typists, filing clerks	Word-processing operators
Adding-machine clerks (insurance industry)	Spreadsheet analysts
Corporate mail clerks	(electronic mail)
Postal workers	(electronic mail)
Middle management positions	(senior staff with data-base access)
Typesetters	Computer-to-laser printing operators
Bank clerks	(automated teller machines)
Telephone operators	(digital phones / switching systems)

whom there is no equivalent job. When human-operated assembly-line jobs are replaced with programmable robots, as is happening in the automobile industry, thousands of people are permanently laid off. The same is true of non-assembly-line manual jobs in industries such as steel, petroleum, paper, or chemical processing. A major steel producer in Hamilton, Ontario, employs 8000 workers at its older steel-making plants. One of its newer, computerized facilities at nearby Nanticoke, which has the same industrial capacity as all the older plants combined, is operated by only 800 people, ten times fewer staff than in the non-computerized plants.

(3) Fewer People Required for Traditional Service Jobs

In areas in which there are equivalent higher-technology jobs to turn to, fewer people will be needed to get the same amount of work done. The banking, insurance, telephone, and printing industries are employment areas in which the number of people required to handle tasks is static or shows slow growth because of the volume-handling capacity of computer-assisted customer service. Both the banking and telephone industries have instituted automated systems to allow customers to use their service without staff intervention.

(4) No Career Path Is Immune

The tasks that can be performed by computer cover all types of jobs—manual labour, managerial, office, and service sector. No career path is entirely immune from potential job displacement. This is the first technology to threaten all career sectors at the same time. By comparison, the invention of the automobile, for example, only affected the area of transportation.

Professional Roles

Even such professions as medicine, law, and education are being altered. Computers can be programmed to accept test data from interns or nurses, suggest a diagnosis, and recommend treatment. A lawyer's memory of relevant precedent cases can be stored in a computer and retrieved within a few seconds. Computers can be programmed to teach any subject, and can do so with infinite patience and individual attention to the learner.

*T*he developers of these computer systems state that new jobs in computer programming, computer manufacturing, word processing, computer operations, numerical-control operating, and computer maintenance are being created. People can retrain for these new types of job. Indeed, a new generation of workers will have to be educated to supply the distinctly different job market created by computer technology. As long as people are willing to move to another job location and retrain when a job is made obsolete, they will continue to survive economically.

During the last four decades, national unemployment statistics have risen, both in absolute numbers and as a percentage of the labour force (referred to as the rate of unemployment). There are several factors that affect unemployment figures: one is an increasing number of women entering the permanent work force (60%), and another is structural unemployment.

Structural unemployment results from changes in demand for labour as technology changes and as shifting demand displaces workers whose skills become obsolete. A variation of this impact is occurring in the car industry. Canadian car manufacturers are steadily adopting robotic technology for assembly-line production. Rather than firing thousands of redundant workers, and angering the labour unions in the process, these plants have left retiring employees' positions vacant. As a result, the "blue collar" work force in the automotive industry is steadily declining in numbers because of computer technology, but this decline is not showing up as structural unemployment.

The rise in unemployment figures also coincides with the increase in popularity of large computer systems in the mid-1960s. (The popular 360 series of IBM mainframe computers debuted in 1964.) These systems were applied to the banking industry, the airline industry, and to the processing of payroll, inventory, and scheduling in government and corporate offices. All these areas were previously much more labour intensive.

Canadian Labour Force Unemployment Rates

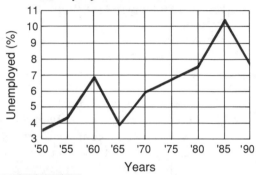

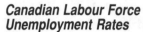

Figure 9.2

This line graph indicates the rising level of unemployment over the past 40 years, which is partly attributable to the negative impact of automation and computers on available jobs.

If the changeover to new computer systems continues to be a slow evolution rather than a rapid revolution, our society may be able to redirect the displaced workers into new and satisfying roles without causing massive unemployment. The newer roles, however, will probably require more technical training and some knowledge of computers.

Even so, a 50-year-old worker whose job disappears because of computers is bound to be skeptical. The news that a company with new technology will employ many people is only good news if you are one of those people, and if you are willing to relocate and retrain to obtain one of those jobs. For many older workers, some of whom show an unwillingness to adapt to computers, permanent unemployment becomes a harsh reality. In addition, it is highly probable that changing job descriptions, corporate takeovers, or changing product demands may force most people to work at several different jobs in their lifetime.

9.6 FRUSTRATION IN DEALING WITH COMPUTER-ORIENTED SYSTEMS

At least once in their lifetime, almost everyone has suffered the frustration of receiving a bill, address label, bank statement, or paycheque with incorrect information. Before computerized customer service became popular, people could explain the situation to the appropriate clerk and have the error corrected with relatively little trouble. Today, an incorrect address label may continue unchanged for several months despite a customer's appeal for revision. In several instances, requests generated by a computer for a bill totalling $0.00 became increasingly threatening even though the customer pleaded that the situation was totally ridiculous. (One customer finally solved the problem by sending a cheque for $0.00.)

These problems are usually caused either by a lack of communication between the computer department and the rest of the organization, or by a programming error, or by clerks who do not understand the computer system.

Large organizations often hire outside companies to process their labels, bills, or cheques. McGraw-Hill of Canada, for example, sends reminder letters to some Canadian magazine customers from their Netherlands operations in Europe. When a customer sends in a request for a correction, the foreign-based company may not hear about it for several weeks. With satellite technology, capable of transmitting information anywhere in the world, such inter-national operations will become more commonplace.

A similar situation of slow communication may also occur simply because the company's own internal computer department is completely isolated from other areas in the same building.

The invoice for $0.00 mentioned earlier was caused by an incomplete computer program. Angry customers have convinced many systems analysts to be more careful in their program designs. There is still a great need for better-trained computer personnel who can understand the complexities of large computer systems and their software.

Clerks who handle customer transactions are usually not the best people to refer to when a correction is needed. They are so used to handling routine transactions that inconsistencies baffle them. Some poorly trained clerks actually believe that computers never make mistakes. As a result, customers who notice an error are told that they are mistaken. When seeking help, customers should go directly to a manager, or the customer service department.

"35 million dollars! I'm afraid our computer is somewhat of a practical joker!"

9.7 ELECTRONIC MONEY

*H*ave you noticed a growing trend toward a cashless society in North America? Company employees rarely see their paycheques. Usually wages are deposited directly into the employee's bank account. Department stores, gas stations, travel agencies, hotels, and restaurants now accept a variety of credit cards. Cheques, still one of the most popular substitutes for money, also have wide acceptance for paying bills. Except for buying groceries, newspapers, and small novelties, cash is slowly declining as a medium of exchange. This trend is leading Canadians toward a cashless society in which the means of exchange may be primarily electronic.

What is taking place is a process of moving money electronically from one place to another with the help of computers and dedicated telephone lines called **electronic funds transfer systems (EFTS)**. Instead of physically transferring money, a bank's computer can be instructed to deduct the money from one account and deposit it in another all within a few seconds.

The latest money substitute is a **debit card** that causes the immediate payment of money from your bank account for any product or service. When a purchase is made, the cashier keys in your identification number and the cost of the item. The electronic cash register, which also acts as a computer terminal, then sends a message to the computer in the head office of your bank. That bank's computer checks your account balance. If the balance is sufficient, the cost of the purchase is automatically deducted from your account and deposited into the store's account. If the balance is insufficient, you will not be allowed to purchase the item.

There is no particular advantage to the customer with this system. Credit cards give you 25 days to pay the debt. Debit cards give you ten seconds. But a debit card does provide the store with immediate funds to restock their merchandise, and it also reduces their need for credit card departments and collection agencies.

There is, however, still a strong emotional dependency on money. People like to see and handle currency because it makes them feel rich. Even though computer technology is capable of storing and moving electronic wealth from one location to another, paper money and coins will probably remain popular for many years to come.

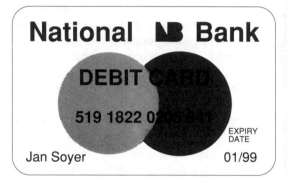

9.8 INVASION OF PRIVACY

*L*arge organizations—government agencies, credit card companies, and corporations—tend to collect information about people. Computers make large data-collection centres possible by providing storage for millions of individual records and retrieving them in a fraction of a second.

Centralized data banks present a problem to individual citizens, however. In some instances, it is fairly easy for government agencies or individuals who have access to a computer network system to obtain a printout on anyone they wish. Several years ago, the R.C.M.P. was accused of tampering with people's mail and illegally tapping telephone lines. As a result of the political controversy, a new investigative group called CSIS (Canadian Security Intelligence Service) was formed. Based in Ottawa, this agency is separate from the R.C.M.P. and directly responsible to the ruling party in the House of Commons. Hidden in buildings behind high wire fences and surveillance cameras, the agency has unhampered access to computer systems, satellite technology, telephones, and electronic mail. Away from the normal scrutiny of news reporters and the public, this civilian government operation can do as it wishes within its political mandate.

Easy access to private information, regardless of the source, can lead to harmful consequences for individuals. Politicians, law enforcement agencies, newspaper reporters, or blackmailers could easily ruin someone's reputation or cause the loss of a job by publicizing personal data. Historical records stored in a computer system may contain a criminal record, evidence of alcoholism, information about drug abuse, school records, medical data, or references to absenteeism or family relations.

In addition, the personal information stored on disk or tape may be false, or simply someone's opinion rather than the facts. Consider the following data summary about an individual.

Note that no item by itself is particularly damaging or abnormal. Yet, taken together, the report presents a fairly negative image.

Computerized records tend to be negative because bureaucracies use the rule of **management by exception** for data collection. This means that only exceptions to everyday behaviour are noted. Ordinary positive comments, which would describe the vast majority of people, would simply take too much space within the computer system. So, aside from exceptionally positive comments, such as "Scholastic Award Winner", they are ignored. It is easier to record only negative comments. Such computerized records, as a result, reflect a very biased viewpoint.

If you were an employer and received the following computerized report about someone, would you hire him or her? How would you react on learning that this was your school principal's data history, or a ten-year summary of a local politician?

Routine Summary of One Individual

SCHOOL RECORDS:

Average marks; reported behavioural problems; one truancy violation; absenteeism rate (18%).

CRIMINAL RECORD:

Four traffic violations;
careless driving (1990).

CREDIT RATING:

Three months overdue account in 1991 resulting in a lowering of credit rating.

BANK ACCOUNT:

Savings Account: $ 4.10
Chequing Account: $ 126.50

MEDICAL DATA:

Surgery, 1989, 1991
Communicable disease, 1992

FAMILY RELATIONS:

Father member of Alcoholics Anonymous; Mother political activist.

*T*here are four rules that should be instituted to protect individuals from misuse of centralized information.

If the privacy issue is ignored, governments may create a society in which people will no longer feel free to do as they wish or to express an opinion for fear of a permanent, negative computerized report. If we let it happen, the Big Brother of George Orwell's book *1984*, in which an oppressive government kept its population under constant electronic scrutiny, may become a reality.

Rules to Protect Citizens

(1) Make Records Secure

The records must be made secure. Unauthorized people must not be allowed to gain access to confidential records.

(2) Searches for Information Must Be Relevant

In addition, the type of information that one is permitted to view must be relevant to the investigation. For example, medical data records should be made available to doctors, but not to newspaper reporters, politicians, or law enforcement agencies. Similarly, it is reasonable to allow educational institutions to share school marks, but not reasonable to make the marks available to agencies that are not concerned with learning. Unfortunately, at the present time, most agencies (government or private) can obtain all kinds of unrelated information on private individuals.

(3) Citizens Must Have Access to Files About Themselves

Citizens must be allowed to review and correct computerized records as well as request the removal of outdated information. Something that happened 20 years ago should not be maintained as a permanent reflection of an individual. People change.

(4) Computer Ombudsman to Represent Individuals

The only way that individual privacy can be maintained is by government legislation. To help enforce the laws, a **computer ombudsman** should be appointed to represent individuals who have been unfairly treated as a result of computerized information. The computer ombudsman should have the power to demand that false information stored in any computer system in the country be updated or removed.

9.9 INTENSITY OF IMPACT OF COMPUTER TECHNOLOGY

"If there is a computer revolution going on, how come I'm not personally affected?" There are two reasons why technology does not affect everyone equally. The first is that it is not being applied to all sectors of the economy with equal intensity. There are progressive stages of computer implementation within the manufacturing and service sectors. Computerized systems are more advanced in industries that have had the money to invest in new equipment. The automobile industry, for example, has made giant strides in the implementation of robotics during the last two economic reces-

Courtesy of Compaq Computer Corporation

Figure 9.3 The size and portability of the laptop computer make it ideal for on-site reporting of news and sporting events. This is one field in which computers are being used in new and different ways.

sions (1981, 1990), when most of its employees were on temporary layoff and the companies had money set aside.

The second reason is that the implementation of new technology tends to appear in stages five to ten years apart. This is sufficient time for companies to develop extra capital to invest, and for the next generation of computer technology to appear with its additional power (usually ten times greater) and new features (smaller size, multi-tasking, networking, voice response, artificial intelligence, robotics, etc.). Each stage involves a greater intensity of application of computer technology than the previous stage.

The chart on the following page illustrates how computer technology is implemented in five different industries—automobile, banking, mail, office, and travel. For each sector, three different stages of computer application are shown, each with a greater impact on categories such as task, career role, and skills required.

Criteria for Three Categories

In a low-impact situation, the task is completed more efficiently or more conveniently. The same career role exists and usually the same person does the job. Little training is involved.

In a medium-impact situation, the task is modified by the introduction of technology. Fewer people are needed to do the job, and employees require retraining to work with the new machines.

In the high-impact situations, the task becomes entirely different. The traditional career role disappears. Previous employees are displaced and must retrain for a new career.

Intensity of Impact of Computer Technology

	LOW IMPACT	MEDIUM IMPACT	HIGH IMPACT
A U T O	Chip-enhanced engines Electronic engine diagnosis	Some robots along assembly line	Cybernated factories
B A N K I N G	Teller terminals	Automated teller terminals	Home banking by computer Electronic funds transfer system between stores and banks
M A I L	Bar code Electronic sorting of letters	Corporate electronic mail Fax machines	Home mailing systems
O F F I C E	Word processing Spreadsheets Data bases	Voice recognition software Rule-based artificial intelligence	Teleprocessing Working at home
T R A V E L	Airport reservation systems Travel agent terminals	Automated reservation terminals in shopping malls	Flight reservations on home computer Vacation selection software for home computers

9.10 COPING WITH LEISURE TIME

*O*ffice computers and programmed industrial robots tend to increase productivity. As businesses produce more products and services, management can afford to negotiate more free time for their employees in the form of a shorter work week and longer vacations.

Leisure time, however, will not affect everyone equally. The reductions in work will apply mostly to employees whose responsibilities can be measured by the number of hours that they spend on the job (rather than what they accomplish). This would include secretaries, clerks, office managers, foremen, and factory workers. Another group, such as salespersons, doctors, politicians, researchers, scientists, inventors, writers, artists, and business executives will probably continue to work longer hours. These people set their own goals and do not mind spending the extra time striving to attain them.

Curiously, increased leisure time is not welcomed by all social groups. Many groups who have recently immigrated, for example, tend to use vacation time working at a part-time job to supplement their income, and to get established in society. Other people find the concept of self worth so closely related to their job that they feel uncomfortable when they are away from work for long periods of time.

North Americans, historically, have regarded non-working people as lazy and nonproductive. As a result, people with increased leisure time often feel guilty about not working.

| Figure 9.4 | The freedom to pursue hobbies is part of the lure of increased leisure time. Professional musicians, artists, and writers may choose longer hours at their art because they enjoy it. |

Courtesy of IBM

*S*ince computerization may increase the amount of time that we spend away from work, it is important that negative attitudes toward leisure begin to change. Societies must be taught to view leisure time and working time with equal respect. Leisure time can be used to indulge in specialized hobbies such as carpentry, sculpting, competitive chess, oil painting, landscaping, gardening, or continued education.

Eventually, people may spend part of their year working for a company and the other part teaching a craft to a group, working at an entirely different type of job, lecturing, travelling, playing for a team, designing a house, spending more time with their children, or writing a book. This is a great way for human beings to spend their lives compared to a lifetime tied to a single routine job. People will have the time to do different and exciting things, rather than just taking brief vacations.

However, although highly educated, active, or self-motivated individuals may view leisure time in this way, less educated or ambitious individuals may use unstructured leisure time very unproductively. Increased drug and alcohol use, disturbance of the peace, violence, theft, burglary, and vandalism could result from these less-disciplined people having more free time. Increased leisure time, coupled with fewer available jobs, may prove a mixed blessing for society as a whole.

9.11 SELECTING ONLY THE BEST APPLICATIONS

*O*ne former advertisement from United Technologies, a corporate conglomerate that manufactures high-technology products for both the military and industry, expressed the following viewpoint about the impact of technology:

> "Ethically, technology is neutral. There is nothing inherently either good or bad about it. It is simply a tool, a servant, directed and employed by people for whatever purpose they want fulfilled."

The point of the advertisement was to convince readers that ethics (the morality of our behaviour) come from the user, not the technology. Following that line of argument, a gun, or a missile with a nuclear warhead, is neither good nor bad in itself. Only when you use a weapon to kill people can it be considered a "bad application". A good application of a nuclear warhead, one supposes, would be as a threat and not the actual use for which it was designed.

According to this philosophy, the applications of computer technology can only be considered morally bad if corporations use

Figure 9.5 The spectre of increased crime and violence as a result of unemployment is one possible outcome of a society in which very few people have full-time jobs.

them in a way that is harmful to people. Corporations, however, claim that reduction in operating costs, and maximization of profits for investors, is what computerization is useful in achieving.

This presents a conflict concerning the use of computerization that industry and society have not yet resolved. There are both good and bad effects from the same process, and political leaders have not considered the consequences. Two false assumptions are being made about computer technology. The first is that its impact is neutral, and the second is that it will always be put to socially useful ends.

Computer Technology Is Not Neutral

No significant technology has a neutral impact on society. As mentioned at the beginning of the chapter, the mass production of automobiles, which began in the 1920s with Henry Ford's Model-T car assembly lines, caused a whole range of positive and negative changes over the years. The pioneer car designers and assembly-line workers could not predict air pollution, traffic congestion, car crashes, the need for inter-provincial highways, oil and gasoline production, and the demand for tires, batteries, and safety glass windows. These side-effects only became problems many years later.

Computer applications are still in their infancy. Yet to come are completely "cybernated" automobile, steel, textile, paper, and petroleum processing plants. Service sector industries may include nationwide electronic mail systems; completely digital computer-switched telephone services; computer-driven subway and train networks; home shopping through computers; intelligent industrial, office, and domestic robots; smart information-retrieval systems for home use with access to cross-indexed data bases; and on-line commercial transactions in law, medicine, political voting, educational training, investments, and banking. The effects of those innovations will not be neutral. They will involve a tremendous displacement of workers, higher levels of structural unemployment, home-based work rather than commuting, and less daily interaction among people.

Not All Applications Are Socially Useful

The second assumption, that this technology will always be applied to socially useful purposes, is also unrealistic. Almost all businesses that adopt computer technology in corporate head offices and factories do so with the goal of increasing profits and competing in international markets. Their last concern is the social impact of their business decisions.

One reason why our society confronts so many unexpected problems is that we tend to develop and adopt new technologies before considering the possible consequences. We should begin with hard questions about what type of society we want, and choose those technologies, and particular outcomes, that serve long-range social and ecological goals. Rather than letting technology shape our destiny, we should exercise control, through federal legislation, over the directions in which technology is taking us, and buffer citizens from the harsher effects of its application.

*I*t is not enough to study the uses for which computers are suited. Any complex technology, if it becomes popular, can cause dramatic changes in society. As individuals, we may not be able to alter the impact that such technology has on our lives. An understanding of its potential, however, will help us to accept and cope with the changes.

Consider the impact of the automobile. It has contributed to the development of highways, suburbs, drive-ins, fast-food chains, traffic lights, petroleum processing, tires, and batteries, as well as automobile manufacturing, air pollution, traffic congestion, and jobs for one-sixth of the North American population.

Computer technology is going to have that kind of widespread impact. It will affect our work habits, job choices, leisure time, rights to privacy, methods of handling money, education, and job productivity, and will increase our capacity to process ever more complex problems.

The most visible impact of computer technology will be the evolution of a distinctly different job market. Many traditional roles will become obsolete, and a great number of workers will be displaced. At the same time, computers will give rise to entirely new electronic software and support industries. Workers must be willing to relocate and re-train to maintain their financial position. If the changeover to new computer systems continues to be a slow evolution rather than a rapid revolution, our society may be able to absorb the displaced workers into new and satisfying roles.

Most of the jobs people will have 20 years from now have not yet been invented. It is possible that most jobs will be computer-related, and that computer technology will employ more workers than the entire automobile industry.

The impact of computer-chip technology is not neutral, nor will it necessarily be put to socially useful purposes. We should begin to ask difficult questions about what type of society we want, and choose those technologies, and particular outcomes, that serve long-range social goals. We should exercise control, through federal legislation, over the directions in which technology is taking us.

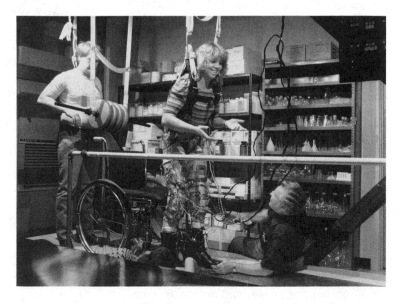

centralized data banks

computer ombudsman

debit card

electronic funds
transfer system (EFTS)

expanded intellectual
achievements

increased productivity

invasion of privacy

job obsolescence

management by
exception

structural
unemployment

CHECKING YOUR READING

*T*hese are general questions that may require factual recall, reading comprehension, and some application of the knowledge gained from this chapter.

Introduction

1. What distinguishes the computer chip from other technologies of the past?

2. List eight things affected by the use of computer technology.

3. Why will things, as we know them today, not stay the same with the increase of computer technology?

4. If we may not be able to alter the impact of such technology, why should we learn about it?

Increased Productivity

5. What is meant by the term "increased productivity"?

6. Describe an example of a role in which computers have increased the productivity of employees.

7. Explain the effect of both engines and computers on human capabilities.

8. What debate has been created by the possibility that computers may someday think for themselves?

Changes in the Job Market

9. Explain the statement "All new technologies cause job obsolescence". Provide three examples of roles that computers will make obsolete.

10. Briefly list four observable patterns of change in the job market caused by computer technology.

What Will People Do?

11. What must people be willing to do when their jobs become obsolete?

12. What has happened to unemployment during the last four decades?

13. Explain what "structural unemployment" refers to, and how this may relate to the use of computers.

14. Under what circumstance will the changeover to new computer systems in our society result in displaced workers finding new jobs?

Frustration in Dealing with Computer-Oriented Systems

15. Explain how some companies that use computers for billing or mailing labels cause problems for customers.

16. Why are company clerks not the best people to talk to about a computer-related error? To whom should you talk? Why?

Electronic Money

17. Define "electronic funds transfer system".

18. (a) How might people make purchases in the future, if they do not carry cash, cheques, or credit cards?
(b) Give an example of how that might work.

19. Of what advantage is the debit card for (a) customers; (b) store owners?

Invasion of Privacy

20. Why might centralized data banks be feared by many individuals? Explain.

21. (a) Why is there a tendency for computerized records to be negative in their description of people?
(b) What effect might this have on potential employers?

22. List four rules that should be legislated to deal with computerized records of people.

23. List the following types of data files. Beside each one, indicate the type of agency or professional group that should have exclusive access to the information.
(a) school marks
(b) medical history
(c) criminal records
(d) credit ratings
(e) tax payments

Coping with Leisure Time

24. In the future, as a result of increasing productivity, who will
(a) have more leisure time?
(b) still want to work "long hours"?

25. Give three reasons why not all people would want more leisure time.

26. Suggest how the following types of people may use the increased leisure time caused by computerized work places:
(a) highly motivated, active, ambitious people
(b) poorly trained, undisciplined, or unambitious people

Selecting Only the Best Applications

27. What is wrong with the logic of this statement?
"Ethically, technology is neutral. There is nothing inherently either good or bad about it."

28. List four effects on society that suggest that computer technology is not neutral.

29. What is one reason why our society confronts so many unexpected problems?

*T*hese questions assume an understanding of the material presented in this chapter, and provide new situations that may require evaluation, analysis, or the application of your newly acquired knowledge.

1. Different types of computer technology, if they become popular, can cause dramatic changes in society. Consider the impact of (a) automobiles and (b) computers in the following ways. For each one of these inventions, list five jobs that it has made obsolete, then list five new jobs that it has created. Use a chart format.

2. This chapter mentions that computers expand our intellectual achievements. Identify three mental capabilities that humans have that a computer can imitate and expand. What type of intellectual activities does the computer allow humans to pursue that we previously could not?

3. Norbert Wiener predicted that "as machines learn, they may develop unforeseen strategies at rates that baffle their programmers, and go beyond the limitation of their human designers." Why do many people find this idea frightening? What can we do about it?

4. Describe the computer hardware, and other devices, that are necessary for (a) a retail store and (b) a bank to establish an electronic funds transfer system.

5. How do messages about customer transactions get to the bank from the retail store? How does this EFT system work if the bank is closed while the store remains open?

6. What advantages do you think EFT provides? Name two disadvantages.

7. George Orwell's novel *1984* described an oppressive government that used a large centralized data bank to keep electronic surveillance over its population. It also manipulated the data base to change the content of history books and newspapers to suit its political goals. Suggest why many people, including science fiction writers, fear the establishment of government-operated, computerized information centres.

8. Suppose that you discovered that a data file about you contained false information, or someone's opinion rather than facts. What would you do? Explain.

9. In the future, increased productivity caused by the use of computers may allow people to work for part of the year, then do something else for the remainder. Suggest three different things (other than watching television or doing nothing) that you would do if you had three months (90 consecutive days) to pursue other activities.

10. Read the following quotation, then answer the questions. "Ethically, technology is neutral. There is nothing inherently good or bad about it. It is simply a tool, a servant, and employed by people for whatever purpose they want fulfilled."

    (a) Why does the quotation seem believable?

    (b) What two assumptions are made about the quotation when it is applied to computer-chip technology?

1. Presentation of a Novel

Many writers have strong fears of the uncontrolled use of computers and robots. Often, science fiction writers include them as either a villain or as part of the story's plot.

Read one of the following stories. Prepare a two-page summary using a word processor. In your summary, identify the role of the computer or robot in the story (as a villain, plot element, or part of the setting) and explain the fear(s) that the author is attempting to communicate to the reader. Include a computer-generated title page.

(a) *2001: A Space Odyssey* by Arthur C. Clark

(b) *Rossum's Universal Robots* by P. Selver and N. Playfair.

(c) *The Humanoids* by Jack Williamson

(d) *1984* by George Orwell

(e) *Life Keeper* by Mike McQuay

(f) *The Cunningham Equations* by Edmondson & Kotlan

(g) Any other science fiction novel, with permission from your teacher, that concentrates on robots or artificial intelligence.

2. Great Thinkers on Computers

(Research Report)

Research information on the ideas about which one of the following people has written. Prepare a two-page, printed summary using a word processor. In your report, concentrate on the person's ideas, rather than their personal history. School library resources may include general knowledge encyclopedias, *The Encyclopedia of Computer Science*, and computer textbooks. Include a computer-generated title page.

Great Thinkers
(a) Norbert Wiener
(b) John von Neumann
(c) Alan M. Turing
(d) Norman Cousins
(e) Arthur L. Samuel
(f) Joseph Weizenbaum

Suggested Titles Available at the Public Library
(a) *Computers and Man* by Richard C. Dorf
(b) *The Computer and the Brain* by John von Neumann
(c) *The Human Use of Human Beings* by Norbert Wiener
(d) *The Computer Prophets* by Jerry Rosenberg
(e) *God and Gotham, Inc.* by Norbert Wiener

3. Futuristic Scenario

Using a word processor, create a two-page scenario of what society will be like if all the computer applications mentioned in the last section in this chapter come true. Your outlook can be positive, negative, or neutral. Include topics like employment, travel, use of money, centralized data banks, entertainment, and home life. Attach a computer-generated title page. *The Futurist* and *Popular Science* magazines may offer ideas.

4. Computer Articles on Future Applications

Find five magazine or newspaper articles that describe how computer applications will take effect in the future. Neatly trim each article to fit on a sheet of white 8 1/2" x 11" paper without folding. Tape or glue to mount. Legible photocopies are acceptable. Cover with a computer-generated title page. Examples of magazines include: *The Futurist, Omni, Popular Science, Time, Newsweek,* and *Maclean's.*

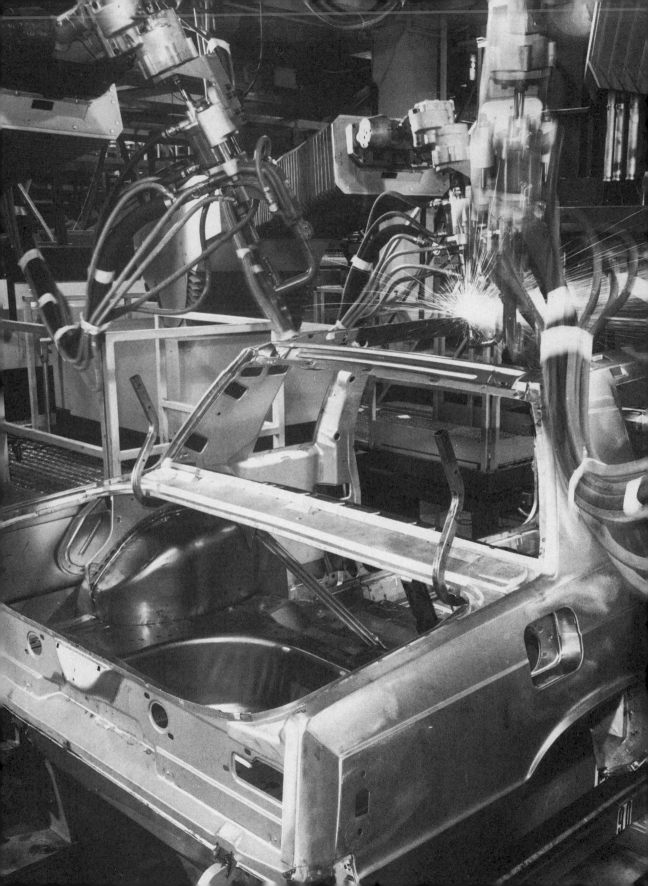

Chapter 10

CONTROVERSIAL ISSUES

CONTROVERSIAL ISSUES
CONTROVERSIAL ISSUES

OBJECTIVES

By the end of this chapter, you will be able to:

1 Describe opposing sides of several controversial issues often avoided by conventional computer scientists;

2 Understand some of the social, legal, and moral issues that are indirectly caused by computers in our society;

3 Understand that people should consider the consequences before embracing new technologies.

66 Every time the cost of labour goes up one dollar an hour, 1000 more robots become economical. 99

Roger B. Smith
Chairman of General Motors

WORKING IN THE WORLD OF COMPUTERS

A. I. Researcher
creates and improves artificial intelligence systems for computers

Bank Auditor
must have a knowledge of accounting and computer software to check the accuracy of a bank's records

Bomb Disposal Expert
uses a remote-controlled robot to pick up and safely remove terrorists' bombs

Specialized Medical Technician
installs and modifies artificial, electronic limbs for patients

Movie Director
understands the techniques of blending computer-generated animation with real-life actors and actresses

Nuclear Power Employee
uses huge computer-driven cranes to remove worn out uranium fuel rods

Nurse
enters medical data into a small medical terminal at a patient's bedside to be analyzed for a diagnosis

Computer Fraud Detective
needs to understand programming techniques used by criminals who embezzle money or goods from a company

Robot Salesperson
sells homeowners domestic robots to handle outdoor and household jobs

Science Fiction Writer
uses computers and robots as part of the setting or plot in his or her novel

*T*his chapter presents several short articles that deal with issues that have aroused much debate over the years. The articles are concerned with the economic, legal, and moral impact computers may have on our society. These are the long-term issues that computer scientists usually do not consider when they design computer systems. Although the issues themselves are serious, their presentation is often positive, and sometimes light-hearted.

Most of the questions that follow the articles are divided into two groups. The first group, entitled *Checking Your Reading*, is concerned only with the reader's understanding. The second group, entitled *Getting at the Issues*, invites the reader to analyze and evaluate the underlying assumptions.

"I think this artificial intelligence stuff is getting out of hand!"

*E*ven before computers became popular, Alan Turing, a British mathematician, had proposed a test for computer intelligence. The **Turing Test** requires that a researcher hook together three computers—one in a room by itself for the test volunteer to use, and the two others in another room for the researcher to use. The object of the test is for the volunteer and the researcher to communicate by computer with each other. They can use any questions and answers they can think up. If, during the test, the researcher switches the communication line to the third computer, which has a program that emulates human thought process, and the volunteer does not notice any difference in the conversation, the third computer and its software would be described as thinking.

One clever application of this test is a program called "Eliza", created by Joseph Weizenbaum, that is capable of carrying on a limited conversation with a human. It uses a search technique that picks out key phrases in your conversation and provides appropriate answers from its data bank. One variation of this idea is a program called "Doctor", which was used to conduct psychiatric interviews by computer with several patients (similar to the Turing Test setup). Afterwards, when the patients were told that they were not conversing with a real psychiatrist, 60 percent refused to believe it.

The above experiments were measured by the single criterion of use of the English language. Human intelligence, of course, involves more than just sentence interpretation. It also includes speech, visual and auditory recognition, creativity, mastery of fine motor movements, memory recall, the ability to learn by experimentation, and the capacity to devise a wide range of problem-solving strategies. Our dominance in these areas, however, is being challenged by a branch of computer research called **artificial intelligence**, which is striving to provide computers with these "human" capabilities.

There is already chess software that uses its own strategies to beat human opponents. Robotic devices can now navigate around objects, climb stairs, or think of ways to build ramps to obtain some object just out of reach. It may be only a short time before characteristics normally attributed to humans—intelligence, intuition, and creativity—will be displayed by computers.

Norbert Wiener, a pioneer in robotic theory, believes that this trend is dangerous. Computers that go beyond the limitations of the people who designed them may become uncontrollable.

An opposing opinion is held by scientist Arthur L. Samuel: the fact that some computers can beat humans at chess and appear to be thinking is irrelevant. The person who created the chess program gave computers that ability. The computer's level of artificial intelligence was decided ahead of time by its designer.

1. What test did Alan Turing propose? What was he trying to prove?

2. What human characteristics may soon be displayed by computers?

3. Why does Norbert Wiener think increased computer intelligence may be dangerous?

4. Why is Arthur L. Samuel not too concerned about "thinking computers"?

Getting at the Issues

5. Is there anything wrong with Turing's test for computer intelligence? Explain.

6. Why, in your opinion, would some patients refuse to believe that the psychiatrist was a machine, rather than a person?

7. Suppose you owned a computer that displayed intelligence, intuition, and creativity. Do you think that it would be a dangerous machine to have around? Explain.

8. In your opinion, can computers think? Give reasons for your answer.

10.3 COMPUTER THEFT

*I*n the past three decades, the existence of mainframe computers and telephone cables has lead to the development of "electronic funds transfer systems", by which banks and corporations move numerical figures representing money from one location to another electronically. The actual cash involved in these millions of transactions is only physically moved once a month between the head offices of the chartered banks with the help of a centralized clearing house.

Bank accounts have become centralized, disk-based computer files that are changed directly by bank employees, or by account holders who use automated teller machines. The speed and convenience deriving from this banking revolution, however, are not without their harmful side effects.

It has been estimated that, since 1965, the total losses due to computer-related crimes have amounted to $600 million, although no one really knows for sure. One study has indicated that the average "take" from a computer-related theft is 43 times as much as from a traditional armed bank robbery. Yet these stories rarely appear in the newspaper or on television. The Criminal Code of Canada specifies up to ten years imprisonment for grand theft, but few suspects are ever charged. Often, the corporate victims fear the bad publicity that court appearances may cause.

One embezzler used a bank's computer to withdraw 20 or 30 cents at a time, at random, from several hundred chequing accounts. The money was then diverted into a dummy bank account which the embezzler had opened at the same bank. The criminal was careful never to divert money from any particular account more than three times a year.

The victims, the bank customers, often assumed the 30-cent difference was due to their own poor arithmetic or a service charge, or simply did not find it worthwhile to argue the point with the bank manager. As a result, little by little, the embezzler became rich.

Another method of electronic theft, called the **salami technique** (a little slice at a time), is almost invisible to both customers and bank personnel. This technique uses a modified computer program to truncate all bank interest calculations. For example, if interest owed to you amounts to $95.845, the computer transfers the $95.84 to your account, and the remaining $0.005 into a dummy account. The thief then patiently waits to collect the growing sum of money.

Computer theft has not been restricted to money. In the early 1970s, officials of the Pennsylvania Central Railroad were surprised to discover that 217 boxcars had disappeared. When U.S. Federal agents finally located them, the boxcars had been repainted and sold to another railway. Someone had been able to reroute the boxcars by providing the company's computer with false information.

In another case, a university student was charged with stealing $1 million worth of electronic equipment from a major telephone company. He had gained access to the company's computerized ordering service with a portable keyboard terminal. Unaware of the situation, the company's own trucks delivered the expensive equipment to open street manholes, where the thief pretended to be repairing underground cables. He then stored the equipment in a warehouse until a sale could be made.

"Our next speaker will talk on the subject of 'the pitfalls of electronic funds transfer systems'."

1. Some people think that computer-related theft is insignificant when compared to losses from ordinary crimes. Is this true? Explain.

2. Give one reason why the facts of computer crimes are generally not made public.

3. How is the "electronic thief" able to embezzle money from so many bank accounts and not get caught?

4. How did the boxcar theft occur?

Getting at the Issues

5. Suggest how an investigator might detect the "salami technique" of embezzlement.

6. Suppose the facts about computer frauds were reported regularly in the newspaper and on television. Explain one negative effect and one positive effect that these reports might have.

7. Explain who suffers when a bank is subject to "electronic theft".

8. What could individual customers do to reduce the number of computer-related crimes? Explain.

10.4 ROBOTS

"Hold it Ribly!" the executive called out. *"I have another parcel for the fourth floor."*

"Yes sir," came the response. Its mechanical rotor stopped and Ribly waited patiently while the executive found room for the package among those already stuffed into its parcel bin.

"OK, off you go," the executive said, and he returned to his office.

Its quiet whirring faded as the robot disappeared down the corridor toward its next delivery point.

The short story above indicates how robots can now be used for mail delivery in large office buildings. Robots are also designed to make and deliver coffee to people at their workstations. In factories, durable industrial robots are gaining popularity by doing such hazardous jobs as welding, spray painting, hot-oven work, and handling of dangerous chemicals, explosives, or nuclear material.

The next generation of robots may be the type designed specifically for home use. These **domestic robots** could provide companionship to children, teach, and do housework. Most likely, they will be programmed with a high level of intelligence, and have the ability to communicate easily in a spoken language.

The capacity of a computer to interact with children was demonstrated several years ago in a New York City hospital. A remote-controlled, interactive, toy robot had remarkable success in radically improving the condition of several autistic children. These are children who, for some reason, refuse to communicate with people, or even respond to the world around them. What amazed a number of psychiatrists was that the children's improvement occurred without traditional psychotherapy. The machine, by being able to talk, respond to touch, comment, explain, and draw pictures, helped the children to come out of their inner world and enjoy being with people.

CHECKING YOUR READING

1. Name two jobs that office robots can perform. Think of another job, not mentioned in the text, that they could also perform in office buildings.

2. Provide examples of jobs that industrial robots are designed to do.

3. What is a domestic robot? What things might it do for the people who own it?

4. Suggest two abilities that domestic robots probably will need.

Getting at the Issues

5. Why do you think that children like to communicate with robots?

6. Suggest some tasks, other than those already mentioned, that robots could assist in performing around the house.

7. Besides the two characteristics mentioned in the article, what other abilities would be helpful if they were programmed into a domestic robot?

8. Some people are genuinely concerned about robots being placed in offices and factories. Suggest some reasons why these people might be worried.

10.5 COMPUTER VIRUSES

A virus is a name for a class of programs that reproduce and infect other programs, analogous to the way a cold virus attacks the human body. Such programs, developed by anti-social and unethical people with technical computer skills, are potentially very costly to the owners of victimized computer systems. Particularly vulnerable are computer owners who use their modems to copy software provided by bulletin board services. Viruses are often hidden inside programs with attractive-sounding names, and once "triggered" into action by some key word or command, systematically begin to destroy the host software on a floppy disk or hard disk.

The potential for disaster is great when you consider the number of operations run by complex computer systems, such as the telephone system, electronic banking, military defence, air traffic control, and nuclear power stations. A Japanese terrorist group, the Red Brigade, specifically includes the destruction of computer systems as one of their objectives. On one occasion, they confused the Japanese computerized commuter train system so badly that a major city was paralyzed for several hours.

One form of virus, called a **worm program**, moves around randomly into any space it can reach. As it moves, it copies itself into the new space and leaves a trail of zeros, thereby destroying any original programs and data files. In less than a second, your entire disk can be corrupted with worm trails.

Another form of virus, appropriately called **Trojan Horse**, derives its name from the legendary giant, wooden horse that was used to hide a group of Greek soldiers. It was left as a gift to the Trojans, who hauled the horse inside their city. At night the soldiers came out of the horse and took control of the city of Troy. Today, a Trojan Horse virus is an apparently useful program that does things in addition to what it is advertised to do. For example, a program might provide a menu for your disk files, but also copy a virus onto your disk. Or it might be a password protection scheme that collects your password and stores it to permit access by an intruder at a later date.

Ironically, the first recorded use of a virus came from India, where a programmer used the concept as a protection scheme to prevent unauthorized copies of his software. Now, unfortunately, viruses are even considered by military intelligence as an effective way of disrupting an enemy's defence system prior to attack.

CHECKING YOUR READING

1. What is a virus?

2. Why are viruses considered to be potentially disastrous?

3. How does a worm program operate?

4. (a) What is a Trojan Horse?
   (b) Give an example of its application.

Getting at the Issues

5. Suppose a travel agency inadvertently copied a virus onto its disk while

using a bulletin board service. What harmful effects might the virus have?

6. What would you tell computer owners to do to protect themselves against virus attacks?

7. Suppose you are a courtroom judge and the following people have been found guilty by the jury. What punishment would you consider appropriate? Explain why in each case.
   (a) A university student who corrupted a military defence program;
   (b) A student who left a worm program on a bulletin board service, causing 400 people to lose their original software investments.

8. If you worked in military intelligence, what computer software owned by your enemy would you consider attacking? Why?

10.6 COMPUTERS AND THE COURTROOM

*D*ependence on computer systems can lead to some unusual shifts in attitude about who is responsible in certain situations. The impact of computers on people's views is illustrated in the following fictional civil cases.

Case One—Medical Diagnosis

Dr. T. Unger, a doctor in a large urban hospital, is being sued for malpractice. This is a situation in which negligence is suspected in the treatment of the patient.

During the court proceedings, it was revealed that Dr. Unger had relied on information from a computer terminal for treatment of the patient. The terminal provided hospital staff with access to a **medical diag-**

nosis program that was designed to make a diagnosis and recommend treatment on the basis of the patient's medical data. The system was thought to be reliable, since it had been used successfully for several years. "Therefore," the defendant's lawyer argued, "the doctor is not the one who is at fault, the computer is."

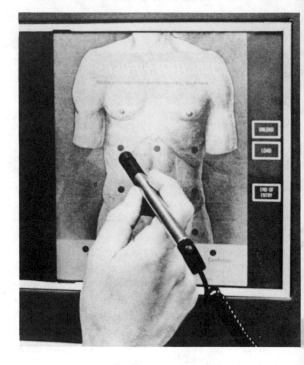

Case One Questions

1. What is a medical diagnosis program?

2. Why does a lawyer think that the doctor is not guilty of malpractice?

3. In your opinion, who is at fault—the doctor or the computer? Explain.

4. Suppose a politician claimed that a decision that resulted in a $100 million loss to the country was actually due to a faulty program in a large computer. What similarity is there between this situation and the lawyer's argument for the doctor? Why would this trend be dangerous for the public?

Case Two—Educational Software

The parents of a child filed a lawsuit against a computer software company that had provided educational diskettes for the child's home computer. The child's parents claimed that she had spent some five hours a week during her preschool year studying the information on the diskettes. At the time, the child appeared bright and alert.

When the child was enrolled in grade one, however, she received very poor marks, and seemed to lack the ability to understand material suitable for the average student. Both the school principal and the classroom teacher suggested that the child's inability to learn may have been caused by improper teaching techniques used by the computer software company.

Case Two Questions

1. Why are the parents suing the computer software company?

2. What makes the parents think that their child is not of below-average intelligence?

3. Besides the computer software company, who else might be at fault? Give reasons.

4. Do you think that a child who enjoys interacting with a microcomputer will automatically succeed in school? Explain. What would you recommend to the parents to help the child?

10.7 ENHANCED HUMAN INTELLIGENCE

Several years ago a fictional television hero called the Six Million Dollar Man was popular, and more recently a movie called *Robocop* contained a similar type of man-machine combination. Such a combination is described as a "cyborg", although many writers have adopted the less harsh term "bionic". A **cyborg** is a person who is partly mechanical and partly organic. Both sections of the body can be controlled by the brain.

There are actually hundreds of **bionic people** in our society. They are patients who have been fitted with electronic eyes, hearing implants, touch-sensitive skin, battery-powered pacemakers, and artificial limbs. These adaptations of the human body require that both the brain and the body's chemical defences accept the foreign object as natural.

The next step in this man-machine evolution may be a tiny computer chip connected to the brain. Such miniature circuits could enhance human intelligence by providing additional memory, or ultra-high-speed processing areas. Imagine the possibilities for gaining "instant knowledge" by implanting a memory circuit containing millions of facts and figures into the brain. A human being could, for the first time, have immediate access to the entire storehouse of human knowledge.

One argument against implanted circuits is that this type of processing and memory capability could just as easily be carried around in the form of a powerful pocket computer.

Other opponents argue that the trend toward more durable and efficient mechanical parts in our body may change the way in which we view ourselves. Instead of considering humans to be valuable living organisms, we might begin to treat each other as merely stylish entities with disposable, replaceable human parts.

CHECKING YOUR READING

1. Define "cyborg". To what other computer-related term mentioned in Chapter 8 is the word cyborg related?

2. Do bionic people really exist? Explain.

3. What may be the next step in this man-machine evolution?

4. What other invention may be used instead of implants? Suggest some capabilities that such an invention should have for it to be useful.

Getting at the Issues

5. Would there be any advantage in having an implanted computer, as opposed to a pocket computer? Explain.

6. In your opinion, should medical engineers continue to experiment with enhanced human intelligence? Explain.

7. Why would the viewpoint that "People may be treated as stylish entities with disposable human parts" be considered a poor outcome of the new technologies?

8. Suppose that you had the opportunity to triple your factual knowledge, and to be able to multiply ten-digit numbers in your head with ease. Would you consider having a circuit implanted to gain that ability?

10.8 THE CONTROLLED SOCIETY

*T*he most persistent fear that writers display in their works featuring computers is also the one most likely to come true: the advent of a society in which computer systems are used to direct and control the population. Naturally, this type of society experiences a loss of privacy and freedom of expression.

Such a fear is reflected repeatedly in the theme or setting of science fiction novels. Sometimes it is the governments that misuse computers to produce distorted societies, such as those depicted in *Robocop*, *The Running Man*, and *Logan's Run*. In other novels, it is the computers themselves that dictate how people are to behave, live, or die. Notable examples include *The Forbin Project*, *2001: A Space Odyssey*, and *Vulcan's Hammer*.

At present, governments have countless information data banks containing statistics on individual citizens, and a growing number of interconnecting computer networks. These data banks include information on taxes, school achievement, criminal records, medical history, births, deaths, marriages, divorces, and records of all financial transactions and bank accounts.

If people were required to carry a plastic identification card at all times, government agencies could determine where you shopped, ate lunch, or went on vacation, which airline you used, and in which hotel you slept. In fact, the "electronic funds transfer system" recommended by computer companies (the use of the plastic bank debit card to pay for everything) is an excellent way to painlessly create such a society. Each time you purchase an item, you leave an electronic trail.

Ironically, it will probably not be a wicked dictatorial government that imposes such a system, but rather a naive, passive population that eagerly embraces a technology without considering the consequences.

1. Describe the fear that many writers have about computers.

2. What do governments already have that would contribute towards a more controlled society?

3. How would a compulsory plastic identification card help suspicious government agencies?

4. Explain the concept of an "electronic funds transfer system".

Getting at the Issues

5. Why would writers, in particular, fear a computer-controlled society? Who else would suffer? Explain.

6. Explain the meaning of the last paragraph in the article, in your own words.

7. Do you believe what was stated in the last paragraph? Give reasons.

8. Suggest some additional ways, not mentioned in the article, by which governments could use computers to gain greater control over their citizens.

*T*he phrase controversial issues here refers to computer applications that have both positive and negative effects on people. The applications may involve economic, legal, or philosophical issues that people cannot agree upon or resolve.

Research into artificial intelligence, for example, is making progress in improving machine intelligence that will permit computers and robots to make decisions on their own without human assistance. Even though such research has many useful applications, many people fear the ultimate consequences of giving up decision-making control to machines.

Electronic transfers representing money transactions between financial institutions and corporations have become commonplace. Customers can transfer money from one account to another and deposit and withdraw funds in seconds using automated teller terminals.

One unfortunate side-effect of this electronic funds transfer system is the misuse of the technology to embezzle or steal money. The silent stealth of crooks using the salami technique or other programming gimmicks to remove funds from people's accounts represents the new breed of bank robber—the computer thief.

Increased dependence on computer systems can lead to some unusual shifts in attitudes about responsibility. Can a doctor who relied on a computer-generated diagnosis of a patient (who subsequently died) legally shift the blame to the computer or programmer?

Movies, such as *Robocop*, illustrate the potential of medical technology to rebuild a human being who has suffered massive injuries with artificial parts. This trend, however, raises doubts about how we would view such people, known as cyborgs. Would they be more or less human? Can they be considered disposable when their usefulness is ended? Could this concept be applied to metallic-enhanced soldiers?

The strongest fear most writers have about computers is of their political use to control a population through electronic surveillance and through restrictions on an individual's rights and freedoms.

"You mean it's going to take two of those just to replace Hartwell?"

artificial intelligence	controlled society	medical diagnosis program	Trojan Horse
bionic person	cyborg		Turing Test
computer theft	domestic robots	salami technique	worm program

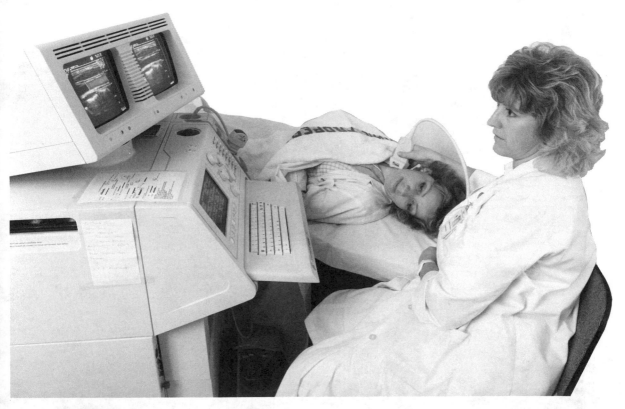

Figure 10.1 Doctors are coming to increasingly rely on computers for assistance in diagnosing patient problems.

Courtesy of Credit Valley Hospital

Chapter 11

THE FUTURE

THE FUTURE
THE FUTURE

66 There are many possible futures. An intelligent society will aim not just for the most promising technological future, but also for the one that will be the most acceptable for its citizens. **99**

OBJECTIVES

By the end of this chapter, you will be able to:

1 Define the following terms: firmware, optical fibre, communication satellites, von Neumann bottleneck, parallel processing, symmetric parallel processing, asymmetric parallel processing, programming shell;

2 Describe some likely changes in computer hardware and software in the next decade;

3 Predict some possible future developments in computers from the year 2000 to 2015;

4 Describe some commercial computer innovations developed in Canada.

WORKING IN THE WORLD OF COMPUTERS

Astronaut
uses computerized guidance controls and information systems on board space shuttles

Communication Expert
understands the operation of satellite and microwave tower technology

CD-ROM Author
uses the skills of an author and a moviemaker to create 54 000 frames of information for an optical disk

Electronic Cartographer
creates interactive maps with zoom capability for use in cars, offices, and homes

Electronic Publisher
assembles text, pictures, and movies onto CD-ROM disks for distribution

Electronic Journalist
collects news stories and pictures for electronic transmission to home terminals

Microprocessor Engineer
designs MPU chips for use in computers and consumer products

Microtechnologist
specializes in the design and use of computer circuits and miniature gears

Political Activist
organizes people to lobby and protest against computer applications that have a negative impact on society

Video Service Developer
organizes a company to provide services to home video data systems

11.1 INTRODUCTION

Computers and related communication technologies are continuously being improved to meet people's rising expectations. About every five and a half years, a new generation of computers is introduced, which usually displays an improvement in speed and reliability by a factor of ten and an increase in memory capacity by a factor of 20. By the year 2015, the computer systems now in use will seem as crude and unsophisticated as the Wright brothers' first airplane.

This chapter is concerned with predictable short- and long-term trends in areas related to computers. Topics include hardware, software, communication networks, and Canadian development, as well as some predictions of directions in which computer applications will go over the next 20 years.

11.2 HARDWARE TRENDS

*I*n the future, mass storage of information will be accomplished with CD-ROM disks. These are devices that store pictures, sound, and text on round metal platters etched by varying laser light patterns. CD-ROMs, currently popular for recording music, have also become a popular medium for archiving large volumes of information, such as encyclopedias, reference books, and company product manuals. Although currently the computer search time can be as long as five seconds, compared to 10 milliseconds for some hard disks, laser disks are a better storage medium for pictures and sound. Even slides and movies can be shown with a CD-ROM system.

Internal Memory

*I*n 1978, the amount of main memory in a microcomputer was 64 K. This was limited by the size of the microprocessor unit (MPU), which determines how much memory can be directly accessed. As microprocessor chips have increased in size, so has the amount of memory they can control. Current microcomputers contain one or two million bytes of main memory and the trend is toward even greater capacity.

Addressable Main Memory

COMPARATIVE SIZE OF MPU	ADDRESSABLE RAM MEMORY
8-bit	64 000 bytes
16-bit	640 000 bytes
32-bit	16 000 000 bytes

Present-day semiconductor devices may give way to three-dimensional **memory cubes**. In other words, a cube of material will be filled with electronic circuits, as opposed to today's two-dimensional electronics that are confined to the flat surface of a chip.

Microprocessors

*M*ost computers today contain only one processor (one MPU chip). This presents a problem in networked computer systems in which several terminals share a common printer and a hard disk, or on individual microcomputers that run software that requires numerous calculations, such as three-dimensional drawing programs, desktop publishing programs, and animation software. In those applications, a single microprocessor cannot keep up with the volume of information to be processed, which slows down the application considerably.

This problem, called the **von Neumann Bottleneck**, is being resolved. Most computers in the future will use multiple processors. When several MPUs operate together to process a set of instructions, the process is called **parallel processing**. There are two approaches to configuring more than one processor on the motherboard—the symmetric approach and the asymmetric approach

Symmetric Parallel Processing

*T*he symmetric approach to multiple-processor systems requires that each processor have an equal role, and equal access to all parts of the computer. The Compaq SystemPro uses this design to allow each of its two processors to share an equal amount of the workload. The following diagram illustrates how three MPUs operating simultaneously share access to both main memory and the input/output channel that connects the motherboard to the computer's peripherals.

Asymmetric Parallel Processing

*I*n the asymmetric approach to multiple-processor systems, a "master" processor assigns specific duties to its "slave" processors, each of which looks after a specific peripheral. One of the slave processors might be assigned to look after the screen, while another might be assigned printer duties or sound generation.

Some of the low-end microcomputers were the first to incorporate this design, mostly because their original 8-bit processors were too slow to handle sound, graphics, and regular processing all at the same time. Commodore's C-64 and Amiga models, and some Atari microcomputers use three separate microprocessors: one controls the screen, one controls the sound, and another acts as the clearing house for all computer traffic. These computers tend to be unrivaled for dazzling three-dimensional graphics and multi-channel sound. The following diagram illustrates how the master processor directs the activities of its slave processors.

Symmetric Parallel Processing

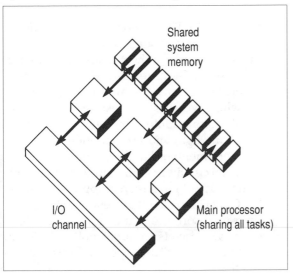

Asymmetric Parallel Processing

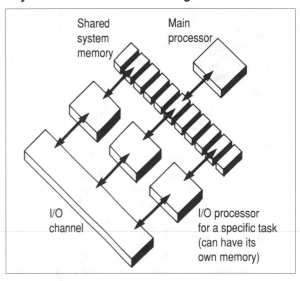

Faster and More Powerful MPUs

*T*here are two major manufacturers that largely control the North American market for microprocessors. Motorola Corporation provides MPUs for Macintosh, NeXT, and Sun microcomputers, and Intel Corporation provides MPUs for Compaq, Dell, and IBM microcomputers. Both manufacturers have been increasing the capabilities and clock speeds of their products about every two to three years. The following chart illustrates the announced trends for Intel.

Intel Microprocessor Development

MPU MODEL	YEAR	NUMBER OF TRANSISTORS	SPEED	MILLIONS OF INSTRUCTIONS PROCESSED/s	APPLICATIONS
80486	1990	1.2 million	33 MHz	15 MIPS	Desktop publishing Networking
80586	1993	5 million	75 MHz	250 MIPS	Animation 3-D graphics
80786	1999	20 million	200 MHz	2000 MIPS	Full-motion video Speech recognition

Super-computers

*S*everal thousand microprocessors can also be set up to operate as one powerful main unit, particularly in some of the high-speed supercomputers. One attempt to simultaneously harness the power of 32 000 MPUs is a cube-shaped processor unit called the "Connection Machine" that processes eight billion operations per second. Another model being developed for the military by the same company (Thinking Machines Inc.) is aiming for a speed record of one trillion operations per second!

Unfortunately, some supercomputers with parallel processors cannot run existing software. They need special instructions by which they divide a problem into many parts and work on them before assembling the answer. They are, however, well-suited to problems such as multiple-point map drawing, weather forecasting, translating satellite signals into complete pictures, and analyzing light and wave motions.

Experimenters have discovered that as electrical circuits are miniaturized, they tend to heat up. Often supercomputers, such as the Cray Computer, have elaborate cooling units to absorb the tremendous heat. Interestingly, if circuits are supercooled, the logic circuits increase their performance about 100 times.

11.3 SOFTWARE TRENDS

*I*n the future, computer technology will make much greater use of **firmware**. Firmware refers to the instructions that are permanently stored on the circuit boards inside the computer system by the manufacturer. As the cost of internal memory decreases, manufacturers will begin to store more and more software in non-erasable ROM (Read Only Memory) chips, rather than keep the programs on disk. Programs such as operating systems (system BIOS), disk and monitor controllers, language processors, and common utilities will become standard firmware in every new computer. This will make computers less complicated to operate and decrease the need for large amounts of external storage.

Computer Languages

*A*t present, computers generally operate with high-level languages that require a fairly extensive training program for potential users. FORTRAN, COBOL, BASIC, Pascal, and Turing are of this nature. Modern COBOL, the most widely used programming language for business applications, and BASIC, the most popular home computer language, are both very similar in format to their first versions of some 20 years ago.

It has been estimated that a typical industrial programmer produces only eight to ten debugged lines of code per day. Although structured design and structured programming are aimed at improving productivity, there is still much improvement to be made. The current trend is to provide a **programming shell**, such as ALICE BASIC or ALICE Pascal, which automatically sets up the top and bottom commands for repetition and selection structures, and shows indentation levels on the screen as the programmer enters the code.

One of the challenges associated with a career in programming is keeping one's skills updated over time. The knowledge and skills acquired by programmers are almost completely obsolete within ten years. When you consider the dramatic changes in hardware design, operating systems, and programming techniques that occurred during the past decade, it is obvious that a continuous upgrading of skills becomes necessary. A programmer who graduated from university 15 years ago, for example, would not have been trained in(or even heard of) microcomputers, laptops, pocket computers, optical disks, parallel processing, modems, multi-tasking, graphical user interfaces (such as Microsoft Windows), three-dimensional graphic software, or structured programming.

As research into artificial intelligence continues, there will be a tendency for computers to respond to human language instructions, and voice-activated systems will become more common.

11.4 COMMUNICATION NETWORKS

*I*t is not just the technology that will change: the way we "normally" do things will change too. People will rely, to a greater degree, on information networks that will move information from one part of the world to another. All forms of communication media will be actively involved in the transmission of computer data. These media include telephone lines, coaxial cable, microwave towers, and orbiting satellites.

Optical fibre, hair-thin glass strands along which laser light can travel, will slowly replace coaxial cable. A single strand of optical fibre can transmit 20 times the data that an ordinary copper wire can carry, and is immune to normal electromagnetic

Figure
11.2

These super-fine strands of optical fibre are more efficient data carriers than the old, bulky coaxial cable they are replacing.

Courtesy of Bell Labs

Figure
11.3

Canada is one of the world's leading suppliers of communication satellites.

Courtesy of NASA

disturbances such as lightning or atomic blasts.

Three **communication satellites** are all that would be needed to completely "wrap" the world in an information network. Their stationary orbits would keep them above the same points on earth at all times. The satellites could then be used to "bounce" messages from one ground station to another. Some day it may be a common occurrence, for example, for a student living in Edmonton to access a computer data base located in London, England, in order to complete a research paper.

The Canadian communications idea innovator, Marshall McLuhan, referred to this system of linking people worldwide through an electronic network as a trend towards a "global village". In the future, people from other continents may become as familiar to us as our next-door neighbours.

11.5 ADAPTING TO AN INFORMATION-RICH SOCIETY

New consumer products and services will arise as a result of the combination of old technologies. For instance, telephone lines, computers, and photocopiers have combined to enable the introduction of fax machine technology, which permits the transmission of pictures and text over great distances.

In an information-rich society, an increasing amount of paper-related information could be electronically transmitted. Cable services could deliver electronic mail and newspapers to your computer monitor.

There would be less need for business travel as access to information became more readily available. Office work could be accomplished through a computer terminal located in the home. Shopping could be done by viewing the latest selections on a video screen, then entering requests to the store's computer by means of a home terminal keyboard.

11.6 HIDDEN HELPERS

Microprocessor chips will be built into most future electronic devices. These **dedicated processors**, so called because they operate on a fixed set of instructions, will improve the reliability and accuracy of most devices, such as radio receivers, televisions, CD-ROM player/recorders, toys, clocks, microwave ovens, refrigerators, and automobile carburetors.

The future trend in automobile design will be to have a computer terminal built into the dashboard, which will provide drivers with map references, suggested routes to avoid traffic congestion, gas consump-

tion ratings, compass directions, and outside weather readings.

It will also be common for new suburban homes to have built-in microprocessors that control the environment. They will automatically control the heating in the winter and air-conditioning in the summer.

Generally, dedicated processor circuits are hidden from view; the user is unaware of their operation. The influence of computers in the home will be more apparent whenever there is the addition of a personal microcomputer or a home terminal. A personal microcomputer can be used for entertainment, office work, or household management. The addition of a modem permits people to access information bulletin boards outside the home.

Figure 11.4 Computerized, in-dash "vehicle information systems" provide the driver with information such as fuel level, outside temperature, and fastest route.

Courtesy of General Motors Canada Ltd.

*S*everal Canadian companies are involved in high-tech hardware and software ventures that are being marketed both in domestic and international markets.

Home Video Data System

*B*ell Canada has launched a home video data system in Montreal and Toronto called ALEX. Access to the system is available in two ways: through your own microcomputer, Bell software, and a 1200-bit or 2400-bit modem, or with a terminal available from Bell at a monthly rental fee. In addition, there is a per-minute charge that varies depending on the service used.

By keying words into a terminal connected to ALEX, the user can tap into any of 300 services, including ones that make airplane reservations, or provide financial information, current events updates, weather forecasts, or sports updates. The user rents or purchases the terminal, and also pays a monthly flat rate plus an additional per-minute charge.

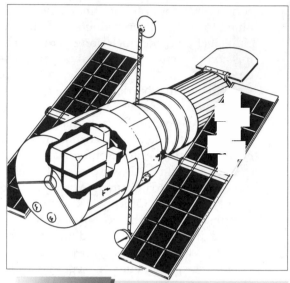

Figure 11.6 The Hubble space telescope, launched in 1990, is powered by solar cell panels, and is directed outward from earth to study our solar system.

Figure 11.5 The "ALEX" network gives customers instant access to 300 services, including banking, airline reservations, and tickets for special events, through a rented computer terminal in their home.

Courtesy of Bell Canada

Pictures from the Hubble Space Telescope

A Canadian software company called Alias Research Inc. (Toronto) wrote the program that translates the signals sent back to earth from the orbiting Hubble Space Telescope into pictures. The software runs on multiple VAX computers (from Digital Equipment Corporation) located in Baltimore.

Alias made its reputation in three-dimensional imaging in the field of motion picture animation by providing the special effects software for Lucasfilm Inc. The filmmaker used the software to create the image of a giant water worm in the academy-award-winning film *The Abyss*. In addition, General Motors, Honda, Volvo, BMW, Mitsubishi, and Volkswagen use Alias software for producing three-dimensional automobile designs.

First Canadian-made Super-computer

*A*n Edmonton-based firm called Myrias Research Corp. designs and builds super-computers. Model SPS-2, the first Canadian-built supercomputer, took six years to develop and uses a parallel processing design. Myrias' units, which are marketed at a price of $1 million, have been sold to the Alberta Research Council for developing oil exploration programs, and to the U.S. Department of Defense for confidential military applications.

Silicon Valley North

*B*ecause of the number of high-tech computer firms established in the Ottawa valley, this area has been dubbed "Silicon Valley North" in comparison to a similar cluster of computer companies in California. Included in the Ottawa region are the developers of a successful illustration program called *Corel Draw* (Corel Corporation), the developers of the *QNX* operating system (used on ICON microcomputers), a circuit board manufacturer (Digital Equipment), and a manufacturer of telephone circuit boards.

World-Famous University Research

*T*wo Canadian universities have become famous for their innovative approaches in the field of computers. The University of Alberta has several people working on the interaction between computer software and optical disks. A program that teaches medical students, for example, includes slides and continuous movie segments and a sound track selected from the optical disk. Pictures can overlay text, or be placed next to the text on the screen.

Waterloo University trains students to develop operating systems, structured languages, programming environments, and computer applications. Several spin-off companies, run by Waterloo graduates, develop manuals, provide training, and offer the software for sale. Sample products include WATCOM BASIC, Pascal, WATFILE, and WATCOM Workbench for both microcomputers and mainframe computer systems.

11.8 LOOKING INTO THE FUTURE

*F*orecasting the future is at best a risky venture. Computer futurists must consider not only the types of hardware that will be available, but also the extent to which a society will be willing to accept a particular computer application.

Although many computer developments are technically possible, not all of them are socially desirable. Just because a manufacturer discovers a new use for a computer, it does not automatically follow that society must accept that particular application.

Many things prevent technical innovations from being adopted by society. For example, if politicians were convinced that industrial robots would lead to massive unemployment, laws might be legislated to prohibit their widespread use. If citizens saw electronic funds transfer systems as being a threat to their future privacy because of the possibility of electronic surveillance, that computer application might not be fully used.

Consider the following chart entitled *Future Computer Developments*. It projects possible technical achievements and applications from the year 1995 to the year 2010. All achievements are given at least a 50% chance of becoming commonplace by a particular year. The approximate years in which developments are expected to occur are indicated along the bottom axis. The higher the item appears relative to the left-hand column, the greater the probability it has of becoming commonplace.

Future Computer Developments

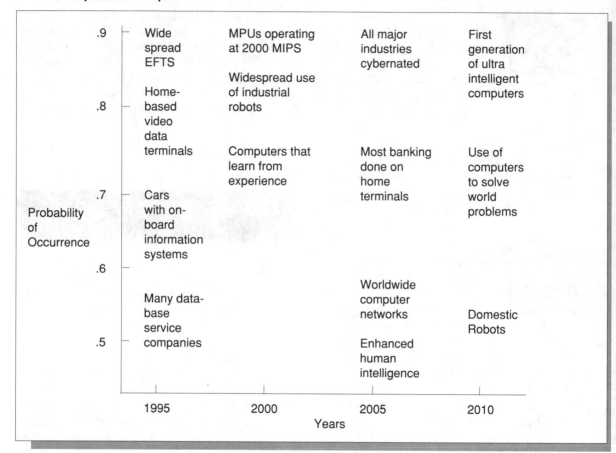

Probability of Occurrence	1995	2000	2005	2010
.9	Wide spread EFTS	MPUs operating at 2000 MIPS	All major industries cybernated	First generation of ultra intelligent computers
.8	Home-based video data terminals	Widespread use of industrial robots		
.7	Cars with on-board information systems	Computers that learn from experience	Most banking done on home terminals	Use of computers to solve world problems
.6			Worldwide computer networks	
.5	Many data-base service companies		Enhanced human intelligence	Domestic Robots

Years

11.9 SMART SKIN

*A*t the University of Pisa, an Italian engineer named Danilo De Rossi has developed an artifical skin for robots. The skin, no thicker than a dime, is composed of layers of rubber, water-swollen gel, and electrodes. This skin may eventually give robots the sense of touch, which is important to their ability to handle objects. They could distinguish between a block of steel and an egg, for instance, and could then apply appropriate pressure to each. The artifical skin is even capable of feeling the tug from a piece of sticky tape.

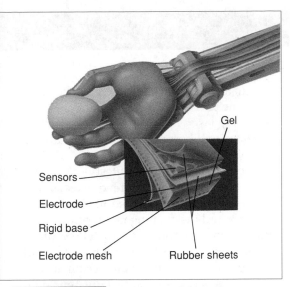

Artificial skin represents one of the components leading towards the development of a completely mobile, intelligent robot for office and industrial use by the year 2010.

11.10 INDUSTRIAL ROBOTS: THE NEW BLUE COLLAR WORKERS

North American and Japanese manufacturers have already begun to use stationary industrial robots to assemble cars, toys, calculators, and computers, and operate entire processing, chemical, and steel plants. Company officials have discovered that reprogrammable robots make excellent workers. They do not sleep, take coffee breaks, or require vacations or retirement benefits.

The problem with using industrial robots on assembly lines is that they displace human workers. Some forecasters have predicted a 25% to 50% reduction in the size of the work force in assembly plant operations every ten years due to this type of technological displacement. By the year 2005, most Canadian assembly line plants may be cybernated and with very few human labourers. What will people do?

One solution may be to reduce the number of hours a person works each week. The standard work week may be reduced to four days instead of five. Also, people may be encouraged to retire at 55 instead of 65. These two changes would spread the available work among more people.

To provide retirement benefits for those who retire early, and be able to pay unemployment benefits to those people who are not working, the company could be required to pay a tax for using robots.

Whatever solutions may be found, the widespread use of industrial robots will create a society profoundly different from the one in which we now live. Human beings may become obsolete as workers on assembly lines. All jobs in this sector may be of the white collar variety—office work, sales, and jobs in various service industries. Fortunately, there are more jobs created by individual ventures in Canada than there are people employed at the big factories. For the unskilled, blue collar factory workers who become displaced by technology, however, there will be difficult years requiring retraining, relocation, and family hardship.

Although many future computer developments are technically possible, not all developments may be socially desirable. Desirable or not, however, when people believe that the adoption of a certain technology is inevitable, that belief can set the stage for a self-fulfilling prophecy. Even though privacy, freedom, and dignity are challenged, individuals may feel powerless to intervene.

It is important, therefore, that computer scientists, educators, industrialists, politicians, and those studying computer systems raise two questions whenever they consider new computer developments. They should not only ask "Is it technically possible?" but also, "Is it socially desirable?"

Computer technology rapidly becomes obsolete as new innovations replace the old. Most of the changes have occurred with the hardware devices and computer circuitry. There is a general trend towards faster, more accurate computers with greater memory capacity.

Computer languages have changed relatively little over the past 30 years. They still remain complex and difficult to learn. For widespread adoption, computer devices will have to respond to natural language instructions that require little or no programming experience by the user. To achieve this, much of the operating system software in the future may be in the form of stored firmware.

Not just the technology will change. People will rely, to a greater degree, on

information networks to move information from one part of the world to another. Optical fibre, laser light, and communication satellites will become the common carriers of global information.

People will adapt their lifestyles to an information-rich society. Video screens and printers may be substituted for home mail delivery and the evening newspaper. Information will be conveyed to fellow office workers by modem just as easily as it would be in person. Home computer terminals will reduce the necessity for the daily, time-consuming, and often frustrating ritual of travelling to work.

Although many future computer developments are technically possible, not all of them are socially desirable. When people believe that the adoption of a technology is inevitable, however, it becomes a self-fulfilling prophecy. Even though privacy, freedom, and dignity may be threatened, individuals will feel powerless to oppose the change.

It is important, therefore, that computer scientists, industrialists, politicians, and those studying computer systems consider two things about new computer developments. They should not only ask "Is it possible?" but also, perhaps more important, "Is it socially desirable?"

asymmetric parallel processing

communication satellite

dedicated processor

firmware

memory cubes

optical fibre

parallel processing

programming shell

symmetric parallel processing

von Neumann bottleneck

CHECKING YOUR READING

*T*hese are general questions that may require factual recall, reading comprehension, and some application of the knowledge gained from this chapter.

Introduction

1. (a) How often does a new generation of computers get introduced?
    (b) What improvements in speed and memory capacity are made with each new generation?

Hardware Trends

2. (a) What type of auxiliary storage device will become increasingly popular in the future?
    (b) Why is this storage medium better than existing media?

3. What trend has lead to increased capacity in computers' main memories?

4. (a) What is the "von Neumann bottleneck"?
    (b) What may remove that problem?

5. Explain "parallel processing".

6. Explain the difference between symmetric parallel processing and asymmetric parallel processing.

Software Trends

7. What will be the positive results of increased use of firmware in computers?

8. How efficient is the average industrial programmer?

9. What is a programming shell?

10. What is one of the challenges of a programming career?

Communication Networks

11. List four media that will be used in the transmission of computer data.

12. What are the advantages of using "optical fibres" in computer networks?

13. Explain how only a few satellites are needed to "wrap" the entire world in an information network.

Adapting to an Information-Rich Society

14. Why might there be less morning traffic on the roads in the future?

Hidden Helpers

15. What new trend in automobiles involves the use of computers?

16. What role might "dedicated processors" play in new suburban homes?

Canadian Computer Innovations

17. What is a home video data system? What is it for?

18. Describe two other notable Canadian achievements in the field of computers.

Looking into the Future

19. List three items from the *Future Computer Developments* chart that will have a very high possibility of occurring by the year 2010. List one item that, in your opinion, will not occur, and explain why.

Smart Skin

20. How is a new development in Italy contributing to the trend towards mobile, intelligent robots?

Industrial Robots: The New Blue Collar Worker

21. (a) What is the problem with industrial robots?
    (b) Suggest three things that might be done to reduce the problem.

22. What is meant by "You should not only ask is it technically possible, but also is it socially acceptable"?

*T*hese questions assume an understanding of the material presented in the chapter, and provide new situations which may require evaluation, analysis, or application of that knowledge.

1. Suppose that you were given the task of designing a microcomputer for the typical Canadian home. What features would you include to make it easy to operate and acceptable to even those families who have little knowledge of computers?

2. In what way does Marshall McLuhan's description of the world as a "global village" seem an appropriate term for the world of the future?

3. Suppose scientists have sent a communication satellite into orbit around the earth. The scientists want the satellite to remain above the same point on the earth at all times so they can "bounce" messages off it. How can this be accomplished, if the earth keeps rotating every 24 hours?

4. Many people believe that the widespread use of industrial robots will cause massive unemployment among blue collar workers. In your opinion, what effects would the widespread use of *domestic robots* (robots in the home) have on society? Give reasons.

5. The *Future Computer Developments* chart shows the "use of computers to solve world problems" as a possible application by the year 2010. Describe several world problems which, in your opinion, computers could be used to solve. Explain why.

6. Obviously, the *Future Computer Developments* chart is incomplete. Many possible items were omitted. Suggest some additional developments that may occur. Classify your suggestions as either "high" or "low" probability.

7. If you had complete control of society today, what would you do to prevent the high unemployment predicted as a result of the widespread use of industrial robots? Why are similar steps not being taken by our society?

8. Draw a two-column chart that illustrates several advantages and disadvantages of allowing networks of electronic funds transfer systems to operate in our country.

1. A Science Fiction Story

Plan and write a science fiction story (use a word-processing program) using computers or robots as characters, or as part of the story's setting. In your plan, consider the possible future computer developments that you could include to add realism to your story. Double space the output, and make the story about two or three pages in length. Cover with a computer-generated title page.

2. Inventing Possible Futures

Futurists often use a technique called a scenario. A scenario is a description of a possible event, such as how the world might appear in the year 2015. Use either a positive or negative viewpoint to describe how you think the world will appear at that time. Include computers as part of the scenario. Double space the output and make your scenario two or three pages in length. Cover with a computer-generated title page.

UNIT 4 COMPUTER PROGRAMMING

This four-chapter unit focuses on computer programming. The first three chapters provide instruction on the three fundamental structures of programming in the popular interpretive computer language, BASIC. The last chapter introduces the widely used commercial compiler, Turbo Pascal. The unit's main aim is to provide the students with the ability to teach the computer to perform new tasks.

The three BASIC chapters are intentionally not computer-specific, to permit the instructor to teach the topics with any available BASIC interpreter (including Applesoft BASIC, Commodore BASIC, IBM BASIC, and GWBASIC), on any microcomputer.

Because WATCOM BASIC differs dramatically in program structures, the chapters on repetition and selection structures are each divided in half to permit users to teach the topics in either traditional or WATCOM BASIC with equal ease.

Chapter 12

SIMPLE SEQUENTIAL STRUCTURES

❝ A wise programmer plans on paper before approaching the keyboard. ❞

OBJECTIVES

By the end of this chapter, you will be able to:

1 Define the following programming terms: immediate mode, programming mode, data, variables, programmer comments, assignment statement, batch-style data entry, interactive data capture, prompt, response, end user, user friendly, library functions, reserved words;

2 Use the following BASIC system commands: RUN, LIST, SAVE, LOAD, and NEW;

3 Use the following BASIC programming commands: REMARK, PRINT, LET, READ, DATA, TAB, INPUT, and INTEGER;

4 Use arithmetic operators to perform calculations in programs;

5 Manipulate information horizontally and vertically on the screen;

6 Design programs with any one of three different styles of data entry: assignment statements, batch-style data entry, and interactive data entry.

WORKING IN THE WORLD OF COMPUTERS

Computer Consultant
advises businesses on which hardware and software to purchase

Computer Teacher
teaches computer languages and problem-solving strategies to students

Freelance Programmer
writes and sells computer software from his or her home to commercial software com-panies

Games Designer
designs and codes games for the software entertainment market

Junior Programmer
works as part of a design team in a large company

Documentor
writes user manuals to accompany software packages

Programming Systems Analyst
analyzes clients' needs and writes specific software to answer them

Robot Programmer
writes programs for robots to follow

Senior Programmer
manages a design team that writes programs for a large company

12.1 INTRODUCTION

*S*ome people prefer to have greater control over the computer than a pre-designed spreadsheet or data-base program might allow. One option is to learn the skills of the people who wrote the software in the first place. The process of writing software is referred to as programming.

This is an introductory chapter on computer programming in a computer language designed for beginners, called BASIC. This section, the first of three chapters, introduces the easiest of three essential structures in programming, **Simple Sequential Structures**, or what some people call "straight-line programming". In this type of structure, the flow of movement through the instruction set is from top to bottom without any lines being repeated, or without any logical decisions being made by the computer.

Typical problems that can be solved with a sequential structure might concentrate on inputting values, performing calculations, and presenting the answer on the screen or as a printout in a neat and readable manner. This pattern of problem solving can be generalized to a simple sequence of INPUT, PROCESSING, and OUTPUT.

12.2 THE BASIC LANGUAGE

*B*ASIC is currently the most popular language for table-top and lap-model computers. Developed by John Kemeny and Thomas Kurtz at Dartmouth College in 1965, it provides an introductory language for hobbyists, professional programmers, and educators.

BASIC is an acronym; that is, a word formed from the first letters of other words, which in this case stands for "Beginners' All-purpose Symbolic Instruction Code". BASIC is widely used with microcomputers and comes in several versions, which means that different models of computers use slightly different commands to perform the same tasks. For this reason, instructions written on one microcomputer may not necessarily run on another model of microcomputer. This chapter makes reference to several versions of the BASIC computer language, including Applesoft BASIC, Commodore BASIC, IBM BASIC, Tandy BASIC, GW BASIC, and WATCOM BASIC.

12.3 ELEMENTS OF A COMPUTER PROGRAM

A **computer program** is a set of instructions that causes the computer to perform certain tasks. The person who plans, writes, and corrects programs for a computer is called a **programmer**.

A computer program usually contains three components: some programmer comments, a set of instructions, and some data (although not all programs need data).

Programmer comments are phrases or sentences inserted into the program to make it easier for a user to understand. They are preceded by a REMARK command, and are ignored when the program is executed. In all versions of BASIC, the abbreviation REM can be substituted, and in some versions of BASIC, the exclamation symbol (!) can be substituted for the REMARK command.

Comments may include a program title, the programmer's identification (student's name and period, for example), the date of the program's completion, and various remarks placed throughout the program to aid the programmer or some other user in interpreting what the various groups of commands are designed to achieve. Sepa-

rating groups of related statements from the rest of the program with spaces and programmer comments is very important when writing computer programs. It makes a program easier to read and modify, if something needs to be altered later on.

Instructions are statements that the computer understands that cause it to perform some type of action. Instructions may include commands, such as "READ", or "PRINT", or longer phrases that require the computer to continue acting until certain conditions are met.

Data can refer to values used in calculations, such as subject marks used to calculate your term average at school. Data can also refer to words, such as names and addresses, that a computer can manipulate.

12.4 GETTING STARTED

*M*ost versions of BASIC require a line number at the beginning of each statement. This helps the computer keep instructions in the proper sequence. Notice that the line numbers in the programs in this text increase at intervals of ten at a time. Leaving sufficient intervals between line numbers helps programmers to modify or to make corrections in computer programs by allowing the insertion of additional lines, in between the existing lines, if required.

```
10 PRINT "COMPUTER PROGRAMMING IS"
20 PRINT "EASIER THAN I THOUGHT!"
30 END
RUN
```

When the program on the previous page is typed into the computer, along with the command RUN, the computer executes the instructions. This means that it performs each step in the program until it runs out of line numbers or encounters the END command. The output will appear like this on the screen.

```
COMPUTER PROGRAMMING IS
EASIER THAN I THOUGHT!
Ready
```

The word "Ready" that appears after a program has been executed is the computer's way of saying that it has completed the task and is ready for something else. Some computers indicate this state of "readiness" by printing "ok" after the program.

If your original program is no longer on the screen, it can be brought back by keying in the word LIST. The list of all the instructions that make up a particular computer program is referred to as a **program listing**. Programmers must use the LIST command frequently. It allows them to look at their program, and also permits corrections to be made in the lines within the program.

Consider this next program, which includes:

(1) the NEW command that is entered before the new lines of instruction are keyed in. This powerful command erases any former programs stored in the computer's main memory, so they will not accidentally be combined with the lines of a new program. (WATCOM BASIC uses the CLEAR command);

(2) some programmer comments to identify the program at the beginning;

(3) several print commands for placing information on the screen.

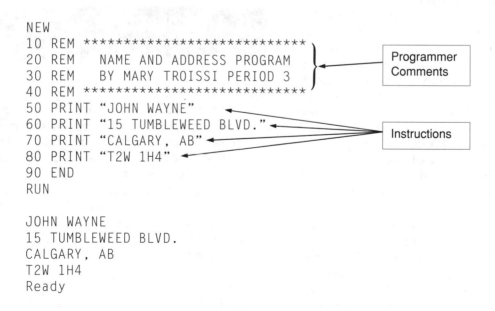

```
NEW
10 REM  ****************************
20 REM    NAME AND ADDRESS PROGRAM
30 REM    BY MARY TROISSI PERIOD 3
40 REM  ****************************
50 PRINT "JOHN WAYNE"
60 PRINT "15 TUMBLEWEED BLVD."
70 PRINT "CALGARY, AB"
80 PRINT "T2W 1H4"
90 END
RUN

JOHN WAYNE
15 TUMBLEWEED BLVD.
CALGARY, AB
T2W 1H4
Ready
```

(Notice that no data is used in this particular program)

12.5 SYSTEM COMMANDS

*C*ertain non-programming commands, called **system commands**, are designed to manipulate the peripherals, such as the display screen or the disk drive, rather than to be used as programming commands. The following chart highlights five system commands that programmers use regularly.

System Commands

COMMAND	WHAT IT DOES	EXAMPLES OF USE
LIST	Displays on the screen all the statements of any program currently in main memory.	LIST LIST 10-50 LIST 100- LIST -100
RUN	Executes any program stored in main memory.	RUN
DELETE	Erases a statement or group of statements from the program.	DELETE 10 DELETE 20-120 DELETE 20- DELETE -20
RENUMBER	Changes the line numbering beginning at ten and incrementing by ten, unless you specify otherwise. (not available in all versions of BASIC)	RENUM RENUM 100, 10 RENUM 100, 10, 200-300
NEW	Clears main memory. (Technically, it resets a memory pointer to the top of main memory, causing the computer to ignore the existence of any items below it.)	Apple: NEW C-64: NEW IBM PC: NEW PET: NEW Tandy: NEW WATCOM BASIC: CLEAR
SAVE	Saves any program stored in main memory onto disk. (You may have to include a disk drive reference such as SAVE "B:file name" or SAVE "2:file name".)	Apple: SAVE file name C-64: SAVE "file name", 8 IBM PC: SAVE "file name" PET: DSAVE "file name" Tandy: SAVE "file name" WATCOM BASIC: SAVE "file name"
LOAD	Loads a program from a disk into the computer's main memory. (You may have to include a disk drive reference, such as LOAD "B:file name" or OLD "2:file name".)	Apple: LOAD file name C-64: LOAD "file name", 8 IBM PC: LOAD "file name" PET: DLOAD "file name" Tandy: LOAD "file name" WATCOM BASIC: OLD "file name"

Design a program that will print the following greeting between two rows of asterisks (*) on the screen. Include an appropriate title and your name as part of the programmer comments, to provide some identification at the top of your program. Save your program on disk with the file name "LOOKS".

Sample Output:

```
*************

HELLO THERE

GOOD LOOKING!

*************
```

12.6 TYPES OF DATA

Data can be classified as an "integer", which is a whole number; or as a "decimal" (also called "floating point"), which is a number containing a decimal point; or as a "character string", which can be any group of letters, numbers, or special characters.

Types of Data

Data Type	Examples
(a) INTEGER	2 100 -15
(b) DECIMAL (floating point)	3.0152 100.50 -16.3
(c) CHARACTER STRING	"Sue Wilson" "75 Main St." "$"

12.7 VARIABLE NAMES FOR DATA

When a programmer wants to add numbers or other types of data to a program, the data must be assigned a special location in main memory. These storage locations can be thought of as a collection of mailboxes, each labelled with a different letter of the alphabet. In this way, the computer has a label to help it remember where data is stored.

Consider the example on the next page, in which the computer is asked to temporarily store two numbers, add them together, and then print the answer. Lines 40, 50, and 60 are referred to as **assignment statements**. The letters "A", "B", and "T" are **variable names** representing storage locations in main memory in which the related numbers are being stored.

When this program is executed, the computer assigns (stores) the value 200 in storage location "A" and the value 300 in storage location "B". The computer is then asked to add the contents of "A" and "B" and store the answer in storage location "T", which represents the total. Since the answer is stored in the box labelled "T", the last line of the program asks the computer to print the contents of that storage location. This results in the answer being displayed on the screen.

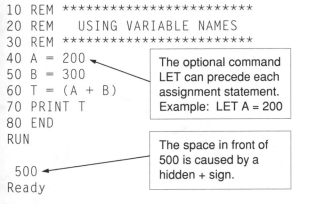

```
10 REM ***********************
20 REM    USING VARIABLE NAMES
30 REM ***********************
40 A = 200
50 B = 300
60 T = (A + B)
70 PRINT T
80 END
RUN

 500
Ready
```

The optional command LET can precede each assignment statement. Example: LET A = 200

The space in front of 500 is caused by a hidden + sign.

Main Memory Trace

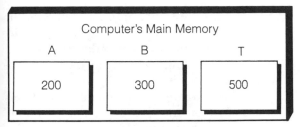

Computer's Main Memory

A	B	T
200	300	500

Words and phrases can be stored in a similar manner to numbers with these exceptions:
(1) the label for the storage location must also have a dollar sign ($) after it, and
(2) the word or phrase being assigned to that storage location must be enclosed within quotation marks (").

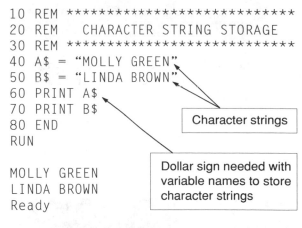

```
10 REM ***************************
20 REM    CHARACTER STRING STORAGE
30 REM ***************************
40 A$ = "MOLLY GREEN"
50 B$ = "LINDA BROWN"
60 PRINT A$
70 PRINT B$
80 END
RUN

MOLLY GREEN
LINDA BROWN
Ready
```

Character strings

Dollar sign needed with variable names to store character strings

12.8 LIMITATIONS TO VARIABLE NAMES

You may have noticed that the variable names in the programs presented so far have been one or two characters long. All versions of BASIC limit the length of the variable names. Apple IIe, Pet, Tandy, and C-64 allow up to 14 characters in their variable names. But these languages will only distinguish differences in the first two letters. This means that names such as "Loan1" and "Loan2" would appear to be the same variable name to the computer and it would not be able to tell them apart. Other languages, such as WATCOM BASIC, which allows up to 31 characters, and IBM BASIC and GW BASIC, which allow up to 40 characters in variable names, will recognize differences anywhere within the variable name. Students should refer to their teacher or to the programming manual that comes with the computer to determine the acceptable length and the number of significant letters in variable names.

12.9 ARITHMETIC OPERATORS

*I*n programming, mathematical symbols representing subtraction, addition, multiplication, and division are called **arithmetic operators**. These symbols are shown below.

Arithmetic Operators

To add numbers	+
To subtract numbers	–
To multiply numbers	*
To divide numbers	/
To raise to the power of	↑ or ^ or **

Notice that the asterisk symbol (*) is used to represent multiplication. This symbol removes the confusion with assignment statements that contain X's, such as T = (X * X). The division symbol (/), called the "slash", is needed to help programmers write assignment statements horizontally, all on one line. For example: A = B/C instead of $A = \frac{B}{C}$, which cannot be accepted by the computer because it does not fit on one line.

The exponential symbol, which means "to the power of", is another operator. The keyboard symbol for the exponential function varies with different computers. Check your computer manual to see which one

applies. For example, 18^3 may be represented as:

18 ** 3 or 18↑ 3 or 18 ^ 3.

The following program contains four examples of assignment statements (lines 130-160). The first two assignment statements introduce data to be used in the program. The second two use arithmetic operators to calculate the amount of interest and the final balance in a bank-loan-related problem.

```
100 REM ***************************
110 REM USING ASSIGNMENT STATEMENTS
120 REM ***************************
130 P = 5000
140 R = .10            Introducing
                       data
150 I = P * R
160 P = P + I
170 PRINT I            Performing
180 PRINT P            calculations
190 END
RUN

 500
 5500
Ready
```

Notice the switch in line numbering in this program from two-digit numbers to three-digit numbers. This is done to keep the program listing even along the left-hand margin.

The assignment statement on line 160 may appear strange to beginning programmers because the equal sign is treated by the computer as a signal to transfer the answer from the right-hand side to the left-hand side, and *not as an equality*. It would be better to think of the equal sign as an arrow directing the computer, as shown in this example.

P ← P + I

As the statement above illustrates, the computer always processes the right-hand side first and then assigns the answer to the variable on the left-hand side.

12.10 ERRORS IN YOUR PROGRAM

*A*n error in a program is called a **bug**. The process of locating the errors and rewriting parts of the program to remove them is referred to as **debugging**.

Errors may appear in two forms. A **syntax error** is a mistake in the coding of the program. It may involve things such as a missing comma or quotation mark, or a spelling mistake in a BASIC command.

A **logic error** is an error in the design of the program solution (also called a computer algorithm). Usually, a program containing logic errors will still execute. The answer, however, may be incomplete or incorrect. To correct a logic error, the programmer must go back to the original plan (your program plan on paper) and rethink the solution.

Consider the example to the right of a logic error. Notice that the syntax of the statements is correct, even though the answer is going to be wrong. Since the variable D has nothing stored in it, the computer calculates line 30 as TOTAL = 50 + 0

```
10 A = 50
20 B = 78
30 TOTAL = (A + D)
40 PRINT TOTAL
50 END
RUN

   50
```

"Where did you learn to debug a program, Haverstraw?"

12.11 BEDMAS RULES

*T*he arithmetic operators (+, -, /, *) are processed in a certain order by the computer. The order of operations can be expressed by a series of rules shown below as **BEDMAS Rules of Operation**. "BEDMAS" is an acronym to help you remember the order.

Notice in the program below how the placement of brackets in identical assignment statements produces different answers because of the Rules of Operation. Calculate the solutions to the two statements mentally, to see how they were reached.

```
100  T1 = 5 * (12 - 10)    Answer = 10

110  T2 = (5 * 12) - 10    Answer = 50
```

BEDMAS Rules of Operation

ACRONYM	WHAT IT MEANS	RULES OF OPERATION
B	BRACKETS	Items inside brackets are processed first.
E	EXPONENTS	Numbers expressed as "to the power" of some other number are calculated second.
D	DIVISION	Items to be divided or multiplied have equal priority. The computer processes
M	MULTIPLICATION	them in the order in which they occur.
A	ADDITION	Addition and subtraction have equal priority. They are processed in the
S	SUBTRACTION	order in which they occur.

Program to Try

(20 mins.)

Design a program that will assign each number to a specific location in main memory, process the following equation, then print the final answer on the screen. Include programmer comments at the top of your program. Save your program on disk with the file name EQUATION.

Data: A = 62.5
       B = 23.2
       C = 50.0

Equation:

$$T = \frac{(A)(B)}{C}$$

12.12 PLACING WORDS WITH YOUR ANSWER

The computer can be instructed to print any word or phrase that is placed within a pair of quotation marks. The items we want printed are called **literals**. These are messages (character strings, alphanumeric strings) found in PRINT statements that are used to print particular words or phrases, such as titles, headings, or sentences to accompany answers generated by the computer. The purpose of literals is to organize and clarify computer output. Note the use of a literal in line 80 of the following program, which is written to calculate the average of three term marks.

```
10  REM  ***********************
20  REM    AVERAGE OF TERM MARKS
30  REM  ***********************
40  M1 = 75
50  M2 = 65
60  M3 = 91
70  A = (M1 + M2 + M3)/3
80  PRINT "THE TERM AVERAGE IS", A
90  END
RUN
THE TERM AVERAGE IS           77

Ready
```

A literal

Actual answer is stored in memory location "A"

12.13 THE COMMA AND SEMICOLON

In the last example, the phrase "the term average is" and the numerical answer "77" both appear on the same line. The space between them is caused by the comma in line 80 (plus an additional space for the hidden + sign).

The Comma

In PRINT statements, punctuation marks are actually spacing commands. On a monitor that has 40 print positions across the screen, the computer divides the screen into four print zones of ten spaces each. On a monitor that has 80 print positions, the computer divides the screen into eight columns of ten. (This distance varies with the version of BASIC being used.)

A comma within a PRINT statement instructs the computer to jump to the next adjacent print zone. This works well if your answers are of the same length, such as a series of numbers, but works poorly if your answers are not of equal length, such as a series of words each containing a different number of letters, or if you have a phrase to accompany your answer.

In WATCOM BASIC there are normally 24 spaces in a print zone. However, you can change the number of spaces in a print zone with the command OPTION PRTZO. (PRTZO is an abbreviation of the words "print zone".) For example, OPTION PRTZO 10 will create eight print zones of ten spaces each on an 80-column screen. This statement should be included at the beginning of your program after the programmer comments.

The Semicolon

A semicolon (;) will leave no space, or one space, depending upon what is being printed. The computer always allows for one space to be left in front of a numerical value for the placement of a plus or minus sign. No space is left if the value is a word or character. This next program illustrates the power of punctuation marks within print statements.

```
100  REM  ******************************
110  REM     SPACING IN PRINT STATEMENTS
120  REM  ******************************
130  R = .10
140  P = 550
150  T = (P * R)
160  PRINT "THE ANSWER WITH A COMMA", T
170  PRINT
180  PRINT "THE ANSWER WITH A SEMICOLON"; T
190  END
RUN
THE ANSWER WITH A COMMA                55

THE ANSWER WITH A SEMICOLON 55
```

A comma forces the cursor into the next print zone

This space is caused by the hidden + sign in front of 55

Program to Try

(20 mins.)

Design a program that will require the computer to use the four subject marks provided, each introduced with an assignment statement, and calculate the total and average marks. Then have the computer print the output exactly as shown to the right. Use programmer comments to identify the title of the program and yourself as the programmer. Save the completed program on disk with the file name MARKS.

Sample Output:

```
SUBJECT MARKS 76    52    90    68

TOTAL MARKS    _____

AVERAGE MARK   _____
```

Figure 12.1
Organizations, such as the Armed Forces, must create their own computer software to meet their specific needs.

Courtesy of Canadian Forces Photo-Vic Johnson

12.14 SCREEN MANIPULATION

*T*he output that appears on the screen can be manipulated vertically and horizontally to allow the programmer to place information at specific points on the screen. The PRINT command appearing by itself in a program statement instructs the computer to leave one blank line on the screen. Several PRINT statements can be linked together with colons to create several blank lines. This feature allows programmers to manipulate the output vertically on the screen.

```
100 PRINT: PRINT: PRINT
```

> This statement instructs the computer to leave three blank rows on the screen and to place the cursor on the next print line.

The question mark (?) is an abbreviation for the command PRINT. This means that the above example, which moves the cursor down three lines on the screen, can also be written like this.

```
100 ?:?:?
```

> This statement creates three blank lines on the screen similar to PRINT:PRINT:PRINT. It is automatically translated into PRINT commands when listed.

12.15 GREATER HORIZONTAL CONTROL

*T*he TAB command can be combined with the PRINT command. TAB's purpose is to move the cursor horizontally to a specific position before printing the information. The TAB command always counts the number of print positions from the left-hand margin of the screen. (Students using WATCOM BASIC should note that a semicolon is required directly after the closing bracket in the TAB).

```
100 REM ************************
110 REM    USING THE TAB FEATURE
120 REM ************************
130 PRINT TAB(10) "NAME"; TAB(25)
    "MARK"
140 PRINT
150 PRINT TAB(10) "ROSE MARIE";
    TAB(25) "90"
160 END
RUN
        NAME            MARK

        ROSE MARIE      90
Ready
```

12.16 CLEARING THE SCREEN

*M*ost computer languages contain a command that clears the screen while leaving main memory intact. This feature is useful to a programmer because it allows the screen to be cleared of any old information before new items are presented. The clear command varies among different versions of the BASIC computer language. This command is usually placed at the top of short programs just after the REMARK

Version of BASIC	Example of Clear Command
Applesoft	10 HOME
Commodore	10 PRINT "  "
IBM PC	10 CLS
Tandy	10 CLS
WATCOM BASIC	10 CALL CLEARSCREEN

statements and before centring commands are executed.

Consider the example to the right of a BASIC program that illustrates where the "clear screen" instruction is placed within a program before commands for vertical and horizontal centring are executed. What do you think would happen if lines 130 and 140 were swapped? The TAB command is currently set for an 80-column screen. What would the TAB be for a 40-column screen?

```
100 REM *********************
110 REM    SCREEN MANIPULATION
120 REM *********************
130 (clear the screen command)
140 ?:?:?:?:?:?:?:?:?:?:?:?
150 PRINT TAB(28) "THIS PHRASE
    IS CENTRED!!"
160 END
```

Program to Try

(30 mins.)

Design a program that will place the following three statements in the exact centre of a cleared screen—that is, centred both vertically and horizontally. Programmer comments must include an appropriate title and programmer identification. Note that "text" is most readable when the phrases are lined up evenly to the left as they would appear in a textbook or a newspaper column. Save the program on disk with the file name FEATHERS.

```
HAROLD'S CHICKEN HATCHERY
89 FEATHERDUSTER BOULEVARD
RUFFLE ROAD, NS
B1S 1A1
```

Data can be introduced into main memory with the READ command as well as with assignment statements. A statement using the READ command assigns the data from the data statements to corresponding variable names within the READ statement. This particular style of entering data into a computer's memory is sometimes referred to as "batch-style data entry" because it is used to group many similar data statements for "batch" or group processing.

```
100 REM ************************
110 REM   BATCH-STYLE DATA ENTRY
120 REM ************************
130 READ N$, M
140 PRINT N$, M              Character string
150 DATA "CAPTAIN KIRK", 92
160 END                      Integer data
RUN
CAPTAIN KIRK 92
Ready
```

Notice that words, as well as numbers, can be used as data. Words are called **character strings** when they are placed in a data statement or an assignment statement because they appear as a string of letters or characters to the computer. The character string "Captain Kirk" is enclosed within quotation marks and the number 92 is not. The comma is used to separate data variables in DATA statements and variable names in READ statements. The comma is not placed at the end of those statements, however.

Character strings can appear both in DATA statements, to provide data for the program, and also in PRINT statements as "literals", to add clarity or organization to the output. In both cases, the character strings are enclosed in quotation marks, but their function within the program is different, which is why they are given two different names—"character string data" and "literals".

Program to Try   (25 mins.)

Design a program that will read your name and age from a data statement and print those items in the exact centre of the screen (horizontally and vertically) under the titles, as shown to the right. Leave a space between the title line and the next print line. Make sure that the screen is cleared before the computer begins printing. Save the completed program on disk with the file name AGE.

Example:

NAME	AGE
Your name	Your age

12.18 INTERACTIVE DATA ENTRY

*S*o far, two methods of entering data into the computer's main memory have been presented—the assignment statement, and the use of READ and DATA statements.

Both of those methods assume that the user knows the values ahead of time, so that they can be inserted into the program as it is being designed. Both also assume that the values will remain the same if the user needs to run the program again.

A third method, referred to as **interactive data entry**, uses the INPUT command to collect new data from the user of the program when the program is being executed. This allows the program to be run repeatedly with new data each time. Consider the following example.

In the program below to the left, line 160 contains the prompt that asks the user of the program what his or her name is. A **prompt** is a statement or command displayed on the screen that requires a response from the user. In this case, the phrase "Enter your name" is the prompt. "Fred", which is what the person at the keyboard keyed in, is called the **response**.

Entering Data on the Same Line

*S*ometimes it is more convenient, when there is room, to accept the response from the user on the same line where the prompt appears. This requires that two different commands be linked together with the combination of a semicolon and a colon (;:), as shown on the next page.

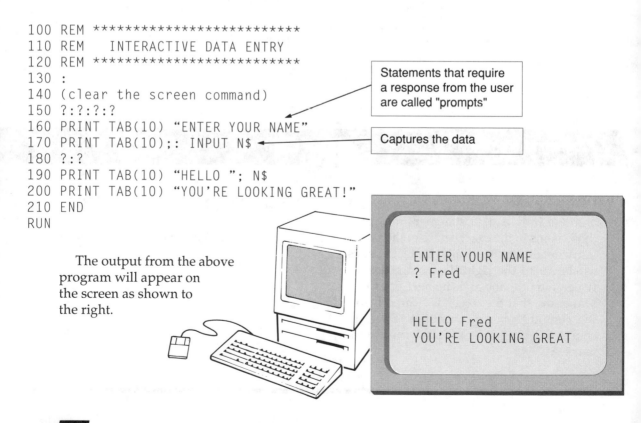

```
100 REM *************************
110 REM    INTERACTIVE DATA ENTRY
120 REM *************************
130 :
140 (clear the screen command)
150 ?:?:?:?
160 PRINT TAB(10) "ENTER YOUR NAME"
170 PRINT TAB(10);:: INPUT N$
180 ?:?
190 PRINT TAB(10) "HELLO "; N$
200 PRINT TAB(10) "YOU'RE LOOKING GREAT!"
210 END
RUN
```

Statements that require a response from the user are called "prompts"

Captures the data

The output from the above program will appear on the screen as shown to the right.

```
ENTER YOUR NAME
? Fred


HELLO Fred
YOU'RE LOOKING GREAT
```

```
100 REM ****************************
110 REM     INTERACTIVE DATA ENTRY #2
120 REM ****************************
130 :
140 (clear the screen command)
150 ?:?
160 PRINT TAB(10) "ENTER YOUR AGE ";:
    INPUT A
170 ?:?
180 PRINT TAB(10) "CONGRATULATIONS, YOU"
190 PRINT TAB(10) "ARE"; A ; " YEARS OLD."
200 END
RUN
```

```
ENTER YOUR AGE ? 17


CONGRATULATIONS, YOU
ARE 17 YEARS OLD.
Ready
```

"Interactive data capture" programs always require more careful screen design than other styles because the programmer is often not the "end user". An **end user** is the person for whom the program is being designed. For example, a team of programmers might design an airline seat reservation system for booking passengers on various flights. The end users of such a program, however, are not the programmers but the many airport clerks who work at the ticket counters. Since the programmers are not available at airports to answer questions from the clerks about the program's operation, it is extremely important that the program be **user friendly**; that is, capable of being run without any difficulty by a person who has little or no computer experience.

Program to Try   (25 mins.)

Design an interactive program that will ask the person at the keyboard for their "favourite candy" and their "present weight". Once the data is captured, have the computer clear the screen, and present the second screen as shown to the right. Save the completed program on disk with the file name CANDY.

First Screen:

```
ENTER YOUR FAVOURITE CANDY ?
licorice

ENTER YOUR PRESENT WEIGHT ?
64 kg
```

Second Screen :

```
YOU ARE LUCKY. USUALLY PEOPLE
WHO EAT LICORICE WEIGH MORE
THAN 64 kg.
```

12.19 USEFUL LIBRARY FUNCTIONS

12.20 TRUNCATING NUMBERS

*M*ost computer languages have in their "library" about a dozen built-in functions, such as INT, LEN, RND, SIN, and COS. A **library function** is a built-in operation related to strings or numbers that BASIC already knows how to perform: you do not have to teach it to the computer when programming. Typically, functions are used within assignment or PRINT statements. This next chart lists some of the common BASIC library functions. On the following page some uses for the INTEGER function are illustrated.

*S*ometimes answers processed by the computer are accurate to several decimal places. Calculating a student's average, for example, may provide an answer such as 81.459125. Some of the more modern computers may give you accuracy to 15 decimal places. This level of accuracy may not be useful as an answer, however. One solution is to use a built-in library function called INT (the abbreviation for INTEGER). Its purpose is to **truncate** (cut off) any decimal places in the answer and just leave a whole number. Notice the different answers provided by the program on the next page when the answer is printed first without the INTEGER function, then with the INTEGER function when calculating a student's term average.

Library Functions

ABBREVIATION	WHAT IT MEANS	WHAT IT DOES
INT	INTEGER	Truncates or cuts off the decimal places in a number
LEN	LENGTH	Determines the number of characters in a character string
RND	RANDOM	Creates a random number within a certain range
SIN	SINE	Creates a particular mathematical wave form
COS	COSINE	Creates a particular mathematical wave form opposite in frequency to a sine curve

```
100  REM  ******************************
110  REM    USING THE INTEGER FUNCTION
120  REM  ******************************
130  AVERAGE = (71.5 + 80 + 64 + 56)/4
140  PRINT AVERAGE
150  PRINT
160  PRINT INT(AVERAGE)
170  END
RUN
   67.875  ◄────────  Regular answer with
                      several decimal places

   67  ◄──────────  Answer with decimal
                    places truncated
```

Rounding Answers to the Nearest Whole Number

Some students may think that the second average in the last example is unfair, because the answer was not rounded up to the nearest whole number.

Here is a simple solution to that situation. Add the value .5 to the average before truncating it. This will create a rounded whole number. The chart that follows the program below illustrates how to round to various levels of accuracy.

```
100  REM  ********************
110  REM  ROUNDING VALUES
120  REM  ********************
130  AV = (71.5 + 80 + 64 + 56)/4
140  PRINT "REGULAR AVERAGE IS"; AV
150  RD = INT(AV + .5)
160  PRINT "ROUNDED AVERAGE IS"; RD
170  END
RUN
REGULAR AVERAGE IS 67.875
ROUNDED AVERAGE IS 68
Ready
```

Rounding Chart

ACCURACY REQUIRED	ROUNDING EQUATION
General format	INT(NUMBER * N + .5)/N
Nearest whole number	INT(NUMBER * 1 + .5)/1
Accurate to one decimal place	INT(NUMBER * 10 + .5)/10
Accurate to two decimal places	INT(NUMBER * 100 + .5)/100
Accurate to three decimal places	INT(NUMBER * 1000 + .5)/1000

12.21 RESERVED WORDS

Every version of the BASIC language has a **reserved word list**. These are words that are part of the vocabulary of the programming language and cannot be used by the programmer for such other purposes as naming variables, files, procedures, or subroutines. Examples of reserved words would be PRINT, READ, DATA, INPUT, INT, and END. If the word is a BASIC programming, system, or library-function command, it cannot be used for something else.

A computer program is a set of instructions that causes the computer to perform certain tasks. It usually contains three components—a set of instructions, data, and programmer comments—although its only compulsory component is instructions. People who write computer programs are called programmers.

The computer distinguishes between system commands (those commands that manipulate hardware peripherals, such as the disk drive, monitor, and printer), and programming commands (those commands included in a computer program). Generally, system commands are used to obtain some immediate response from the hardware, and are not preceded by line numbers. Programming commands, on the other hand, are used to create a long-lasting set of instructions for future use, and must be preceded by line numbers (in most versions of BASIC) to be retained in main memory.

Data, the values used by a computer program, can be divided into three categories—integers, decimals, and character strings. Any one of these forms of data can be entered into a computer's memory with the assistance of a computer program. The program temporarily stores each separate piece of data in a location containing a unique and non-repeating label called a "variable name".

Calculations can be performed with the help of assignment statements, mathematical symbols called "arithmetic operators", and some rules of behaviour, referred to as the BEDMAS Rules of Operation. Notably, the equal sign is not to be read as an equality, but rather as a transfer of information from right to left.

Data can be entered into the computer in three different ways: assignment statements (equations), READ and DATA statements (batch-style data entry), and interactive data entry.

Library functions are a specific set of commands that can be used to modify numerical data or character strings within an instructional statement. A typical application might be to use the INT function as part of a rounding routine for answers involving finances.

Shoe

arithmetic operator	end user	prompt
assignment statements	instructions	reserved word list
batch-style data entry	integer	response
BEDMAS Rules of Operation	interactive data entry	rounded
bug	library function	simple sequential structures
character string	literals	syntax error
computer program	logic error	system commands
data	program listing	truncate
debugging	programmer	user friendly
decimal	programmer comments	variable name

SYSTEM COMMANDS

DELETE	NEW	RUN
LIST	RENUMBER	SAVE
LOAD		

PROGRAMMING COMMANDS

(CLEAR THE SCREEN)	INTEGER	READ
DATA	LET	REMARK
END	PRINT	TAB
INPUT		

*T*hese are general questions that may require reading comprehension, factual recall, and some application of the knowledge gained from this chapter.

The BASIC Language

1. BASIC is an acronym. Explain what "acronym" means, and then translate the acronym BASIC.

2. Why do instructions that are written for one computer not necessarily run on another computer?

3. Name and briefly explain the three elements of most computer programs.

4. Suggest some uses for programmer comments in a program.

System Commands

5. What is a system command? Give two examples.

6. Explain the function of each of these system commands:
   (a) RUN
   (b) LIST
   (c) SAVE
   (d) NEW (or CLEAR)
   (e) DELETE

7. Suppose that a student keyed in the command NEW (or CLEAR on some computers) intending to clear the screen. What would happen to that person's program?

8. If you had a 20-line program numbered by intervals of ten (10, 20, 30, 40, etc.), how could you get the computer to display only the top four lines of the program?

9. Give an example of how you would perform the following actions on a program titled "program_one".
   (a) Save it on disk.
   (b) Retrieve it from disk.

Types of Data

10. Identify the types of data the following items represent:
    (a) 1456
    (b) 18.95
    (c) "Fred Twilliger"
    (d) "********"

Variable Names for Data

11. To what does the term "variable name" refer?

12. What difference is there between variable names that store numbers and ones that store words?

13. For the following items, suggest appropriate variable names that will clearly indicate what they represent.
    (a) hours worked
    (b) rate of pay
    (c) employee's name
    (d) employee's gross pay
    (e) employee's net pay

14. What programming hint can be applied to the selection of variable names?

Arithmetic Operators

15. What does the following expression require the computer to do? A = 10

16. What is an arithmetic operator? Give four examples.

17. Explain why the following assignment statement, which at first glance appears illogical, is acceptable to a computer: $T = T + 2$

18. Explain what is wrong with this assignment statement: $B * D = AN$

Errors in Your Program

19. What is a "bug" in your program?

20. Explain the difference between a "syntax error" and a "logic error".

BEDMAS Rules of Operation

21. What does the acronym BEDMAS mean?

22. Using the BEDMAS rules, calculate the value of "AN" in this expression where $B = 6$, $C = 10$, $D = 5$, $E = 3$, and $F = 4$.
$AN = B + C / (D - E) * F$

Placing Words with Your Answer

23. What is a "literal"?

24. Write a one-line BASIC statement that will have the computer print the phrase "The answer is" and the answer currently stored in memory location "T" on the same line.

25. Commas (,) and semicolons (;) produce different spacing effects when used in print statements. Explain the difference.

26. Write a one-line BASIC statement that will print your first name and age on the same line with only a single space between them.

Screen Manipulation

27. How can a programmer instruct a computer to begin printing a phrase on the fourth line from the top of the screen?

28. Write a one-line BASIC statement that will instruct the computer to print the phrase "The total is" 25 spaces in from the left-hand margin of the screen.

29. Using line ten as the line number, write a BASIC statement that will clear the screen on a typical computer in your class.

Batch-Style Data Entry

30. Write a one-line BASIC statement that will read the following data into main memory. DATA "Ian Cordiner", 89

31. Write a one-line BASIC statement that will provide the data for the following READ statement related to a report card: 10 READ N$, A, B, C, D

Interactive Data Entry

32. Explain what the words "prompt" and "response" refer to when working with interactive programs.

33. In BASIC, write a suitable prompt that asks for a student's height, and also write a separate statement that captures the user's response.

34. In BASIC, write a prompt asking a person's weight, and then capture the response on the same line where the prompt appears.

35. Explain the term "end user" as it applies to interactive programming.

36. What is meant by "a user-friendly program"?

Useful Library Functions

37. What is a "library function"? Give two examples.

38. Explain what happens when you instruct a computer to "truncate" a number with two decimal places.

39. Calculate the values to the following items:
    (a) INT(562.49)
    (b) INT(.29)
    (c) INT(1.59)
    (d) INT(150.55)

40. State whether or not these words would be acceptable variable names in your microcomputer's version of BASIC. If they are not suitable, explain why.
    (a) AVER1
    (b) INPUT
    (c) PROGRAM_FOURTEEN

*T*hese questions assume an understanding of the material presented in this chapter and provide situations that may require evaluation, analysis, or the application of your newly acquired knowledge.

Variable Names and Assignment Statements

1. Rewrite these expressions as equations so that they can be understood and processed by a computer.

   (a) $I = \dfrac{(P)(R)}{T}$

   (b) $\dfrac{(M1 + M2 + M3)}{3}$

   (c) 25 to the power of 5

2. Substitute the values provided in these questions and give the solutions.
   Values: A = 60; B = 2.50; C = 15
   (a) TOTAL = (A * B)/C
   (b) TOTAL = A * (B/C)
   (c) ANS = (A/C) - B

3. Write a one-line BASIC assignment statement that will calculate a student's average based on the following three marks. (Note: your statement cannot have any numbers in it. Assume the marks have already been assigned to variables.)

   ENGLISH 67, MATHEMATICS 65, COMPUTERS 81.

Placing Words with Your Answer

4. Rewrite the following BASIC statements so that all the syntax errors (errors in grammar, punctuation, and spelling) are removed.

   (a) `100 PRINT THE ANSWER IS ... N`
   (b) `200 DATA , 13, KAREN KASIK,`

(c) `150 READ N$; A; B`
(d) `60 A - B = T`
(e) `70 TOTAL = (A)(B)`

5. Write the corrected version of this program.

```
100 REM "  *************************" .
110 REM "   LENA HOWARD PD. 4
110 PRINT ************************
```

6. Write the corrected version of this program.

```
10 REM ****************************
20 REM GEORGES AUGUSTINE PD.2
30 REM "****************************
40 READ
50 T = A + B + C
60 PRINT THE ANSWER IS T
70 DATA 14, 12, 20,
80 END
```

Batch-Style Data Entry

7. Find the syntax errors in this setup and correct them.

```
100 READ N, M$
110 DATA JOAN LINSTROM, 87
```

8. Write the corrected version of this program.

```
100 REM *************************
110       BANK INTEREST PROBLEM
120       VALERIE EMARD     PD.1
130 REM *************************
140 READ P, R
150 I = (P)(R)
160 P : P + I
170 PRINT I, T
180 DATA 650, .10
END
```

9. Write a short program that will read the following five numbers into main memory, then print them.

Data: 67, 90, 82, 77, 60

10. In BASIC, show how these two items of data—"FRED" and the value "90"—can be entered into a computer system, using the following methods.
(a) Assignment statements
(b) Batch-style programming
(c) Interactive Data Capture

Interactive Data Capture

11. Write a two-line program that will ask a person's name and capture the response on a separate line.

12. Write a short program that will ask for the first names of four people and capture each of the responses on a different line, one underneath the other.

13. Write a BASIC statement that will ask for a person's hair colour, and capture the response on the same line as the prompt.

14. Write a short program that will ask for a person's name, then respond with the following phrase... "WELL _____, HAVE WE GOT A GIFT FOR YOU!"

*T*hese problems will require analysis and planning on paper before entering and testing them on the computer. Programs must contain all the elements of good programming style and output should appear in the middle of a cleared screen, unless otherwise indicated. Save your programs on disk for future reference.

1. Term Report Card

A teacher wants an interactive report card program that will accept any student's name and four subject marks, and then print a screen-version of a report card similar to the one shown below. The average must be a value calculated by the computer.

Sample Output:

```
        REPORT CARD


    STUDENT: Fran Fisher

    MARKS 65 71 52 75

    TERM AVERAGE = 65.75
```

2. Secretary's Salary

The office secretary worked 40 hours last week at a rate of pay of $8.65 per hour. Deductions from earnings included income tax (24% of gross pay), Canada Pension (7% of gross pay) and Unemployment Insurance (2% of gross pay). Print the following answers with the phrases indicated.

Sample Output:

```
    GROSS PAY = $

    TOTAL DEDUCTIONS = $

    NET PAY = $
```

3. Calorie Burner

A four-slice pizza contains approximately 375 calories per slice. A person jogging one kilometre uses up about 62 calories per kilometre. Design an interactive program that will ask a person how many pieces of pizza he or she has just eaten and then say how far it will be necessary to jog to "burn off" those calories. Centre the output in the middle of a cleared screen.

Sample Output:

```
HOW MANY PIECES OF PIZZA DID
YOU EAT?

YOU MUST JOG          KILOMETRES

TO USE UP THOSE CALORIES.
```

Other foods that can be substituted in the problem:

Chocolate Bar	270 calories
Doughnut	150 calories
Hamburger	344 calories
Chocolate Chip Cookie	50 calories

4. Overdue Books

The school librarian wants a simple program to calculate the fines for overdue books. Design a program that will prompt the librarian for "number of books borrowed" and "number of days late". Have the computer print the amount of your fine if overdue books are charged $0.15 per day.

Sample Output:

```
******** OVERDUE BOOKS ********

NUMBER OF BOOKS BORROWED :

NUMBER OF DAYS LATE :

OVERDUE LIBRARY FINE : $
```

5. Fast Asleep

The average person tends to sleep about 7.5 hours per night. In a lifetime, this can amount to a great deal of time spent sleeping. Design an interactive program that will ask the user's name and age. Then have the program calculate and display the output as shown below in the middle of a cleared screen.

Sample Output:

```
******************************************
PERSON'S NAME :

TOTAL HOURS TO-DATE IN LIFETIME =   HRS.

TOTAL HOURS SPENT SLEEPING       =   HRS.
******************************************
```

6. The Bank Loan

George Thompson has obtained a one-year installment loan from a Winnipeg credit union. The principal of the loan is $12 500, and the rate of interest is 9.75% per year, calculated annually. Plan an interactive program that will furnish the output shown below. The program must be able to accept any principal amount and any rate of interest and it must calculate the information shown in the output. The final output must be centred on a cleared screen. All answers must be accurate to two decimal places. Use the data provided for George Thompson to test your program.

Sample Output:

```
*************************************
DOLLAR AMOUNT OF INTEREST = $

TOTAL AMOUNT TO BE REPAID = $

EQUAL MONTHLY PAYMENTS    = $
*************************************
```

7. Canada Savings Bonds

Kim Simpson has purchased five Canada Savings Bonds from a local bank at a par value of $1000 each. The bonds stipulate an annual rate of interest of 8.85%, with an annual interest payment sent directly to the bearer. Design an interactive program that will accept any value of bonds and any annual rate of interest. Then have the computer calculate and print the following output in the centre of a display screen. Use the above figures as test data.

Sample Output:

```
*****************************
CANADA SAVINGS BOND INVESTMENT

TOTAL INVESTMENT = $

RATE OF INTEREST = %

ANNUAL INTEREST  = $
*****************************
```

8. The Park Renovations

The Ottawa Parks Department is considering fencing in a section of land for use as a recreation area. The Parks Director wants to install a protective fence around the perimeter of the field and seed the area with a high-quality grass seed. As a summer helper, you have been chosen to determine the perimeter, area, fencing, and seeding costs of

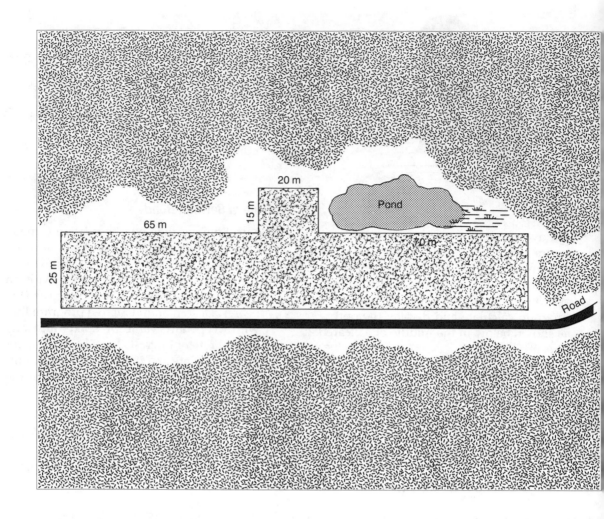

this field. The fencing is priced at $6.25 per running metre and the seed costs $16.50 for 100 square metres. The park area is shown in the above diagram.

The output should appear as follows in the middle of a cleared screen. Notice that all equal signs are lined up under one another.

```
*************************************************

                PARK RENOVATIONS

PERIMETER          = METRES

AREA               = SQUARE METRES

COST OF FENCING = $

COST OF SEEDING = $


*************************************************
```

9. The Air Conditioner

Use the metre ruler to measure the dimensions of the classroom (length, width, and height). Using the measurements of the classroom, design a program that will calculate the volume of air in the room, and the amount of time it would take each of two different sizes of air conditioners to cool the room. A brochure on air conditioners states that a 1500 W model will cool 2.5 cu. metres of air per hour whereas a 3000 W model will cool 5 cu. metres of air in the same time.

Sample Output:

```
****************************************

AIR CONDITIONER COMPARISON

ROOM VOLUME IN CU. METRES =

TIME TO COOL WITH 1500 W =

TIME TO COOL WITH 3000 W =


****************************************
```

Chapter

13

REPETITION STRUCTURES

REPETITION STRUCTURES
REPETITION STRUCTURES

❝ People who write programs without considering the cost of debugging and modification are similar to golfers completing a game without counting the strokes. Neither group is very effective in its performance. ❞

OBJECTIVES

By the end of this chapter, you will be able to:

1 Define the following terms: repetition structure (loop structure), counters, accumulators, destructive read-in, data file, nested loops;

2 Identify problem situations in which a repetition structure is required for the solution;

3 Use the following BASIC programming commands: FOR...NEXT, FOR...NEXT STEP; or, in WATCOM BASIC: LOOP...ENDLOOP, WHILE...ENDLOOP;

4 Design programs that make use of independent counters and accumulators for performing calculations within a repetition structure;

5 Design repetition structures that count in intervals of other than one, or that count backwards;

6 Design programs that use a repetition structure to read and print information stored in a series of data statements.

WORKING IN THE WORLD OF COMPUTERS

Assembly-Language Programmer
writes computer programs in machine-level language

CAI Programmer
writes educational software to train students in skills or concepts

Communications Programmer
creates programs that permit various communication devices to exchange information

Computer-Language Engineer
develops interpreters and compilers for specific computer systems

GUI Engineer
designs graphical user interface programs, such as Windows, to make computers easier to use

Industrial Programmer
writes short programs for dedicated processors in home appliances

Medical Systems Consultant
advises hospitals on which hardware and software to use

Operating Systems Engineer
develops operating systems for specific microprocessors

13.1 INTRODUCTION

*T*his chapter introduces **repetition structures**, which are also referred to as "loop structures" or "loops". These are statements in a program that cause the computer to repeat a series of steps until some task has been completed. Because computer programs usually contain many repeated operations, the repetition structure is one of the most common structures used in programming.

13.2 WHEN TO USE REPETITION STRUCTURES

*T*he key to recognizing the need for such a structure is to identify situations in which the same process needs to be repeated several times. Programming statements that most often get repeated in programs include assignment statements that perform calculations, READ statements, and PRINT statements.

Suppose you were asked to design a program that would read and print the name and age of one student. A simple, sequential, straight-line structure would be adequate. However, if the problem stated that the names and ages of several students were to be read and printed, a loop structure would be more useful. To process several names, the READ and PRINT statements can be enclosed within a loop that makes the computer perform those particular actions over and over until the last name and age have been printed. (Notice that lines containing data begin with the number "500". This makes it easy to distinguish data from programming commands, should you need to go back and make corrections.)

```
100 REM ***************************
110 REM   SOLUTION WITHOUT A LOOP
120 REM ***************************
130 READ N1$, M1, N2$, M2, N3$, M3,
    N4$, M4
140 PRINT N1$, M1
150 PRINT N2$, M2
160 PRINT N3$, M3
170 PRINT N4$, M4
500 DATA "FRED", 17
510 DATA "MARIA", 18
520 DATA "SUSAN", 16
530 DATA "TONY", 15
540 END
```

> Programs that require repeated actions are well-suited to repetition

```
100 REM **********************
110 REM   SOLUTION WITH A LOOP
120 REM **********************
130 (beginning of loop)
140 READ N$, A
150 PRINT N$, A
160 (end of loop)
500 DATA "FRED", 17
510 DATA "MARIA", 18
520 DATA "SUSAN", 16
530 DATA "TONY", 15
540 END
```

> In a loop, the task of multiple READS and PRINTS is reduced to two statements

In general, the secret to identifying the need for a loop in a program solution is to ask yourself the following question.

Identifying the Need for a Loop

"Are there any steps that must be repeated several times?" If the answer is "yes", then a loop structure will be part of your solution.

Students who have access to computers that understand the WATCOM version of BASIC should now turn to the middle of this chapter (page 273), where their section begins.

TRADITIONAL BASIC SECTION

*T*his section describes the details of loops as found in Applesoft BASIC, Commodore BASIC, IBM BASIC, and GW BASIC.

13.3 LOOPS

*I*f we were to define a loop structure more precisely by how it operates, we would state that a **loop** refers to a set of instructions that a computer is required to repeat until a certain test condition is met. A **test condition** is that part of the loop instruction that allows the computer to exit from the loop when the condition is satisfied. In the loop shown to the right, the test condition is the loop's upper limit, which in this case is the value "5".

Each loop contains a top control statement, such as "FOR C = 1 TO 5", and a bottom control statement, such as "NEXT C", which together control what is to be processed and how many times the process should be repeated. For example, the loop to the right requires the computer to print the phrase "Happy Birthday" five times.

In the top line of the loop structure, "FOR C = 1 TO 5", the programmer can choose any variable name to label the storage area in main memory which will be used to "count" how many loops are being processed. The variable name "C" is being used in the above loop as the counter.

The top control line instructs the computer to set or initialize the counter at the value "1" and to continue processing the contents of the loop until the counter has exceeded "5".

The middle line in the above loop is a single print statement containing the phrase

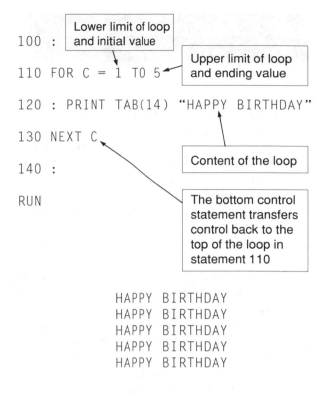

```
100 :    Lower limit of loop
         and initial value

110 FOR C = 1 TO 5    Upper limit of loop
                      and ending value

120 : PRINT TAB(14) "HAPPY BIRTHDAY"

130 NEXT C           Content of the loop

140 :

RUN                  The bottom control
                     statement transfers
                     control back to the
                     top of the loop in
                     statement 110
```

```
HAPPY BIRTHDAY
HAPPY BIRTHDAY
HAPPY BIRTHDAY
HAPPY BIRTHDAY
HAPPY BIRTHDAY
```

"Happy Birthday", which represents the content of the loop.

The bottom line, "NEXT C", is the control statement that transfers control, after each pass through the loop, back to the top control statement "FOR C = 1 to 5", until all required loops are completed.

It is good programming style to indent statements contained within the loop. This can be achieved by placing a colon (:) after the line number and indenting with the space bar before typing the rest of the statement. Also, blank lines created by colons are placed before and after the loop structure to make the loop structure stand out from the rest of the program. Isolating the loop in this way, as well as indenting the contents of the loop, makes a program more readable, so that items needing repair or modification are easier to locate.

13.4 INDEPENDENT COUNTERS

Some programming techniques require a counter that is not part of the loop process. Because it is separate from the loop, it is called an **independent counter**. For instance, one might be used to change the Year or Month in a program, or simply to number the various lines of output. Independent counters are inserted into a program as assignment statements. For example, the current year can be displayed by giving the variable "Y" (representing Year) a starting value, such as 1990, and then using the counter "Y = Y + 1" to change the year.

Consider this second example of a loop structure, in which the computer is instructed to print all the years beginning with 1990 and continuing for a period of eight years. Notice that the independent counter must be initialized before the loop begins, as in statement 140.

```
100 REM ************************
110 REM   WORKING WITH COUNTERS
120 REM ************************
130 :
140 Y = 1990
150 FOR C = 1 TO 8
160 :   PRINT Y
170 :   Y = Y + 1
180 NEXT C
190 :
200 END
RUN
 1990
 1991
 1992
 1993
 1994
 1995
 1996
 1997
Ready
```

Program to Try   (30 mins.)

Design a program that will use a loop to calculate and print both the year and how old you will be in that year, for a period of ten years beginning with the current year. Place the titles "Year" and "Age" over the columns, as shown to the right. Save your completed program on disk with the file name AGE.

Sample Output:

YEAR	AGE
1991	17
1992	18
1993	19

*A*n **accumulator** is an assignment statement similar to a counter, except that, while a counter always adds a constant value, such as "1", an accumulator can add a variable with a different value each time. For example, the statement "T = T + C" repre-

sents an accumulator that adds the value of the variable "C" to the storage area in main memory represented by the letter "T". In this loop, all the numbers from one to ten are being added to get a final total.

In the program below, the answer from the accumulator is not displayed until the very end of the program. An alternative method is to display the answer each time a value is added to the accumulator. The next "Program to Try" illustrates that approach.

```
100 REM *********************
110 REM    USING ACCUMULATORS
120 REM *********************
130 :
140 T = 0
150 FOR C = 1 TO 10
160 :   T = T + C
170 NEXT C
180 :
190 PRINT TAB(15) "THE TOTAL OF THE NUMBERS IS"; T
200 :
210 END
RUN
```

Accumulators must be initialized outside the loop

```
        THE TOTAL OF THE NUMBERS IS 55
```

Program to Try

(30 mins.)

Design a program containing a loop structure that will calculate and print the balance in a bank account at the end of every year for ten years. The account currently contains $5000, and the bank pays 8.5 percent interest, calculated annually. The output should appear centred on a cleared screen. Save your completed program on disk with the file name BALANCE.

Sample Output:

YEAR	BALANCE
1990	$5425
1991	$—
1992	$—

13.6 LOOPS AND READ AND DATA STATEMENTS

*L*oop structures work well with problems in which you are required to read in multiple similar data statements. For example, suppose that the data contains a list of five student names with their corresponding term marks and that you are required to have these items printed. In this situation, since the number of data statements is known ahead of time, simply set the maximum number of loops equal to the number of data statements. If you set the loop maximum for a quantity higher than the number of data statements, this error message will appear: "Out of data".

Long lists of similar information with items arranged in the same order are often referred to as **data files**. The data file in the program below contains student names and term marks. Each line of data represents a record. Each record, in this case, is divided into two fields of information—a student's name, and their mark.

Destructive Read-In

*E*ach time the loop structure is executed, the information contained in one data statement is stored in the memory locations "N$" and "M". The contents of these two memory locations are printed before the next data statement is read. As each succeeding student name and mark is read, the information previously held in those two memory locations is erased (destroyed). This process of erasing the previous contents of a memory location and re-using the same spaces for some other data is called **destructive read-in**. It is useful for reading in great quantities of data while using few memory locations and very little coding.

```
100 REM ******************
110 REM NAMES AND MARKS
120 REM ******************
130 REM N$ = STUDENT NAME
140 REM M = TERM MARK
150 REM C = LOOP COUNTER
160 :
170 (clear the screen command)
180 ?:?:?:?
190 :
200 FOR C = 1 TO 5
210 :    READ N$, M
220 :    PRINT TAB(10) N$; TAB(30) M
230 NEXT C
240 :
250 DATA "LISA REHAK", 78
260 DATA "RICHARD GERRARD", 81
270 DATA "BECKIE KNIGHT", 73
280 DATA "HEATHER SMITH", 75
290 DATA "JEREMY GREVEN", 76
300 :
310 END
```

Data file with five records

Design a program that will print a list of items sold in the school store, along with the quantity in stock. Have the items listed under their appropriate headings, as shown to the right. Make sure the output is centred on a cleared screen. Save your completed program on disk with the file name CANDY.

Sample Output:

```
PRODUCT NAME   QUANTITY
 Licorice         12
 Jujubes          25
 Sours            15
```

Data:

Licorice	12	Sours	15	Mints	18
Jujubes	25	Chewing Gum	10	Chocolates	12

13.7 USING THE STEP FEATURE

One modification of the regular loop structure is to include a STEP command at the end of the top loop-control statement. The step command modifies the way in which the loop counter "counts". The counter can be made to count two at a time, in fractions, or even backwards.

The sample program to the right illustrates how a loop can be made to count backwards.

```
100 REM ********************
110 REM   COUNTING BACKWARDS
120 REM ********************
130 :
140 FOR C = 10 TO 1 STEP -2
150 :   PRINT C
160 NEXT C
170 :
RUN
 10
 8
 6
 4
 2
Ready
```

> Notice that the upper and lower limits are reversed when counting backwards

Effect of Step Modifications

MODIFICATION	EFFECT ON COUNTING
STEP 2	Counts two at a time
STEP .5	Counts 1/2 at a time
FOR C = 10 TO 1 STEP -1	Counts backwards one at a time. This loop would be initialized with a high rather than a low number.

Design a program that will instruct the computer to count from 1 to 20 but list only the odd numbers; that is, 1, 3, 5, etc. Centre the output in the middle of a cleared screen under the heading "Odd Numbers". When that task is completed, modify the program so that the odd numbers are printed in descending order from 20 to 1; that is, 19, 17, 15, etc. Save your completed program on disk with the file name NUMBERS.

END OF TRADITIONAL BASIC SECTION

*S*tudents who are not reading the section on WATCOM BASIC should now turn to page 280.

WATCOM BASIC SECTION

13.3W LOOPS

*I*f we were to define a loop structure more precisely by how it operates, we would state that a **loop** (repetition structure) refers to a set of instructions that a computer is required to repeat until a certain test condition is met. A **test condition** is that part of the structure which allows the computer to exit from the loop when the condition is satisfied.

Each loop contains a top control statement, "LOOP", and a bottom control statement, "ENDLOOP", which together control what is to be processed and how many times the process should be repeated. For example, the loop shown in the following sample program requires the computer to print the phrase "Happy Birthday" five times.

The programmer chooses any variable name to label the storage area where the computer can keep "count" of how many loops are being processed. The variable name "C" is being used here as the counter. Line 110 sets the beginning value for the counter. This is called **initializing the counter**.

The "LOOP...ENDLOOP" structure is set to print five lines of the phrase "Happy Birthday", 14 spaces in from the left-hand margin of the screen. The statement "IF C >= 5 THEN QUIT" is the test condition for allowing the computer to exit from the loop once the "count" has reached or exceeded the value of five. The statement "C = C + 1" adds one to the counter each time a loop is processed. The "ENDLOOP" statement transfers control back to the "LOOP" state-

ment, after each pass through the loop, until all the required loops are completed.

It is good programming style to indent statements contained within the loop. Also, blank lines created by colons are placed before and after the loop structure to make it stand out from the rest of the program. Isolating the loop in this way, as well as indenting the contents of the loop, makes a program more readable and makes it easier to locate items needing repair or modification.

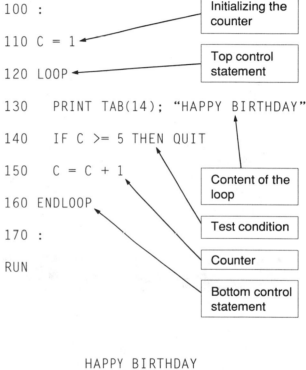

```
100 :

110 C = 1

120 LOOP

130    PRINT TAB(14); "HAPPY BIRTHDAY"

140    IF C >= 5 THEN QUIT

150    C = C + 1

160 ENDLOOP

170 :

RUN
```

Initializing the counter

Top control statement

Content of the loop

Test condition

Counter

Bottom control statement

```
          HAPPY BIRTHDAY
          HAPPY BIRTHDAY
          HAPPY BIRTHDAY
          HAPPY BIRTHDAY
          HAPPY BIRTHDAY
```

```
100 REM ***********************
110 REM   WORKING WITH COUNTERS
120 REM ***********************
130 :
140 Y = 1990
150 C = 1
160 LOOP
170     PRINT Y
180     Y = Y + 1
190     IF C >= 8 THEN QUIT
200     C = C + 1
210 ENDLOOP
220 :
230 END
RUN
 1990
 1991
 1992
 1993
 1994
 1995
 1996
 1997
Ready
```

Some programming techniques require a counter that is not part of the loop process. Because it is separate from the loop, it is called an independent counter. For instance, one might be used to change the Year or Month in a program, or simply to number the various lines of output.

Independent counters are inserted into a program as assignment statements. For example, the current year can be displayed by giving the variable "Y" (representing Year) a starting value, such as 1990, and then using the counter "Y = Y + 1" to change the year.

Consider this second example of a loop structure in which the computer is instructed to print all the years beginning with 1990 and continuing for a period of eight years. Notice that the independent counter must be initialized before the loop begins, as in statement 140.

Program to Try   (30 mins.)

Design a program that will use a loop to calculate and print both the year and how old you will be in that year for a period of ten years beginning with the current year. Place the titles "Year" and "Age" over the columns as shown to the right. Save your completed program on disk with the file name AGE.

Sample Output:

YEAR	AGE
1990	17
1991	18
1992	19

An **accumulator** is an assignment statement similar to a counter, except that, while a counter always adds a constant value, an accumulator can add a variable with a different value each time. For example, the statement "T = T + C" represents an accumulator that adds the value of the variable "C" to the storage area in main memory represented by the letter "T". In this loop, all the numbers from one to ten are being added to get a final total.

In the program below, the answer from the accumulator is not displayed until the very end of the program. An alternative method is to display the answer each time a value is added to the accumulator. The next "Program to Try" illustrates that approach.

```
100 REM *********************
110 REM    USING ACCUMULATORS
120 REM *********************
130 :
140 T = 0     ◄─────────────────────  Accumulators must
150 C = 1                             be initialized outside
160 LOOP                              the loop structure
170     T = T + C
180     IF C >= 10 THEN QUIT
190     C = C + 1
200 ENDLOOP
210 :
220 PRINT TAB(15); "THE TOTAL OF THE NUMBERS IS"; T
230 :
240 END
RUN

        THE TOTAL OF THE NUMBERS IS 55
```

Program to Try

(30 mins.)

Design a program containing a loop structure that will calculate and print the balance in a bank account at the end of every year for ten years. The account currently contains $5000, and the bank pays 8.5 percent interest, calculated annually. The output should appear centred on a cleared screen. Save your completed program on disk with the file name BALANCE.

Sample Output:

YEAR	BALANCE
1990	$5425
1991	$———
1992	$———

*L*oop structures work well with problems in which you are required to read in multiple similar data statements. For example, suppose that the data contains a list of five student names with their corresponding term marks, and that you are required to have these items printed. In this situation, since the number of data statements is known ahead of time, simply set the maximum number of loops equal to the number of data statements. If you set the loop maximum for a quantity higher than the number of data statements, this error message will appear: "Out of data".

Long lists of similar information with items arranged in the same order are often referred to as **data files**.

The data file in the program at the bottom left contains student names and term marks. Each line of data represents a record. Each record, in this case, is divided into two fields of information—a student's name, and their mark.

Destructive Read-In

*E*ach time the loop structure is executed, the information contained in one data statement is stored in the memory locations "N$" and "M". The contents of these two memory locations are printed before the next data statement is read. As each succeeding student name and mark is read, the information previously held in those two memory locations is erased (destroyed). This process of erasing the previous contents of a memory location and re-using the same spaces for some other data is called **destructive read-in**. It is useful for reading great quantities of data while using few memory locations and very little coding.

```
100 REM ************************
110 REM    LIST OF STUDENT NAMES
120 REM ************************
130 REM    N$ = STUDENT NAME
140 REM    M = TERM MARK
150 REM    C = LOOP COUNTER
160 :
170 CALL CLEARSCREEN
180 ?:?:?:?
190 :
200 C = 1
210 LOOP
220       READ N$, M
230       PRINT TAB(30); N$; TAB(50); M
240       IF C >= 5 THEN QUIT
250       C = C + 1
260 ENDLOOP
270 :
280 DATA "LISA REHAK", 78
290 DATA "RICHARD GERRARD", 81
300 DATA "BECKIE KNIGHT", 73
310 DATA "HEATHER SMITH", 75
320 DATA "JEREMY GREVEN", 76
330 :
340 END
```

Data file with five records

Design a program that will print a list of items sold in the school store, along with the quantity in stock. Have the items listed under their appropriate headings, as shown to the right. Make sure the output is centred on a cleared screen. Save your completed program on disk with the file name CANDY.

Sample Output:

```
PRODUCT NAME   QUANTITY
Licorice         12
Jujubes          25
Sours            15
```

Data:

| Licorice | 12 | Sours | 15 | Mints | 18 |
| Jujubes | 25 | Chewing Gum | 10 | Chocolates | 12 |

13.7W MODIFYING THE LOOP STRUCTURE

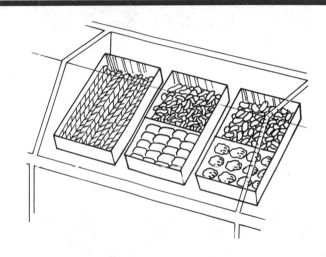

*T*he counter in the loop structure is the key statement that allows a programmer to modify the way a loop "counts". The loop structure can be made to count two at a time, in fractions, or even backwards.

Effect of Changes in the Counter

MODIFICATION	EFFECT ON COUNTING
C = C + 2	Counts two at a time
C = C + .5	Counts 1/2 at a time
C = 10	Counts backwards one at a time. The loop would be initialized with a high number rather than a low one.
C = C - 1	

The sample program to the right illustrates how a loop can be made to count backwards.

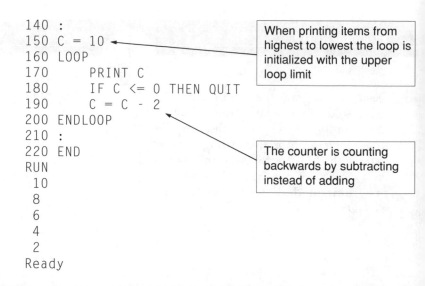

```
140 :
150 C = 10
160 LOOP
170     PRINT C
180       IF C <= 0 THEN QUIT
190       C = C - 2
200 ENDLOOP
210 :
220 END
RUN
 10
 8
 6
 4
 2
Ready
```

When printing items from highest to lowest the loop is initialized with the upper loop limit

The counter is counting backwards by subtracting instead of adding

Program to Try   (30 mins.)

Design a program that will instruct the computer to count from 1 to 20 but print only the odd numbers; that is, 1, 3, 5, etc. Centre the output in the middle of a cleared screen under the heading "Odd Numbers". When the task is completed, modify the program so that the odd numbers are printed in descending order from 20 to 1; that is, 19, 17, 15, etc. Save your completed program on disk with the file name NUMBERS.

13.8W ALTERNATIVE LOOP STRUCTURE

A variation of the "LOOP...ENDLOOP" structure is the "WHILE...ENDLOOP" structure. It has the advantage of having the test condition built into the top control statement. Everything else is the same. Notice that instead of the "equal to" sign in the test condition, a combination of the "less than" and "equal to" symbols is used. In the sample program below, the "<=" symbols tell the computer that the loop should continue to execute as long as the counter has a value less than or equal to ten.

```
100 :
110 C = 1                    Initialize the counter
120 WHILE C <= 10            Top control statement
130    PRINT TAB(10); "HAPPY BIRTHDAY!"
140    C = C + 1             Counter
150 ENDLOOP   Bottom control statement
160 :
```

Design a program that will use the "WHILE...ENDLOOP" structure to read the data file in the same order as shown to the right, and calculate "Total Sales" for each item. Have the computer display the output centred on a cleared screen under the headings "Qty. Sold", "Product", "Unit Price", and "Total Sales", in that order. Save your completed program on disk with the file name SALES.

Data:

PRODUCT	QTY. SOLD	UNIT PRICE
Stereo LPs	20	$ 8.95
Cassettes	35	7.95
Blank Cassettes	12	4.50
Cassette Holders	3	14.25
Tape Cleaner Units	1	10.00
Compact Disks	8	14.95

END OF WATCOM BASIC SECTION

The repetition structure, which is also called a loop structure, or simply a loop, is made up of program statements that cause the computer to repeat a series of steps until some test condition is satisfied. A test condition refers to some preset limit that allows the computer to exit from the loop.

The key to recognizing the need for such a structure is to ask yourself the question "Are there any items that must be repeated several times?" If the answer is yes, then a loop structure will be part of the solution. Programming statements that are most often repeated include assignment statements performing calculations, and READ and PRINT statements.

Each loop structure contains the following elements: an initial value, sometimes called the lower limit of the loop; an ending value, sometimes referred to as the upper limit of the loop (which allows the computer to exit from the structure once the limit has been reached); some method of counting, either implied within the top control statement, or explicit as an assignment statement; and a bottom control statement that transfers control back to the top control statement.

Loop structures are excellent methods for reading and processing items from a data file. A data file is a set of records that contain similar information, with each record in the file arranged in the same order.

For example, a data file might include a list of several data statements, with each statement containing the name of a student followed by that student's term mark.

Reusing the same memory locations with different data during the execution of a program is called "destructive read-in". During this process, each new set of data erases the previous contents of the storage areas. This is a useful method for reading great quantities of data while using few memory locations and very little coding.

Because computer programs usually contain many repeated operations, the repetition structure or loop is one of the most common structures used in programming.

"It's amazing how this place empties at 5 o'clock!"

accumulator

counter

data file

destructive read-in

field

independent counter

initializing the counter

loop (repetition structure)

record

test condition

Traditional BASIC Commands

FOR...NEXT
FOR...NEXT STEP

WATCOM BASIC Commands

LOOP...ENDLOOP
WHILE...ENDLOOP

*T*hese are general questions that may require reading comprehension, factual recall, and some application of the knowledge gained from this chapter.

When to Use Repetition Structures

1. What type of programming statement most often gets repeated?

2. Using a specific example of your own, show how loops can reduce the number of lines used in a program.

3. What question can a programmer ask that will determine if a loop is needed in a program solution?

Loops

4. Write a short loop that will print the phrase "Happy Birthday" ten times. Leave plenty of writing space above and below the loop for the labels required by the next question.

5. Label the following items on the loop structure you have created in the previous question.
   (a) top control statement
   (b) bottom control statement
   (c) contents of the loop
   (d) lower loop limit
   (e) upper loop limit

(f) line that does the counting

(g) line that contains the test condition to allow the computer to exit from the loop

Independent Counters and Accumulators

6. Using an example, explain the purpose of an "independent counter".

7. What instruction must accompany all independent counters and accumulators before the loop structure can begin?

8. What do counters and accumulators have in common?

9. How do counters and accumulators differ?

10. Suppose that the accumulator "T = T + C" is inserted inside a loop structure that uses the variable "C" to count, and that the loop is increasing two at a time. What value will the accumulator have if it is initialized with the value 100 and the loop structure has executed three times?

Loops and READ and DATA statements

11. When would the error message "Out of data" appear?

12. How can an "Out of data" error be corrected?

13. What is a data file? Give an example of your own design, using four data statements with two items in each.

14. Explain how "destructive read-in" works.

15. Suppose that you had a data file containing ten student names. If you could not use the destructive read-in technique for main memory storage, what alternative method could you use to read all ten names?

*T*hese questions assume an understanding of the material presented in this chapter and provide situations that may require evaluation, analysis, or the application of your newly acquired knowledge.

When to Use Repetition Structures

1. Read each of the following descriptions, then state whether or not a loop will be required as part of the solution. If a loop is needed, then suggest what the contents of the loop should be.

(a) A student wants to print the phrase "Happy Birthday" in the middle of a cleared screen.

(b) You need a program that will calculate the interest and year-end balance, each year for ten years, on $5000 deposited in a term account with an interest rate of 8% per year.

(c) A student wants to have the phrase "Hello Good Looking!" appear as a running list on the display screen.

(d) You need a program that will calculate the year-end interest and the new balance for a $50 000 investment earning 10.5% interest, calculated annually.

(e) Design a program that will read and print the names and term marks of the first five students in a data file.

Loops, Independent Counters, and Accumulators

2. After studying one of the loops at the top of the next page, give specific answers to each of the questions below.

Traditional BASIC

```
100 :
110 FOR C = 1
    TO 13 STEP 2
120 : PRINT
    "HELLO"
130 NEXT C
140 :
```

WATCOM BASIC

```
100 :
110 C = 1
120 WHILE C <= 13
130 PRINT "HELLO"
140 C = C + 2
150 ENDLOOP
160 :
```

(a) What is the lower limit of the loop?

(b) What is the upper limit of the loop?

(c) After the second loop, what would be the value of "C"?

(d) How many times will the word "hello" appear on the screen?

(e) How could you modify the loop to make the computer print twice as many "hellos" without inserting another print statement or modifying the existing one?

3. Design a short interactive program that will prompt the user for a year in the future and then print a list of the years from the current year to the year specified in response to the prompt.

4. Design a loop structure that will print the value of the loop counter in one column and the output from the accumulator "T = T + C" beside it in another column. The variable "T" begins with a value of 500, and the upper limit of the loop is 15.

Loops and READ and DATA Statements

5. Design a loop structure that will read and print the names of the following automobiles and their approximate costs. If you are aware of recent price changes, alter the amounts.
    Data:

Camaro IROC-Z	$25 500
Corvette	$55 000
Firebird Trans Am	$28 000
Mazda RX7 Turbo	$30 000
Porsche 944 Turbo	$75 500
Toyota Supra	$38 000

6. Design a loop structure that will read in all the items of information from each of the following data statements, but print only the first and the third items. To prove that all items were read in, after the list is completed, print all items from the last entry.

    Data:

Janice	F	16
Anthony	M	15
Ian	M	17
Marcie	F	16
Bertrund	M	15
Kimberly	F	18

7. Design a loop structure that will print all the numbers from 0 to 100 in intervals of ten; that is, 0, 10, 20.

8. Design a loop structure that will count backwards. The loop is to print the year and your age beginning with the current year and age, and continue until the loop reaches the year in which you were born.

*T*hese problems will require analysis and planning on paper before entering and testing them on the computer. Solutions must contain all the elements of good programming style and appear in the middle of a cleared screen, unless otherwise indicated. Question 5 is a challenge problem.

1. My, But She's Growing!

A human baby tends to grow at a rate of 3% per week for the first half year. Plan a program that will print the weight of a baby each week for 13 weeks. The baby's weight at birth was 3.57 kg. The answers should appear under the headings, as shown. After the kilogram chart is completed, convert the final answer into pounds (1 kg = 2.197 lb.).

Sample Output:

```
WEEK                  BABY'S WEIGHT
1                        3.57
2                         --
3                         --
WEIGHT IN POUNDS =
```

2. Braking Distance

The braking distance for the average car is 0.06 times the square of the car's speed; that is, $D = (0.06 * S^2)/3.28$. Design an interactive program that will prompt the user for the minimum and maximum speeds (expressed to the nearest ten km/h) that the chart is to display. Then have the computer print the braking distances for speeds in intervals of ten for all speeds from the minimum to the maximum, as specified by the responses to the prompts. The output should appear on two separate screens as shown.

First Screen

```
MINIMUM SPEED
(Enter amount between 0 and 140) ?
30
```

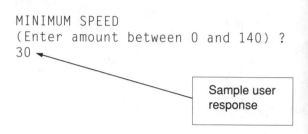

Sample user response

Second Screen

```
MAXIMUM SPEED
(Enter amount between 0 and 140) ?
100
```

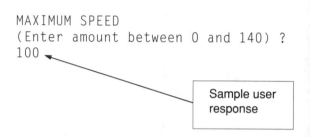

Sample user response

Second Screen

```
*** BRAKING DISTANCE CHART ***

SPEED              BRAKING DISTANCE
                       (in metres)


30                        —
40                        —
                          —
                          —
90                        —
100                       —
```

3. The TV Survey

Grinwald and Associates, a marketing research firm that you work for, has been hired by a TV network to determine which sitcom has the largest audience. A telephone survey of 2300 viewers is made, asking them which sitcoms (including re-runs) they watched during the past week. Design a program that will use the data collected from the survey to create a chart with the following headings—"TV Show", "Audience", and "Percentage Market Share".

Data:

TV Show	Audience
Alf	250
Cosby Show	300
Designing Women	250
Family Ties	290
Kate & Allie	275

(Make up five more entries)

4. Strange-looking Animals

Design a program to read the data containing the names of strange-looking animals and the country or location in which they are found. The output should appear on alternate lines in the form of a repeated sentence, with the data being used to fill in the blanks. The sentences should begin two lines after the title "Strange-looking Animals", as shown, and should appear double spaced on the screen.

Sample Output:

```
***** STRANGE-LOOKING ANIMALS *****

You can find a/an _____
in _____
```

Data:

Platypus	Australia
Aardvark	Africa
Moose	Northern Canada
Tapir	Brazil
Llama	Peru
Armadillo	United States
Gnu	Southern Africa
Horned Narwhal	Arctic Ocean
Kangaroo	Australia
Dromedary	Northern Africa
Bison	Northern Canada
Tasmanian Devil	Tasmania

5. The Mortgage Dilemma

One problem with purchasing a home is that interest rates often increase the payments to a level beyond the reach of the average wage earner. The Walkers, for example, have $85 000 of their mortgage left to pay on their home. The current interest rate is 11.5%, compounded annually. The Walkers can only afford to make payments totalling $8600 per year. Assuming that the bank adds the accrued interest before deducting the annual payment, design a program to print a chart as shown for a period of 15 years, illustrating the Walker family's dilemma.

YEAR	INTEREST	BALANCE
1	$ -----	$ -----
2	$ -----	$ -----
3	$ -----	$ -----

Chapter 14

SELECTION STRUCTURES

SELECTION STRUCTURES
SELECTION STRUCTURES

66 As the machines improve...we shall begin to see all the phenomena associated with the terms "consciousness," "intuition," and "intelligence." It is hard to say how close we are to the threshold, but once it is crossed, the world will not be the same. 99

Marvin Minsky
Scientist, Massachusetts Institute of Technology

OBJECTIVES

By the end of this chapter, you will be able to:

1 Understand the following programming concepts: test conditions, relational operators, key to the search;

2 Identify problem situations in which selection structures would be required as part of the solution;

3 Write programs containing single and multiple decision structures;

4 Write interactive programs employing user input as the key to a search.

WORKING IN THE WORLD OF COMPUTERS

Computer Animator
designs computer-generated animated movies for studios

Computer Photographer
combines photography skills and computer knowledge to capture pictures generated by a computer

Computer Security Consultant
analyzes complex computer systems to prevent breaches of security

Computer Code Cryptographer
encodes and decodes secret computer messages for the military or special services

Expert-Systems Designer
combines a specific set of knowledge, such as law, with an intelligent data system

Manager of Information Services
manages centralized computer systems for large organizations

Program and Media Librarian
files and retrieves tapes and disks to support a mainframe computer system

Simulation Programmer
designs software that simulates the conditions of specific real-life activities, such as the operation of a nuclear power plant

14.1 INTRODUCTION

*T*his chapter introduces **selection structures**, which are also referred to as "decision structures", or simply "decisions". These are statements in a program that cause the computer to perform some kind of action based on a comparison between two or more data items. It is this logical decision-making power that gives computers their peculiar ability to "think".

14.2 WHEN TO USE A SELECTION STRUCTURE

*T*he key to recognizing the need for a selection structure is to identify problems in which certain data must be selected from a data file. Quite often, the repetition structure and the selection structure are combined in problems having varying data.

For example, if you were asked to design a program that would read and print the names and term marks of five students, a repetition structure would be adequate to accomplish that task. However, if only the names of those students with a passing term mark were to be displayed, both a repetition structure and a selection structure would be required.

Compare the following two programs that read and display the contents of five data statements. The first program simply displays every item of data that it reads into main memory. The second program, however, selects and displays only those students who received a term mark greater than or equal to 50.

```
100 REM  ***********************
110 REM    SOLUTION WITHOUT A
120 REM    SELECTION STRUCTURE
130 REM  ***********************
140 :
150 (beginning of loop)
160       READ N$, M
170       PRINT N$; M
180 (end of loop)
190 :
500 DATA "JIMMY", 87
510 DATA "WANDA", 48
520 DATA "LUCIA", 70
530 DATA "PETER", 91
540 DATA "KRIS", 45
550 END
RUN
JIMMY 87
WANDA 48
LUCIA 70
PETER 91
KRIS 45
```

The above program reads and prints five data records without any screening. The next program uses a selection structure to select only passing students.

```
100 REM  ***********************
110 REM    SOLUTION WITH A
120 REM    SELECTION STRUCTURE
130 REM  ***********************
140 :
150 (beginning of loop)
160       READ N$, M
170       (selection structure
            print only if M => 50)
180 (end of loop)
190 :
500 DATA "JIMMY", 87
510 DATA "WANDA", 48
520 DATA "LUCIA", 70
530 DATA "PETER", 91
540 DATA "KRIS", 45
RUN
JIMMY 87
LUCIA 70
PETER 91
```

In general, the secret to identifying the need for a selection structure in a program solution is to ask yourself the question posed on the right.

Students who have access to microcomputers using the WATCOM version of BASIC should turn to the middle of this chapter (page 298), where their section begins.

Students who have access to microcomputers using the WATCOM version of BASIC should turn to the middle of this chapter (page 298), where their section begins.

Identifying the Need for a Selection Structure

"Do you wish to use or display only specific items from the data provided?" If the answer is "yes", then a selection structure will be part of your solution.

Figure 14.1 Documentation manuals are valuable to programmers who work with complex software systems. Final drafts of program descriptions, planning diagrams, and program listings are indexed, bound, and stored for future reference.

Courtesy of Digital Equipment Corporation

TRADITIONAL BASIC SECTION

*T*his section is designed for students who have access to microcomputers that use a traditional BASIC interpreter based on a version developed by Microsoft International, such as Applesoft BASIC, Commodore BASIC, IBM BASIC, and GW BASIC.

14.3 UNDERSTANDING DECISION STATEMENTS

*T*he "IF...THEN" statement provides the computer with logical decision-making power. It can be inserted into any program that needs to sort information to solve a problem. Each decision statement is made up of two parts. The first part is a **test condition**, which is a comparison between a given variable and some preset variable or number. The comparison is made with the help of one of six different symbols called **relational operators**, such as "greater than"

or "equal to". It is possible to make such comparisons because the machine reduces each symbol or character to a different binary number (which is made of patterns of the two digits 0 and 1). When the computer compares the letters "A" and "B", for example, the letter "A" will appear different from the letter "B" because it has a different numeric value. The characters and their numeric values are usually listed in an ASCII chart (pronounced askee). The chart at the bottom of this page illustrates the different types of comparisons that can be made.

The second part of the decision statement is some action that the computer must perform if the comparison is true. All comparisons are either TRUE or FALSE. If they are true, the specified action must be performed. If they are false, that action is not performed, and the computer moves on to the next statement in the program.

There are several possible instructions that can be used to complete a test condition. Notice the way the "IF...THEN" statement is set up in each of these examples.

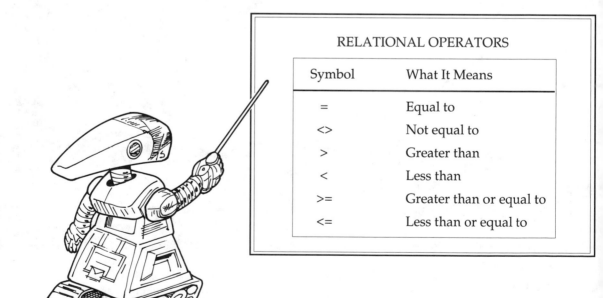

RELATIONAL OPERATORS

Symbol	What It Means
=	Equal to
<>	Not equal to
>	Greater than
<	Less than
>=	Greater than or equal to
<=	Less than or equal to

IF STATEMENT	OUTCOME IF THE TEST CONDITION IS TRUE
IF M >= 50 THEN END	The program would stop executing.
IF M >= 50 THEN GOTO 250	The computer branches directly to statement number 250 in the program.
IF M >= 50 THEN PRINT "PASSED"	The computer prints a character string enclosed within quotation marks.
IF M >= 50 THEN C = C + 1	The computer processes the equation.
IF M >= 50 THEN PRINT	The computer leaves a blank line.

Analyze the following sample program and see if you can predict what the final output will be as each data variable is screened by the decision statement.

The "IF...THEN" statement in this following example compares the value stored in a memory location labelled "M" with the number "50". If the value is equal to or greater than 50, the computer is instructed to print "passed". If the value stored in "M" is less than 50, the computer is instructed to ignore the print command. All decision statements have two possible alternatives.

```
100 REM ******************************
110 REM    SELECTING ITEMS FROM A LIST
120 REM ******************************
130 REM    M = MARK
140 REM    C = LOOP COUNTER
150 :
160 FOR C = 1 TO 4
170 :    READ M
180 :    If M >= 50 THEN PRINT TAB(24) "PASSED"; M
190 NEXT C
200 :
210 DATA 60, 37, 71, 49
220 END
RUN
```

Test condition

If the test condition is true, the PRINT action is taken. If the test condition is false, the PRINT action is ignored

```
                    PASSED 60
                    PASSED 71
```

14.4 SELECTION BY MATCHING NUMBERS

*O*ne way of selecting specific items from a list is to compare numerical data with a preset number or range of numbers. Any item of numeric data that matches the preset number or range of numbers is accepted by the decision statement, and some specific action is taken. Any data that does not match the preset limits is ignored.

The program below uses a decision statement to select all the honour students from a list of five classmates. Even though two items of information, the name and the mark, are provided for each student, only the mark is important in the design of the

"IF...THEN" statement. Essentially, the decision statement is set up to select items according to whether they fall within the range of numbers equal to or greater than 75.

Statement 220 provides the test condition. Its function is to compare each mark that is read into the processor with the value 75. If the test condition is met (true), the computer is instructed to print both the student's name and mark. If the test condition is not met (false), the print instruction is ignored and the computer continues to process the remaining data.

As a challenge, see if you can figure out how many names of students listed in the data section would be printed if the test condition were modified to read "IF M > 70 THEN..." in the program below.

```
100 REM ***************************
110 REM    SELECTING HONOUR STUDENTS
120 REM ***************************
130 REM    N$ = STUDENT NAME
140 REM    M = STUDENT MARK
150 REM    C = LOOP COUNTER
160 :
170 (Clear the screen command)
180 ?:?:?:?:?:?:?:?:?:?
190 :
200 FOR C = 1 TO 5
210 :    READ N$, M
220 :    IF M >= 75 THEN PRINT TAB(20) N$, M
230 NEXT C
240 :
500 DATA "POLLY ESTER", 78
510 DATA "DAN DRUFF", 67
520 DATA "LEAH TARD", 74
530 DATA "LINDA HAND", 81
540 DATA "BARBIE KEW", 76
550 END
RUN
```

```
POLLY ESTER 78
LINDA HAND 81
BARBIE KEW 76
Ready
```

Design a program that will read in all of the following inventory items and their quantities, and have the computer print the name and quantity of all products with amounts less than 50. The output should be centred on a cleared screen with the following titles. Hint: Have the computer print the titles *before* the loop begins.

Data:

Hockey Sticks	48	Shoulder Pads	21
Hockey Pucks	56	Goalie Pads	8
Hockey Helmets	49	Black Tape	38
Goalie Sticks	15	White Tape	62

Sample Output:

```
PRODUCT          CURRENT QUANTITY

Hockey Sticks          48
Shoulder Pads          21
```

14.5 SELECTION BY MATCHING WORDS

"*I*F...THEN" statements can also be used to compare words or letters from a data file to cause some action to be taken if a match is found. In this example, the decision structure is searching for the word "engineer", which appears under the heading "Job Title" in a list of job applicants. If the word appears, the applicant's name is printed. If the word is not discovered, the computer ignores the print command.

```
100 REM ************************
110 REM    COMPARISON WITH WORDS
120 REM ************************
130 REM    N$ = PERSON'S NAME
140 REM    J$ = JOB TITLE
150 REM    C = LOOP COUNTER
160 :
170 FOR C = 1 TO 3                    Test condition
180 :    READ N$, J$
190 :    IF J$ = "ENGINEER" THEN
         PRINT TAB(20) N$, J$
200 NEXT C
210 :
500 DATA "RALPH TWILLIGER",
    "PROGRAMMER"
510 DATA "SUSAN WILSON", "ENGINEER"
520 DATA "JUDY SMITH", "DESIGNER"
530 END
```

The name is printed only if the test condition is true

```
RUN
SUSAN WILSON ENGINEER
```

Design a program that will read in all the data on famous people, their roles, and their countries of residence. Then display only the names and roles of Canadian personalities. The output should appear in two columns in the middle of a cleared screen under the titles "Famous Canadians", and "Roles That Made Them Famous".

Data:

Phil Collins	Singer/Musician	England
Gordon Lightfoot	Singer/ Song-writer	Canada
Anne Murray	Singer	Canada
Alexander Coville	Realistic Painter	Canada
Margaret Atwood	Novelist/Poet	Canada
John Polanyi	Nobel Prize Winner	Canada
Pierre Berton	Writer/TV Personality	Canada
David Suzuki	Scientist/Author	Canada
Barbara Frum	TV Journalist	Canada
Elizabeth Manley	Figure Skater	Canada
Tom Cruise	Actor	U.S.A.
Conrad Black	Financier	Canada
Alannah Myles	Singer	Canada
Robert Bateman	Naturalist Painter	Canada
Genevieve Bujold	Actress	Canada

14.6 INTERACTIVE SEARCHES

*T*he decision structure can also be used as part of the "screening for suitability" process within interactive programs. The program can prompt the user for a word or number that acts as the **key to the search**. In other words, the decision structure uses that particular word or number to screen or search through all incoming data from the data statements, and will accept and display only information related to the specific item requested by the user. The program on the next page, simulating a doctor's medical file, illustrates the "key to the search" function that the decision statement performs.

Each time this program is executed, the user (doctor or nurse) can key in a new request for a patient's name that the program then uses as the "key to the search" to scan through all the medical records. To enter another name, the program must be run again.

Upper- and lower-case letters were used in the above example to differentiate between the prompt from the program and the input from the doctor. However, in actual programming, the search can be "case sensitive", which means that the computer thinks that Dewitt is an entirely different person from DEWITT. Adjust your programming to compensate for this difference.

```
100 REM ********************
110 REM   INTERACTIVE SEARCH
120 REM ********************
130 :
140 REM N$ = PATIENT'S NAME
150 REM M$ = MEDICAL PROBLEM
160 REM R$ = SEARCH REQUEST
170 REM C = LOOP COUNTER
180 :
190 (clear the screen command)
200 ?:?:?:?:?:?:?:?:?:?
210 PRINT TAB(20) "ENTER PATIENT'S LAST NAME ";: INPUT R$        Key to the search
220 ?:?
230 :
240 FOR C = 1 TO 5
250 :   READ N$, M$
260 :   IF N$ = R$ THEN PRINT TAB(20) M$
270 NEXT C
280 :
500 DATA "WILSON", "MILD STROKE"
510 DATA "JARVIS", "BACK INJURY"
520 DATA "WONG", "HEAD INJURY"                Medical records
530 DATA "JAZVEC", "CHRONIC ARTHRITIS"
540 DATA "DEWITT", "SKIN ABRASIONS"
550 END
```

Sample Output:

```
ENTER PATIENT'S LAST NAME ? Dewitt


SKIN ABRASIONS
```

Design an interactive flight-information program that will provide ticket clerks (or customers) with flight times and gate numbers of any of six flights to particular cities. The display screen must have the six cities listed across the top, and must prompt the user for one of those cities. The program then searches on that key for the appropriate flight time and gate number, and displays them as shown in the example below.

Sample Output:

```
        FLIGHT-RESERVATION SYSTEM

VANCOUVER   MONTREAL   ST. JOHN'S

TORONTO     HALIFAX    CALGARY

WHAT CITY ? Halifax          ← Key to the search

DEPARTURE TIME: 8:15 p.m.

GATE NUMBER:       21        ← From data files
```

14.7 MULTIPLE DECISIONS

*S*ome programs require several decision structures—for example, a program that screens several different factors from a list of data. The program on the next page illustrates the use of two "IF...THEN" statements in the same solution.

In this program, the first decision statement selects only those students who are in grade 11. The second decision statement selects only those students who achieved grades of 80 percent or better. Any data meeting those two criteria gets printed by line 250. All other data is rejected. Notice how the "IF...THEN" statements are set up to screen for what they do not want rather than what they want. Screening to eliminate unacceptable data is usually easy. Have a second look at the Grade 11 Honour Student program. State what output this program would generate if the test condition in line 240 were rewritten to read "IF A < 70 THEN GOTO 260".

```
100 REM  *******************************
110 REM      GRADE 11 HONOUR STUDENTS
120 REM  *******************************
130 REM    N$ = STUDENT NAME
140 REM    G = GRADE LEVEL
150 REM    A = AVERAGE FOR THE YEAR
160 REM    C = LOOP COUNTER
170 :
180 (Clear the screen command)
190 ?:?:?:?:?:?:?:?:?:?
200 :
210 FOR C = 1 TO 5
220 :    READ N$, G, A
230 :    IF G < > 11 THEN GOTO 260
240 :    IF A < 80 THEN GOTO 260
250 :    PRINT TAB(20) N$, A
260 NEXT C
270 :
500 DATA "FREDDIE LAKER", 11, 71
510 DATA "JUNE POSSIUM", 11, 83
520 DATA "ALICE GOSHAM", 10, 92
530 DATA "TOM LATHAM", 11, 90
540 DATA "ANNA KNIGHT", 11, 85
550 END
RUN
```

> First decision rejects all data with grades other than grade 11

> Second decision rejects all data with marks less than 80

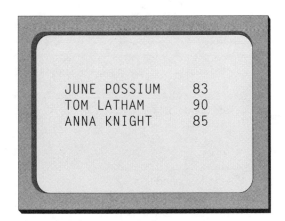

```
        JUNE POSSIUM    83
        TOM LATHAM      90
        ANNA KNIGHT     85
```

END OF TRADITIONAL BASIC SECTION

*S*tudents not reading the section on WAT-COM BASIC should now turn to page 308.

WATCOM BASIC SECTION

*T*his section describes the more powerful features of the specific interpreter called WATCOM BASIC.

14.3W UNDERSTANDING SELECTION STRUCTURES

*T*he "IF...ENDIF" structure provides the computer with logical decision-making power. It can be inserted into any program that requires information be screened for suitability. Each selection structure has at least three statements. The first statement is a "test condition", which is a comparison between a variable and some preset word or number. The comparison is made with

the help of one of six different symbols called "relational operators", such as "greater than" or "equal to".

The second statement in the selection structure, which is wedged between the "IF" and "ENDIF" statements, gives the action that the computer must perform if the comparison is true. All comparisons are either TRUE or FALSE. If they are true, the specified action must be performed. If they are false, that action is not performed, and the computer moves on to the next statement in the program outside the selection structure.

The last or bottom statement is the "END IF" statement, which informs the computer where the selection structure ends.

Analyse the following program and see if you can predict what the final output will be as each data variable is screened by the selection structure.

```
100 REM *****************************
110 REM    SELECTING ITEMS FROM A LIST
120 REM *****************************
130 REM    MARK = STUDENT MARK
140 REM    C = LOOP COUNTER
150 :
160 C = 1
170 WHILE C <= 4
180     READ MARK
190 :
200     IF MARK >= 50          ◄──────────  Test condition
210         PRINT TAB (24); "PASSED"; MARK
220     ENDIF
230 :
240     C = C + 1
250 ENDLOOP
260 :
270 DATA 60, 37, 71, 49
280 END
RUN
```

If the test condition is true, the PRINT action is taken. If the test condition is false, the PRINT command is ignored

```
                    PASSED 60
                    PASSED 71
```

In the preceding program segment, the "IF...ENDIF" structure is the decision structure. It provides the computer with two possible outcomes or actions based on a test condition. A **test condition** is a comparison of two or more items using a relational operator, such as "greater than or equal to" or "less than or equal to". The "IF...ENDIF" structure in the above example compares the value stored in the memory location labelled "MARK" with the number "50". If the value stored in "MARK" is greater than 49, the computer is instructed to print the word "passed". If the value stored in "MARK" is less than 50, the computer is instructed to read another value from the data file.

Relational Operators The chart below right illustrates the different types of comparisons that can be made inside a BASIC statement. The symbols used for comparisons are called **relational operators**. They are used to define how one item relates to another. This comparison is possible because the machine reduces each symbol or character to a different binary number (which is made of patterns of the two digits 0 and 1). When the computer compares the letters "A" and "B", for example, the letter "A" will appear different from the letter "B" because it has a different numeric value. The characters and their numeric values are usually listed in an ASCII chart (pronounced askee).

There are several possible commands that can be used in the "IF...ENDIF" structure. Consider the chart on the next page, illustrating several possible selection structures and their outcome when the test condition is true.

These examples illustrate a variety of instructions the computer can process as an outcome if the test condition is true. Programmers are not restricted to only one statement, but can insert several lines between the "IF" and "ENDIF" commands, if desired.

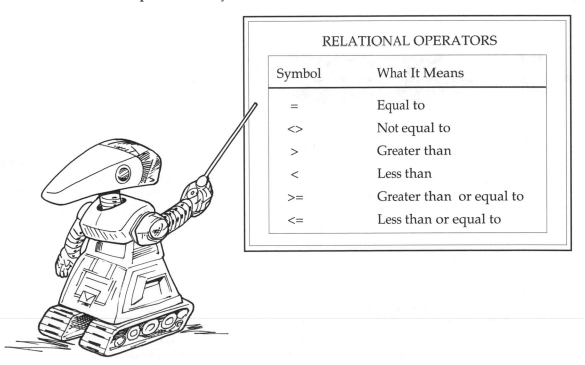

RELATIONAL OPERATORS

Symbol	What It Means
=	Equal to
<>	Not equal to
>	Greater than
<	Less than
>=	Greater than or equal to
<=	Less than or equal to

SELECTION STRUCTURE	WHAT WOULD HAPPEN IF THE TEST CONDITION WERE TRUE
| ```
IF M >= 50
    READ N$
ENDIF
``` | The computer reads an item from data. |
| ```
IF M >= 50
    PRINT "PASSED"
ENDIF
``` | The computer prints the literal enclosed within the quotation marks. |
| ```
IF M >= 50
    C = C + 1
ENDIF
``` | The computer processes the assignment statement. |
| ```
IF M >= 50
    PRINT
ENDIF
``` | The computer leaves a blank line. |

14.4W SELECTION BY MATCHING NUMBERS

*O*ne way of selecting specific items from a list is to screen numerical data with a preset number or range of numbers. Any numeric data that matches the preset number or range of numbers is accepted by the decision statement, and some action is taken. Any data that does not match the preset limits is ignored.

The program on the next page uses a decision statement to select all the honour students from a list of five classmates. Even though two items of information are provided about each student—name and mark, in this case—only the mark is important in the design of the "IF...ENDIF" structure. Essentially, the decision statement is set up to select items if they fall in the range of numbers equal to or greater than 75.

Statement 240 provides the "test condition". If the test condition is true, statement 250 will be executed. If the statement is false, line 250 will be ignored. The function of the test condition, in this case, is to compare each mark that is read into the processor with the value 75. The computer is instruct-ed to print both the name and mark of every student who has a mark greater than or equal to 75.

As a challenge, see if you can figure out how many names of students listed in the data section will be printed if the test condition is changed to "IF MARK > 70" in the program to the right.

```
100 REM ****************************
110 REM    SELECTING HONOUR STUDENTS
120 REM ****************************
130 REM    NAME$ = STUDENT NAME
140 REM    MARK = STUDENT MARK
150 REM    C = LOOP COUNTER
160 :
170 CALL CLEARSCREEN
180 ?:?:?:?:?:?:?:?:?:?
190 :
200 C = 1
210 WHILE C <= 5
220     READ NAME$, MARK
230 :
240     IF MARK >= 75
250         PRINT TAB(24); NAME$, MARK
260     ENDIF
270 :
280     C = C + 1
290 ENDLOOP
300 :
500 DATA "POLLY ESTER", 78
510 DATA "DAN DRUFF", 67
520 DATA "LEAH TARD", 74
530 DATA "LINDA HAND", 81
540 DATA "BARBIE KEW", 76
550 :
560 END
RUN
```

```
    POLLY ESTER    78
    LINDA HAND     81
    BARBIE KEW     76
```

Design a program that will read in all of the following inventory items and their quantities, and have the computer print the name and quantity of all articles with quantities less than 50. The output should appear centred on a cleared screen with the titles shown in the sample output below. Set the loop counter to match the number of sets of data to be read in.

Sample Output:

```
ARTICLES            CURRENT QUANTITY
Hockey Sticks            48
Shoulder Pads            21
```

Data:

Hockey Sticks	48	Shoulder Pads	21
Hockey Pucks	56	Goalie Pads	8
Hockey Helmets	49	Black Tape	38
Goalie Sticks	15	White Tape	62

14.5W SELECTION BY MATCHING WORDS

"IF...ENDIF" statements can also be used to compare words or letters from a data file and cause some action to be taken if a match is found. In this example, the decision structure is searching for the word "engineer" in a list of job applicants. If the word "engineer" appears, the applicant's name is printed. If the word "engineer" is not discovered, the computer ignores the print command.

If the test condition is true, the job and the person's name will be printed. Otherwise, the PRINT command is ignored

```
100 REM ************************
110 REM    COMPARISON WITH WORDS
120 REM ************************
130 REM    NAME$ = PERSON'S NAME
140 REM    JOB$ = JOB TITLE
150 REM    C = LOOP COUNTER
160 :
170 C = 1
180 WHILE C <= 3
190     READ NAME$, JOB$
200 :
210     IF JOB$ = "ENGINEER"
220       PRINT TAB(20); NAME$, JOB$
230     ENDIF
240 :
250     C = C + 1
260 ENDLOOP
270 :
500 DATA "RALPH TWILLIGER",
        "PROGRAMMER"
510 DATA "SUSAN WILSON", "ENGINEER"
520 DATA "JUDY SMITH", "DESIGNER"
530 END
RUN

        SUSAN WILSON    ENGINEER
```

Design a program that will read in all the data on famous people, their roles, and their countries of residence. Then, display only the names and roles of Canadian personalities. The output should appear in two columns in the middle of a cleared screen under the titles "Famous Canadians" and "Roles That Made Them Famous".

Data:

Phil Collins	Singer/Musician	England
Gordon Lightfoot	Singer/Song-writer	Canada
Anne Murray	Singer	Canada
Alexander Coville	Realistic Painter	Canada
Margaret Atwood	Novelist/Poet	Canada
John Polanyi	Nobel Prize Winner	Canada
Pierre Berton	Writer/TV Personality	Canada
David Suzuki	Scientist/Author	Canada
Barbara Frum	TV Journalist	Canada
Elizabeth Manley	Figure Skater	Canada
Tom Cruise	Actor	U.S.A.
Conrad Black	Financier	Canada
Alannah Myles	Singer	Canada
Robert Bateman	Naturalist Painter	Canada
Genevieve Bujold	Actress	Canada

14.6W INTERACTIVE SEARCHES

A decision structure can also be used as part of the "screening for suitability" process within an interactive program. The program can prompt the user for a word or number that acts as the "key to the search".

In other words, the decision structure uses that word or number to screen or search through all incoming data from the data statements and will accept and display only information related to the specific item requested by the user. The program on the following page, which simulates a doctor's medical file, illustrates the "key to the search" function that the decision statement performs.

```
100  REM  **********************
110  REM    INTERACTIVE SEARCH
120  REM  **********************
130  :
140  REM    NAME$ = PATIENT'S NAME
150  REM    PROBLEM$ = MEDICAL PROBLEM
170  REM    REQUEST$ = SEARCH REQUEST
180  REM    C = LOOP COUNTER
190  :
200  CALL CLEARSCREEN
210  ?:?:?:?:?:?:?:?:?:?
220  PRINT TAB(20); "ENTER PATIENT'S LAST NAME ";: INPUT REQUEST$
230  ?:?
240  :
250  C = 1
260  WHILE C <= 5
270      READ NAME$, PROBLEM$
280  :
290      IF NAME$ = REQUEST$
300          PRINT TAB(20); PROBLEM$
310      ENDIF
320  :
330      C = C + 1
340  ENDLOOP
350  :
500  DATA "WILSON", "MILD STROKE"
510  DATA "JARVIS", "BACK INJURY"
520  DATA "WONG", "HEAD INJURY"
530  DATA "JAZVEC", "CHRONIC ARTHRITIS"
540  DATA "DEWITT", "SKIN ABRASIONS"
550  END
RUN
```

Key to the search

Medical records

Sample Output:

```
ENTER PATIENT'S LAST NAME ? Dewitt


SKIN ABRASIONS
```

Each time the program on the previous page is executed, the user (doctor or nurse) can key in a new request for a patient's name, which the program then uses as the "key to the search" as it scans through all the medical records. To enter another name, the program must be run again.

Upper- and lower-case letters were used in the above example to differentiate between the prompt from the program and the input from the doctor. However, in actual programming, the search can be "case sensitive",which means that the computer thinks that Dewitt is an entirely different person from DEWITT.

One way of dealing with a case-sensitive program is to use a WATCOM library function called "LWRC", which is an abbreviation of the words "lower case". For example, the following WATCOM statement, "IF LWRC$(NAME$) = LWRC$(REQUEST$)", can be substituted in line 290 in the preceding program. Then the computer will convert both variables into all lower-case letters before comparing for a match.

Program to Try

(45 mins.)

Design an interactive flight information program that will provide ticket clerks (or customers) with the flight times and gate numbers of any of six flights to particular cities. The display screen must have the six cities listed across the top, and prompt the user for one of those cities. The program then searches on that key for the appropriate flight time and gate number and displays them as shown in the example to the right.

Sample Output:

```
FLIGHT RESERVATION SYSTEM


VANCOUVER      MONTREAL      ST. JOHN'S

TORONTO        HALIFAX       CALGARY


WHAT CITY ? Halifax                        Key to the
                                           search

DEPARTURE TIME: 8:15 p.m.

                                           From data
GATE NUMBER: 21                            files
```

14.7W MULTIPLE DECISIONS

*S*ome programs require several decision structures—for example, a program that screens several different factors from a list of data. The program on the following page illustrates the use of two decision structures, one within the other in the same solution. Data that meets the condition of the first decision is then screened by the second decision. See if you can predict what output this program will produce.

```
100 REM  ***************************
110 REM    GRADE 11 HONOUR STUDENTS
120 REM  ***************************
130 REM    NAME$ = STUDENT NAME
140 REM    GRADE = GRADE LEVEL
150 REM    AVERAGE = AVERAGE
160 REM    C = LOOP COUNTER
170 :
180 CALL CLEARSCREEN
190 ?:?:?:?:?:?:?:?:?:?
200 :
210 C = 1
220 WHILE C < 6
230     READ NAME$, GRADE, AVERAGE
240 :
250     IF GRADE = 11
260 :
270         IF AVERAGE > 79
280             PRINT TAB(20); NAME$, AVERAGE
290         ENDIF
300 :
310     ENDIF
320 :
330     C = C + 1
340 ENDLOOP
350 :
500 DATA "GUY DROLET", 11, 85
510 DATA "MONICA TAYLOR", 11, 83
520 DATA "GEORGE HOPKINS", 10, 92
530 DATA "DAN RYAN", 11, 90
540 DATA "BRIAN SCINTO", 11, 71
550 :
560 END
RUN
```

```
        GUY DROLET      85
        MONICA TAYLOR   83
        DAN RYAN        90
    Ready
```

In the above program, the decision statement selects only those students who are both in grade 11 and have achieved grades of 80 percent or better. Any data meeting those two criteria gets printed by line 280. All other data is ignored and the computer is instructed to continue with the loop. When one decision structure is combined within another, this procedure is called a **nested decision structure**.

14.8W IF...ELSE...ENDIF

*D*ecision structures can also be used to take different actions, depending on the results of the test condition. The "IF...ELSE... ENDIF" structure provides two alternative actions. Suppose, for example, that it is necessary to divide a list of students into the number who are passing and the number who are failing.

The program below left reads each data item one at a time, adding the value of one to the PASS counter if the number is greater than 49, or adding the value of one to the FAIL counter if the number is less than 50. The output would appear as shown in the bottom right corner.

```
100 REM *********************
110 REM    PASS/FAIL PROGRAM
120 REM *********************
130 :
140 CALL CLEARSCREEN
150 ?:?:?:?:?:?:?:?
160 :
170 PASS = 0
180 FAIL = 0
190 C = 1
200 WHILE C <= 10
210     READ NUM
220 :
230     IF NUM < 50
240         FAIL = FAIL + 1
250     ELSE
260         PASS = PASS + 1
270     ENDIF
280 :
290     C = C + 1
300 ENDLOOP
310 :
320 PRINT TAB(20); "NUMBER OF STUDENTS WHO PASSED ="; PASS
330 PRINT
340 PRINT TAB(20); "NUMBER OF STUDENTS WHO FAILED ="; FAIL
350 DATA 67,43,90,78,81,50,63,49,40,75
360 END
```

"I think you should be more explicit here in step two."

Sample Output:

```
NUMBER OF STUDENTS WHO PASSED = 7

NUMBER OF STUDENTS WHO FAILED = 3
```

END OF WATCOM BASIC SECTION

*D*ecision statements (or structures) give computers their peculiar ability to "think". They can be inserted into programs where logical comparisons are required and alternative actions can be taken as a result of the comparison. The logical comparisons are performed by symbols called "relational operators", such as greater than (>) or less than (<). It is possible to compare numbers, letters, or even special characters, because each keyboard symbol has a numeric value that is created when the computer converts all its instructions into binary numbers for machine handling. Most BASIC computer manuals have an ASCII (pronounced as-kee) chart as a guide to the numeric values of each character.

The part of the decision that does the comparison is called the "test condition". It can compare data variables with a constant or with some other variable. The decision statement (or structure) can be completed with several types of instructions, such as print commands, equations to be processed, or transfer requests.

Multiple decisions can be used in the same program to screen for several desired or undesired conditions in the data. Each decision will have its own outcome.

The secret to identifying the need for a selection structure is to ask yourself—"Do you wish to use or display only specific items from the data provided"? If the answer is yes, then a selection structure will be part of your solution.

"Where's the clown that set up this program?"

interactive searches

key to the search

multiple-decision structures (nested decision structures)

relational operator

single-decision structure

selection by matching numbers

selection by matching words

selection structure

test condition

PROGRAMMING COMMANDS

Traditional BASIC Commands

IF...THEN

WATCOM BASIC Commands

IF...ENDIF

IF...ELSE...ENDIF

CHECKING YOUR READING

*T*hese are general questions that may require reading comprehension, factual recall, and some application of the knowledge gained from this chapter.

Introduction

1. How can you tell if a problem solution will require a selection structure?

2. What other programming structure often combines with the selection structure in program solutions?

3. What question can you ask yourself that will help you to identify the need for a selection structure?

Understanding Decision Statements (or Structures)

4. Explain what a "test condition" does in a programming statement.

5. How many results or actions are possible from a single decision? Give an example of a decision statement or decision structure, and explain the results from that decision.

6. What is a relational operator? Give three examples of relational operators.

7. Suggest four general actions that the computer could take as a result of a test condition.

Selection by Matching Numbers

8. Explain to what the programming concept "selection by matching numbers" refers.

9. Write a decision statement or decision structure that will compare the contents of memory location "A" with the value "16". If the two are equal, print the phrase "Age 16".

10. Write a decision statement or decision structure that will screen numerical data and print only data that is greater than 100.

Selection by Matching Words

11. Explain the programming term "selection by matching words".

12. Write a decision statement or decision structure that will compare the contents of a main memory storage area with the word "French". If the test condition is true, have the computer print the phrase "Mother tongue - French".

13. Write a decision statement or decision structure that will screen incoming data containing names and job titles, and print only those names carrying the job title "programmer".

Interactive Searches

14. Explain to what the term "key to a search" refers in interactive programming.

15. Give an example of a "key to a search".

16. Explain what "case sensitive" means, and invent your own example to illustrate the concept.

Multiple Decisions

17. To what does the term "multiple decisions" refer in programming?

18. Suggest an example of a program that will use more than one decision.

19. Write a short programming module that will screen the following list of data and print the names of only those job candidates who are 16 years of age or older and can type.

Data:

Susan Wallace	17	electrical
John Thompson	16	typing
Kim Yagar	16	typing
Sandhya Chari	15	typing

*T*hese questions assume an understanding of the material presented in this chapter and provide situations that may require evaluation, analysis, or application of that knowledge.

1. Write a decision statement or decision structure that will print the word "passed" if the value stored in memory location "M" is greater than 25.

2. Write a decision statement or decision structure that will perform the calculation C = C + 1 if the value in memory location "T" is less than 50.

3. Rewrite either version of the following program to remove all syntax and logic errors. The program is supposed to print 0, 5, 15, 20—leaving out the answer 10 from the series.

Traditional BASIC

```
10 T = 0
20 FOR C = 0 TO 20
30 T = T + C
40 C = C + 5
50 NEXT T
```

WATCOM BASIC

```
10 TOTAL = 0
20 C = 0
30 WHILE C < 25
40     TOTAL = TOTAL + C
50     C = C + 5
60 END
```

4. Rewrite either version of the following program to remove all syntax and logic errors. The program is supposed to read in all data and print only the names of students who are in grade 11.

Traditional BASIC

```
10 FOR C = 1 TO 4
20 READ N$, G
30 IF G < 11 PRINT N$
40 DATA "BRIAN", 11
50 DATA "SUSAN", 11
60 DATA "WENDY", 12
70 DATA "JULIAN", 11
```

WATCOM BASIC

```
10 C = 0
20 WHILE C < 5
30     READ N$, G
40     IF G < 11
50     PRINT N$
60 DATA "BRIAN", 11
70 DATA "SUSAN", 11
80 DATA "WENDY", 12
90 DATA "JULIAN", 11
```

5. Design a short program module that will read all of the following data and print the names and quantities of only those items with quantities greater than 50.

Data:

Chalk brushes	11
Yellow Chalk	83
White Chalk	450
Metre Sticks	18
Pencil Sharpeners	3

6. Design a program module that will generate and print all the numbers from 0 to 20 except the number 10.

7. Design a program module that will count by fives and print all the numbers in a series from 5 to 50 except the number 20.

Multiple Decisions

8. Design a program module that will read in the following data and print only the numbers that are greater than 49 but less than 100.

   Data: 62, 23, 91, 79, 75, 45, 67, 50, 57, 68

9. Design a program module that will print all the numbers from 1 to 20 with the following exceptions: instead of printing the answer 10 or the answer 20, print the phrase "next group".

10. Design a program module that will read all of the following data and print only the names of students whose extra-curricular activities include either basketball or soccer.

   Data:

   Vernon Miles, basketball, soccer
   Mila Turner, council, track & field
   Ted Sheehan, soccer, football
   Randy Zimmerman, basketball, scouts
   Leisa Fleming, basketball, cheerleaders
   Nijola Sernas, basketball, track & field

PROGRAMMING PROBLEMS

*T*hese problems will require analysis and planning on paper before you enter and test them on the computer. Solutions must contain all the elements of good programming style. You may want to save them on disk for future reference. Teachers may require printer output instead of screen output.

1. Criminal Record

The Fredricton Police Station wants a program that will allow constables to request records on all criminals who are guilty of any one of three specific crimes. The file contains the name, offence, and conviction date of each criminal. Design an interactive program that will prompt the user for the specific type of crime. The program is to search the criminal record file and print complete statistics on all criminals who were found guilty in that particular category. The output screen must include a title and column headings as shown.

Sample Output:

```
 *** CRIMINAL SEARCH PROGRAM ***

WHAT CATEGORY ? Theft

NAME          OFFENSE CONVICTION DATE

Bugs Malone    Theft January 5, 1981
Louise Lurche  Theft July 7, 1985
```

Data:

Bugs Malone	Theft	January 5, 1981
Jim Slicer	Assault	May 1, 1952
Louise Lurche	Theft	July 7, 1985
Slippery Sally	Theft	March 23, 1986
Wilma Grinch	Arson	April 1, 1983
Edie Striker	Assault	August 25, 1986
Red Dillinger	Theft	September 16, 1975
Wally Lightfinger	Theft	June 9, 1963
Wippy the Torch	Arson	August 5, 1988
Al Heavyhander	Assault	October 30, 1988

2. Baseball Draftees

For every baseball player eligible to be drafted, a record has been prepared showing his name, age, position, and batting average. Design a program that will read in one data record at a time, and select and print the statistics of only those players who are at least 25 years old and have a batting average of 280 or better.

Sample Output:

```
***** SELECTED DRAFT CHOICES *****

NAME          AGE POSITION   AVERAGE

George Latham 26  Third Base  290
Watch T. Ball 25  Short Stop  305
```

Data:

George Latham	26	Third Base	290
Morley Simpson	21	First Base	120
Watch T. Ball	25	Short Stop	305
Wally Badman	23	Catcher	208
Legs Wasserman	25	L. Field	321
Mo Zachowski	26	R. Field	256
Don Ferris	27	Second Base	271
Bill Notcham	25	Pitcher	218

3. Mortgage Holders

The manager of a major lending institution has asked you, the company's chief programmer, to design a program that will list monthly all delinquent mortgage holders requiring immediate action. The list should contain the names and loan balances of only those customers who have balances over $50 000 and have been delinquent (have not made payments) for three months or longer. The output should appear on a cleared screen under the titles as shown.

Sample Output:

```
CUSTOMER         OVERDUE BALANCE

Peter Pauper       $152 900
Wilma Oddley       $ 53 500
```

Data:

Peter Pauper	$152 900	4 months
Wilma Oddley	$ 53 500	3.5 months
Joan Jamison	$ 49 700	4 months
George Grimley	$ 50 100	3 months
Heather Handout	$ 80 000	1 month
Cash McCall	$ 75 600	0 months
Tony De Peso	$ 60 000	6 months
Mary Meanly	$ 73 000	3.5 months

4. Shipping Rates

Packages are shipped from Toronto to Halifax by rail at the following rates: for packages up to 100 kg - $0.65/kg; for packages exceeding 100 kg - $0.80/kg. Plan a program that will read the following customer names and their package weights, one set at a time, and produce the chart as shown. Shipping costs must be accurate to two decimal places.

Sample Output:

```
CUSTOMER        PACKAGE     SHIPPING
                WEIGHT      COST

G. Hagen        114.0       $71.10
G. Augustin     120.0       $ ____
```

Data:

CUSTOMER'S NAME	PACKAGE WEIGHT (kg)
G. Hagen	114.0
G. Augustin	120.0
N. Casey	210.5
E. Prokop	34.0
P. McHugh	98.0
J. Parekh	55.5
B. Herd	40.65
T. Smith	58.0
K. Kasik	321.0
T. Viola	69.0

5. The Cosmetic Company

A cosmetic company that sells products door-to-door pays its sales staff a percentage of their total sales for the month. The company keeps a record of each salesperson's name and total monthly sales. If sales are under $1000, a 9.5 percent commission is paid. If sales are $1000 or over, an 11 percent commission is paid. Design a program that will read in the name and monthly sales total for each person and print a complete list containing the name of the salesperson, total sales, and the dollar amount of commission for every seller. At the end of the list, have the computer calculate and print the two totals as shown. All dollar answers must be accurate to two decimal places.

Sample Output:

```
SALESPERSON       MONTHLY   COMMISSION
                  SALES

Rena Bruni        $1 250    $137.50
Marilyn Conrad    $3 600    $ _____

TOTAL SALES = $
TOTAL COMMISSIONS = $
```

Data:

SALESPERSON	MONTHLY SALES
Rena Bruni	$1 250
Marilyn Conrad	$3 600
Doris Flynn	$ 960
Kyu Hong	$2 890
Roger Breese	$ 975
Dorothy Barnes	$ 500
Jennifer Dabic	$3 200
Julio Estefan	$1 300
Cathy Renaud	$1 650
Emilia Bialik	$ 865

6. Medical Diagnosis

Interns at a general hospital want a program that will allow them to key in data on a patient (in response to prompts from the program) to determine whether the person has a cold, bronchitis, or pneumonia. The interactive program will present "yes" or "no" questions, such as "Does the patient have a sore throat?" "Signs of chest congestion?" "Does the patient have a fever?" "Any chest pains?" The total number of "yes" responses will determine which diagnosis and which recommended cure the program is to display. Possible cures can include throat lozenges, aspirin, a cold remedy, an antibiotic, and bed rest. You decide which total is best associated with each output. A sample display is shown on the next page.

Sample Output:

```
*************************************************************
              MEDICAL DIAGNOSIS PROGRAM

1. DOES THE PATIENT HAVE A SORE IHROAT? No
2. SIGNS OF CHEST CONGESTION? Yes
3. DOES THE PATIENT HAVE A FEVER? Yes
4. ANY CHEST PAINS? Yes
   POSSIBLE DIAGNOSIS: Pneumonia
   RECOMMENDED CURE:   Bed Rest
                       Aspirin
                       Antibiotic
*************************************************************
```

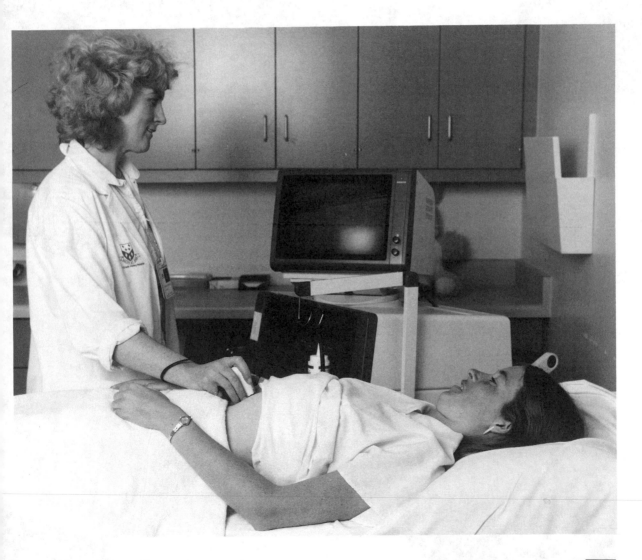

Chapter

15

AN INTRODUCTION TO TURBO PASCAL

TO TURBO PASCAL

66 The decade-old Three-Mile Island (nuclear power plant) disaster...is still being cleaned up by a six-wheeled, one-armed robot named Rover. 99

Mark Kemp
Freelance Author
Discover Magazine

OBJECTIVES

By the end of this chapter, you will be able to:

1 Define the following programming terms: algorithm, control statement, counter, loop, variable declaration;

2 Use the following Pascal system commands: EDIT, COMPILE, RUN;

3 Use the following Pascal programming commands: PROGRAM, VARIABLE, WRITELN, BEGIN...END, READLN, CLRSCR, FOR...DO, REPEAT...UNTIL, IF...THEN, IF...THEN...ELSE;

4 Design programs that use one or more of these program structures: sequential, repetition, selection.

WORKING IN THE WORLD OF COMPUTERS

CAM Engineer
specializes in the design of computer-aided manufacturing facilities

Computing Contractor
contracts time and programming skills on an hourly basis to companies that need temporary help

Econometric Forecaster
uses computer models to forecast how well the economy will be doing in the future

Expert Systems Specialist
uses rule-based artificial intelligence systems to design specific applications

Industrial Robot Salesperson
sells robotic devices to manufacturing companies

Project Manager
leads a team of in-house planners and programmers to solve corporate computer problems

Space Station Computer Specialist
operates and monitors the environmental and information-systems computers in a space station

Technical Support Analyst
assists a development team with computer hardware, peripheral devices, and tools to install new computer systems

15.1 INTRODUCTION

Pascal is a programming language that was developed in the early 1970s by the Swiss computer scientist Nicklaus Wirth. It was named for the 17th-century French mathematician and philosopher, Blaise Pascal. There are several incompatible versions of the Pascal programming language on the market, including Microsoft Quick Pascal, Turbo Pascal, and WATCOM Pascal. This chapter concentrates on the commercially popular Turbo Pascal Version 3.01, this being a widely used version. Later versions will vary. However, the material given here will enable you to write fairly complex programs, and will also provide a solid foundation of knowledge for further exploration of the language.

Pascal represents a category of language processors called **compilers**. This means that programs are written and executed in two distinct stages: the edit and compile stage, and the run stage. Only when a program is completely written and compiled will it run, or will run-time error messages be displayed. When mistakes are found in Turbo Pascal, the software returns the user to the editor automatically, as soon as the escape key is pressed.

An error in a computer program is referred to as a **bug**, and the process of finding and removing errors is called **debugging**.

There are two kinds of errors encountered when writing programs. A **syntax error** is a mistake in the grammatical rules of the language. Syntax errors include spelling mistakes in command words, missing semi-colons at the ends of statements, and incorrect arrangement of symbols within a statement. These types of errors are "flagged" by the compiler and pointed out to the programmer. Syntax errors always prevent the program from executing.

A **logic error** refers to an error in the design of the program that leads to incorrect output, although the program does execute. Examples include incorrect equations, data, or phrases. Logic errors can be difficult to locate because they are not "flagged" by the compiler. Also, the user often mistakenly thinks the output is automatically correct simply because it is displayed without any compilation errors.

15.2 STEPS IN PROBLEM SOLVING

Good programmers always plan first, and program second. You should never sit down at the computer and simply begin keying in Pascal code. This leads to bad design and poor output. The program solution to a problem, called the **algorithm**, is best achieved by following a series of five steps.

1. **Problem Analysis**

   Consider the problem carefully and determine what is expected as output from the computer. Using ordinary sentences, describe the expected output clearly and unambiguously.

   Example:

   PRINT THE PHRASES "GROSS PAY = $" AND "NET PAY = $", ALONG WITH THEIR RESPECTIVE VALUES, CENTRED ON A CLEARED SCREEN.

2. **List Known Values**

   List all known values provided by the problem. Assign these values to specific variable names.

   Example: HOURS := 40 RATE := 8.50

3. Plan an Algorithm

On paper, outline the steps you will take to arrive at the expected output. You may wish to number the steps to indicate their order of appearance. Consider the following example of a simple planning technique called "pseudocode" (meaning false code, so called because it does not execute).

Example of a Pseudocode Algorithm

1. Program Header
2. Programmer Comments
3. Variable Declarations
4. Begin Command
5. Accept Input from Keyboard
6. Perform Calculations
7. Print Output
8. End Command

4. Code the Solution

Convert the lines of the program into the language of Pascal following the appropriate syntax rules. Key the coded solution into the computer using the Edit module of Turbo Pascal.

5. Execute and Debug the Program

When the algorithm has been coded and entered into the Pascal editor, instruct the computer to compile and run the program. Analyze the output for correctness, and debug any syntax errors. Then run the program using test data for which you have hand-calculated the correct output. Do this for a variety of data, being sure to pick difficult cases as well as easy ones. If the computer output is not correct, it means that you have logical errors, so debug them. Repeat this process until all errors are removed and the program delivers the correct output.

"Hope you like tea. We don't have a coffee algorithm yet."

15.3 GETTING STARTED

When the Turbo Pascal language is loaded into your computer, you will see an opening "copyright line" which asks the question, "Include error message (Y/N)?" Enter the letter "Y" for "Yes" so that error diagnostic messages will be displayed when syntax errors are spotted. These will help you locate and correct mistakes.

The next screen that appears is Turbo Pascal's main menu. Each of the highlighted letters represents an option that the programmer can select.

```
Pascal Main Menu

Logged drive: A
Active directory: \

Work file:
Main file:

Edit Compile Run      Save
Dir  Quit compiler    Options

Text: 0 bytes
Free: 62024 bytes

>
```

15.4 COMPONENTS OF A SAMPLE PROGRAM

A Pascal program typically has four sections, each with a different purpose. The following program (which you may wish to key in on a test run) illustrates the four components. In order to begin, you must select the letter "W" (Work file) from the main menu, and key in the program's file name, which the computer will use to identify the program. Next select the letter "E" to call up the Editor. Be sure that you are in the Insert mode.

To test the program, hold down the control (CTRL) key with your left hand while tapping the "K" and "D" keys (in that order) with your right hand.

This returns you to the main menu, which provides the menu prompt symbol ">". Next press "C" for "Compile". If there are no error messages, the compile messages will appear on the screen as shown on the next page. This means that your program has compiled correctly. The actual numbers that appear will vary, and this information can generally be ignored.

Sample Program

```
PROGRAM FILE_NAME (OUTPUT);          ← Program Header

(***************************************)
(* SAMPLE PROGRAM BY BOB PHILLIP PD.3 *)  ← Programmer Comments
(***************************************)

VAR
    NAME : STRING[20];               ← Variable Declaration

BEGIN
    CLRSCR;
    WRITELN ('ENTER YOUR FULL NAME');
    READLN (NAME);
    WRITELN;                             Body of the Program
    WRITELN ('HELLO ', NAME);
    WRITELN ('NICE TO MEET YOU!');

END.
```

```
Compiling
    18 lines

Code:        000B paragraphs ( 176 bytes), 0D1D paragraphs free
Data:        0004 paragraphs (  64 bytes), 0FD8 paragraphs free
Stack/Heap: 7A57 paragraphs (501104 bytes)

>
```

Next, at the menu prompt, type the letter "R" for "RUN". The program then executes and produces output as shown to the right in the top left-hand corner of your screen.

```
ENTER YOUR FULL NAME
JOHN SMITH

HELLO JOHN SMITH
NICE TO MEET YOU!
```

15.5 USING THE EDITOR TO MAKE CORRECTIONS

*T*he original draft of your Pascal program and subsequent corrected versions are made with the help of a particular text-editing program referred to as the "editor". When your program has been keyed in and compiled, Pascal's syntax checker scans it for syntax errors. If a syntax error is encountered during the compile stage, the process is stopped, and a specific error message appears. Only one error is flagged with each compilation. If you have ten errors, you will have to compile the program ten times, and make corrections each time, before the program will be acceptable for execution.

If you press the Escape (ESC) key after an error message is displayed, the editor automatically reappears along with the program that you keyed in, with the cursor placed at (or close to) the spot where Turbo Pascal believes the error occurred. Because of limitations in the "error-finding" capabilities of Pascal, some of the trickier errors may be flagged in the wrong spot. A missing semicolon (;) at the end of a line, for example, may be flagged at the start of the next line; a variable that is undeclared near the top of the program might be flagged where it is being used, much further down in the program.

On the next page there is a table showing some of the keys used to manipulate the editor when correcting errors in your program.

Special Editing Keys

KEYS	WHAT KEYS DO
BACKSPACE	Erases the character to the left of the cursor
CTRL Y	Erases the line on which the cursor is sitting
CTRL K D	Returns to the main menu prompt
CURSOR ARROWS	Move the cursor in any of four directions on the screen
DEL	Deletes the character at the cursor position
END	Moves the cursor to the end of a programming statement
ESC	Returns control to the editor after an error message has been displayed
INSERT	Toggles the editor between the insert mode and the overwrite mode
RETURN	When the insert mode is active, this creates a new line and puts the cursor at its beginning. When the overwrite mode is active, the cursor is just moved to the beginning of the current line. (This same effect can be achieved by pressing the HOME key.)

15.6 TOP OF THE PROGRAM

*T*he top section of your program contains a mandatory statement called the **program identifier**. It is made up of three sections: (1) the command "PROGRAM", (2) the file name, and (3) what is expected of the results. In most cases the word "OUTPUT" inserted in parentheses (round brackets) is used to indicate that the answer is to appear on the screen. Consider the following example.

Example of a Program Identifier

```
PROGRAM SAMPLE_1 (OUTPUT)
```

| Command | File name | Display on screen |

The next section in a typical Pascal program is composed of **programmer com-**ments. These are optional lines that do not get processed when the program is executed. They permit the programmer to insert reference information about the program, such as its title, author, and perhaps the author's class or period. Each line of programmer comments must begin and end with a rounded bracket and an asterisk, similar to the examples shown here.

(a) Three-Line Program Identification

```
(*****************************************)
(* SAMPLE PROGRAM BY JOE IVY  *)
(*****************************************)
```

(b) Four-Line Program Identification

```
(*************************)
(*     SAMPLE PROGRAM       *)
(*     PETE SIMPSON PD.2    *)
(*************************)
```

(c) Descriptive Phrasing

```
(* This program illustrates
annual bank interest. *)
```

Some programmers may wish to use three or four statements to provide program identification, or descriptive phrases to describe a program's purpose. It is also good practice to use additional comments to separate different sections of longer programs, and to identify their purpose within the program.

15.7 TYPES OF VARIABLES

*T*here are four different types of data that the Pascal language recognizes. Each type must be declared near the top of your program, after the programmer comments.

Types of Data

Type of Data	Example	Declaration
(a) Letters	A	CHAR
(b) Words	Jennifer	STRING[8]
	Chairs	STRING[6]
(c) Whole Numbers (no decimals)	10	INTEGER
(d) Decimal Numbers	10.50	REAL

For example, suppose that a problem requires that you ask for a user's name, age, and term average (accurate to one decimal place). A sample declaration for the variables in such a program might be as follows:

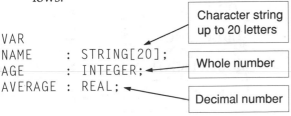

```
VAR
NAME    : STRING[20];
AGE     : INTEGER;
AVERAGE : REAL;
```

Character string up to 20 letters

Whole number

Decimal number

15.8 BODY OF A PROGRAM

*T*he main section of your program starts with the command "BEGIN" and stops with the command "END". There is no punctuation after "BEGIN", but there must be a period after the command "END" (if it is the last one in the program.) All statements in the program (not including the programmer comments or VAR) must be separated by a semicolon (;). This is a bit tricky—it means that each statement must end with ";" if it is followed by another program statement. After the commands "VAR" and "BEGIN", statements are indented five spaces. Consider this example of the main body of a program.

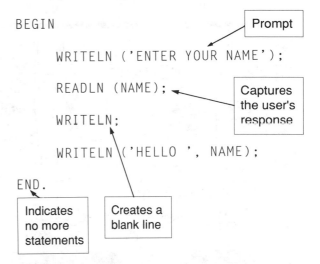

```
BEGIN
     WRITELN ('ENTER YOUR NAME');
     READLN (NAME);
     WRITELN;
     WRITELN ('HELLO ', NAME);
END.
```

Prompt

Captures the user's response

Indicates no more statements

Creates a blank line

Write a program that clears the screen, then asks for the user's name, age, and grade. Leave two spaces before printing that information between two rows of stars.

Sample Output:

```
ENTER YOUR NAME
George Smithers

ENTER YOUR AGE
16

ENTER YOUR GRADE
11


***************
GEORGE SMITHERS
AGE 16
GRADE 11
***************
```

"I figure it will pay for itself in the money we'd save on chalk."

—WAN

15.9 CALCULATIONS

*I*n Pascal, mathematical calculations can be performed in separate statements, or in the statement that does the printing. For clarity, only separate statements will be shown in this chapter. The mathematical symbols for manipulating data are shown in the chart of arithmetic operators.

Arithmetic Operators

FUNCTION	SYMBOL
ADDITION	+
SUBTRACTION	-
MULTIPLICATION	*
DIVISION	/

The following expressions are examples of the valid use of arithmetic operators, assuming that the variables have been declared. The answers to these statements are always stored in the variable on the left of the ":=" sign.

```
TOTAL := 15 * 10;
AVER := (MARK1 + MARK2 + MARK3
+ MARK4)/4;
SUM := (TOTAL - 12);
```

Figure 15.1 Scientific, engineering, and mathematical calculations are easily generated with Pascal programs.

Courtesy of Computing Canada

15.10 FORMATTING THE OUTPUT

Pascal is capable of providing answers with as much as ten-digit accuracy. However, most solutions require less precision. Instructing the computer to limit the number of digits and the number of decimal places in numeric answers is called **formatting the output**. Notice the differences in output when the following statements are executed.

Comparison of Unformatted and Formatted Output

```
AVER := 60.445;
WRITELN ('THE AVERAGE IS ', AVER);
WRITELN ('THE AVERAGE IS ', AVER:4:1);
```

Four-character output (three digits and the decimal point) with one-decimal-place accuracy

Output:

```
THE ANSWER IS 60.445000000E+01
THE ANSWER IS 60.4
```

Integers can also be formatted to indicate how many print positions you wish the number to occupy. This technique is helpful when the number of digits in the value changes from line to line, as in the series 8, 9, 10. It may prove helpful, in certain situations, to format the output to its largest expected number of digits so that the results on different lines will be correctly aligned.

```
MONTHS := 12
WRITELN ('NUMBER OF MONTHS =', MONTHS:2);
```

Sample Program Using Calculations

In the Hamburger Restaurant program below, the total cost of any order can be calculated, assuming Hamburgers are $2.25 each.

```
PROGRAM HAMBURGER (OUTPUT);
(**********************************)
(*    HAMBURGER RESTAURANT PROGRAM    *)
(**********************************)
VAR
      PRICE : REAL;
      TOTAL : REAL;
      NUMBER : INTEGER;

BEGIN
      CLRSCR;
      PRICE := 2.25;
      WRITELN ('ENTER NUMBER OF HAMBURGERS ');
      READLN (NUMBER);
      TOTAL := PRICE * NUMBER;
      WRITELN;
      WRITELN ('TOTAL COST OF ORDER = $', TOTAL:5:2);

END.
```

Defines TOTAL as a five-digit number with two decimal places

The calculation line "TOTAL := PRICE * NUMBER;" is referred to as an **assignment statement** because it assigns the answer to the variable "TOTAL" on the left-hand side. The variable "TOTAL" is then printed with a phrase in the second last statement and truncated to two-decimal-place accuracy. The output will appear as follows.

```
ENTER NUMBER OF HAMBURGERS
3

TOTAL COST OF ORDER = $ 6.75
```

Program to Try

(40 mins.)

Design a restaurant program, similar to the example in the previous section, that allows the customer to order any combination of French Fries ($1.25 each), Onion Rings ($1.75 each), or Hamburgers ($2.25 each). Then the program is to calculate and print the total cost of the order.

15.11 LOOPS

There are situations in programming where some action must be repeated several times. For example, you may wish to leave numerous lines blank before printing answers, or to require the computer to repeat a calculation, such as an interest calculation on a bank loan. This can be performed with a process called a **loop** or **repetition structure**. Most computer languages have more than one command for repeating a series of statements: this chapter illustrates two methods available in Turbo Pascal.

The FOR... DO Loop

If only one line needs to be repeated within a program, the "FOR...DO" command may be helpful. It causes the one statement immediately following to be repeated a set number of times.

The "FOR...DO" statement is made up of three components: (1) a variable, (2) an initial value, and (3) a final value, as illustrated in the next example. The computer is instructed to count from one to ten, using "COUNTER" as a variable name for the main memory storage area in which the computer keeps track of the count.

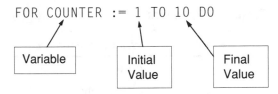

Suppose that you prefer to have the output from a program appear several lines down from the top of the screen to improve its readability. This can be accomplished with a FOR...DO statement. Consider the "Moving Down" example that follows.

```
PROGRAM MOVINGDOWN (OUTPUT);
(*******************************)
(*    MOVING DOWN FROM THE TOP    *)
(*******************************)

VAR
        COUNTER : INTEGER;

BEGIN
        CLRSCR;
        FOR COUNTER := 1 TO 10 DO
                WRITELN;

        WRITELN ('HAPPY BIRTHDAY');

END.
```

The output from this program would be the phrase "HAPPY BIRTHDAY" printed once on the tenth line down from the top of the screen.

15.12 REPEAT...UNLESS

A second type of loop can be used to repeat any number of statements enclosed within the two commands "REPEAT" and "UNTIL". The variable "C" (or the word "COUNT", or any declared variable selected by the programmer) may be used to keep track of the number of times the loop is processed.

There are three components to the counter—its initial value, the counter itself (C := C + 1), and the test condition, which checks to see if the counter has reached its preset upper limit.

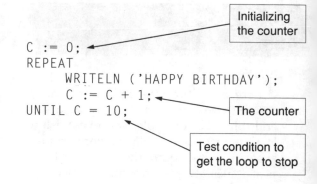

```
C := 0;
REPEAT
    WRITELN ('HAPPY BIRTHDAY');
    C := C + 1;
UNTIL C = 10;
```

Initializing the counter

The counter

Test condition to get the loop to stop

In the above example, the last statement checks to see if the counter has reached the upper limit of ten with each "pass". If it has, the loop process stops; otherwise, the loop continues to print the phrase "Happy Birthday".

Program to Try   (30 mins.)

Design a program that will print the phrase "PASCAL IS EASY!" ten times, with each line numbered sequentially. The output will appear five lines from the top of a cleared screen. All phrases, including the last one, are to be evenly aligned.

Sample Output:

```
1 PASCAL IS EASY!
2 PASCAL IS EASY!
```

15.13 CONTROL STATEMENTS

Control statements, also referred to as "selection structures" or "decision statements", permit a programmer to compare one value or variable to another and to provide appropriate action based on the comparison. Six **relational operators** can be used to compare values.

Relational Operators

Symbol	What It Means
=	Equal to
>	Greater than
<	Less than
>=	Greater than or equal to
<=	Less than or equal to
<>	Not equal to

To form an expression containing a relational operator, two variables (or values) of the same type must be placed on opposite sides of the relational operator. Assuming that the variables have been properly declared, the comparisons shown in the table below are valid.

This simple control structure will perform the action contained in the statement placed directly after the "THEN" command if the comparison is true; otherwise, it will ignore the action and continue with the rest of the program.

In this sample program, a student's grade is checked for a passing mark of 50 or greater. If the value falls in that range, the phrase "Congratulations, you passed!" is printed.

```
PROGRAM GRADES (OUTPUT);
(***************************)
(*    MARK CHECK PROGRAM    *)
(***************************)

VAR
    MARK : INTEGER;

BEGIN
    CLRSCR;
    WRITELN ('ENTER YOUR MARK');
    READLN (MARK);
    WRITELN;

    IF MARK >= 50
        THEN WRITELN ('CONGRATULATIONS, YOU PASSED!');

    WRITELN;
    WRITELN ('END OF PROGRAM.');

END.
```

```
ENTER YOUR MARK
52

CONGRATULATIONS, YOU
PASSED!

END OF PROGRAM.
```

Examples of Control Structures

CONTROL STRUCTURE	WHAT WILL HAPPEN IF THE TEST CONDITION IS TRUE
IF M < 50 THEN F := F + 1;	The value one is added to the counter "F"
IF M >= 50 THEN WRITELN ('PASSED');	The word "Passed" is printed
IF ENTRY = PASSWORD THEN WRITELN ('ACCEPTED');	The word "Accepted" is printed
IF VALUE > 100 THEN WRITELN;	A print line is left blank

15.14 IF...THEN...ELSE

A more powerful version of the control structure is the "IF...THEN...ELSE" command, which causes the computer to perform one action if the comparison is true, and perform a different action if the comparison is false. Consider the modification below of the program given on page 329.

Notice that there is no semicolon after the IF or THEN statements, only after the ELSE statement. This ensures that the computer will treat those three lines as a complete unit.

```
BEGIN
    IF MARK >= 50
        THEN WRITELN ('CONGRATULATIONS, YOU PASSED!');
        ELSE WRITELN ('SORRY, TRY HARDER NEXT TIME.');

    WRITELN;
    WRITELN ('PROGRAM COMPLETED.');

END.
```

Program to Try   (20 mins.)

Design a program that will begin output on a cleared screen, five lines down from the top, and ask the user for a numerical four-digit password. If the password is correct, the program should print the words "PASSWORD CORRECT". If the password is not correct, the program should print the words "PASSWORD INVALID". Regardless of what action is taken, have the computer leave two blank lines before printing the final phrase "PROGRAM COMPLETED".

15.15 CENTRING OUTPUT ON THE SCREEN

*T*o improve the appearance and readability of output, most users require that the output be centred rather than appear at the left-hand side of the screen. Earlier in the chapter, it was noted that the "FOR...DO" loop can be used to move output downwards. Strings containing blank characters (created with the space bar) can be used to centre items horizontally on a print line.

To centre any phrase, you should create a tab equal to forty spaces minus half the number of characters in the phrase. Suppose that the title FAMOUS ROCK GROUPS (which contains 18 characters including the spaces) is to be centred on a print line. An entire print line can hold 80 characters, with a half-way point of 40. The calculation (40 - 9 = 31) indicates that exactly 31 spaces are to be left blank to centre that particular phrase.

```
VAR
    TAB31 : STRING[31];
BEGIN
    TAB31 := ('                               ');
    CLRSCR;
    FOR C = 1 TO 4 DO
        WRITELN;

    WRITELN (TAB31, 'FAMOUS ROCK GROUPS');

END.
```

The use of the variable TAB is arbitrary, but appropriate because its purpose is to move the cursor a specified number of spaces before printing. The number on the end of the variable name reminds the programmer of the length of the space. You can use as many different tabs as are required, as illustrated in this Centring Columns program.

```
PROGRAM CENTRING (OUTPUT);
(***********************)
(*    CENTRING COLUMNS    *)
(***********************)

VAR
    TAB12 : STRING[12];
    TAB14 : STRING[14];
    TAB25 : STRING[25];
    C : INTEGER;
    NUM : INTEGER;
    SQUARE : INTEGER;

BEGIN
    TAB12 := ('            ');
    TAB14 := ('              ');
    TAB25 := ('                         ');
    CLRSCR;

    FOR C := 1 TO 6 DO
        WRITELN;

    WRITELN (TAB25, 'NUMBER', TAB12, 'SQUARE');
    WRITELN (TAB25, '------', TAB12, '------');
    WRITELN;

    NUM := 1;
    REPEAT
        SQUARE := NUM * NUM;
        WRITELN (TAB25, NUM:3, TAB14, SQUARE:4);
        NUM := NUM + 1;
    UNTIL NUM = 11;

END.
```

```
        NUMBER           SQUARE
        ------           ------
          1                1
          2                4
          3                9
          4                16
          5                25
          6                36
          7                49
          8                64
          9                81
         10               100
```

Design a program that will clear the screen and centre the two columns of output both vertically and horizontally under the headings DAY and BALANCE. Leave one line space after the headings. The first column is to represent days of the week for 15 days. The second column is to represent the a-mount owed at the end of each day on an unpaid credit card balance of $500, given that the daily interest rate is 0.000767. Include a "$" sign with each balance (accurate to two decimal places), and align the figures under the headings.

15.16 ARRAYS AND WORD LISTS

*T*here are several instances in which lists of words and numbers are required by the user. For example, a teacher might need a list of student names and marks, or a bank manager might need a list of customers and their loan balances.

Pascal requires the use of one-dimensional arrays to collect lists of data interactively, store them temporarily in main memory, and then display them in an attractive manner. A one-dimensional array is a physical space (similar to a column) in main memory capable of holding a list of either numbers or words. It can be referred to with a single file name.

To inform the Pascal compiler that arrays are to be set up, you must declare them at the top of the program.

Declarations for Arrays

```
VAR
NAMES : ARRAY [1..10] OF STRING[20];
MARKS : ARRAY [1..10] OF INTEGER;
```

Essentially, this tells the computer to set up two columns in main memory: one called NAMES, which is to contain up to ten names, each of which can be 20 characters long, and one called MARKS, which is to contain up to ten whole numbers.

A loop is required when collecting data interactively to store in these two arrays. Notice the loop counter appears inside square brackets after each array name.

This counter numbers each of the entries to position them inside the array.

Loop to Enter Data into Arrays

```
C := 0;
REPEAT
    CLRSCR;
    WRITELN ('ENTER NAME');
    READLN (NAMES[C]);
    WRITELN;
    WRITELN ('ENTER MARK');
    READLN (MARKS[C]);
    C := C + 1;
UNTIL C = 5;
```

With each pass of the loop, the computer clears the screen and then prompts the user for a name and mark. This process is repeated five times. The names and marks are stored in two separate arrays, similar to the example on the next page.

Sample One-Dimensional Arrays

NAMES(C)	MARKS(C)
SUSAN JENKINS	89
TOM DERRINGER	50
WAYNE NEUTON	71
LISA BIALEK	76
BILL MINOR	95

A second loop is required to print the arrays. The contents are printed in the order in which they were originally entered.

Loop to Print Contents of Arrays

```
C := 0;
REPEAT
    WRITELN (MARKS[C]:3, TAB10, NAMES[C]);
    C := C + 1;
UNTIL C = 5;
```

The "Sample Arrays Program" on the following page illustrates the entire sequence for collecting lists of names and marks for later display in chart form.

Notice that in the output loop, the marks are printed first to help line up the names. The content of each loop is printed under the appropriate heading.

```
PROGRAM ARRAYS (OUTPUT);
(*****************************)
(*      SAMPLE ARRAY PROGRAM      *)
(*****************************)

VAR
      NAMES : ARRAY[1..10] OF STRING[20];
      MARKS : ARRAY[1..10] OF INTEGER;
      TAB8 : STRING[8];
      TAB10 : STRING[10];
      TAB20 : STRING[20];
      C : INTEGER;
      X : INTEGER;

BEGIN
      TAB8 := ('        ');
      TAB10 := ('          ');
      TAB20 := ('                    ');
      C := 0;
      REPEAT
          CLRSCR;
          FOR X := 1 TO 10 DO
             WRITELN;

          WRITELN ('ENTER STUDENT`S NAME');
          READLN (NAMES[C]);
          WRITELN;
          WRITELN ('ENTER MARK');
          READLN (MARKS[C]);
          C := C + 1

      UNTIL C = 5;

      CLRSCR;
      WRITELN (TAB20, 'MARKS', TAB8, 'STUDENTS');
      WRITELN;

      C := 0;
      REPEAT
          WRITELN (TAB20, MARKS[C]:3, TAB10, NAMES[C]);
          C := C + 1;

      UNTIL C = 5;

END.
```

> Note the switch in punctuation to avoid closing quotation

*P*ascal is a compiled programming language. This means that the program is written and executed in two distinct stages: the edit and compile stage, and the run stage.

Users may encounter syntax errors (errors in grammar, spelling, and punctuation) and logic errors (mistakes in the program's design) when creating new programs. However, Pascal will only flag the syntax errors and does so one at at time.

Programmers should always plan first, and program second. The solution to a problem, referred to as an algorithm, is best achieved by following a series of five steps: (1) analyze the problem, (2) list the known values, (3) plan an algorithm, (4) code the solution, (5) execute, test, and debug the program.

Pascal programs contain four sections: a mandatory "program header", an optional programmer comment section (used for identification), a section in which all variables (and constants) are declared, and the body of the program, recognizable by its "book-end" commands "BEGIN" and "END".

All program solutions can be developed using combinations of the three essential programming structures: sequential structures (straight-line sections), repetition structures (loops), and selection structures (control statements).

"I don't understand all that stuff he said between 'Good Morning, Class' and 'That concludes my lecture for today'."

KEY CONCEPTS AND VOCABULARY

algorithm
arithmetic operator
assignment statement
bug
compiler
control statement
counter
debugging
editor
formatting the output
logic error
loop (repetition structure)
program header
program identifier
programmer comments
prompt
relational operator
syntax error
user response
variable declaration

PROGRAMMING COMMANDS

ARRAY
BEGIN...END
CLRSCR
FOR...DO
IF...THEN
IF...THEN...ELSE
INTEGER
PROGRAM
READLN
REAL
REPEAT...UNTIL
STRING
VARIABLE
WRITELN

EDITOR COMMANDS

COMPILE
EDIT
RUN

*T*hese are general questions that may require reading comprehension, factual recall, and some application of the knowledge gained from this chapter.

Introduction

1. (a) What category of programming languages does Pascal represent?
   (b) Name the two distinct stages programmers must follow when using Pascal.

2. (a) What is a "bug"?
   (b) Explain the difference between a "syntax error" and a "logic error".

Steps in Problem Solving

3. Define "algorithm".

4. List the five steps for problem solving with Pascal.

Components of a Sample Program

5. Name the four components of a typical Pascal program.

6. What combination of keys invokes the Main Menu?

Using the Editor to Make Corrections

7. When your program is being compiled, for what is the Pascal language searching?

8. Describe one of the trickier syntax errors to locate in Pascal. Explain why it is difficult to find.

9. Which keyboard keys perform the following actions?
   (a) moves cursor in any direction
   (b) erases character to the left of the cursor

(c) moves the cursor to the end of a programming statement
(d) returns control to the editor

10. Write a sample "program identifier" and label its three parts.

11. (a) What is the purpose of "programmer comments"?
    (b) Write an example of a three-line program identification for a payroll program written by Darcie Daines in Pd. 3.

Types of Variables

12. What is the difference between an integer and a real number?

13. Provide the correct variable declarations for these items of data:
    (a) SUM := 130.54
    (b) VALUE := 50
    (c) GROUP := ('MUSICIANS')
    (d) LETTER := ('Z')

14. In general terms, explain what the probable content of these data variables will be, if the following represent their variable declarations.
    (a) TOTAL : REAL
    (b) AGE : INTEGER
    (c) PRODUCT : STRING[10]

Body of a Program

15. Explain what these two program statements do.
    WRITELN ('ENTER TEMP');
    READLN (TEMP);

16. Write a two-line program that will prompt the user to enter his or her name and then capture the response.

Calculations

17. What is an arithmetic operator?

18. Write single-line Pascal assignment statements that will perform the following calculations. (Variable names represent stored values.)
(a) Multiply the following data: VALUE1, VALUE2.
(b) Calculate the total of the following values: 150, 178, 291, 526.
(c) Find the average of the totals for the following four subjects: ENG, MATH, BUS, COMP.

Formatting the Output

19. To what does the phrase "formatting the output" refer?

20. Given a data value of "TOTAL := 150.145", how can you format the variable in a WRITELN statement to provide:
(a) a REAL answer with two-decimal-place accuracy?
(b) an INTEGER answer?

21. Write two lines of a program using a "FOR...DO" loop that will leave ten lines blank.

22. Write a "FOR...DO" loop that will print the phrase "Happy Birthday" five times.

REPEAT...UNTIL

23. Write a "REPEAT...UNTIL" loop that will add the contents of the counter with each pass of the loop to get a final total.

24. What will the outcome of this loop be? Why?
```
C := 0;
REPEAT
     WRITELN (C);
UNTIL C = 10;
```

Control Statements

25. What is a "relational operator"?

26. Explain what this control structure will do.
```
IF MARK < 50
      THEN F := F + 1;
```

IF...THEN...ELSE

27. What does the "IF...THEN...ELSE" control statement require the computer to do?

Centring Output on the Screen

28. State the rule for centring phrases or titles on the screen.

29. Write a one-line Pascal statement that will centre the phrase "Canadian Companies" on an 80-column print line.

Arrays and Word Lists

30. Define "one-dimensional array".

*T*hese questions assume an understanding of the material presented in this chapter, and provide situations that may require evaluation, analysis, or application of the newly acquired knowledge.

Introduction

1. Identify each of these programming mistakes as either a syntax error or a logic error.
    (a) missing semicolon at the end of a statement
    (b) equation based on a wrong assumption
    (c) incorrect data
    (d) misspelled command

Types of Variables

2. Write the correct declarations for each of these data variables:
    (a) INV := 1678
    (b) OBJECTS := ('TABLES')
    (c) MARK := 75
    (d) ENTRY := ('A')
    (e) VALUE := 60.95

Body of a Program

3. Write the body section of a Pascal program that requires a user to enter their age and captures the response.

4. Write the body section of a Pascal program that requires a user to enter two different values, captures those entries, leaves two blank lines, then prints out those two values on the same print line.

Formatting the Output

5. Write the body section of a Pascal program that assigns the following two values to variable names, adds the values, and prints the answer accurate to two decimal places.
    Data: 278.50, 350.25

6. Write the body section of a Pascal program that accepts any four subject marks, calculates the average mark, and prints the phrase "AVERAGE IS =" along with the mark, accurate to one decimal place.

REPEAT...UNTIL

7. Write a "REPEAT...UNTIL" loop that prints these two phrases one after the other, with a space between each pair, five times.
    Phrase One — "I'M CAUGHT IN A LOOP"
    Phrase Two — "NO I AM NOT"

8. Rewrite this loop to remove the seven errors it contains.
    ```
    K := 0;
    REPEAT;
        WRITELN ('ENTER A VALUE');
        READLN (VALUE)
        C := C + 1
    REPEAT UNTIL
    ```

Control Statements

9. Write a control structure using the "IF... THEN" statement that would check for a mark greater than 79 and print the word "Honours" if the mark falls in that range.

10. Write a control structure using "IF...THEN... ELSE" statements that checks if a person is older than 16. If the comparison is true, print the phrase "ACCEPTABLE FOR TEAM"; otherwise, print the phrase "NOT OLD ENOUGH".

Arrays and Word Lists

11. Write a loop structure (as part of a furniture store inventory program) that will clear the screen and ask the user for the name and quantity of 15 different items. (Example: tables, 20).

These problems will require analysis and planning on paper before you enter and test them on the computer. Solutions must contain all the elements of good programming style.

1. Light as a Feather

The mass of a planet determines its gravity, and therefore the weight of a person standing on the surface. An astronaut, for example, would feel lighter standing on a small planet than on a larger one.

Design a program that will determine how much a person would weigh on various planets. Assume that their weight relates directly to the planet's size. The masses of the following planets are expressed as a per-centage of the earth's mass: Moon 16%, Mars 38%, Venus 85%, Jupiter 264%. The program will ask the user for their weight as a starting figure, and produce the following chart, centred on a cleared screen.

Sample Output:

PLANET	WEIGHT
Earth	- - - -
Moon	- - - -
Mars	- - - -

2. Population Growth

Hamilton's population is 320 000 and it is growing at a rate of two percent annually. Waterloo's population is 50 000 and it is growing at the rate of 15 percent annually. List the year and the population of each city until the population of Waterloo is greater than Hamilton's population. The output is to appear centred on a cleared screen.

Sample Output:

YEAR	WATERLOO	HAMILTON
19—	50 000	320 000
19—	—	—
19—	—	—

3. Test Diagnostic Program

A geography teacher has asked you to design a Test Diagnostic Program that will accept any 15 test marks from the keyboard and produce the following output. The statistics are to be used to help the teacher design better tests.

```
*****************************************
NUMBER OF PASSING STUDENTS =
NUMBER OF FAILING STUDENTS =
AVERAGE MARK FOR THE CLASS =
*****************************************
```

4. Gas Consumption

A major oil company knows that a typical compact car consumes 4.76 litres of gas every hour if it travels at 50 km/h. For each additional 10 km/h in speed, the car will consume an extra 0.5 litres per hour.

The marketing department wants a table that will illustrate the relationship between *speed* and *gas consumption*. The chart is to display speeds in intervals of ten, ranging from 50 to 100 km/h. The program will ask for the local price of regular gas per litre before printing the chart centred on a cleared screen.

5. Loan Payment Schedule

The manager of a local bank has hired you to write a loan payment schedule program. This schedule shows the total amount that must be repaid by customers on loans kept for 12, 24, or 36 months. The interest rate is 1.5%, compounded monthly. The amounts borrowed are shown in the sample output that follows. All repayment figures must contain a "$" sign and be accurate to two decimal places.

Sample Output:

```
LOAN AMOUNT     12     24     36

$ 1 000
$ 1 500
$ 2 000
$ 5 000
```

PROBLEMS THAT REQUIRE ONE-DIMENSIONAL ARRAYS

6. Software Inventory

The president of an educational publishing company needs a report on the company's computer software inventory. Design a program that will accept the data from the keyboard and print an inventory listing as shown, including a figure representing total inventory.

Sample Output:

```
            SOFTWARE INVENTORY
TITLE                          QUANTITY

Easy Write                       150
File-It                           62
_____                          _____

TOTAL INVENTORY =
```

Data:

Easy Write	150
File-It	62
Disk Doctor	10
Better BASIC	9
Music Master	12
Image Maker	60
Accu-Spell	6
Design Shop	135
Math Whiz	25
Word Pro	30
Grade Manager	125
Money Manager	18

7. The Flower Shop

Heather Thompson, who operates a retail flower shop where she sells cut flowers and potted plants, enters her weekly sales figures into her microcomputer for analysis. Design a program that will read her sales figures into arrays, calculate the total sales for each type of flower, and print the result with the headings shown in the following sample output.

Sample Output:

NAME	PRICE	QTY. SOLD	TOTAL SALES
Daffodils	$12.50	12	$ —

Data:

NAME	PRICE	QTY. SOLD
Daffodils	$12.50	12
African Violets	$10.00	3

Tulips	$ 8.50	6
Red Roses	$25.00	10
Sweetheart Roses	$18.50	13
Orchids	$15.00	4
Carnations	$ 5.50	2
Mixed Stems	$13.50	18
Begonias	$ 9.50	4
Chrysanthemums	$10.50	7

8. Foreign Exchange

(Requires a newspaper)

The head office of a large international bank wants a daily list of the prices of world currencies. The output will include the country, its currency, and the quoted prices of its currency based on Canadian dollars, accurate to four decimal places. Design a program that will accept the data from the keyboard, store it in arrays, and then print it in a table, as shown below.

Sample Output:

```
      FOREIGN EXCHANGE TABLE
COUNTRY          CURRENCY        PRICE

Sweden           Krona          0.1974
```

Currencies to be Researched:

Sweden, Saudi Arabia, United States, Japan, England, U.S.S.R., China, France, Italy, Mexico, India, Greece.

A

Accumulator
An assignment statement that adds a variable to some pre-defined total. Example: BAL = BAL + INTEREST.

Acronym
A word or short form derived from the first letter (or letters) of each word in a phrase or name. Typically, no period follows the letters when typewritten.Example: CRT (which stands for Cathode Ray Tube).

Ada
A computer language developed at the U.S. Department of Defense. It is a structured language similar to Pascal. It was named after Ada Lovelace, Lord Byron's daughter, who was a major intellectual inspiration and patron of Charles Babbage's Analytical Engine.

Aiken, Howard (1900-1973)
In affiliation with IBM, Aiken built an electromechanical computer called the Mark 1.

Algorithm
A general name for any set of well-defined rules or procedures for the solution of a problem. Can be expressed diagrammatically like a flowchart, in pseudocode, or as a computer program.

Alphanumeric
A term for any set of alphabetic letters (A through Z), numbers (0 through 9), and special characters (-, +, /, $, etc.) that can be machine processed.

ALU
An acronym for Arithmetic Logic Unit, a section on the microprocessor chip. The logic circuitry designed to perform operations such as addition, subtraction, multiplication, and division. Also, it can perform logical comparisons, such as "Is A > B?"

Ambience
A software package that provides a user-friendly screen display for the selection of system functions on an ICON microcomputer. This user interface provides rectangles and squares that can be highlighted and selected with a trackball pointing device.

Analog Computer
A device that measures physical quantities such as air pressure, temperature, or velocity, and compares the measurement to some preset level. The device usually triggers some system into action if the comparison is not equal. Example: a thermostat measuring room temperature.

Animation Software
An application program that permits live-action movement of graphic images on the screen.

Application Programs
Programs often tailored to the user's needs. These programs perform tasks unrelated to the operation of the computer itself. Examples: word-processing, spreadsheet, file-manager, or payroll programs.

Arithmetic Operator
A symbol used to indicate a math operation such as "+" for addition.

Artificial Intelligence
The ability of a computer to make decisions on its own. Early experiments involved rule-based decision making, in which a computer made decisions based on a pre-defined set of rules. More advanced research concentrates on heuristic abilities that permit the machine to learn on its own by trial and error and pure logic. Included in this broad definition are programs that perform visual pattern recognition, speech synthesis, robotic movement, and game theory. Also called machine intelligence.

ASCII
An acronym for American Standard Code for Information Interchange. Originally a 7-bit code, it is used in keyboards and computer circuitry to represent data. Also available in an 8-bit code called ASCII-8. Pronounced "askee".

Assignment Statement
An algebraic mathematical expression that requires the computer to perform whatever action is on the right-hand side of the equal sign and store the result in whatever variable name is shown on the left-hand side of the equal sign.

Asymmetric Parallel Processing
A multiple-processor computer in which a "master" processor assigns specific duties to its "slave" processors.

Audio Response Unit
Computer circuitry and a speaker capable of imitating human speech as a form of computer output.

Automated Teller Terminals
Computer terminals often located on the outside wall of banks, credit unions, and trust companies to process banking transactions by machine. Typically, they have nicknames to encourage greater customer acceptance, such as Johnny Cash or The Green Machine.

Auxiliary Memory
Extra storage devices, such as magnetic disk drives or optical drives, that can be added to a computer system for long-term file storage.

B

Babbage, Charles (1792-1871)
A British mathematician and inventor. He designed a "difference engine" for calculating algorithms to 20 decimal places, and an "analytical engine" that was the forerunner to the modern digital computer. His designs were ahead of the technology of his day.

Bar Graph
A graph with an X and a Y axis, composed of groups of vertical or horizontal bars each representing specific values.

BASIC
An acronym for Beginner's All-Purpose Symbolic Instruction Code. A computer language designed in 1964 to provide an introductory language for people without a background in computer studies. Presently, it is the most popular computer language used in desktop, laptop, and pocket computers. Available in several incompatible versions from different companies, including Applesoft BASIC, Commodore BASIC, IBM BASIC, GWBASIC, True BASIC, and Waterloo BASIC.

Batch Processing
A method of grouping together repetitive jobs of a similar nature to facilitate their simultaneous processing. Example: processing paycheques for employees.

BEDMAS
A memory-assisting acronym that indicates the order in which a computer performs various mathematical tasks within an assignment statement. It stands for "Brackets, Exponents, Division, Multiplication, Addition, Subtraction".

Binary
A number system composed of just two numbers, zero and one. Currently, all computers process information coded in some form of binary representation. Examples: $101 = 5$; $1010 = 10$.

Bionics
The study of living systems for the purpose of relating their characteristics to the development of mechanical and electrical hardware. Primary applications are in medical research, particularly the creation of artificial limbs. A bionic man would be a person with artificial parts.

BIOS
An acronym that means "Basic Input Output System". This is part of the operating system that handles and controls peripheral devices. This routine is stored in a ROM chip in certain computers to assist the computer in accessing the disk drive and the rest of DOS when the computer is first turned on.

Bit
A binary digit. One storage position in a computer memory circuit that can either be "on" or "off". Several bits are required to represent a number or letter in a computer system.

Boldfaced
The darkening of printed characters to highlight certain items within a document, often achieved by double printing the characters (in dot matrix printers).

Boot
The startup process of a computer system. Many computer systems lacking a hard disk require a special disk with "boot instructions" to be inserted before the machine is turned on.

Bubble Memory
A type of computer memory circuit that uses an electromagnetic field to store and move magnetic spots (called domains) around a tiny chip of magnetic material. The domains resemble tiny bubbles when viewed through a microscope; hence its name. Designed as a sequential access device. Also called magnetic bubble memory. Texas Instruments, the originator of the idea, withdrew from the project after investing $50 million into its research.

Bug
A term used to denote an unidentified mistake in a computer program or system, or malfunction in a computer hardware component. Common usage: "There's a bug in my program."

Business Graphics
A term referring to graphical displays created from values in a spreadsheet, such as bar, circle, and line graphs. Also called value graphics.

Business Letter
A formal style of printed communication between business people.

Byte
The number of bits needed to code one character (a letter, number, or symbol) in a computer. Commonly eight bits plus a check bit would represent one byte.

C

CAD Engineer
An engineering graduate who uses computer-aided-design software to make two- and three-dimensional drawings and blueprints.

CAI
An acronym for computer-assisted instruction. A software application that provides self-paced lessons and testing. Examples: Learn to Type program, or a history or science lesson.

CD-ROM
See optical disk.

Cell
A space created by the intersection of a row and column in a spreadsheet. A space in which data or formulas can be stored.

Cell Address
The location of a particular cell within a spreadsheet, indicated by its column letter and row number, such as B1, or C10.

Centralized Data Banks
The concept of combining several different data files of information into one massive cross-indexed data base, accessible by a variety of government agencies or organizations. Combined files might include tax, medical, social security, and legal history.

CGA
A designation for the lowest resolution in colour computer monitors. The acronym means Colour Graphics Adapter, and refers to the circuit board required to operate the monitor.

Character String
Any group of characters treated as a unit of data within a computer program including letters, digits, punctuation marks, and symbols. The term was developed by pioneer computer scientists who had difficulty getting computer languages to manipulate words as data.

Checksum
A method of adding the number of bits required to internally represent a computer program. Its purpose is to assist the verification of programs transferred between storage devices and the main memory, or vice versa.

Circle Graph
A circular graph that displays values (shown as a wedge in the circle) expressed as a percentage of a whole amount. Also called "pie chart".

Clip Art
Pre-drawn images stored on disk that can be used in desktop-publishing or word-processing programs.

Clip-Art Library
A disk file containing pre-drawn clip art.

Clipboard
A holding place in memory for the temporary storage of text or graphics within an art or word-processing program.

Closed Architecture
A microcomputer design that typically does not allow user modification of the factory-installed circuit boards, or its operating system, to improve performance.

COBOL
An acronym for Common Business-Oriented Language, a high-level computer language originally developed for business data-processing applications by Grace Hopper.

Coding
The process of writing a program solution into some particular computer language. Writing programs after the planning has been completed.

COM
An acronym for Computer Output Microfilm unit—devices that reduce computer output to miniature images on film for future reference. Also an abbreviation in DOS for communication channel, a reference to which auxiliary port is being used for input or output.

Common Data Carrier
A communication medium, such as telephone lines or microwave towers, that is routinely used to transmit computer data.

Communication Satellite
An earth-orbiting device capable of relaying communication signals over long distances.

Computer-Aided Design (CAD)
The use of computers and high-resolution monitors to design architectural or engineering drawings, usually in three-dimensional perspective. A replacement for the pen and paper method of drafting blueprints.

Computer Applications
The uses that people find for computers. Examples: word processing, spreadsheets, payroll.

Computer Architecture
The main design features of a computer, including housing shell, layout of motherboard and daughterboards, and whether or not the user is allowed to access and modify the circuit boards.

Computer Generation
A group of computers using a specific design that is characteristic of that era. A term generally used to identify each major technological innovation in the computer industry.

Computer Graphics
Images including graphs, artistic designs, cartoons, or maps drawn with specialized software.

Computer Language
A set of instructions, construction, and syntax rules that are needed to communicate with a particular computer system. Examples: BASIC, COBOL, FORTRAN. Appears in two varieties: interpreters, and compilers. Also called a language processor.

Computer Model
A series of mathematical equations that represent variables in a real-life situation based on a set of assumptions. By altering the variables in the model, a researcher can determine the effect on the entire situation. May be represented as numerical figures or as a dynamic or static graphical display. Example: A model that lets researchers examine the effect of a toxic substance entering the bloodstream. Also called a computer simulation.

Computer Ombudsman
An appointed official who can intervene in any civil matter on behalf of individuals who have been unfairly treated as a result of incorrect computerized information.

Computer Operator
A person who plans and makes certain that a mainframe computer system operates correctly and without delays.

Computer Program
See program.

Computer Programmer
A person who uses problem-solving skills to plan and code computer programs and has a thorough knowledge of the rules of some particular computer language.

Computer Simulation
See computer model.

Computer System
A computer with its various peripherals and software.

Computer Terminal
A general name for any input/output device directly linked by cable, phone line, microwave tower, or some other transmission medium into a computer system. A group of terminals and their host processor are together referred to as a network.

Computer Theft
The use of a computer to embezzle, steal, or commit fraud. For example, a thief uses a computer terminal to steal money from other people's accounts by illegally transferring amounts from one account to another.

Computer Virus
A destructive program hidden on a disk, or within a larger program, that will surface under certain conditions and often permanently damage data or its host program. Similar to a human virus, a computer virus can infect and make a computer "sick". It is speculated that the coding of viruses began as a simple copy-protection routine in India in the early 1980s.

Console Station
A general name for an interactive computer terminal containing a keyboard and visual display screen.

Control Unit
The hardware logic circuitry that controls the sequence of operations in a program. A section on the MPU chip.

Conversational Programming
See interactive data entry.

Copyediting
Finding and correcting errors in printed materials and writing corrections on the printout.

Counter
An assignment statement in which a constant value is added to some pre-defined total. Used to keep track of some series of events, such as a loop process.
Example: $C = C + 1$

CP/M

An operating system developed by Digital Research Inc. for early microcomputers in the late 1970s. Refers to Control Program for Microcomputers. Replaced by DOS or UNIX in most microcomputers today.

CPU

See processor unit.

Crop

To reduce the size of a picture or clip art by cutting out unwanted materials along the edges.

CRT

An acronym for Cathode Ray Tube. An electronic output device that visually displays answers on a screen. Resembles a television set in appearance. Also called monitor, or (in Britain) a video display terminal (VDT).

Cursor

The lighted, blinking underscore or square on a computer screen that informs the user where the computer's attention is currently focused.

Cybernation

A combination of the words cybernetics and automation. It refers to a computer-controlled factory that employs automated devices, such as industrial robots, to produce assembly-line products. The term was coined by Norbert Wiener.

Cyborg

A person who is partly mechanical or electrical and partly organic, with both parts controlled by the brain. A bionic person. Example: fictional character Robo Cop.

D

Data

The values or variables used in computer programs. Can be numeric, alphabetic, or both.

Data Base

A large collection of separate but related files of data.

Data-Base Manager

A software program that allows a computer to select parts of several different but related files and combine them to form a report.

Data-Entry Clerks

People who enter information directly into a computer system (onto disks), using a keyboard terminal and visual display screen to edit the entries before they are stored.

Data File

A collection of information stored as a single unit, and represented by a unique file name. In data-file management, a data file contains similar records of information about a common topic.

Data Processing

A phrase that traditionally refers to the application of computers to process information related to the operation of a business. Examples: accounting, production figures, inventory update, payroll.

Data-Processing Manager

A person who is responsible for the successful operation of a computer department. The person hires the data-processing staff, supervises their training, recommends the purchase of new equipment, and prepares the annual department budget.

Data Structure

A pre-defined organizational model that specifies relationships between multiple files in a data base. The way in which a data base is organized. Examples: hierarchical data structure, network data structure, or relational data structure.

Debit Card

A plastic card, similar in size and format to a credit card, that causes an immediate reduction in a customer's bank account when a purchase is made.

Debug

To detect, locate, and remove all mistakes in a computer program.

Dedicated Processor

A miniature logic chip with a limited set of instructions that aids in the operation of some device, such as a digital watch or a microwave oven.

Demand Report

A request to the computer to select information from several files and combine them in a particular order before displaying them to the user. Usually applied to reports on one item or individual.

Desktop-Presentation Software

Software that allows the user to create an on-screen presentation, similar to a slide show. Useful for demonstrations at trade shows, conventions, and lectures.

Desktop Publishing

The use of a computer system to design, edit, and print professional-looking documents, such as brochures, newsletters, magazines, manuals, and catalogues that contain graphics, columnar text, and enlarged headings.

Destructive Read-In

The repeated use of a limited number of variable names to store a large amount of data in main memory. Only a certain set of data is processed at one time. Once that set has been processed, a new set is read into main memory, overwriting (and therefore erasing) the previous set of data.

Disk Directory

A list of all the files stored on a disk by file name.

Diskette

A circular disk composed of flexible, mylar plastic and a thin coating of metallic oxide. It stores information by means of coded magnetic spots. Comes in four sizes measured by diameter — 8", 5 1/4", 3 1/2", and 2". Coined by IBM in the United States in the early 1970s.

Disk Formatting

The preparation of a new disk for use in a particular computer system. The process creates a number of circular tracks, pie-shaped sectors, and an index for the disk drive to use. Formatted disks are machine specific and cannot be transferred to another type of computer.

Document

A general name for printed output from a computer, particularly from word-processing or desktop-publishing software. Includes memos, business letters, reports, assignments, essays, manuals, catalogues, etc.

Documentation

Various items related to a computer program that are stored together in an organized manner for future reference for programmers.

Document Outliner

A program that allows the user to plot and arrange the main points of an article or story prior to writing it. Typically this software presents "bullets" to highlight the main points, and then displays additional details indented from the bullets.

Document Title

The title or name at the top or beginning of a report.

Domestic Robots

Robots designed for use in the home.

DOS

An acronym for Disk Operating System. A general name for any collection of external programs that operates a particular computer system and is stored on disk. Also, more specifically, an operating system designed by Microsoft Corporation Limited, and made popular due to its use on IBM microcomputers. Micros using this system are referred to as DOS machines.

Draft Document

A rough, printed version of a document suitable for editing, but not for handing in.

E

EBCDIC

An acronym for Extended Binary Coded Decimal Interchange Code. An 8-bit code used to represent data in computers. EBCDIC can represent up to 256 distinct characters. Pronounced "ebb see dic".

Editing

The correction of mistakes or changes made in a document to improve its style, accuracy, content, or appearance.

EFTS

An acronym for Electronic Funds Transfer System. It refers to a network of computer systems that allows funds to be immediately deducted from a person's bank account.

EGA

One of several designations indicating the resolution and clarity of a colour computer monitor. The acronym, coined by IBM, means Enhanced Graphics Adapter and refers to the circuit board required to operate the monitor.

Electromechanical

A device that is partly electrical and partly mechanical.

Electronic Mail

The immediate electronic transfer of letters, memos, or invoices from one location to another using networked computers.

End User

The intended user for a completed computer program; the individual or group for whom the program is being written.

ENIAC

The first completely electrical computer in North America, designed between 1943 and 1946 by John Mauchly and J. Presper at the University of Pennsylvania. It is considered to be a landmark leading to the development of many electronic computer designs, and paving the way for the "computer revolution". Acronym for Electrical Numerical Integrator and Calculator.

EOF Check
An acronym for End-Of-File check. This is a statement within a program that tells the computer to check for a specific record in a list of data. The purpose of this statement is to prevent an infinite loop from occurring during the reading process.

EPROM
An acronym for Erasable, Programmable, Read-Only Memory. It is a semiconductor memory chip that can be erased with ultraviolet light.

Ergonomics
The study of the design features of computer equipment and furniture to make them easier for humans to use.

Error Diagnostics
Messages from a language processor indicating that a programming error has occurred.

F

Family of Fonts
A group of fonts, each slightly different, but all based on the same typeface.

Fibre Optic Cable
Cable made of fine strands of glass along which laser light can travel and carry coded information. It is an improvement in information-carrying capacity over metallic coaxial cable, and it is unaffected by magnetic surges.

Field
An area within a data record in which a specific type of information is stored. Examples: Name and Address fields in a student record.

File
A collection of related records treated as a unit and stored under the same file name. Example: A list of all credit card customers. File types include data, program, command, and operating-system files and can be recognized by their dotted abbreviations, such as .dat, .prg, .com, and .sys attached to the end of the file name.

File Maintenance
The process of keeping files up to date by adding, deleting, or modifying records within them.

File Manager
A software package that facilitates the creation, deletion, storage, and retrieval of data files one at a time.

File Name
A word or phrase used by people and the computer to identify a particular file.

File Server
A network controller containing a high-capacity storage device, such as a hard disk, that allows several work stations to share access to files stored on it or to share a common printer.

Firmware
Instructions permanently stored inside a computer system by the manufacturer in the form of non-erasable read-only memory chips. Also called stored logic or micro-programs.

Fixed-Point Arithmetic
Arithmetic involving whole numbers (integers). There are no fractions.

Flat-Bed Scanner
See page scanner.

Flight Simulator
An imitation cockpit of an airplane or other flying craft that is used to train pilots. A computer is used to create visual and motion effects as the pilot manipulates the flight instruments.

Floating-Point Arithmetic
Arithmetic involving decimal fractions. This is a necessary feature for scientific and business applications.

Flowchart
A diagrammatic program planning technique composed of geometric shapes and directional arrows. Can be designed with the help of a plastic flowchart template.

Flowchart Template
A plastic stencil used to draw the special symbols and shapes used in flowchart design.

Font
A complete set of letters, numbers, or characters of a particular typeface displayed in a specific shape and size. Usually appears as part of a family of fonts which permits variations on the same typeface, such as italic, boldface, or drop shadow.

Footprint
The amount of space that the base of a personal computer or printer takes up on a table top.

Format
The specific way values are shown in a cell, column, or row of a spreadsheet. The values may include commas, dollar signs, and several decimal place accuracy.

Forms-Design Software
An application program used to create ruled business forms, such as invoices and sales slips. Once the documents are created, they can be printed or displayed as a data-entry template to a file management system. Examples include *Formtools* and *Formworx*.

Formula
A statement stored in a particular cell of a spreadsheet that instructs the computer to perform some calculation using values found within the spreadsheet.

Formula Replication
The copying of a formula from one cell to another in a spreadsheet with automatic adjustments for row and column references.

FORTRAN
A combination of the words FORMULA TRANSLATION, it was one of the earliest computer languages and was originally designed for use by engineers, scientists, and the military on mainframe computers.

Free-Style Drawing Software
A general category of software that permits the drawing of original artwork.

Function
A process that is pre-defined by the software and represented by a single command word, such as ROUND for rounding a number, or INTEGER for turning a real number into a whole number.

G

Gigabyte
A billion bytes. Usually refers to the memory capacity of some auxiliary storage medium.

GIGO
An acronym for Garbage In-Garbage Out. Refers to the necessity for accurate input to a computer system in order to arrive at the correct answer.

Grammar Checker
Software that searches documents for grammatical errors and highlights them, along with an explanation, for the user to consider changing. More helpful in technical or business documents than in fiction writing.

Graphic Layout
The positioning of graphics, borders, and fonts on the page of a document to achieve a pleasing appearance and effective delivery of content.

Graphics-Assembly Software
A general category of programs that contain files of pre-drawn borders, images, and fonts that the user selects and assembles into a suitable layout before printing. Examples include *The Print Shop* and *Print Master*.

H

Hacker
A person who spends all of his or her time programming or working with a computer. Also used as a pejorative word to mean an unethical, self-taught computer expert who enjoys breaking into secured systems or protected software.

Hand Scanner
A hand-held input device, about the size of a mouse, that is used to transfer images or words directly from a page into main memory. Requires a special circuit board inside the computer.

Hard Copy
See printout.

Hard Disk
A high-speed, circular, magnetic storage medium that allows direct-access storage and retrieval of data. The read/write magnetic heads float above the disk on a cushion of air created by the disk's movement.

Hardware
All the electrical, mechanical, and magnetic parts that make up a computer system. Examples: monitor, keyboard, printer, circuit boards, and electrical wires.

Headline
In desktop publishing, this refers to a major column heading for an article. It typically occupies the same number of columns as the article itself. If it is the width of the entire document, it is called a "banner headline".

Hollerith, Herman (1860-1929)
A statistician with the U.S. Census Bureau who designed a method of storing coded information on cardboard cards in the form of rectangular punched holes. The code and the computer card-handling machines were purchased by IBM in 1929.

Hopper, Grace (1906-)
A mathematician and programmer with the U.S. Naval Reserve who developed programs for the Mark 1 and early Univac computers. A pioneer in the field of computer languages, Hopper wrote the first practical "compiler" programming language, called COBOL.

Horizontal-Format File Manager
A file-manager program that requires that any data entered and any record displayed appear as a single horizontal line across the screen.

Hung

A word to describe a computer system that appears to be doing nothing, although it is in the middle of a program. This state can be caused by a programming error such as an infinite loop or an incomplete INPUT command. Also, the system may be waiting until the user turns on a peripheral device, such as a printer.

Hybrid Computer System

A combination of analog and digital computers. Analog devices usually act as peripherals while the digital computer provides the processing instructions for the system. Example: automatic feedback systems on a cybernated assembly line.

HyperCard

A combination of an authoring system and a simple data base developed originally for Macintosh computers.

I

IBM

An acronym for International Business Machines Ltd., a company that has dominated the mainframe computer market for 30 years because of superior marketing strategies and innovative designs.

Icon

A graphic representation of some object, such as a tool, file, or command displayed on a screen as an option for the user to select with a pointing device.

ICON Microcomputer

A networked microcomputer system designed and built to specifications provided by a Canadian educational market.

Idea Generator

Software that uses a variety of strategies to assist writers in planning and developing their work. Useful for overcoming the "writer's block".

Idiot-Proofing

The process of designing procedures to handle unexpected responses from the user of a conversational program to prevent the program from "crashing".

Immediate Mode

Communicating directly with the computer without the use of programming statements or statement numbers.

Independent Counter

An assignment statement within a loop structure that is not related to the control of the loop process.

Industrial Robots

Robotic devices with interchangeable, multi-purpose arms and reprogrammable memories that can perform a given task repeatedly and with great efficiency. Used in factories for welding, spray painting, moving heavy materials, and product assembly.

Infinite Loop

A situation in which a computer continues to follow a series of instructions without a logical way of stopping. Also called an endless loop.

Information Organizer

A general name for any paper-planning sheet that provides an outline to assist programmers in the analysis and development of their algorithm for a computer program.

Initializing the Counter

Some loop structures require that a separate assignment statement be placed immediately before the loop to provide a starting value for the loop counter. Example: C = 0.

Input Device

A general name for any hardware device that can be used to enter information into a computer system. Examples: keyboard, voice recognition unit, graphics tablet.

Input Medium

The material, such as floppy or hard disks, on which information is stored prior to input into a computer system.

Instructions

In programming, these refer to statements that tell a computer how to perform a particular task.

Integer

A whole number that may be positive, negative, or zero. It does not have a fractional part.

Integrated Circuits

Miniature electrical circuits etched in a tiny chip of silicon or some other material.

Integrated Software

A collection of software applications that permit the passing of text, graphs, and artwork between each other.

Intel

A major manufacturer of microprocessor (MPU) chips for computers. Each series of chips has a designated number to indicate its power and relative speed, such as 8086, 8088, 80286, 80386, 80486, and 80536. Used predominately by IBM and other DOS microcomputer manufacturers.

Interactive Data Entry

A particular technique of writing computer programs that requires the end-user of the program to make active responses to the instructions that appear on the screen. Programs which use the INPUT, GET, READLN, or INKEY$ command to collect new data for entry at the moment the program is being executed. Also called conversational programming.

Interactive Processing

A type of processing involving continuous dialogue between the user and the computer. As the user makes an entry, the computer immediately responds.

Interactive Searches

The process of entering keywords that the program uses to find particular items in a data file.

Interpreter

A specific category of language processor that decodes and reacts to each statement, one at a time, as it is being executed. Any single statement can be executed and checked for errors to provide instant feedback to the programmer. Almost all personal computers use a BASIC interpreter as their language processor.

Italics

A common font within a family of fonts of a particular typeface. Characters are slanted to the right, rather than aligned vertically. Typically used to highlight names of books, movies, titles, or other items within a document.

J

Job Obsolescence

The elimination of jobs due to the introduction of new technology that requires less manpower or a different set of skills and knowledge than the current workers possess.

Joystick

A type of pointing device that controls the movement of the cursor on the screen. Popular for manipulation of graphic images in arcade-style games.

K

K

An abbreviation for kilobytes. A measure of storage capacity for disks and main memory. One K of memory is equivalent to 1024 bytes of memory, but is usually rounded to even units of 1000 when approximating.

Key to the Search

The criteria, usually a word or number, used by a program to search for and locate a specific record.

Key to the Sort

The criteria, usually a word or number, used by a file manager or data-base manager to arrange data into some particular order, such as alphabetical or numerical order. Usually software will ask you from what "field" you wish the data to be sorted. What you enter in reply to that question is the key to the sort.

Keywords

In information retrieval, a keyword refers to a special label identifying which document or information is to be retrieved.

L

Label

A column or row heading in a spreadsheet, or axis titles in a graph.

Language Processor

See computer language.

Laptop Computer

A portable computer with a collapsible or folding display screen, full keyboard, disk storage capacity, and long-term battery power. Resembles a briefcase with a handle when folded.

Laser Printer

A printer that uses the technologies of a photocopier and computer circuitry to reproduce high-resolution text and graphics on plain sheet paper. Available in small, desktop models and large, floor-standing models.

Library Functions

Pre-written subroutine programs in a computer language to make programming easier. Examples: SIN, COS, RANDOMIZE, and RENUMBER functions.

Light Pen

An electrical input pointing device that resembles a pen, and is used to select items from a screen menu, or to sketch graphic images on a graphics tablet or directly onto the screen.

Line Drawing

Simple two-dimensional artwork composed of lines and shading, such as a cartoon character.

Literal

A character string used as output in a PRINT statement. Example: "THE NET PROFIT = $".

Logic Error

An error in program organization such as instructions entered out of sequence, or an illogical request. Logic errors usually do not stop a program, but generally provide incorrect or unwanted answers.

Logical Operators

Programming commands used to combine or reject alternative items in a decision-making process. Examples: AND, OR, NOR.

Loop

A series of instructions that the computer is required to repeat until a certain test condition is met. Also called repetition structure.

M

Machine Intelligence

See artificial intelligence.

Mainframe Computer System

The largest type of computer system, it derives its name from its oversized processing unit. Each of the computer's basic functions (input, processing, output, storage, and control) usually has its own separate floor-model machine which operates at very high speeds. Often the entire computer system will occupy a small room.

Main memory

The part of a computer that stores programs and data while the computer uses them. Also called primary memory or internal memory.

Management by Exception

A time-management concept that specifies that a manager should concern himself or herself with only the exceptions to the rule, or items requiring immediate attention, and ignore the rest.

Mark 1

The first electromechanical computer, developed under the direction of Howard Aiken at Harvard University.

Mauchly, John (1907-)

Co-inventor with J. Presper Eckert of a computer system called ENIAC, which was America's first completely electrical computer. It weighed 30 tonnes and contained 18 000 glass, gas-filled vacuum tubes.

Mechanical Layout

The assembly of elements, such as graphic images, titles, and text, on a page for maximum effect and a pleasing appearance, using scissors and glue or tape.

Mechanical Mouse

A hand-manipulated pointing device that glides on a trackball contained in its "belly" to control the movement of the cursor on the screen.

Medical Diagnostic System

A rule-based artificial intelligence program with access to medical data that can assist nurses, interns, and doctors in diagnosing medical problems and recommending cures.

Megabyte

One million bytes. Refers to disk or main memory storage capacity.

Megahertz (MHz)

The number of millions of cycles per second that a microprocessor chip is capable of performing. A numerical efficiency rating indicating the chip's processing power relative to other MPUs of the same model number.

Memo

A brief, printed or handwritten inter-office communication, usually unsigned, between colleagues or professional people typically within the same organization. Abbreviation for memorandum.

Memory Cubes

A memory module that stores data in a three-dimensional cube instead of in a flat two-dimensional wafer.

Menu

A screen of options that lists the various programs or files that the user can select by entering a keyword, number, letter, or pointing with the cursor. Similar in concept to a restaurant menu. Whatever you order will be brought to you.

Microcomputer

A desktop model computer, usually composed of three components—keyboard, monitor, and processor unit. The most popular category of computer system, the microcomputer is used in offices, classrooms, and homes.

Microelectronics

A new technology devoted to the design and fabrication of miniaturized integrated circuits.

Microprocessor Unit (MPU)

A complete computer on a chip, and the heart of any computer. An integrated logic chip that contains memory registers, a control unit, and an arithmetic logic unit. Major manufacturers include Intel and Motorola.

Microsecond

One-millionth of a second, or 1×10^{-6}.

MIPS Rating
A numerical figure that describes the absolute speed of an MPU in millions of instructions per second. Used to compare the processing power of different microprocessors.

Motherboard
The main circuit board that channels the flow of information and distributes electrical power to the various parts of the computer system. It usually forms the base of the computer's inner shell. However, it takes a vertical position in vertical tower-style processor units.

Motorola
A major American manufacturer of microprocessor (MPU) chips for computers. Each new series of chips has a designated number to indicate its relative power and speed, such as 68020, 68030, and 68040. Predominate users of Motorola MPU chips are Apple Computer, Inc. in its Macintosh computers, NeXT Computers, Sun Systems, and Commodore Amiga.

Mouse
A hand-manipulated pointing device that glides over the surface of a desk and controls the directional movement of the cursor on the screen.

Mouse Pad
A pad of special desktop material for a mouse to ride upon. For a mechanical mouse, the material is made of rubber. For an optical mouse, the material is a smooth, reflective, metallic material.

Mouse Tail
The cord that attaches a mouse to the processor unit.

MPU
See microprocessor.

Multimedia Computer
A computer that integrates several different media as part of its design, such as disk storage, optical storage, sound capabilities, and video input. Examples: Commodore Amiga and NeXT Computers.

Multiple Decision Structure
A programming module that contains more than one decision structure. Also called nested decision structure.

N

Nameplate
In desktop publishing, this refers to the title of a newsletter, or of a newspaper. Often contains a logo, fancy typefaces, and other information, such as the publishing date and the selling cost.

Nanosecond
One billionth of a second, or 1×10^{-9}.

Network Controller
A device containing logic, memory circuits, and software that allows several workstations to access common peripherals or each other.

Neumann, John von (1903-1957)
A brilliant mathematician who created the concept of input, processing, and output for computer design.

Neural Networks
A radical departure in computer architectural-logic design that mimics the interconnected neurons of the human brain by using thousands of processors simultaneously.

Newsletter
A document printed periodically that contains information of interest to a particular group or profession.

Norton Rating
A numerical figure used to compare the relative processing power of an MPU chip to that of the original IBM PC (1981) with an 8088 chip operating at 4.7 MHz. Example: an 80480 chip with a clock speed of 25 MHz has a Norton rating of 40, which means it is 40 times as fast as the original IBM PC.

Number Cruncher
A phrase applied to supercomputers or fast microcomputers designed to process huge volumes of mathematical calculations at high speed (billions of computations per second). Useful for weather forecasting, computer modeling, computer-aided design, spreadsheets, and military applications.

Numerical Control Operator
This person translates the details of a blueprint into computer commands and stores them for later recall by a computer-controlled machine, which then follows the instructions to cut, grind, and shape raw material into a finished product.

O

Open Architecture
A design feature that allows users to make additions or substitutions to factory-installed circuit boards, or to a computer's operating system.

Operating System
A program designed by the manufacturer that supervises the way in which a computer handles information. Its function is analogous to that of a traffic director. Examples: CP/M, DOS, UNIX, QNX.

Optical Disk
A hard, circular reflective platter used as a high-capacity storage medium. It can be used to store thousands of frames of information in the form of still pictures, motion pictures, textual material, or sound tracks, any of which can be accessed by the computer system for playback. Also called laser disk, optical disk, and CD-ROM.

Optical Fibre
Hair-thin glass strands along which laser light can travel. A medium for transmitting information in the form of light.

Optical Mouse
A hand-manipulated pointing device with two tiny holes in its "belly". One hole emits a laser light, the other captures the laser light once it has bounced off a special reflective surface. It is an input device that controls the movement of the cursor on the screen.

Output Device
A general name to describe any hardware device that can be used to display answers, output, or information generated by a computer. Examples: monitor, printer, voice response unit.

P

Page Scanner
A flat-bed input device resembling a small photocopier that digitizes and transfers an entire page of text or artwork directly into main memory.

Paint Program
Free-style drawing software that permits the creation of new graphic images on the screen, or the modification of old ones, using special screen "drawing tools".

Parallel Processing
The use of two or more MPUs in a computer to process data simultaneously. The computer divides work up among the chips for faster execution. Useful for situations that have huge amounts of data coming in from different sources simultaneously, such as data collection from multiple weather stations, or from several military outposts.

Pascal
A partly structured programming language developed in 1971 by the Swiss computer scientist Nicklaus Wirth that is available in several non-compatible versions. Named after the seventeenth-century inventor and mathematician, Blaise Pascal. Best suited for mathematical or engineering applications.

Peripheral
Any device attached to the processor unit of a computer. Examples: printer, plotter, external memory device, joystick, keyboard.

Picosecond
One trillionth of a second, or 1×10^{-12}.

Pixel
A word meaning "picture element", the smallest unit of a graphic image on a computer monitor. Paint programs and graphics tablets usually allow the user to alter an image pixel by pixel.

Plotter
An output device capable of producing fine-line diagrams, graphs, and blueprints. A pen is mounted on a mechanism that can be positioned anywhere on the paper under the control of a computer program. Can work all four directions on the paper by either moving the drum on which the paper sits, or the drawing pens.

Pocket Computer
A portable, hand-held, programmable computer with keypad and small viewing screen.

Pointing Device
A generic name for an input device that controls the directional movement of the cursor on the display screen. Examples: joystick, mouse, trackball, game paddle.

Port
An input or output receptacle in the processing unit into which cables from peripheral devices can be plugged to connect them to a computer system.

POS Terminal
A Point-Of-Sale terminal. These are the specialized electronic cash registers used in department stores and grocery stores that also serve as interactive computer terminals to a mainframe computer.

Powers, James (1917-)
A statistician with the U.S. Census Bureau who developed a method of coding information onto cardboard cards for ease of machine handling. His ideas were adopted by the Sperry Rand Corporation (now Unisys).

Predictive Report
A report generated by mathematical equations to forecast trends and to assist planners in making decisions about the future. Examples: probability of rain (weather); probability of part failure (NASA control).

Printout
Computer output that is printed on paper.

Process Control
The ability of a computer to operate machinery external to the computer system itself. Example: computer-run chemical processing plant.

Processor Unit
The main housing protecting the circuit boards in a computer. Includes motherboard, MPU chip, main memory, and adapter cards that operate peripherals. Also called CPU when applied to mainframe computer systems.

Program
A series of instructions written in computer language designed to guide the computer, step by step, through some process.

Program Listing
A complete list of all the statements in a particular computer program displayed on the screen or printed on paper. Used primarily for debugging programs.

Programmer
A person who plans and codes solutions into a form that a computer can understand. This person requires problem-solving skills and a thorough knowledge of some programming language.

Programmer Comments
Non-executable statements inserted into a program to make the program easier to understand. In BASIC, the command REM or the symbol "!" denotes a comment. In Pascal the symbols "(* *)" denote a comment.

Programming Shell
A mask or template that is superimposed with software on the screen to assist programmers in writing structured code. Example: *Alice BASIC*.

PROM
An acronym for Programmable Read-Only Memory. It refers to a blank memory chip which can be programmed permanently by a hobbyist or a computer manufacturer.

Prompt
A phrase on the screen that "prompts" or instructs the user to perform some particular task. Example: "KEY IN YOUR NAME".

Proofreading
Reading a printed document, comparing it to the original handwritten version or previous draft, and noting errors that must be corrected.

Proofreading Symbols
Standardized notations used to identify and describe mistakes that need correcting in a document. Also include symbols to indicate any changes required to improve a document's appearance.

Pseudocode
Literally translated, it means "false code". It refers to a paper-planning technique that roughly outlines the steps to the solution of a computer program. Short phrases are used to describe the steps.

R

RAM
An acronym for Random Access Memory. It is an erasable semiconductor memory chip used to temporarily store computer programs and data. Nicknamed "user memory".

Record
A complete entry about one topic or one person within a file.

Relational Operator
A symbol used in programming, spreadsheets, and data bases that defines a relationship between two items. Symbols include $<$, $>$, $=$, $>=$, $<=$, $<>$.

Repetition Structure
See loop.

Report Generation
The organization of information selected from one or more files into a formal document to meet some particular need. Example: The use of a data base to select and print information about one student or employee.

Reserved Words
Words in a programming language that are command words and cannot be used as variable names. Examples: READ, PRINT, INT.

Response
Whatever the user replies when faced with a prompt from an interactive data-entry program. In the following example, John Smith is the response. Example: KEY IN YOUR NAME: John Smith.

ROM

An acronym for Read-Only Memory. This is a semiconductor memory chip used to store programs as a permanent part of the computer system. Typically, manufacturers store operating systems, video display instructions, or computer languages in them. Nicknamed "factory memory".

ROM Cartridge

A storage device similar in appearance to an audio cassette containing a circuit board and permanent programs. Mostly used for computer games.

Rotate

To turn an image around on the screen, usually in 90-degree intervals.

Round Off

To truncate a particular number to a specified level of accuracy, such as two-decimal-place accuracy, and increase the last digit by one if the subsequent digit was 5 or greater. Example: 56.18502 rounded to two decimal places would be 56.19.

S

Screen Dump

A printout of exactly what appears on the screen. A feature available on most DOS computers that have a special PrtSc key on the keyboard.

Script Editor

A special editor in desktop-presentation software that permits several independent frames of information to be linked together into a slide series, along with fancy ways of introducing frames, such as fading, overlapping, or side wipes.

Scrolling

Shifting an image on the screen vertically or horizontally to reveal part of a document that is currently beyond the borders of the screen. Used in spreadsheets, word processing, and computer languages.

Searching

The process of looking for an item specified by the user within a file.

Selection by Matching Numbers

A decision module in programming that uses a number as a key to the search.

Selection by Matching Words

A decision module in programming that uses a word as the key to the search.

Selection Structure

A set of instructions with a definite beginning and end that requires the computer to compare two or more items. The computer is then provided with alternative programming choices based on the results of the comparison. Also called decision structure.

Semiconductor Memory

The type of integrated circuit typically found in most computers. The circuits are composed of layers of partially conductive metals and non-conductive insulators.

Sequential Access

A process of searching an entire file from beginning to end, one record at a time, until the requested item is located.

Shadow Effect

A shading technique used in artwork to give the viewer the illusion that an image is three-dimensional.

Simple Sequential Structure

A straight line segment of a program which contains no decisions or loops.

Simulated Artificial Intelligence

A clever application of conversational programming techniques to give the user the impression that the computer is thinking for itself. A controversial use of this type of programming was popularized by MIT professor Joseph Weizenbaum, whose program ELIZA and its psychiatric variation, called DOCTOR, were developed in the 1960s.

Size

In graphic software, this verb refers to changing the dimensions of a graphic by enlarging or shrinking it.

Soft Copy

A rarely used term meaning output displayed on the screen. Also referred to as a "readout" in pocket computers.

Software

All the instructions that make a computer operate in a required manner. A general name for computer programs.

Software Vendor

A business that sells application programs to people who own computers.

Sorting

The arrangement of records within a file into some particular order, such as alphabetical or numerical, based on a particular field.

Spaghetti Programming
A name applied to unstructured programs that use a great number of GOTO statements. Spaghetti programs are very difficult to debug if they contain major errors in programming logic.

Spelling Checker
Software that scans a document for spelling mistakes, highlights them, and displays alternatives for the user to select.

Spreadsheet
A software application that displays a large grid of rows and columns on the screen. The place of intersection of a row and column is called a cell. Each cell has the capability of accepting and storing formulas, and of rapidly processing tables of numbers. The advantage of this type of program is that it automatically recalculates the entire spreadsheet when new variables or formulas are entered into the grid.

Spreadsheet Analyst
A person who uses electronic spreadsheets to analyze numerical data. Examples: people who work in budget, accounting, finance, and research departments, and people who work in insurance companies.

Spreadsheet Cycle
A series of logical steps that spreadsheet users take when faced with a new problem.

Statement
A line of code in a computer program.

Status Line
A line at the top or bottom of a word-processing, spreadsheet, or data-base screen that indicates information about the current document.

Stored Program Concept
The idea of entering and storing a program into main memory before executing it.

String Variable
A series of characters (letters, numbers, or special symbols) used as a variable in a computer program. Typically, it is a word or a name, and usually it requires double quotation marks at each end.

Strip Coding
Patterns of coloured stripes on railway rolling stock designed to be read by optical scanners placed along the tracks. The code provides data by which a computer can identify the type, owner, manifest, and destination of the railway car.

Structural Unemployment
Groups of people who are permanently unemployed because of the introduction of new technologies which have made their particular set of skills and knowledge obsolete.

Structured Programming
A systematic way of planning and coding computer programs. They are organized into blocks of code that are highlighted with spaces placed before and after each block to improve readability. Inside repetition and selection structures are indented for easier identification.

Subroutine
A small program that performs some particular function. It is usually separated from the main program, and is called into action whenever needed.

Supercomputer
A term applied to the fastest of the mainframe computer systems, such as the Cray computer.

Symmetric Parallel Processing
A computer system with multiple MPUs in which each processor has an equal role and equal access to all parts of the computer. Requires a special, non-traditional operating system to function.

Syntax Errors
Errors in the grammatical rules of a particular computer language that include spelling, punctuation, brackets, special symbols, and arrangement of those items within a statement.

System Analyst
A person who recommends ways of improving office routines, computer forms, or anything related to the application of a computer system.

System Commands
Instructions that require the computer to do something in immediate mode. Examples: LIST, DELETE.

System Crash
A phrase used to describe an undefined computer malfunction that has caused the computer to stop running, as in: "The system has crashed", or alternatively "The system is down".

System Software
Programs usually created by the computer manufacturer that are required to run a computer. Examples: BIOS, operating systems, video display BIOS, and computer languages.

System Software Programmer
A highly trained programming specialist who develops operating systems and computer languages for computer manufacturers or software companies.

T

Teleprocessing
Any processing done at a distance from the terminal and user. Example: A computer terminal can gain access to the processing power of a computer several kilometres away.

Teller Terminals
Interactive computer terminals designed to be used by tellers in financial institutions to process banking transactions.

Template
A software mask on a computer screen used to aid data entry or data display. This type of shell is used in several types of programs including word processing, spreadsheets, data bases, and desktop publishing.

Test Condition
A statement within a repetition structure that provides the computer with a logical way to exit from the structure once a certain test condition is met. When missing, the structure becomes an "infinite loop".

Test Run
A reliability check on a newly created system (in programming or template software) performed by entering and executing sample data.

Text
The wording in an article, story, or manuscript.

Text Editor
A simple word-processing program that allows the user to manipulate and edit information displayed on the computer screen. Lacks many functions of a full word-processing package.

Thesaurus
Software that provides alternative words to the one highlighted on the screen. Useful for varying language or increasing the accuracy of the wording within a document.

Three-Dimensional
Appearing to have the three dimensions length, width, and depth. Images that appear real enough to touch.

Time Sharing
A method of sharing a computer facility with several users at the same time. A technique used by banks, gasoline stations, and airlines.

Truncate
To drop digits of a decimal number, which lessens the number's accuracy. Example: If 4.62987 is truncated to two-decimal-place accuracy, it would appear as 4.62.

Turing, Alan (1912-1954)
A British mathematician who proposed an intelligence test for computers based on word recognition and word response capabilities.

Two-Dimensional
Appearing to have only two dimensions, such as length and width, but no depth.

Typeface
Lettering of a specific style, such as Times Roman or Helvetica, used in publishing documents. Typeface names are copyrighted, which causes almost identical typefaces to be named differently in different software.

U

Underlining
A method of highlighting items within a word-processed document by drawing a line under them.

UNIVAC 1
The first mass-produced model of a general-purpose computer in the United States. Originally manufactured by Sperry Rand Corporation.

UPC
An acronym for Universal Product Code. It refers to a patch of dark and light vertical lines such as the ones found on grocery products. It contains coded information to assist with inventory control and re-ordering.

User Friendly
A term used to describe hardware or software that can be learned intuitively, without help from a manual, tutorial, or instructor.

User Prompts
Messages embedded in an interactive data-capture program that require a response from the user of the program. Example: "Key in your name".

V

Value
A numerical figure (real or integer) used as data.

Variable Name
A letter or keyword invented by the programmer to be assigned to represent the storage location of a particular variable or set of variables.

Variables
Data in a computer program that can vary in different circumstances, such as in a loop structure that requires different names and grades with each pass. Contrasted to a constant, such as the grade needed to pass, that does not change with additional runs of the program.

Vertical-Format File Manager
A file manager that accepts data entry and displays single records vertically using the full height of the screen. The field names are often aligned, one underneath the other, at the left-hand margin.

VGA
High-resolution colour-monitor designation, which means "Virtual Graphics Array". Higher resolution than either the CGA or EGA monitors.

Video Digitizing
The transferring of subjects (images) from a video camera to a computer system.

Videodisk
See optical disk.

Visual Impact Chart
A page divided into several equal sections that illustrates the areas in which readers typically focus their attention during a quick scan of the sheet.

Voice Recognition Unit
An input device that accepts the human voice as input into a computer system.

von Neumann Bottleneck
A slowing down of the transfer of data within a computer system because all data must be funneled through a single processor. Named after John von Neumann, an American mathematician who first postulated the single processor computer configuration in the 1940s.

W

WATFILE
An information management system (data base) developed by the University of Waterloo that is capable of combining information from several different but related files to form one report.

Watson, Thomas J. (1914-1956)
The president of IBM until 1952.

Weizenbaum, Joseph (1923-)
An American professor at Massachusetts Institute of Technology who gained fame through the development of a simulated artificial intelligence program called ELIZA and the philosophy behind it, described in a book titled *Beyond Human Reason*.

Wiener, Norbert (1894-1964)
An American scientist who coined the word "cybernetics". The founder of this new branch of science, he believed that many thought processes could be determined mathematically and adapted for use in computers.

Window
A viewing area on a screen that permits the user to view a particular file. On a multi-tasking system, several windows, with different files in each one, can be opened simultaneously.

WINDOWS
A specific, multi-tasking operating system with a graphical user interface for DOS microcomputers, designed by Microsoft Corporation. Permits several viewing areas (windows) to be opened and operated simultaneously on the same screen.

Word Processing
This refers to the use of a computer system to key in, edit, store, and print documents, such as memos, letters, manuals, etc.

Word Processing Operator
A person who operates a word-processing system.

Word Wrap
The automatic return of the cursor to the beginning of the next line, when the right-hand margin is reached, bringing with it any word that is too long to fit within the margins of the previous line. A feature in word processing and desktop publishing.

Workstation
A terminal on a shared network that employees or students work at doing similar tasks.

WYSIWYG
A screen-design feature that allows the user to see exactly how the page will appear when it gets printed. An acronym for "What You See Is What You Get".

Note to user: **Boldface** page numbers indicate where a term is explained or defined. Page numbers in *italics* indicate the location of a photograph or illustration.

A

Accumulator, **275**
Addressable main memory, *218*
ALEX, 224
Algorithm, **318**
   pseudocode, 319
ALU, **10**
Analog computer, **15**
Animation software, **122**
Application software, **12**
Arithmetic operators, 242, *324*, 325
Artificial intelligence, 205, 222
Artificial intelligence programmer, **20**
Assignment statements, **240**
Asymmetric parallel processing, 219
Automated teller terminal, 168
Auxiliary memory, **8**

B

Bar graph, 74
BASIC, **236**
   line numbers, 237-38
BEDMAS Rules of Operation, 234-*44*
Bionic people, 211
Bit mapping, **7**
Boldface, **39**
Bug, **243**, 318
Bulletin boards, 173

Business graphics, **72**-74
Business letters, 48-*49*
Byte, **8**

C

CD-ROM, **9**
CD-ROM disks, 218
Cell, 62
Centralized data banks, 188
Character strings, 249
Circle graph, **74**
Clip art, **118**
   reasons for using, 137
Clip-art editor, 137
Clip-art libraries, 136
Clipboard, **149**
Closed architecture, **16**
COBOL, 23
Comma, **245**
Communication networks, 222
Communication satellites, 222
Compilers, **318**
Computer
   courtroom applications, 210-11
   digital, types of, 13
   enhanced human intelligence, 211
   evolution of, 20-23
   future developments, *226*
   generations, 25-26
   languages, **11**, 221-22
   thinking capacity, 204-205
   in university research, 225
Computer-aided design (CAD), 121-22
Computer-aided design specialists, **19**
Computer-assisted instruction (CAI), 169

Computer application programmer, **18**
Computer applications, **162**
   consumer products, 172-73
   in factories, 164-65
   office administration, 162-64
   research tool, 165-67
   retail sales and banking, 167-69
   selecting best only, 194-95
   teaching functions, 169-70
   traffic control, 170-72
Computer graphics, **114**, 136-37
   newsletter, 136-37
Computer languages, 11, 221-22
   BASIC, **236**
   Pascal, **318**
Computer model, **165**-66
Computer ombudsman, 190
Computer programs, **237**
   errors in, 318
Computers, social effects of
   controlled society, 212
   electronic money, 188
   frustrated customers, 187
   increased productivity, 182
   intellectual achievements, 183
   intensity of impact, 191-*92*
   invasion of privacy, 188-90
   job market changes, 184-*85*
   leisure time, 193-94
   selecting applications, 194-95
Computer system, **4**
   functions of, 5-10
   hybrid, **15**, 166-67
Computer theft, 206
Computer viruses, 209
Control statements, 238, *329*
Control unit, **9**, **10**
Copyediting, **41**

Semicolon, **245**
Shadow effect, **115**
Silicon Valley North, 225
Simple sequential structures, 236
Sizing (images), 137
Software, **4**
  application, **12**
  system, **11**
  graphics, 114-19, 121-22
  high-end word processing, **149-50**
  integrated, **148-49**
  trends, 221-22
Spelling checker, **44**
Spreadsheet, *64*
  building, 66-69
  business graphics, 72-74
  commands, 69, 70, 71
  cycle, 74-75, 76-77
  formulas, 63-64, *65*
  label, **63**
  and problem solving, 76
  reusable templates, **66**
  types of information, 63-65
  value, **63**
  viewing on screen, 63
Spreadsheet analysts, **18**
Status line, **34**
STEP command, 271
Storage, **8-9**
Strip coding, 170
Structural unemployment, 186
Supercomputers, 220, *221*, 225
Syntax error, **243**, **318**
Symmetric parallel processing, 219
System commands, **239**
Systems software program-
  mers, **20**

T

Teller terminals, 168
Template, **66**, **91**
  horizontal-format, *92*

pre-designed, 133-34
  vertical-format, *92*
Test condition, **267**, 273, 298
Test run, **100**
Text, **135**
Thesaurus, **44**
Trackball, **6**
Trojan Horse, 209
Truncating numbers, 252-53
Turing Test, 204
Typefaces, *138*-39

U

UNIVAC 1, 24
Universal Product Code (UPC), 167
Underlining, **39**
User friendly, **118**, 251

V

Variable names, **240**
  limitations to, 241
Vertical-format file managers, **90**, *91*
Video digitizing, **114**
Videodisks, **9**
Viruses, 209
Voice input, **6**
Voice output, **8**
von Neumann Bottleneck, 219

W

WYSIWYG, **39**, 132
WATCOM BASIC, 273, 298
Window, **34**
Word processing, **34**
  business letters, 48-*49*
  cycle, 40-41
  document protection, 43
  formatting diskette, 38
  memos, writing, 46-47
  print features, 39
  screen, *35*

screen editing, 36-37, 41
software programs for, 44-45
typeover vs. pushright mode, 36-37
viewing documents, 34-35
Word processing operator, **17-18**
Word wrap, **35**
Worm program, 209